"Look at Me and Be Appalled"

Biblical Interpretation Series

Editors-in-Chief

Paul Anderson (*George Fox University*)
Jennifer L. Koosed (*Albright College, Reading*)

Editorial Board

A. K. M. Adam (*University of Oxford*)
Nijay Gupta (*Portland Seminary*)
Amy Kalmanofsky (*Jewish Theological Seminary*)
Jennifer Knust (*Duke University*)
Sara Koenig (*Pacific Seattle University*)
Vernon Robbins (*Emory University*)
Annette Schellenberg (*University Wien*)
Johanna Stiebert (*University of Leeds*)
Duane Watson (*Malone University*)
Christine Roy Yoder (*Columbia Theological Seminary*)
Ruben Zimmermann (*Johannes Gutenberg-Universität Mainz*)

VOLUME 190

The titles published in this series are listed *at brill.com/bins*

"Look at Me and Be Appalled"

Essays on Job, Theology, and Ethics

An Interdisciplinary Dialogue

By

Samuel E. Balentine

BRILL

LEIDEN | BOSTON

Library of Congress Cataloging-in-Publication Data

Names: Balentine, Samuel E. (Samuel Eugene), 1950- author.
Title: "Look at me and be appalled" : essays on Job, theology, and ethics /
 by Samuel E. Balentine.
Description: Leiden ; Boston : Brill, [2021] | Series: Biblical
 interpretation series, 0928-0731 ; volume 190 | Includes bibliographical
 references and index.
Identifiers: LCCN 2020057598 (print) | LCCN 2020057599 (ebook) | ISBN
 9789004453456 (hardback) | ISBN 9789004459212 (ebook)
Subjects: LCSH: Bible. Job—Criticism, interpretation, etc.
Classification: LCC BS1415.52 .B347 2021 (print) | LCC BS1415.52 (ebook)
 | DDC 223/.106—dc23
LC record available at https://lccn.loc.gov/2020057598
LC ebook record available at https://lccn.loc.gov/2020057599

Typeface for the Latin, Greek, and Cyrillic scripts: "Brill". See and download: brill.com/brill-typeface.

ISSN 0928-0731
ISBN 978-90-04-45345-6 (hardback)
ISBN 978-90-04-45921-2 (e-book)

Copyright 2021 by Samuel E. Balentine. Published by Koninklijke Brill NV, Leiden, The Netherlands.
Koninklijke Brill NV incorporates the imprints Brill, Brill Hes & De Graaf, Brill Nijhoff, Brill Rodopi,
Brill Sense, Hotei Publishing, mentis Verlag, Verlag Ferdinand Schöningh and Wilhelm Fink Verlag.
Koninklijke Brill NV reserves the right to protect this publication against unauthorized use. Requests for
re-use and/or translations must be addressed to Koninklijke Brill NV via brill.com or copyright.com.

This book is printed on acid-free paper and produced in a sustainable manner.

For Tricia and Barry

•••

Friendship is a sacred appellation
(COLERIDGE)

••
•

Contents

Preface XI
Acknowledgments XIII
List of Figures XV
Abbreviations XVI

PART 1
Prologue: From Eden to Uz

1 **"For No Reason"** 3
   1 Job and Israel's "Grammars of Creation" 7
   2 "For No Reason" 13
   3 Some Concluding Ruminations on the Enigma of Evil 20

PART 2
Job and His Friends: "What Provokes You That You Keep on Talking?"

2 **Who Will Be Job's Redeemer?** 29
   1 Looking for the Redeemer through Job's Eyes: Job 19:21–29 30
   2 Looking for Job's Redeemer through the Eyes of the Artist: Gilding the Metaphor of Resurrection with "the Edge of Felt Conjecture" 38
   3 The Theodicists' Perspective: Remembering or "Dismembering" Job? 46
   4 Who Then Will Be Job's Redeemer? 49

3 **"Let Love Clasp Grief Lest Both Be Drowned"** 52
   1 Models of Friendship 53
   2 And Jesus Said, "Which of These Three, Do You Think Was a Neighbor to the Man?" 66

VIII   CONTENTS

4   "What Are Human Beings That You Make So Much of Them?"
     Responses and Counter-Responses from Job, Prometheus,
     and Frankenstein   72
     1   "Job Is the Prometheus of the World"   73
     2   The End of the Promethean Myth?   79

5   "What Provokes You That You Keep on Talking?"   83
     1   Pastoral Care 101   84
     2   "What a Bunch of Miserable Comforters!"   91
     3   "Look at Me and Be Appalled, and Lay Your Hand on
          Your Mouth"   93

     PART 3
     Job and the Priests: "Look at Me and Be Appalled"

6   Job as Priest to the Priests   107
     1   Priestly Imagery in the Prologue and Epilogue of Job   110
     2   Inside the Priestly Rituals: Job's Affliction and Contention   118
     3   Job's Challenge to the Priestly System   126

7   Job and the Priests: "He Leads Priests Away Stripped" (Job 12:19)   133
     1   A Framing Perspective: The Priestly Profile of Job in the Prologue
          and Epilogue   136
     2   Concluding Reflections: "He Leads Priests Away Stripped"   144

8   "My Servant Job Shall Pray for You"   146
     1   The Conventional and Salutary View of Job as Intercessor   147
     2   The Nonconventional and Salutary View of Job as Intercessor   152
     3   Concluding Discernments: to Pray ("As My Servant Job Has") or
          Not to Pray?   160

     PART 4
     Traumatizing Job: "God Has Worn Me Out"

9   "Ask the Animals, and They Will Teach You"   165
     1   Creation's Ambiguous Truths   166
     2   Conflicting Discernments   167
     3   The Celebration of "Un*man*-aged Freedom"   172

CONTENTS

10   Inside the "Sanctuary of Silence": The Moral-Ethical Demands
     of Suffering   175
     1   Inside the Sanctuary of Silence   175
     2   Job as a "Test Case" for the Sanctuary of Silence   180
     3   "Inside the House, an Archaic Rule; Outside, the Facts
         of Life"?   187

11   Traumatizing Job   194
     1   The Old Testament's Lexicon of Trauma   194
     2   "Have You Considered My Servant Job?"   196
     3   Traumatizing Job   201

     PART 5
     Out of the Whirlwind: "Can You Thunder with a Voice Like God's?"

12   "What Are Human Beings, That You Make So Much of Them?"
     Divine Disclosure from the Whirlwind: "Look at Behemoth"   209
     1   Primordial Questions: "What Are Human Beings, That You Make
         So Much of Them?"   210
     2   Divine Disclosure: "Look at Behemoth"   214
     3   Job's Final Response: "Now My Eye Sees You"   224

13   "Will You Condemn Me That You May Be Justified?" – The Character
     of God in Job   229
     1   The Character of God in the Prose Tale of Job   231
     2   The Character of God in the Divine Speeches   240
     3   Which God Should We Emulate?   244

14   The Joban Theophany and the Education of God   247
     1   "Then the Lord Answered Job Out of the Whirlwind"   249
     2   The "Critical Inquisitiveness" of Rhetorical Questions   250
     3   God as Rhetor   252
     4   Dueling Banjos   255

X   CONTENTS

PART 6

Preaching Job and Job's God: "Listen Carefully to My Words"

15   Moral Rebellion or Reverent Submission? (Job 23:1–9, 16–17)   259

16   Preaching Job's God   265

17   The Church of Saint Job   273

      1   Ruminations on What Goes on Inside the Church of
           Saint Job   274

      2   Ruminations on What Goes on Inside the Church of the
           "Lectionary Job"   283

      3   Can You Tell Me How to Find the Church of Saint Job?   290

PART 7

Epilogue: "All's Well That Ends Well" ... or Is It?

18   Re(reading) Job's Story in a Post-Holocaust World   295

      1   "You ... Did Not Comprehend the Extent of Your
           Sleeping Power"   301

      2   "We Won't Allow Your Blood to Be Covered"   307

      3   "We Know His [Job's] Story for Having Lived It [...]. Whenever We
           Attempt to Tell Our Own Story, We Transmit His"   310

      4   "Have You Considered My Servant Job?"   317

      Scripture Index   321

Preface

This book brings together published and unpublished articles on Job written over two decades. The majority were originally presented or published in academic settings; about one third of them were also delivered in a somewhat modified form in a variety of congregational venues. The blend of the academic and the theological has been characteristic of my work over the last four decades; I have been unwilling to uncouple rigorous exegesis from robust theological reflection. I have also consistently aspired to connect and integrate biblical motifs with a wide range of art forms, including fiction, poetry, drama, music, art, and iconography. The book of Job has long been an especially rich reservoir for such attention. As Mr. Zuss says to Nickels in Archibald MacLeish's *J.B.*, "there's always someone playing Job." The essays here exemplify how much I have learned about Job from 'exegetes' of all kinds.

The essays are reproduced here as they were originally published. The style and format, therefore, will not be uniform. The tenor and tone of the essays will differ, some will be more academic and formal, others more personal and interactive, although I trust no less substantive.

I have arranged them here in sections, primarily according to what in retrospect seems to be an appropriate thematic focus. I hope this will serve as a guide for those who may want to connect the essays with the conventional thematic outline of the book of Job: Prologue (Job 1–2), Job and his Friends (Job 3–37), the Divine Speeches (Job 38:1–42:6); and the Epilogue (Job 42:7–14). In the end, however, the categorizing of the essays is rather arbitrary. Almost any one of them could be relocated; suffering like Job's – no less than the effort to understand it – transgresses all boundaries.

It has been interesting and revealing (at least for me) to track the trends and trajectories in my thinking about Job over these many years. I look over my own shoulder and see myself returning again and again to issues that have constantly itched at my sensibilities. In this regard, the lead essay is appropriately placed. What are we to think about a God who, according to the Joban story, is complicit in the death of seven sons and three daughters "for no reason" (Job 2:3)? From first encounter to this day these three words have been the most unsettling I have ever encountered in my journey with God and Job. Like Job, I have tried to wrestle the question to the ground, to pin it underneath the weight of some invincible solution that does not mock clear-eyed truth and integrity. Like Job, I have insisted on arguing with God (Job 13:3). At best, I have learned something about what the English novelist Sebastian Faulks calls "the grandeur of human insignificance." The affirmation does not quiet my disquiet but it has sustained me through years of trying to comprehend the incomprehensible. "Don't write what you know," the National Book Award winner Colum McCann advises those who sit down to the blank page every day, "write toward what you *want to know*."

I am grateful to Jennifer Koosed for including the book in the Biblical Interpretation Series and to Liesbeth Hugenholtz at Brill, who has facilitated the project from beginning to end. I want to thank the students who have walked this Joban trail with me over many years, especially Tricia Vesely and Barry Huff. I have been their teacher; now, I am their student. With enormous pride and high expectations, I dedicate this book to them.

Acknowledgments

I am grateful to the publishers for permission to publish the following:

"For No Reason," *Interpretation* 57 (2003), 349–369

"Who Will Be Job's Redeemer?" *Perspectives in Religious Studies* 26 (1999), 269–289

"Let Love Clasp Grief Lest Both Be Drowned," *Perspectives in Religious Studies* 30 (2003), 381–397

"Job as Priest to the Priests," *Ex Auditu* 18 (2003), 29–52. Used by permission of Wipf and Stock Publishers

"Job and the Priests: 'He Leads Priests Away Stripped,'" in *Reading Job Intertextually*, ed. K. Dell (Library of Hebrew Studies/Old Testament Studies 574; New York, London: T & T Clark, 2013), 42–53

"My Servant Job Will Pray For You," *Theology Today* 58 (2002), 502–518

"Ask the Animals and They Will Teach You," in "And God Saw that It Was Good." Essays on Creation and God in Honor of Terence E. Fretheim, eds., Frederick J. Gaiser, Mark A. Throntveit, *Word and World Supplement Series 5* (2006), 3–11

"Inside the Sanctuary of Silence: The Moral and Ethical Demands of Suffering," in *Character and Ethics in the Torah: Moral Dimensions of Scripture*, eds., M. D. Carroll, J. Lapsley (Louisville: Westminster John Knox, 2007), 63–80

"Traumatizing Job," *Review and Expositor* 57 (2003), 349–369

"'What Are Human Beings, That You Make So Much of Them?' Divine Disclosure From the Whirlwind: 'Look at Behemoth,'" in *God in the Fray: A Tribute to Walter Brueggemann*, eds., T. Linafelt, T. Beal (Minneapolis, MN: Fortress Press, 1998), 259–278

"The Joban Theophany and the Education of God," in *Theology of Hebrew Bible Volume 2: Texts, Theological Readers, and Their Worlds*, eds., Soo J. Kim, David Frankel, Marvin A. Sweeney (Atlanta: Society of Biblical Literature, 2021), forthcoming.

"Job 23:1–9, 16–17," *Interpretation* 53 (1999), 290–293

"Preaching Job's God," *Journal for Preachers* 36 (2013), 22–27

"The Church of Saint Job," *Review and Expositor* 96 (1999), 501–518

"(Re)reading Job's Story in a Post-Holocaust World," in Samuel E. Balentine, *Have You Considered My Servant Job? Understanding the Biblical Archetype of Patience* (Studies on Personalities of the Old Testament; Columbia, SC: University of South Carolina Press, 2015), 202–220

Figures

2.1   Vittore Carpaccio (c. 1455–1523/26). *Meditation on the Passion of Christ* (c. 1490) Oil and tempera on wood. John Stewart Kennedy Fund, 1911. Courtesy of the Metropolitan Museum of Art, New York   42

2.2   Marc Chagall, "Job with Background of Geometricized Christ á la Cimabué." Courtesy of Artists Rights Society   44

3.1   William Blake, "Job's Comforters." National Gallery of Art/Wikimedia Commons   55

3.2   William Blake, "Job Rebuked By His Friends." National Gallery of Art/ Wikimedia Commons   56

5.1   Jean Fouquet (c. 1415–1481). "Job and His Comforters." *The Hours of Etienne Chevalier, Office of the Dead*. Musée Condé, Chantilly, France. (Credit: Saiko, Wikimedia Commons, CCA-SA 3.0)   86

5.2   Pierro della Francesca, "The Resurrection," c. 1462–1464. Palazzo Communale, San Sepolchro. Full view (Credit: Wikimedia Commons, PD-old)   101

5.3   Pierro della Francesca, "The Resurrection," detail of Christ's face   102

6.1   "Saint Job as Priest," church of Saint Martin, Wezemaal. Credit: Barry Huff, personal photograph   109

6.2   "Saint Job as Priest," Mayer van der Bergh Museum, Antwerp. Credit: Barry Huff, personal photograph   131

8.1   Taddeo Gaddi (1300–1366). "Job Intercedes for his Friends." 1355. Fresco Camposanto Monumentali di Pisa Archivio Fotographico Opera Primaziale Pisana. Credit: Samuel E. Balentine, personal photograph   150

8.2   "Job Prepares to Fight." 9th c. Illumination. Saint John Monastery, Patmos (Credit: Bibilotheque du Monastere St. Jean le Theologien, Patmos)   154

8.3   "Job Interrupts God." Vatican Museum, Rome. © Biblioteca Apostolica Vaticana. Gr 1231, fol 19v/Wikimedia Commons   158

15.1   Ossip Zadkine (1888–1967). "The City Destroyed." (1954). Bronze statue, Rotterdam. Credit: National Portrait Gallery, London, UK/Wikimedia Commons   263

17.1   Main portal to the church of San Giobbe. Credit: Samuel E. Balentine, personal photograph   274

Abbreviations

ABD	*Anchor Bible Dictionary*
AV	Authorized Version
BETL	Bibliotheca ephemeridum theogicarum louvaniensium
BI	*Biblical Interpretation*
BZAW	*Beihefte zur Zeitschrift für die alttestamentlische Wissenschaft*
CANE	*Civilizations of the Ancient Near.* Edited by J. Sasson. 4 vols
CBQ	*Catholic Biblical Quarterly*
CBQMS	*Catholic Biblical Quarterly Monograph Series*
ER	*Encyclopedia of Religion*
ExAud	*Ex Auditu*
HAR	*Harvard Annual Review*
HBT	*Horizons in Biblical Theology*
HUCA	Hebrew Union College Annual
FRLANT	*Forschungen zur Religion und Literatur des Alten und Neuen Testaments*
IBC	*Interpreter's Bible Commentary*
ICC	*International Critical Commentary*
JAAR	*Journal of the American Academy of Religion*
JAOS	*Journal of the American Oriental Society*
JBL	*Journal of Biblical Literature*
JJS	*Journal of Jewish Studies*
JQR	*Jewish Quarterly Review*
JR	*Journal of Religion*
JSOT	*Journal for the Study of the Old Testament*
JSOTSup	*Journal for the Study of the Old Testament, Supplement*
KAT	Kommentar zum Alten Testament
LHBOTS	*Library of Hebrew Bible/Old Testament Studies*
NIB	*The New Interpreter's Bible*
OTL	*Old Testament Library*
RevExp	*Review and Expositor*
SHBC	Smyth and Helwys Bible Commentary
SR	Studies in Religion
ThTo	*Theology Today*
TOTC	*Tyndale Old Testament Commentaries*
TLOT	*Theological Lexicon of the Old Testament.* Edited by E. Jenni, C. Westermann. 3 vols

ABBREVIATIONS

VT	*Vetus Testamentum*
WBC	Word Biblical Commentary
WW	*Word & World*
ZA	*Zeitschrift für Assyriologie*
ZAW	*Zeitschrift für die alttestamentliche Wissenschaft*

PART 1

Prologue: From Eden to Uz

CHAPTER 1

"For No Reason"

Cosmos, i.e., pain raved in me with a diabolical tongue.[1]
CZESLAW MILOSZ

• • •

To sum up: 1. The cosmos is a gigantic fly-wheel making 10,000 revolutions a minute. 2. Man is a sick fly taking a dizzy ride on it. 3. Religion is the theory that the wheel was designed and set spinning to give him the ride.[2]
H. L. MENCKEN

• •
•

"We have no more beginnings." With these words George Steiner offers an epithet for the grave that marks the twentieth century.[3] No more beginnings – the words convey the eulogy we speak over the corpse of a century swallowed up in the hideous barbarity of warfare, disease, deportation, ethnic cleansing, and political murder, to name only a few of the headline evils. We have struggled valiantly to find a toehold in the dizzying fly-wheel of this cosmos. We may take some satisfaction in having sustained the "thirst for explanation, for causality"[4] through centuries of increasingly sophisticated and well-defined philosophical and theological skepticism.[5] At the insistence of Nietzsche, Camus, and Dostoevsky, we have learned how to be comfortable, sometimes even faddish, by asking how to live in this world *without* God. With Eli Wiesel, whose struggles with the Holocaust have been generally more palatable than some, like Primo Levi, who could not muster even Wiesel's strained faith, we learned to be at home, questioning how to live in this world without God *and*

---

1 C. Milosz, "Notes" in *New and Collected Poems 1931–2001* (New York: HarperCollins, 2001).
2 H. L. Mencken, "Coda," in *Smart Set* (1920).
3 G. Steiner, *Grammars of Creation* (New Haven and London: Yale University Press, 2001), 2.
4 Ibid., 3.
5 On the skeptical tradition to which we are heir, see F. Baumer, *Religion and the Rise of Skepticism* (New York: Harcourt, Brace, 1960).

© SAMUEL E. BALENTINE, 2021 | DOI:10.1163/9789004459212_002

without justice. But the victories have been pyrrhic at best. We enter the twenty-first century with a "core-tiredness," a fatigue of dashed hope that leaves us sitting at the bar after the last call, still thirsting for a drink that time refuses us: "The dishes are being cleared. Time, ladies and gents, time." As Steiner notes, "Valediction is in the air."[6]

It only adds another verse to the same dirge to note that Steiner wrote these words before the tragic events we have come to call simply 9/11. Our current alarms – at thousands of men and women consumed in the flames of the World Trade Center, at the corporate meltdown of Enron, WorldCom, and United Airlines, at the devastation of Africa and Asia by the AIDS virus – push our anxieties to another level. Not only is the question about God and justice up for grabs. The question now is, Can we survive? To underscore the bankruptcy of our traditional resources, the Roman Catholic Church sits in the docket of public condemnation, guilty of abusing innocent children ... and trying to cover it up. That a report on July 9, 2002 that ministers in a Baptist church in Texas beat a young boy into unconsciousness for having read the wrong Bible verse was no longer headline news is a measure of how dulled our expectations of the church have become. Buried in the back pages of our papers, it was just another story. Read today, tossed in the recycle bin tomorrow. Ho-hum.

One thing does seem to have changed. In the aftermath of 9/11, the word "evil" has forced its way back into the vocabulary of public discourse with a vengeance. I say "back" into public discourse in recognition of the judgment one finds in the *Oxford English Dictionary*. The dictionary distinguishes between a strong and a weak meaning for the word "evil." The weak version, signifying something that is unpleasant, disagreeable, or offensive, is interchangeable with, indeed typically superseded by, the word "bad." The strong sense of the word – something that is wicked, monstrous, morally depraved – "is little used in modern English"; as applied to persons, the word "evil" has become "obsolete." Whether one agrees or not with this judgment, there can be little doubt that, after 9/11, the word "evil" has now become firmly entrenched in our common lexicon.[7] The charge has been led by President George W. Bush, who has used the bully pulpit to apply the labels "evil," "evil ones," and "evildoers" to individuals (Osama bin Laden, Saddam Hussein), groups (Al-Qaeda, Taliban, and other terrorist organizations), and countries (Iraq, Iran, and North Korea,

---

6 Steiner, *Grammars of Creation*, 3.

7 For further discussion, see the collection of articles in D. Parkin, ed., *The Anthropology of Evil* (Oxford: Basil Blackwell, 1985), especially D. Pocock, "Unruly Evil," 42–56, and A. Macfarlane, "The Root of All Evil," 57–76.

the "axis of evil"). Bush has called for a global campaign to "eliminate" evil from this world.

Whatever the flaws and dangers in President Bush's rhetoric,[8] his flat application of these labels has clearly mobilized the country. As long as a particular act is viewed as only "bad," as long as its consequences are merely unpleasant or unfavorable, there is likely to be little or no response to it. Perhaps the act was justified. Perhaps the consequences were unintended. Perhaps, as we sometimes say with a shrug, "no harm, no foul; play on." However, once there is a consensus that an act has gone too far, that it has breached the boundary between what is merely unfortunate and what is gross or heinous, labeling it "evil" becomes a call to action. To do nothing in the face of what is viewed as evil is the moral equivalent of condoning it, of being complicit in it. In essence, to do nothing in the face of evil is to take on the attributes of evil, consciously or not.[9]

North Americans have, therefore, embarked on the journey through the twenty-first century with a tense and paradoxical convergence of perceptions. On the one hand, I believe Steiner is correct. Our collective fatigue is enormous: we limp more than we run; relinquish more than we fight for; and doubt more than we believe. On the other hand, ours is a taut lethargy. We feel in our gut that we are tiptoeing through landmines. One wrong step, one careless oversight, one inadvertent association, and we may be blown to smithereens. The new channel for our fearfully honed *Angst* is "The Department of Homeland Security." The new military strategy that seeks to calm our national insecurity is "pre-emptive interdiction," a thinly veiled threat to strike first and ask questions later.

It is instructive that Steiner is by no means resigned to valediction, despite his assessment. Finding it "difficult to believe that the story out of *Genesis* has ended,"[10] he searches for the "grammars of creation" that may yet beget new life, new hope, new faith. His quest recalls the wide-eyed ardor of Anne Sexton's lead poem in the collection *The Awful Rowing Toward God*:

---

8   In my judgment, there are many, and they are serious.

9   This line of argumentation appears frequently in D. Parkin, "Entitling Evil: Muslims and Non-Muslims in Coastal Kenya," in *Anthropology of Evil*, 224–25.

10   Steiner, *Grammars of Creation*, 335.

I was stamped out like a Plymouth fender
into this world....

but I grew, I grew,
and God was there like an island I had not rowed to....

I am rowing, I am rowing
though the oarlocks stick and are rusty
and the sea blinks and rolls
like a worried eyeball,

but I am rowing, I am rowing,
though the wind pushes me back
and I know that that island will not be perfect,
it will have the flaws of life,
the absurdities of the dinner table,
but there will be a door
and I will open it
and I will get rid of the rat inside me,
the gnawing pestilential rat.
God will take it with his two hands
and embrace it.[11]

Steiner and Sexton, along with all who row against the wind toward that distant island of hope we call God, are following in the wake of Job. He, too, searches for the grammar of creation. He too learns the hard lesson that such grammar stutters with life's absurdities. He too is presented with a door that, by any measurement, is as easily left closed as open, for it is inscribed with the warning that it opens into a world where God is complicit in evil "for no reason" (Job 2:3). This essay reflects on what we might learn by following Job's passage through this door. Toward this end, the essay will address 1) Job's stretching of Israel's "grammars of creation"; 2) God's admission that evil happens "for no reason," an admission that threatens to subvert Israel's fundamental convictions about covenant partnership with God; and 3) some concluding ruminations on why Israel's sacred scriptures should include such a story, and why, or if, this story seeds any new beginnings for our common life "east of Eden."

---

11   From "Rowing," from *The Awful Rowing Toward God*, by Anne Sexton. Copyright 1975 by Loring Conant, Jr., Executor of the Estate of Anne Sexton. Reprinted by permission of Houghton Mifflin Company. All rights reserved.

"FOR NO REASON"

1   Job and Israel's "Grammars of Creation"

Paul Ricoeur has argued that, of all human experiences, evil is most clearly rooted in the myths of creation.[12] When nature convulses with earthquake, flood, or famine, when disease strikes unawares, when a child dies, the universal existential response is "Why?" Are such experiences simply built into the natural order of a world going through its rhythmic, if often ravaging, cycles, or are they distortions of this order? Are such experiences predictable? Are they consequentially associated with punishment that has been triggered by illegal, unethical, or simply unwise behavior? Or are they unpredictable, illogical, irrational, and thus beyond any reasonable mode of comprehension? All such questions, and a host of others, comprise the aggregate cry of lamentation in response to the experience of suffering. Creation myths, couched as primordial descriptions of the way the world works and therefore of how human beings may understand and order their lives in this world, are the first and most generative resource for addressing these questions. It is axiomatic that no culture – more precisely no religion – can dispense with creation stories. As E. Durkheim noted long ago, "there is no religion that is not a cosmology."[13] Ancient Israel is no exception.

The comments below will focus on Job's probing of Israel's grammars of creation. Space permits no more than a few summary discernments about Israel's two principal creation myths, Genesis 1 and Genesis 2–3, and one major reverberation of these myths, Isaiah 40–55, which is also pertinent for Job's grappling with the enigmas of evil.[14]

The grammar of creation in Genesis 1 (the Priestly account traditionally dated to the sixth-fifth centuries BCE) may be summarized with the words "very good" (Gen 1:31). The opening credo of this account, "In the beginning

---

12   P. Ricoeur, *The Symbolism of Evil* (Boston: Beacon, 1967) esp. Part II, 161–346, and idem, "Evil," *ER* 5:199–208.

13   E. Durkheim, *The Elementary Forms of Religious Life* (New York: Macmillan, 1915), 21. For a concise discussion of the importance of cosmological reflection in biblical religion, see R. A. Oden, "Cosmogony, Cosmology," *ABD* 1:1162–1171.

14   Hebrew scriptures contain multiple creation myths, which is not surprising when one considers that ancient Israel's history spans more than a thousand years and diverse political, social, economic, and religious contexts. The similarities and differences in these accounts underscore the fact that Israel constantly scrutinized its creation traditions, in accord with the pressing realities of an ever-changing world, sometimes preserving them, sometimes questioning them, and sometimes modifying them. For a typology of Hebrew cosmogonic myths, see D. Knight, "Cosmogony and Order in the Hebrew Tradition," in *Cosmogony and Ethical Order*, ed. R. W. Loven and E. E. Reynolds (Chicago: University of Chicago Press, 1985), 134–37.

God," serves as a call to praise the Creator who has spoken into existence, without opposition, an orderly and purposeful world in which every living creature may attain and enjoy its fullest potential. This credo anchors the Priestly summons to human beings, created in God's image, to be good stewards of the very good world of God's hopes and expectations (1:26–30). There is no mention of the threat of evil in Genesis 1. God has created an edenic world, a paradise that invokes, sustains, and rewards unceasing, unfettered celebration.

Genesis 2–3, the so-called Yahwist creation account conventionally dated to the ninth century BCE, shifts the emphasis from the perfection of God's creation to deficiencies in the garden of Eden that both invite and require attention if the world is to fulfill its God-given potential.[15] Some of the limitations – the lack of vegetation, rain, and cultivators of the ground (2:5) – are not negative, because God supplies all that is necessary through a dynamic partnership with human beings, who are commissioned to "tend and keep" God's garden of possibilities (v. 15). One limitation, however, portends a much more difficult challenge. God has planted the "tree of the knowledge of good and evil (*ra'*)" (v. 9) but has blocked access to this tree with a primordial prohibition that carries a severe penalty: "You shall not eat, for in the day you eat of it you shall die" (v. 17). According to this creation story, the way human beings respond to God's limitations on their "knowledge of good and evil" determines whether they secure or forfeit their place in the garden.[16]

As Genesis makes clear, human beings make the wrong choice when they succumb to the temptation to possess the knowledge of good and evil, for this leads to their banishment from the garden. The grammars of creation, thus, must now be enlarged by the word "sin." Following upon the stories of Adam

---

15   On the importance of deficiency and provision as defining themes in Genesis 2–3, see T. Boomershine, "The Structure of Narrative Rhetoric in Genesis 2–3," *Semeia* 18 (1980), 113–29; W. P. Brown, *The Ethos of the Cosmos: The Genesis of Moral Imagination* (Grand Rapids: Eerdmans, 1999), 135–37.

16   The meaning of the merism "good and evil" typically evokes from commentators a number of qualifications, which conclude by cautioning readers to understand that it denotes a comprehensive knowledge enabling human beings to make wise and autonomous decisions concerning what is in their own best interests. This understanding, it may be argued, is supported by the use of the merism elsewhere in the Old Testament, e.g., Deut 1:39; 2 Sam 14:17, 20; 19:36. The phrase does not – so this line of argument goes – refer to an ontological knowledge of good and evil in the moral sense, nor does it shed any direct light on the question of the origin of evil. While this is an important caution to bear in mind, it is also instructive to note that whatever referents are involved, the idiom "good and evil" describes knowledge that God possesses and that humans do not. As such, the knowledge of "good and evil" is another critical and ultimately decisive shortage in the world that God has created, a shortage, from God's perspective at least, that humans must learn to live with.

"FOR NO REASON"

and Eve, the genealogy of sin escalates from Cain and Abel to Noah, when "every inclination of the thoughts of their hearts was only evil" (*ra'*) (v. 5). The only recourse left to a grieving God, according to this tradition, is to subsume the world in a flood and start over again (Gen 6–8). As Ricoeur puts it,

> The intention of the Adamic myth is to separate the origin of evil from that of good, in other words, to posit the radical origin of evil distinct from the more primordial origin of the goodness of all created things; man *commences evil* but does not commence creation.[17]

Lurking at the edges of the account in Genesis 2–3, however, is an invitation to theological reflection from another perspective. The serpent provides the temptation to eat from the forbidden tree by insinuating that God's prohibition is arbitrary at best – why is it wrong for human beings to discern between good and evil? – and self-serving at worst – God forbids it only because God does not want to share this knowledge with anyone else (3:4). The temptation to view the prohibition as irrational is underscored by the dialogue that ensues once the transgression has occurred. When challenged to explain their acts, the man blames the woman, and the woman, in turn, blames the serpent (w. 12–13). The text leaves only the serpent without someone to blame, thus forgoing any further probing for originating causes. But the reader knows that the serpent might justifiably have defended itself by simply shifting the blame to God.[18] It was God, after all, who created both the forbidden tree and the tempting serpent. Genesis 2–3 does not pursue the vexing theological questions encoded in this "blame game." The possibility, however remotely conceived, that God is somehow implicated in the evil that undoes the world is nevertheless now on the radar.

The author of the poems in Isaiah 40–55 may have been among the first of the biblical writers to appropriate and expand upon the two creation myths in Genesis. Perhaps, as the aphorism goes, "necessity was the mother of invention," for this author addressed an audience submerged in Babylonian exile. By any measurement, it was an experience that threatened to bury Israel's convictions about God and the world beneath the rubble of Jerusalem's smoldering ashes. Israel survived this experience, its faith "faint, but strongly faint,"[19] in no

---

17   Ricoeur, "Evil," 203 (emphasis added).

18   Cf. D. N. Fewell and D. M. Gunn, "Shifting the Blame: God in the Garden," in *Reading Bibles, Writing Bodies: Identity and the Book*, ed. T. K. Beal and D. M. Gunn (London: Routledge, 1997), 16–33.

19   For this suggestive phrase, see J. Wood's review of John Updike's *In the Beauty of the Lilies*, in *The New Republic* (May 27, 1996), 30.

small part because this author persuasively linked Israel's hope for redemption to God's abiding promise to "create" a new beginning from the "chaos" into which Israel's world had plunged.[20] The new beginning is envisioned as a new Eden, resplendent with trees (note the seven species listed in 41:17–20; cf. 44:1–5) bearing fruits of "justice" and "righteousness" (e.g., 45:8) that transform Israel's withered landscape into a fertile garden teeming with the possibilities of life. Unlike the Yahwist's garden, which contained a forbidden tree of knowledge, Isaiah's new Eden is a majestic grove that invites all people to understand what God is about (e.g., 41:20; 48:6–8).[21] It is in effect, as William P. Brown has noted, a "victory garden,"[22] for it proves, in advance of the reality, that God will claim victory over Israel's enemies (44:24–45:25) and will restore Israel to its land (41:17–20; 42:13–17; 43:16–21; 49:8–12). From the seeds of this assurance, the prophet's successor extends creation imagery to the transformation of Zion (62:1–4, 10–12), a transformation that grounds God's ultimate promise of "new heavens and a new earth," where sorrow, weeping, and injustice will be no more (65:17–25; cf. 66:20–24).

Embedded within Isaiah's vision of the new Eden are two insights into the enigma of evil that Israel must know and understand. The first is that God's capacities as "Creator of the ends of the earth" (40:28) extend to the farthest boundaries imaginable, perhaps even beyond: "I form light and create darkness, I bring prosperity (šālôm) and create disaster/evil (raʿ); I am the Lord who does all these things" (45:7). No matter how one may interpret God's assertions in this verse, it is hard to excise from this verse what seems to be a primary implication: God is ultimately responsible for whatever merits the label "evil."[23]

---

20 Commentators have often noted that creation language and creation theology are important in Isaiah 40–55. Words for "create," "make," or "form" occur with notable frequency, e.g., bārā (17×), yāṣar (14×), ʿāśah (24×), pāʿal (5×). The word for "chaos" (tôhû), which occurs for the first time in Gen 1:2, occurs in Isaiah 40–55 more frequently than any other biblical book. For further discussion, see, e.g., C. Stuhlmueller, *Creative Redemption in Deutero-Isaiah* (Rome: Pontifical Biblical Institute, 1970); B. C. Ollenburger, "Isaiah's Creation Theology," in *ExAud* 3 (1987), 54–71; R. Clifford, "The Unity of the Book of Isaiah and Its Cosmogonic Language," *CBQ* 55 (1993), 1–17.

21 On the importance of the botanical imagery within Isaiah's vision of Israel's new creation, see Brown, *The Ethos of the Cosmos*, 229–69.

22 Ibid., 246.

23 More than three decades have passed since C. Westermann wryly noted, "It is hard to see why this verse does not bother commentators more than it seems to do" (*Isaiah 40–66* [Philadelphia: Westminster, 1969] 161). More recent work indicates that this verse has indeed "bothered" a number of commentators, some of whom have offered interpretations that would effectively mute the question of God's responsibility for evil, especially in any ontological sense. Several works by Terence Fretheim emphasize God's use of specific and less than perfect human agents, in Isaiah's case Babylon, to shape divine judgment

"FOR NO REASON"

In the words of George Eliot's character, Adam, "Evil's evil, and sorrow's sorrow, and you can't alter its nature by wrapping it up in other words."[24]

A second insight is no less instructive. Brown has noted that the botanical imagery so crucial to the poet's overarching vision of the new creation is also appropriated in the figure of the "suffering servant," who models for Israel the appropriate response to God's plan for the restoration of justice and righteousness. In contrast to the desirable but forbidden tree in the garden of Eden, the servant figure is an utterly undesirable but commendable bearer of knowledge. He accomplishes God's redemptive purposes not like a mighty cedar but like a tender "sapling" (*yônēq*, 53:2; NRSV "young plant"), rooted in nothing more secure than patience, trust, and silent endurance of suffering he does not deserve.[25] Before the God who creates both prosperity and disaster/evil, before the God who oversees the "perversion of justice" that brings about his demise (53:8), before the God who wills to "crush him with pain" (v. 10), the servant bows in humble obedience, even to death (v. 12).

In Isaiah's grammar of creation, Eden's trees have been pruned by the trauma of exile. God's primordial commission to "tend and keep" the garden still hovers over all, but the commission is more freighted. As Eliot's Adam goes on to observe, "no story is the same to us after a lapse of time; or rather, we who read it are no longer the same interpreters."[26] In the gap between the promises of Eden and the destruction of Jerusalem, Israel must learn to entrust its future to the God who declares, "I create evil," then measures fidelity by submission to suffering. Who can faithfully tend such a garden as this? It is little wonder that Israel responds with incredulity: "Who can believe what we have heard?" (53:1).

The author of the Prologue in Job 1–2 seems well acquainted with each of the creation accounts outlined above. Like the Priestly account of God's creation of "the heavens and the earth" in Genesis 1, the report of Job's beginnings in the land of Uz unfolds in a sequence of six scenes alternatively set in heaven and earth.[27] Scene One (1:1–5) describes Job's world as a seemingly perfect

---

(e.g., "Divine Dependence Upon the Human: An Old Testament Perspective," *ExAud* 13 [1997] 6–9; idem, "Divine Judgment and the Warming of the World: An Old Testament Perspective," *WW*, Supplement Series 4 [2000], 25–27).

24   G. Eliot, *Adam Bede* (London: Penguin, 1980), 529.

25   Brown, *The Ethos of the Cosmos*, 258.

26   Eliot, *Adam Bede*, 529.

27   Job 1:1–5; 1:6–12; 1:13–22; 2:1–7a; 2:7b–10; 2:11–13. On the verbal and thematic parallels between Job 1–2 and Genesis 1–3, see S. Meir, "Job I–II: A Reflection of Genesis I–III," *VT* 39 (1989) 183–93. On creation theology generally in Job, see L. G. Perdue, *Wisdom in Revolt: Metaphorical Theology in the Book of Job*, JSOTSup 112 (Sheffield: Almond, 1991); idem, *Wisdom and Creation: The Theology of Wisdom Literature* (Nashville: Abingdon, 1994), 123–92.

recapitulation of primordial Eden. The stage is set for life that is in complete harmony with God's cosmic design. Like Adam, Job exemplifies God's hopes and expectations for humankind; by God's own assessment, "there is no one like him on the earth" (1:8; 2:3). His family, along with his contingent of servants and possessions, confirms that Job, like Adam, has realized the primordial commission "to be fruitful and multiply" and to have "dominion" over everything that has been entrusted to him (cf. Gen 1:22, 28). Moreover, like Adam's garden, Job's world is pristine; there is no intrusion of evil anywhere. Even if there were, the narrator reports, and God confirms, Job would always "turn away" from evil without hesitation (Job 1:1, 8; 2:3).

The land of Uz bears a striking, though troubling, resemblance to the Yahwist's garden in Genesis 2–3. Temptation plays a role in Job's world. It comes not in the form of God's serpent but by one of God's heavenly messengers called "the satan" (*haśśaṭān*) who serves God by investigating the claims of those who profess fidelity to God. God, not the satan, initiates the conversations in which the temptations occur (Job 1:7; 2:2). Still more unsettling is the report that God, not Job, yields not once but twice to the satan's suggestion that Job's world be turned upside down (1:12; 2:6). Unlike Adam, who chose his own course by electing to eat the forbidden fruit, Job has no say in what is about to happen to him; he is the unwitting target in a gambit not of his own choosing. Although the means to the end is different, the outcome of the temptation leaves Job in much the same situation as the primordial couple, only worse. The loss of his wealth and possessions and his affliction with horrible physical suffering leave him sitting among the ashes, perhaps as the LXX suggests, outside the city, where society consigns the destitute and the rejected. To these losses is added one more, which escalates Job's suffering beyond anything recorded for Adam and Eve: his seven sons and three daughters are dead (1:18–19). By the end of Job 2, the "garden of Uz" has become little more than "paradise lost."

The Prologue's report of Job's response to what befalls him also reflects Isaiah's insights into the enigma of evil. At the beginning of Job's story, he successfully "turns away from *evil*" (*ra'*; 1:1). By the end of the Prologue, the friends arrive to comfort one upon whom "evil" (*rā'āh*, 2:11; NRSV "troubles") has fallen, a direct result of God's having been "provoked to destroy him" (2:3). Nevertheless, from beginning to end, Job endures everything with grace, poise, and above all, unscathed fidelity to God. When informed of the death of his children, he falls on the ground and worships, secure in the wisdom of traditional piety: "Naked I came from my mother's womb, and naked shall I return there; the Lord gave, and the Lord has taken away; blessed be the name of the Lord" (1:21; cf. Eccl 5:15; Sir 40:1). When his wife urges him to curse God, he

"FOR NO REASON" 13

immediately dismisses her with a rhetorical question that presumes full acceptance of God's declaration in Isa 45:7: "Surely, if we accept the good from God, should we not also accept the evil" (*ra'*, 2:10; NRSV "bad"). One might well argue, as J. Janzen has done, that Job's enduring faith identifies him as a fellow traveler with Isaiah's suffering servant. The Prologue launches Job on a journey of discovery whose end result is the knowledge that innocent suffering is a divine calling that should be accepted and embraced.[28] It is but a short step from this portrait of Job as suffering servant to the New Testament's commendation of the "patience of Job" as the model for Christian piety (James 5:11).

For all these connections with Israel's probing of creation's affirmations and mysteries, the author of the Joban Prologue has opened a "crack in the door,"[29] inviting, if not requiring, an investigation that threatens to subvert even the most trusted response to evil. The wedge in the door is the candid admission that God has moved to destroy Job "for no reason" (*ḥinnām*; 2:3). This admission hangs over the rest of Job's story, indeed, over the rest of all our stories, like the sword of Damocles. The swath it threatens to cut through our convictions is that, despite our best aspirations to fidelity, the forces that can destroy us are restrained by nothing more than a horsehair, and this resides in the hands of a God who often seems cruelly capricious. The sword may fall at any time, and when it does, we are plunged, ready or not, into a world that seems to hold "no more beginnings."

2 "For No Reason"

The Prologue describes two scenes in the heavenly council that involve conversations between God and the satan concerning Job's fate (1:6–12; 2:1–6). The imagery draws upon Mesopotamian and Canaanite parallels in which royal attendants – in this case the satan – stand before the king in order to report on their activities and receive the king's instructions. In the ancient Near Eastern context, such a council meeting would take place on New Year's Day, when the rhythmic patterns of the created order are suspended in the breach between past and future, old and new. On this liminal day, the council assesses the year that has passed and decides the destinies of nations and peoples for the year that approaches. Against this backdrop, the Prologue suggests that Job's world

---

28   J. G. Janzen, *Job*, IBC (Atlanta: John Knox, 1985), 254–59.

29   For this description of Job's contribution, see D. Penchansky, *The Betrayal of God: Ideological Conflict in Job*, Literary Currents in Biblical Interpretation (Louisville: Westminster John Knox, 1990), 83.

is under review. Decisions, made without Job's consultation, will define his life and that of his family. Job's response will contribute, for good or for ill, to the maintenance of the new creation that God and the council have designed.

God initiates the first council scene with two questions, the second of which sets the ensuing drama in motion: "Have you considered my servant Job? There is no one like him on the earth, a blameless and upright man who fears God and turns away from evil" (1:8). The satan responds to God's boast about Job's piety with two counter questions. The first is a general probe of *Job's* motives: "Does Job fear God for nothing (*ḥinnām*)" (1:9). The question assumes the answer that should follow. As one translation puts it, "Doesn't Job have a good reason for being so good?"[30] Of course, Job serves God for a good reason. The satan's second question is a more specific challenge of *God's* motives: "Have you not put a fence around him and all that he has, on every side?" (1:10). The "fence" is an image for divine protection and safety, which if removed leaves one vulnerable to the chaos that ranges freely beyond its borders (Isa 5:1–7; cf. Ps 80:8–13). The most suggestive analogue for the earthly fence is the firmament that holds back the primordial waters of chaos in order to create a space where human beings can live and prosper (Gen 1:6–9; cf. Job 38:8–11).[31] The satan's question implies that God has defined Job's world and protected his life in a way that guarantees Job's unmitigated devotion. Is it not the case, the satan asks, that if God were to remove this protective border and permit affliction to enter Job's world, then Job's piety would change? If Job were cursed with brokenness and loss, then, the satan wagers, he would respond to God in kind: "He will curse you to your face" (1:11). This initial exchange ends with divine consent and a conferral of authority. God will remove the fence, relinquishing Job and "all that he has" into the satan's power. There is one restriction: the satan must stop short of laying hands on Job himself (1:12).

The second scene in the heavenly council (2:1–7a) begins with preliminary questions from God that repeat almost verbatim the first conversation. The repetition provides a sense of narrative tranquility in the aftermath of the calamities the satan has now inflicted upon Job (1:13–19). In spite of all that has transpired, Job remains the same as before. One new detail emerges, however, and it sends the story spinning in a new direction. God concedes to the satan that the destruction Job has experienced thus far has happened because "you have incited me against him, to destroy him for no reason" (2:3). The admission effectively puts the satan's question in 1:9 back on the table for further inspection. If, as God concedes, no connection exists between Job's conduct and

---

30   S. Mitchell, *The Book of Job* (New York: HarperCollins, 1992), 6.

31   Janzen, *Job*, 39.

God's treatment of him, and if, as God boasts, Job still clings to his piety, does this not confirm that his devotion is truly unconditional? The satan responds by inviting God to permit an escalation of Job's suffering to another level. The satan challenges God once more to "stretch out" the hand (2:5; cf. 1:11), this time extending Job's affliction to his bone and flesh. The wager is that if God exacts the price of physical pain and suffering in exchange for love, then Job will refuse payment. Like Ivan in Dostoevsky's parable of the Grand Inquisitor, Job may be expected to conclude that fidelity to God in a world of untold misery simply costs too much: "We cannot afford to pay so much for admission."[32] Once more God agrees to the challenge and places Job at the satan's disposal, this time with the proviso that the satan must stop short of taking his life (2:6).

Two details concerning God's concession in Job 2:3 require further comment.

1) The verbal construction "incite against" (*swt* [hiphil] + *bĕ*) means to stir up someone to an action against another that would not have occurred without provocation (cf. 1 Sam 26:19; 2 Sam 24:1; Jer 43:3). Job 2:3 is the only place in the Hebrew Bible where this construction is used with God as the object of the verbal action. God says to the satan, *you* have provoked *me*. The concession heightens interest in the story in two ways. First, in the opening scene of the council, God, not the satan, initiates the conversation about Job, thus setting in motion the course of actions that follow. By all indications, God is in full control of what has transpired. The second council scene, however, suggests that the conversation about Job is more complex than it appears. As the titular head of the council, God now seems to be receiving instructions, not giving them. The two reports thus stand in tension with each other. Who exercises the controlling influence in the council, God or the satan? Second, the admission that God can be provoked to do something that might not have occurred without some external pressure invites reflection on the nature of God. Can God be coerced, manipulated, perhaps even tricked? The Prologue does not linger over such questions. But in the ensuing dialogues, Job will confront them squarely with his insistence that innocent suffering places God, not the victim, on trial.

2) God admits to having been provoked to act against Job "for no reason" (*ḥinnām*). The adverb *ḥinnām*, "needlessly, without purpose, for nothing," occurs 32× in the Old Testament. In the majority of cases, the word occurs in contexts that are theologically benign, e.g., in commercial transactions with the meaning "at no cost" or "gratis" (Gen 29:15; Num 11:15; Isa 52:3; Jer 22:13), actions that are "in vain" because they do not accomplish the intended results (Ezek 6:10; 14:23; Mal 1:10; Prov 1:17), or actions that are "without warrant" because they are illegal or unjust (Pss 35:7; 109:3; 119:161). The occurrence

---

32   F. Dostoevsky, *The Brothers Karamazov*, tr. D. Magarshack (London: Penguin, 1958), 287.

16   CHAPTER 1

of *hinnām* in Job 2:3, far from being theologically benign, sets in motion an act that would elsewhere be associated with sin and therefore discouraged and condemned. The wisdom admonition in Proverbs 1 clarifies the matter (cf. Prov 3:30; 24:28; 26:2):

> My child, if sinners entice you, do not consent.
>   they say, "Come with us, let us wait for blood;
> let us wantonly (*hinnām*) ambush the innocent;
> like Sheol, let us swallow them (*niblā'ēm*)[33] alive ..."
>   vv. 10–12a

> my child, do not walk in their way,
>   keep your foot from their paths
> for their feet run to evil (*ra'*) ...
>   vv. 15–16

The report that God has set about to destroy Job for no reason, like a nefarious sinner who ambushes the innocent, is in my judgment perhaps the single most disturbing admission in the Old Testament, if not in all scripture. The hermeneutical space it leaves open for interpretations that explain or exonerate God's behavior is small indeed.[34] Seven sons and three daughters are dead – at God's instigation and with God's permission – for no reason. Perhaps Coleridge was right. The very existence of the Book of Job proves that the Bible

---

33   The same verbal root (*bala'*) is used to describe God's treatment of Job in Job 2:3: "you incited me against him to *destroy him (leballe'o)* for no reason."

34   The syntax of Job 2:3 permits different readings. Depending on the placement of the adverbial expression *hinnām*, the sentence states either that the test the *satan* has proposed has been "in vain" because Job clearly clings to his faith, despite what the satan has encouraged God to do, or that God has afflicted Job "for no reason," that is, God has acted capriciously. D. J. A. Clines is one of the few commentators who have addressed the matter. While conceding that there is no cause "in Job himself" for what he has suffered, Clines argues that this "does not mean that the suffering is meaningless or gratuitous." What is really at issue is not God's character but rather "the truth that lies at the heart of the moral universe (a truth badly misconstrued by popular religion and professional wisdom alike)," namely, that "it is indeed possible for a righteous person to suffer gratuitously." In other words, what is placed under review here is the connection between piety and prosperity. The Prologue's objective is to make clear, once and for all, that "the law of retribution has been broken" (*Job 1–20* [Dallas: Word, 1989], 42–43). Such an interpretation merits careful consideration. At the end of the struggle to understand this verse, however, the Prologue to Job's story reports that his seven sons and three daughters are dead, and it still insists, in my judgment, that faith must reckon with the relationship between the words "God," "evil," and "for no reason."

"FOR NO REASON"

is an utterly human production, because God would never have written such a powerful argument against himself!

William Scott Green has offered a cogent assessment of the potential subversion of faith that the Book of Job represents.[35] He measures Job against three traits that distinguish Judaism from other religions of antiquity – monotheism, covenant, and cult – and concludes that in each case Job "conforms neither neatly nor fully" to what might be expected, perhaps even required, of a book deserving a place in the Hebrew Bible. Indeed, one might well conclude that Job wields its way into Hebrew scripture with a blunt axe. Although the presence of the satan figure in Job 1–2 certainly clouds the issue of monotheism,[36] Green notes that the greater stress comes from Job's challenge to Israel's revered convictions about the covenant and the cult.

The *covenant* defines Israel's distinctive relationship with God. Perhaps the most remarkable feature of the covenant is its enduring validity in the face of seemingly insurmountable odds. From God's perspective, the covenant is a gift that anchors God's relentless commitment to stay in relationship with Israel, come what may. When Israel fails to live up to the covenantal requirements for obedience, God sustains the partnership through judgment tempered by grace and the promise of forgiveness. From Israel's perspective, God can be trusted to keep covenantal promises, a conviction that Israel understands as an invitation to approach God not only with praise and penitence but also with lament and protest.[37]

---

35 W. S. Green, "Stretching the Covenant: Job and Judaism," in "Have You Considered My Servant Job?" ed. S. E. Balentine, special issue, *RevExp* 99 (2002), 569–77.

36 Although I will not track the issue here, Job's challenge to Israel's staunch monotheism merits close investigation. One might argue, for example, that evil presents a particularly acute challenge for each of the three monotheistic religions: Judaism, Christianity, and Islam. Christianity and Islam have the advantage, if we may call it that, of mining the resources of Judaism. In this respect, it is instructive to note that both Christianity and Islam assign responsibility for evil to a devil figure, although they do so in different ways. Christianity affirms that the devil works under restrictions imposed by God (John 12:31; Rev 12:9; 20:1–3), who assures that Christ will ultimately triumph in the battle (Heb 2:14–15; 1 John 3:8). Islam, at least in some traditions, depicts Satan (Iblis, Shaytan) more as a tragic figure worthy of God's redemption than a corrupt figure who should be condemned (e.g., P. J. Awn, *Satan's Tragedy and Redemption: Iblis in Sufi Psychology* [Leiden: E. J. Brill, 1983]). Of the three monotheistic religions, as far as I am aware, only Judaism's sacred texts contain a story like Job's that dares to concede God's complicity in evil "for no reason." One might well argue that Job's contribution to Israel's legacy is the invitation to wrestle with the specter of *unethical*, not *ethical*, monotheism.

37 On Israel's daring cross-examination of God's hiddenness, ambiguity, and negativity, see W. Brueggemann, *Theology of the Old Testament: Testimony, Dispute, Advocacy* (Minneapolis: Fortress, 1997), 317–403.

18   CHAPTER 1

There is one stress point, however, that leaves Israel's convictions about the covenant vulnerable to collapse: the specter of God acting arbitrarily. Even at the far limits of human understanding, where the Keeper of the covenant declares, "I will be gracious to whom I will be gracious, and I will show mercy on whom I will show mercy" (Exod 33:19), Israel trusts that God will act in ways that sustain life, not whimsically destroy it. The report of God's behavior in the Prologue stretches even this trust beyond the breaking point. Green makes the point with numbing clarity:

> In God's exchange with the Adversary, which sets the stage and conditions for Job's suffering, it is clear that the issue is not how God will remain steadfast in the face of Israel's weakness and backsliding, but the reverse. How can the discrete Israelite – and therefore Israel as a people – maintain loyalty in the face of God's caprice? The Prologue establishes that Job's suffering is both gratuitous and deliberate. He suffers not despite his righteousness but because of it. His pain is not accidental, but rather an act of divine will – the result of God's boastfulness and a response to the pedestrian provocation of a secondary divine being. God's allowing of the Adversary to afflict Job is neither subtle nor mysterious. It is crude and religiously pointless, an extreme case of covenant violation. *Nothing in the structure of the covenant prepares Job – or Israelite readers of the book, for that matter – to deal with this kind of behavior.*[38]

To borrow from an observation made by James Wood, divine capriciousness reduces "Life-under-God" to little more than "pointlessness posing as a purpose."[39]

Job also stretches Israel's understanding of the *cult*. Grounded in a Priestly vision of reality, the cult understands that humans have the capacity to diminish the "very good" world God has created and to transgress the covenant that defines Israel's place within this world, either deliberately or inadvertently. It also believes that humans can take concrete action, through the complex of

---

38   Green, "Stretching the Covenant," 573–74 (emphasis added).

39   The full citation from J. Wood ("The Broken Estate: The Legacy of Ernest Renan and Matthew Arnold," in *The Broken Estate: Essays on Literature and Belief* [New York Random House, 1999] 254) is still more scathing: "Life-under-God seems a pointlessness posing as a purpose (the purpose, presumably, being to love God and to be loved in return); life-without-God seems to me also a pointlessness posing as a purpose (jobs, family, sex, and so on – all the usual distractions). The advantage, if it can be described as one, of living in the latter state, without God, is that the false purpose has at least been invented by man, and one can strip it away to reveal the *actual* pointlessness."

"FOR NO REASON" 19

rituals in the tabernacle and temple, to expiate their sins and to repair both the world and the covenant with God that provides their identity within it. The cultic system, however, does not envision and cannot address the possibility that God might contaminate the world and vitiate the covenant with Israel for no reason. There is no prescribed sacrifice that atones for *God's* malfeasance, no ritual that requires *God's* repentance.[40] Measured against this vision of reality, the Prologue in Job threatens to render the cult null and void. Once it is established that God has afflicted Job both willfully and gratuitously, the cult has nothing to offer him. Green spells out the consequences as follows:

> Thus, from a cultic or halakhic perspective, there is nothing Job can do to repair his relationship with God. Sacrifice, repentance, and any religious behaviors that develop from them are nugatory under these circumstances. Job cannot atone for a transgression he did not commit. No offering, no change of heart, can appease divine caprice or undo an affliction that happens for no reason It is probably no accident that Job's speeches nowhere explore a cultic option as a solution to his miseries.[41]

---

40   Although the biblical text only hints at the possibility of God's repentance for "evil" (*ra'ah*; e.g., Jer 42:10), the rabbis dare to press the thought. In a recent editorial that reflects on yet another Palestinian suicide bomber who killed innocent persons in Jerusalem, S. Boteach cites one particularly instructive example. Writing during the high holy days of Yom Kippur, Boteach recalls the story of Rabbi Levi Yitzchak of Berditchev. On the eve of Yom Kippur, after standing with his back to the congregation for more than two hours, Rabbi Yitzchak turned to his congregation and explained ("Is It Time For G-d to Teshuvah?" *Tikkun*, September–October 2002, 68–69): "I want to bring you into the conversation I was having with G-d. 'I come here before you on Yom Kippur, the Day of Atonement to ask that You atone for my sins.' But then it suddenly struck me that in the past year, I haven't brought any plagues upon any part of the world. Nor have I made any woman a widow. Nor have I made any child an orphan. Nor have I caused anyone to go bankrupt and thereby not be able to sustain and support their children. Yet G-d has done all these things. And then it struck me, why isn't He coming to us and asking *us for* our forgiveness? So, I said to G-d, 'In the past year, I have caused no death. I have brought no plagues upon the world, no earthquakes, no floods. I have made no women widows, no children orphans. G-d, you have done these things, not me! You should be asking forgiveness from me. So I'll make a deal. You forgive us, we'll forgive you, and we'll call it even.'" Boteach then concludes his editorial with these words: "We need more Jewish Jobs who, when afflicted by G-d, not only look internally at what sinful actions might have caused their suffering, but also look outward and rail and thunder against the seeming divine injustice. 'By G-d who has deprived me of justice, who has embittered my life, as long as there is life in me ... my lips will speak no wrong.... Until I die I will maintain my integrity' (Job 27:2–5)."

41   Green, "Stretching the Covenant" 574–75. Although it may be true that "Job's speeches nowhere explore a cultic option," it is instructive to note that the Prologue and Epilogue

In sum, the book of Job invites the observation that God's gift of the covenant is a poker chip played in a game where the "house" manipulates the odds. It threatens to reduce Israel's cultic system to sacramental nonsense. Given the wreckage that Job makes of Judaism's most distinguishing traits, we can hardly avoid wondering how this book gained a place in Israel's scriptures and why it survived.

3   Some Concluding Ruminations on the Enigma of Evil

Steiner closes his search for the grammars of creation with these words: "We have long been, I believe that we still are, guests of creation. We owe to our host the courtesy of questioning."[42] If we are still the "guests of creation," and if in fact our host has something worthwhile to teach us about the enigma of evil, as Ricoeur argues, then it is important to ask what we are supposed to learn from the creation texts surveyed above.

The Priestly description of creation is and remains an alluring summons to believe in a "very good" world. Without its promise, we would yield in resignation to a world daily flattened by hard experiences. For all its allure, however, the world of Genesis 1 remains a vision, still attainable, but not yet realized. It is an important part of our creation story, but it is not the whole story.

Genesis 2–3 is the part of our sacred story that keeps us mindful of the blessing and burden of our common life "east of Eden." We are blessed and empowered by the responsibility to "tend and keep" the garden of God's possibilities. In partnership with one another and with God, we are not only authorized but also ennobled to be good stewards of creation's needs. But we also know that we are burdened by failure and culpability. There are limitations, according to this story, to what we can know. Inexplicably, mysteriously, and to our constant peril, these limitations have to do with the knowledge of good and evil. We may, and we often do, protest that these limitations are unreasonable. Why, after all, we say with Yeats, has God decreed that "man can embody the truth, but he cannot know it"? We may, and we do, fashion sophisticated versions of the primordial blame game. But whether we explain our indulgences in the name of Augustine's free will or deflect our responsibility in the name of Calvin's predestination, we know that we must now go about our vocation in the world east of Eden. Until God says differently, the way back to what was

---

frame the book of Job with cultic imagery. For the possibility that Job's story challenges and perhaps necessitates a reformation of the Priestly system, see S. E. Balentine, "Job as Priest to the Priests," *ExAud* 18 (2002), 29–52.

42   Steiner, *Grammars of Creation*, 338.

lost remains blocked by the flaming swords of the cherubim. In the meantime, creation's grammar requires that we learn the words "knowledge of good and evil" and "you shall not eat."

Shouldering responsibility for evil is a heavy, if necessary, load for humans to bear. Even when sin triggers the covenant's prescribed and mutually agreed upon penalties, even when contrite hearts acknowledge guilt and respond with repentance, there are some experiences of suffering and loss that seem wholly disproportionate to any reasonable definition of justice, divine or otherwise. The exile was such an experience for Israel. How should a community of faith, even one convicted of sin by the steady drumbeat of its own prophetic preaching, respond to a world where the holy temple has been destroyed; the promised land has been torched; and a whole nation has been consigned, as far as the eye can see, forever, to eke out an existence in the shadow of God's absence? Ezekiel articulates the despair that pushes hope to the margins: "The days are long, and every vision has perished" (Ezek 12:22).

Perhaps nothing less than Isaiah's summons to believe in God's abiding capacity to create a new Eden could command a hearing in such a wasteland of vanquished visions. But Isaiah's message also suggests that creation's promise must offer something more than a garden where evil is not even recognized as a threat (Genesis 1). If he is to command a hearing among people who can no longer find any credible or actionable instruction in the old notion that they are solely responsible for the evil that destroys their world (Genesis 2–3), this prophet must find new words. Isaiah expands the Genesis creation accounts with two new discernments. The first is a new addition to God's repository of "I am" statements: "I am the Lord, and there is no other.... I bring prosperity and create evil" (45:6b–7). With this declaration, God lends an extra pair of shoulders to the task of bearing the burden of evil, effectively sharing with human beings the responsibility "for all these things." The second is the disclosure that God has provided Israel a model for servant suffering that promises to redeem the "perversion of justice" with blessings inviolable, even by death (Isa 53:8, 12). These two additions to Isaiah's creation theology invite, in turn, a new addition to Israel's repository of "You are" confessions: "Truly, you are a God who hides himself, O God of Israel, the Savior" (45:15). This response marks a pivotal juncture in Israel's understanding of what God is doing in a world now submerged in the abyss between good and evil. It is the only place in Hebrew scripture that combines in one taut and indissoluble confession the assertions that God is a hiding God and that God is a saving God.[43] From this point forward, Israel lives

---

43   The text of Isa 45:15 is difficult and open to different interpretations. For the issues and a defense of the reading proposed here, see S. E. Balentine, "Isaiah 45: God's 'I Am,' Israel's 'You Are,'" *HBT* 16 (1994), 103–20.

with the truth that life in relation to God can never be reduced to one part of this confession without the other. Although I do not think Pascal grasped the full import of Israel's discernment, his classic exegesis of this confession lays claim on us still: "Any religion that does not affirm that God is not hidden is not true."[44]

Each of the creation texts surveyed above offers an important perspective on the enigma of evil. But none of them is adequate for the tragedies that befall Job. Even Isaiah's stretching of creation theology falls short of the mark. When God says, "I create evil," there is no reason to suspect that the words "for no reason" are part of the equation. When God commends the servant model of vicarious suffering, who would (or could) believe that God means seven innocent boys and three innocent girls will be killed to make the point? "Job's world," as Brown has said, "is etched in the blood of a crime scene,"[45] and, we may add, the fingerprints on the assault weapon belong to God. If ever there was a time when reality seemed to demand the concession that there are "no more beginnings," surely it was the day when God convened the heavenly council meeting with the question, "Have you considered my servant Job?"

It is therefore enormously instructive to note that Job's story invites, if not requires, God to speak another word about creation. God's words from the whirlwind (Job 38–41) are meant to offer Job a clearer understanding of the world God has created. Moreover, when God is finished, Job is reported to have a clearer understanding of his place within this world (42:2–5). To the exasperation of almost every reader and interpreter of this book, however, what Job is supposed to have learned from God is far from clear. The majority of commentators interpret God's speeches as a definitive rebuke of Job for presuming to understand the complexity of the world. According to this interpretation, God's objective is first to silence Job's complaints (40:3–4) and then to coerce from him a confession of sin that cedes all authority, however unfathomable, to God (42:6). Despite the considerable merits of this interpretation, it remains vulnerable to the complaint that it leaves us with little more than a divine summons to moral indifference. No one has raised the charge more pointedly, I believe, than Cynthia Ozick:

> So the poet, through the whirlwind's answer, stills Job.
>
> But can the poet still the Job who lives in us? God's majesty is eternal, manifest in cell and star. Yet Job's questions toil on, manifest in death camp and hatred, in tyranny and anthrax, in bomb and bloodshed. Why

---

44   B. Pascal, *Pensées* (London: Penguin Classics, 1966), 103.

45   Brown, *The Ethos of the Cosmos*, 319.

"FOR NO REASON" 23

do the wicked thrive? Why do the innocent suffer? In brutal times, the whirlwind's answer tempts, if not atheism, then the sorrowing conviction of God's indifference.

And if we are to take the close of the tale as given, it is not only Job's protests that are stilled; it is also his inmost moral urge. What has become of his raging conscience? What has become of loving kindness? Prosperity is restored; the dead children are replaced by twice the number of boys, and by girls exceedingly comely. But where now is the father's bitter grief over the loss of those earlier sons and daughters on whose account he once indicted God? Cushioned again by good fortune, does Job remember nothing, feel nothing, see nothing, beyond his own renewed honor? Is Job's lesson from the whirlwind finally no more than the learning of indifference?[46]

Swimming against this tide of conventional interpretation, I have argued in another place that God's objective in speaking about creation is not to silence Job.[47] If this were true, why does God continue with a second speech (40:6–41:34) after Job has already yielded in silence (40:5)? Nor can the objective be to wrench from Job a confession of sin.[48] If this were true, why does the book conclude with God saying, "You [friends] have not spoken of me what is right, as my servant Job has" (Job 42:7, 8)? It seems plausible to me that the purpose of God's instructions about creation, especially the instructions to pay particular attention to Behemoth and Leviathan – creatures that God has endowed with the virtues of power, pride, dominion, and fierce determination to resist domestication – is to summon Job to take his stand with them in the fight against injustice, even if it means that Job must file suit against the creator of the world for crimes against humanity. I remain convinced that this interpretation has merit, but I concede that it does little to alleviate the abiding shock of God's admission that everything, including Job's new understanding of the way world works, has happened "for no reason." At the end of the day, Job's seven sons and three daughters are still dead. Surely if God is God, their deaths must count for more than a statistic.

---

46 C. Ozick, "The Impious Impatience of Job," in *Quarrel and Quandary* (New York: Alfred A. Knopf, 2000), 72.

47 S. E. Balentine, "'What Are Human Beings, That you should Make So Much of Them?' Divine Disclosure from the Whirlwind: 'Look at Behemoth'," in *God in the Fray: A Tribute to Walter Brueggemann*, ed. T. Linafelt and T. K. Beal (Minneapolis: Fortress, 1998), 259–78.

48 For an alternative interpretation of the conventional rendering of Job 42:6, see S. E. Balentine, "My Servant Job Shall Pray For You," *ThTo* 58 (2002), 511–13.

24   CHAPTER 1

There is no meaningful rebuttal to the brutal truth that on this side of Eden the words "evil" and "for no reason" have invaded our public discourse and our (mostly unspoken) creeds of faith. I wonder whether writing a forty-third chapter to the book of Job might be a way out of the conundrum. If the biblical writers had only recorded one more divine speech at the end of the book, perhaps we would hear God say to Job,

> I've had you on my mind for a thousand years
> To thank you someday for the way you helped me
> Establish once for all the principle
> There's no connection man can reason out
> Between his just deserts and what he gets.
> Virtue may fail and wickedness succeed.
> 'Twas a great demonstration we put on.[49]

But then, who is to say that such an effort, no matter how imaginative, would end up any different than Robert Frost's ingenious "Masque of Reason," with a wink and a nod that leaves us both smiling and frowning at God's failure? Or maybe we should turn our imagination to rewriting the Joban Prologue, this time omitting the words "for no reason." But then, the effort to understand why God requires the payment of dead children as proof of fidelity would still compel us, willingly or not, to speak the words "for no reason." If we cannot manufacture answers or even explanations – whatever hermeneutical strategies we employ – we can at least know that when life forces us to bang on the door marked "for no reason," we are following in the footsteps of God.

Perhaps "no answer" is, in the end, *the* answer. In his biography of G. K. Chesterton, Gary Wills adds an appendix that addresses Chesterton's imaginative but baffling Joban parable, *The Man Who Was Thursday*. With commentary that applies both to the end of Chesterton's novel and to the conclusion of its biblical model, Wills offers the following assessment:

> [T]here is one thing worse than giving no answer. And that is to give an answer. That would turn God into a theologian, reducing Jehovah to the level of Job's friends. The author of God's speeches in the Book of Job is the first person we know of to realize that the only theology worth having is the one that forswears theodicy. The riddling rabbi in the whirlwind

---

49   Excerpt from "A Masque of Reason," from *The Poetry of Robert Frost* edited by Edward Connery Lathem. Copyright 1945 by Robert Frost, © 1973 by Lesley Frost Ballantine, © 1969 by Henry Holt and Company. Reprinted by permission of Henry Holt and Company, LLC.

"FOR NO REASON" 25

obviously has answers, but not any small enough to dispense. To find them we would have to go back with him to the drawing board and understand Behemoth's linkages. Or set up the sun's timetable for it. The world says, even to us, more than anything we can say in "defense" of it. Any of God's things is a secret too deep to be fathomed – though Job is rewarded for trying. Because he is the best of God's things.[50]

The final poem in Anne Sexton's collection "The Awful Rowing Toward God" is titled "The Rowing Endeth." The words are for me an inviting and deeply haunting punctuation for these ruminations.

I'm mooring my rowboat
at the dock of the island called God....

"It's okay," I say to myself,
with blisters that broke and healed
and broke and healed –
saving themselves over and over....
I empty myself from my wooden boat
and onto the flesh of The Island.

"On with it!" He says and thus
we squat on the rocks by the sea
and play – can it be true –
a game of poker.
He calls me.
I win because I hold a royal straight flush.
He wins because He holds five aces.
A wild card had been announced
but I had not heard it
being in such a state of awe
when He took out the cards and dealt.
As he plunks down His five aces
and I sit grinning at my royal flush,
He starts to laugh,
the laughter rolling like a hoop out of his mouth
and into mine,
and such laughter that He doubles right over me

---

50   G. Wills, *Chesterton*, 2nd ed. (New York: Doubleday, 2001), 289.

laughing a Rejoice-Chorus at our two triumphs.
Then I laugh, the fishy dock laughs
the sea laughs. The Island laughs.
The Absurd laughs.[51]

When I sit with Job on the ash heap, I catch a glimpse of his need to keep rowing toward God. When at last he docks at the island called God, his friends surrounding him, a new family celebrating with him a restoration of prosperity he never thought possible, I believe I can understand how he might have concluded that he had been trumped in a poker game in which God's wild card secured the win before the first bet was placed. I believe I understand why Sexton would use the word "Absurd" to describe the end of the journey. I am not so sure about the laughter, though. When I look through Job's eyes on the lifeless bodies of dead children whose laughter round his table is gone forever, it is hard for me to imagine that either he or God is smiling. On this point, I am chastened by the tragic reminder that Sexton completed these poems in February 1973 and then committed suicide in the fall of 1974.

I remain instructed, however, by another reminder. The book of Job concludes the story that began with "for no reason" by reporting that Job lived until his death "old and full of days" (42:17). I want and need to believe that he did so in the full and painful recognition that the grammar of creation is always composed with the words "evil," "for no reason," and "God." It is this last word that insists creation's grammar may still provide a lexicon of faith. If we are to live our days as faithful heirs of Job's legacy and God's, even if that legacy deserves the label "absurd," I see no other recourse but to keep rowing. Such it seems to me is the imperative of the faith journey east of Eden.

We shall not cease from exploration
And the end of all our exploring
Will be to arrive where we started
And know the place for the first time.[52]

---

51   From "The Rowing Endeth," from *The Awful Rowing Toward God*, by Anne Sexton. Copyright 1975 by Loring Conant, Jr., Executor of the Estate of Anne Sexton. Reprinted by permission of Houghton Mifflin Company. All rights reserved.

52   Excerpt from "Little Gidding," in *Four Quartets*, copyright 1942 by T. S. Eliot and renewed 1970 by Esme Valerie Eliot, reprinted by permission of Harcourt, Inc.

PART 2

Job and His Friends: "What Provokes You That You Keep on Talking?"

∴

CHAPTER 2

Who Will Be Job's Redeemer?

The question posed in the title of this essay invites reflection from three perspectives. First, the question is Job's. It is textually rooted in his story as recorded in Job 19:21–29. To hear what he says we must tune ourselves to his brokenness and loss, his abandonment by friends and by God, his pained passion and urgency. Who is the redeemer Job needs? Who is the redeemer he expects? Who is the redeemer he finds?

Second, the question has captured the imagination of artists whose exegesis takes the shape of the musical score, the canvas, or the fresco. Their discernments are seldom seriously considered by biblical scholars, even though it is clear they have an enormous hold on the popular understanding of Job's story. For example, who can read Job's words in 19:25 – "I know that my Redeemer lives" – without hearing the echo of the glorious soprano aria in Handel's *Messiah*: "For now Christ is risen from the dead"? It is legitimate and important to recognize that this exegesis draws upon Paul's distinctly Christian affirmation in 1 Cor 15:21, hence that it may go beyond what Job could have known. But if for this reason we simply dismiss Handel to the margins of our considerations, then we risk becoming not only invulnerable to the hermeneutics of imagination but also disconnected from those who sense that Job's story is bigger than what we can safely tuck away in our scholarly judgments.

Third, the question about Job's redeemer deserves a place in the discussion of theodicy. Such an assertion may at first strike readers as unnecessary, for surely Job's pursuit of God and justice ought to ensure that his story has a prominent place in our thinking about these critical issues. It may come as a surprise to some, therefore, that this has not really been the case. As Terrence Tilley has noted, part of the problem of theodicy, what he calls "the evils of theodicy," is that theodicists have in fact typically ignored Job's story and silenced his voice.[1] If Tilley is correct, and I believe there is substantial evidence to suggest that he is, then we would do well to reconsider how our theodicies might be different if we find a place for what Job has to say about his redeemer.

---

1 Terrence W. Tilley, *The Evils of Theodicy* (Washington, DC: Georgetown University Press, 1991), 89–112.

© SAMUEL E. BALENTINE, 2021 | DOI:10.1163/9789004459212_003

30 CHAPTER 2

1   Looking for the Redeemer through Job's Eyes: Job 19:21–29

Job's speech responds to Bildad's description in chapter 18 of the fate of the wicked. Bildad has argued with supreme confidence that the "tent" (*'ōhel*) of the wicked will be destroyed (18:6, 14, 15; cf. 8:22), but concerning Job's "tent," that is, Job's place in the world, he said not a word. Job now insists that if the moral order of the world is to be assessed truthfully, his place within it must be factored into the judgment. He directs Bildad and his friends to look closely at his "tent" (*'ōhel*; 19:12), surrounded and under siege by God, and he raises hard questions that challenge his comforters and their question-free view of the world: "How long?" (v. 2); "Why?" (v. 22).[2] He begins by rebuking the friends for repeatedly arguing with him as if he were the guilty party (vv. 2–5). He would have them "know" (v. 6) that it is God's behavior that makes a mockery of justice, not his. God has attacked him ruthlessly and without restraint (vv. 7–12), and God has caused his family and friends to abandon him (vv. 13–20). What Job needs from his friends is compassion (v. 21: "have pity," "have pity"), not condemnation, and he would have them "know" (v. 29) that if they continue to attack him, the judgment they obtain will be their own (vv. 21–29).

Two further observations are pertinent as an introduction to this speech. First, each pericope of the speech is clearly addressed to the friends: v. 2: "How long will you (plural) torment me?" v. 6: "know (plural) that God has put me in the wrong;" v. 21: "Have pity on me ... O you my friends." For the first time since he spoke from the ash heap, Job does not address God. He has cursed and complained in God's hearing (Job 3), but God has not answered. He has summoned God to court (Job 9–10), but God has not answered. He has prepared a case against God and presented it as if God were listening (Job 12–14), but God has not answered. He has charged God with criminal assault and appealed to heaven for a witness (Job 16), but God has not answered. Job has much more to say, of course, and he will continue to cock his ear toward heaven for the response that may yet come, but for now he has said all he knows how to God. When next he addresses God directly, it will be to insist once again on his innocence and to complain once more that when he cries out God does not answer him (30:20–23).

---

2 In the Book of Job it is Job who asks the hard questions about God and the world God has created. The friends are typically willing to question only Job. From their perspective God is beyond question. See further, W. A. M. Beuken, "Job's Imprecation As the Cradle of a New Religious Discourse," in *The Book of Job*, ed. W. A. M. Beuken (Leuven: University Press, 1994), 67.

In the midst of friends who listen without compassion and a God who gives every indication of not listening at all, Job would have good reason to give up all hope. Indeed, he now surmises that it is his "hope" that God has targeted for destruction (v. 10). This makes a second feature of his speech all the more surprising. In the middle of the last pericope (vv. 21–29), sandwiched between vexed contemplation of friends who are "pursuing" and "persecuting" him (vv. 22, 28), Job speaks of a "redeemer" who will rise and testify to his innocence (vv. 25–27). These verses are perhaps the most well known in the whole of the book. They are also among the most difficult to interpret. For the moment, we may suspend discussion of the difficulties in order to appreciate that such verses are present at all. In the midst of everything Job "knows" about brokenness and loss, in the midst of everything he "knows" about God's silence, cruelty, and indifference, Job declares emphatically that he "knows" something beyond these things as well. However, one interprets these verses, it is Job's hope for "something beyond" that makes this speech far more than just another response to one of the friends.

Job's closing words begin with a plea (vv. 21–22) and end with a warning (vv. 28–29). Both the plea and the warning are addressed to the friends, who have been Job's principal audience since the beginning of his speech. Moreover, there are rhetorical links between verses 21–22 and 28–29 that tie the beginning and end of this last pericope together. Job questions why his friends "pursue" (v. 22: *rādap*) him; if they continue "pursuing" (v. 28: *rādap*; NRSV: "persecute") him, they will suffer the consequences.

Despite these clues for reading verses 21–29 as a whole piece, it has long been the practice to isolate verses 23–27 and to accord them a theological significance that virtually guarantees their relationship to the literary context will be lost. This is especially true for verse 25, which is perhaps the most famous sentence in the Book of Job: "I know that my Redeemer lives." Within the Christian tradition this verse can hardly be read apart from the nexus of faith that associates it with Christ and the promise of resurrection. Nevertheless, it is important to bear in mind that in its context Job's affirmation is framed by persecution. From his perspective this persecution comes both from God (vv. 6–20) and from friends who act "like God" (v. 22). If it is Job's hope for a redeemer that imagines a transformation of life's framing realities, it is also the persistent claim of these same realities on his life that works to frustrate, confine, and deny that hope.

The structure of this last pericope argues against severing the connection between reality and hope. A full appropriation of Job's hope for a redeemer depends on recognizing with him the abiding tension of living between *what is* and *what might be*. The temptation is to weight *what might be* so heavily that

32 CHAPTER 2

what is no longer factors into the balance of faith's equations. One strategy for resisting this temptation is to suspend for a time the discussion of Job's redeemer and place his plea (vv. 21–22) and warning (vv. 28–29) at the forefront of our analysis. Once this frame is in place, the hope that *stands at its center* and *yearns for its transformation* can be assessed.

1.1   *The Frame for Job's Hope (19:21–22, 28–29)*

There is a steady and logical progression of thought in these four verses that invites one to ponder what their meaning would be *if* they were taken as a single unit. Job appeals to the friends for different treatment (v. 21), questions them about their persecution of him (v. 22), cites their own reasons for persecuting him as evidence against them (v. 28), then warns them of the penalty they will pay for what they have done (v. 29). Job's lawyer-like movement from appeal to warned punishment is surprising on several counts.

For one who has just described himself as assaulted, stripped, ostracized, and barely clinging to life, Job now seems unexpectedly vigorous. His language is peppered with imperatives, questions, and conclusions that suggest he still has the strength and resolve to speak forcefully.

– He *demands* that the friends change their way of responding to him. His call for them to "have mercy," or "take pity" (v. 21a: *honnunî* [2x]) may be only sarcastic. He has never before asked for their mercy, and he has no reason to expect it from them now. It may also be an ultimatum to "Shut up!" As Clines has suggested, "the biggest favor he [Job] can believably ask of them now is to stop hounding him or persecuting him by continuing their speeches. He does not want their pity so much as their silence."[3]

– He *interrogates* them about their reasons for persecuting him (v. 22: "Why?"), then proceeds to *deduce* their motive and *challenge* it as a flat contradiction of the truth. They believe they are acting "like God," and like God they come after him with a vengeance, because they believe "the root of the matter" lies in him (v. 28). The truth is, as Job has tried to make clear to them, it is "God who has put me in the wrong" (v. 6).

– He *warns* them (*gûrû lākem*; "fear for your lives") that persecuting an innocent person is an act worthy of punishment (v. 29). Previously Job has admonished the friends to know that if they give perjured testimony in his case they can expect to be cross-examined not only by him but also by God (13:7–12). Now he would have them know that their actions against him will be dealt with by the "sword," a symbol for punishment that is comprehensive and fatal (cf. Isa 27:1; Jer 27:8; 44:13).

---

3   David J. A. Clines, *Job 1–20*, Word Biblical Commentary (Dallas, TX: Word, 1989), 453.

WHO WILL BE JOB'S REDEEMER?

Even more surprising is what seems to be generating Job's energy. He has already conceded that "there is no justice" (v. 7), and yet with the last word of this speech he indicates that the pursuit of justice is precisely what continues to drive him forward (v. 29: "there is a judgment"). There is a subtle but important tension between Job's concession about the impossibility of justice and his resolve nonetheless to declare it a certainty. He is convinced that there is no justice for an innocent person like himself, because *God* will not answer his petition for vindication. Yet, when he ponders the justice of his friends' behavior he states without reservation that there will be a judgment that finds them guilty. What is not clear, however, is who will be the agent of this justice. There is no reason to assume that Job believes God will be the agent, for God's silence on these matters seems to be an established fact. Moreover, Job does not once address God in this speech, so if there is to be justice Job seems to expect that it will have to come from some other source.

It is instructive to note in this regard that for the first time since chapter 3 Job does not end his speech by longing for death. His desire is now for something different; he yearns for the validation of the words "there is a judgment." With his resolve now focused on justice rather than death, a new possibility, faintly conceived and barely imaginable, begins to suggest itself to Job. In the midst of abandonment by God and persecution by friends, perhaps the one who must assume responsibility for justice is none other than Job himself. Such a thought of course seems utterly impossible. The pain of his persecution is too deep. The silence of God is too final. The evidence that there is no justice is too overwhelming. When Job comes to the end of this speech these are the hard realities that frame his life. If there were not something more one suspects that these realities would press and squeeze until they exacted from Job a different conclusion than the one with which this speech ends: there is *no* judgment. But these framing realities are not the whole. Something more has inched into the speech, even though there is virtually no room for it in the midst of all that seems to be fixed and settled.

1.2 *The Center of Job's Hope (19:23–27)*

From deep within an existence framed by persecution Job dares to hope for something more. He articulates this hope in several ways, each of which is shaped by the abiding tension between what he *needs*, what he *knows*, and what he *experiences*.

What Job *needs* is some way to keep his plea for justice alive (vv. 23–24). He has argued the case for his innocence with the friends, but they have been unable or unwilling to accept the merits of his claim. He has appealed to God for a fair and just hearing, but God has refused to answer him. He has screamed

34   CHAPTER 2

out "Violence!" in the hope that somewhere on earth there is a place where
the cry of the unjustly accused is not covered up and denied, but "there is no
justice" (v. 7; cf. 16:18). What he needs now is a record of his claim on justice
that will survive in spite of rejection and denial. He yearns for his testimony
to be "written" (*kātab*), "inscribed" (*ḥāqaq*), and "engraved" (*ḥāṣab*; literally,
"hewn out;" cf. NJPS: "incised"). Exactly how Job envisions the writing process
is unclear, but the sequence of these verbs, each one signifying a means of
preservation more permanent than the last, indicates that he desires a record
that cannot be erased. It is to last "forever," beyond the friends' rebuke, beyond
God's silence, beyond his own unanswered cries for justice.[4]

What Job *knows* is stated emphatically: "I, I know my redeemer lives" (v. 25).
Although the grammar that conveys this assertion is clear enough, the meaning of what Job says has been the subject of enormous debate. The unfortunate decision of NRSV and other modern translations to capitalize "redeemer"
obscures this debate by inviting the Christian community to assume that the
one to whom Job refers is Christ. The world in which Job lives, however, and
what he "knows" within (and beyond) this world stands at a far remove from
what Christians may "read back" into his assertion. This is not to deny that
Job (or the poet) may have said more than he knew or that a Christian perspective adds faith assertions that may enlarge what Job could have known.
Nonetheless, when the community of faith recognizes that what Job "knows"
is hard to determine exactly, it keeps itself mindful that the journey from
"redeemer" to "Redeemer" is long and complex, not quick and automatic.

Job *knows*, that is, he "firmly believes" a) that his "redeemer" (*gōʾēl*) lives and
b) that "at the last he will stand upon the earth" (v. 25). Both assertions merit
close attention. The term *gōʾēl* comes primarily from the field of family law. It
designates the nearest male relative – brother, paternal uncle, cousin – who is
duty-bound to protect and preserve the family when his kinsman is unable to
do so. The responsibilities of the *gōʾēl* include buying back family property that
has fallen into the hands of outsiders (Lev 25:25–28; Ruth 4:3–6; Jer 32:6–8),
redeeming a relative sold into slavery (Lev 25:47–49), marrying a widow to provide an heir for her dead husband (Ruth 3:12–13; 4:5), and avenging the blood

---

4   Job's words suggest a stone monument of some type. One possibility is a tomb inscription
    hewn in the rock that marks his burial place (cf. K. Galling, "Die Grabbenschnft Hiobs," *Die
    Welt des Orient* 2 [1954–1959], 3–6). Whatever Job may have intended, his words have become
    an important source for epitaphic sentiments. This is especially true of the eighteenth cen-
    tury, when citations from the Book of Job appear more frequently on tombstones, burial
    vaults, and mausoleums than anywhere else. For discussion and examples, see, Jonathan
    Lamb, *The Rhetoric of Suffering: Reading the Book of Job in the Eighteenth Century* (Oxford:
    Clarendon Press, 1995), 274–300.

of a murdered relative (Num 35:19–27; Deut 19:6–12). In religious usage God is described as the *gōʾēl* of those who have fallen into distress or bondage (e.g., in Egypt: Exod 6:6; 15:13; Ps 74:2; in Babylon: Isa 43:1, 14; 49:7–9). It is noteworthy that God's responsibilities as *gōʾēl* include pleading the case (*rîb*) for those too helpless or too vulnerable to obtain justice for themselves (Ps 119:154; Prov 23:11; Jer 50:34; Lam 3:58).

This range of referents for *gōʾēl* invites an important question: who is the redeemer in whom Job believes? Does he expect a family member to come to his aid? His description of the way family and kin have deserted him (vv. 13–20) indicates that he knows his *gōʾēl* is unlikely to be found among them. Does he expect God to be his *gōʾēl?* What he *knows* about God could hardly give him reason to believe God will be any more help than his family. He *knows* that a mere mortal cannot possibly win a suit against God (9:2), that God will not regard him as innocent (9:28), that God's secret purposes for him are sinister (10:13), and that he can only obtain vindication if God agrees to give up terrorizing him long enough for him to plead his case (13:18–21).

Given his despair over the way both family and God have failed him, it is more likely that Job believes his *gōʾēl* is a third party litigator who will stand between him and his accusers (both divine and human) and argue his case for acquittal. He has explored this possibility on two previous occasions. In 9:33 he imagined that there might be an impartial "arbiter" (*môkîaḥ*) who could mediate the differences between him and God, but then he dismissed the idea as impossible. In 16:19 he returned to the idea of a heavenly "witness" (*ʿēd*) who would take his side in God's court and give testimony to the truth of his claim.

On that occasion his words were both more urgent and more desperately hopeful: "even now, in fact, my witness is in heaven." Now Job returns for a third time to the idea that someone, a *gōʾēl*, will come to his defense *against God* and the *friends*. It appears that his hope is again for a heavenly figure, perhaps an intercessory angel similar to the one Elihu mentions in 33:23–24. But it must be conceded that the one who acts as Job's defense attorney is no more precisely identified than is the *satan* who serves as God's prosecutor.[5] What is clear, however, is that for the first time Job does not dismiss the idea out of hand or express it with caution. Now he states emphatically that his redeemer lives and that in the end ("at the last") the redeemer will be successful in obtaining his vindication.

Job *knows* that his redeemer lives. The interpretive question is *when* does he believe the redeemer will rise to his defense? The adverbial expression "at the

---

5 Cf. Norman Habel, *The Book of Job*, The Old Testament Library (Philadelphia: Westminster, 1985), 306.

last" (*'aḥărôn*, v. 25b) indicates that Job's vindication will take place at some future time. The following line – "after (*'aḥar*) my skin has been destroyed" (v. 26a) – suggests a time after Job's death. Job has previously wondered if death might be a temporary state, after which God would summon him to return to a new and fully restored life (14:13–17). It is possible that this idea of a post-mortem renewal finds further expression in 19:26b–27, which can be taken as a description of Job's "re-fleshed" existence after death, when at last he will see God. From a Christian perspective it may indeed be tempting to interpret Job's vindication "at the last" as an embryonic witness to resurrection. That this is Job's belief, however, is unlikely for several reasons. Although he contemplates renewal after Sheol, he ultimately rejects it as a hope that is utterly without foundation. The truth is that God "destroys" that hope just as certainly as "the waters wear away the stones" (14:18–22). Job states succinctly the only truth he knows: "mortals lie down and do not rise again; they will not awake or be roused out of their sleep" (14:12). Moreover, Job has become increasingly adamant that a post-mortem vindication would not satisfy the imperative for justice. Those who die as victims leave a legacy of nothing more than death. There must be some place among the living where the cry for justice gets a hearing (16:18). If there is not, then the voice that speaks from the grave does not celebrate hope; it mourns its loss: "Where then is my hope? Who will see my hope?" (17:15).

A more satisfactory approach lies along the lines proposed by Clines.[6] He argues for differentiating between what Job *knows* or *expects* (vv. 25–26a) and what he *desires* (vv. 26b–27). Job knows that a redeemer will rise and vindicate him after his death. But what he most desires is justice while he is alive. He wants to be present when his case comes before the court; he wants to testify on his own behalf; in short, he wants to see God for himself (cf. 13:15–16). The tension between what Job knows and what he desires can be captured by rendering the *conjunction* (*waw*) in the middle of verse 26 as "but" rather than "then" and the following verbs ("imperfects" in Hebrew) as expressing a wish or desire rather than a prediction. The *disjunction* at the middle of verses 25–27 may then be reflected as follows:

> I, I know that my redeemer lives, and that at the last he will stand upon the earth – after my skin has been thus destroyed. *But* I *would see* (*'eḥezeh*) God from my flesh. I, I *would see* (*'eḥezeh*) for myself. My eyes *would see* (*rā'û*), not another's.

---

6 Clines, *Job 1–20*, 461–462. For a similar approach see Habel, *The Book of Job*, 479.

The disjunction between what Job knows and what he desires places the redeemer's role in a different light. Job's certainty about the future does not lessen his desire for the present. At the heart of that desire are two things: the presence of God and justice. From this point forward Job says no more about arbiters or witnesses or redeemers. Instead, he intensifies his quest to find God (Job 23) and to argue his innocence before the Almighty with a force that requires response (Job 31). It is tempting to jump to the end of Job's story to see the outcome of his quest, for there we learn that at last God appears to Job (chapters 38–41) and at last Job "sees" God (42:5). Whether this ending satisfies his pursuit of justice must remain for now an open question. In the meanwhile Job must grapple with what he needs and what he knows and *what he desires* in the midst of what he experiences.

Finally, what Job *experiences* is utter exhaustion (v. 27c). "My heart faints within me" is literally "My kidneys wear out in my bosom."[7] At one level the expression signifies the overwhelming emotional fatigue that drains Job's passion for carrying on with the struggle, for the kidneys, like the heart, are the symbolic center of intense affections and desires. At a more basic level the kidneys are a vital and extremely sensitive part of the human anatomy. They are important in maintaining the balance of fluid and salt that stabilizes the body at a tolerable degree of acidity. When that balance is lost the body is threatened, and if the kidneys cannot act to restore equilibrium the consequences can be fatal. Job of course does not speak with the expertise of a medical internist. His knowledge comes from other sources. He does know, however, what it is like when the kidneys are under attack. God's archers have targeted him for destruction; their arrows pierce his "kidneys" (16:13). It is out of that experience and all that it portends that Job speaks about the dangerous imbalance between God's hostile presence in his life and his emotional and physical capacities to withstand it.

To conclude this discussion of verses 21–29 we may return once more to the tension between reality and hope that frames Job's closing words. Job is hemmed in by persecution that has no end in sight (vv. 21–22, 28–29). Without some intervening hope this hard reality will constitute the full measure of what he knows and has already declared to be fixed and settled: "there is no justice." But the structure of this final pericope insists that life must not be read straight through from one reality to the next. Buried deep within Job's consciousness is the hope for something more (vv. 23–27). This hope is real, and it beckons him onward. There is a redeemer, and Job can be certain that in the end the declaration about life will be more than what the present allows him to say.

---

7   Marvin H. Pope, *Job*, The Anchor Bible (Garden City, NY: Doubleday and Company, 1965), 147.

38   CHAPTER 2

Even so, a future justice is a justice delayed, and in the meantime the realties that wage war on hope grind away without interruption. Although Job's hope cannot be thwarted, he does concede that there is no obvious stimulus for it to exercise its passions, *unless* somehow *he* can sustain its aspirations *by his own resolve*. Toward that end, when he turns once more to face the persecution that defines his life he speaks against it with a new-found imperative: be warned, "there is a judgment" (v. 29). Between the reality that "there *is no* justice" and the determination that "there *is* a judgment" there is a vast chasm. On the far side of that chasm is the redeemer, already proclaiming victory. In the middle of that chasm, where victory is hard to see, is Job. Whenever the gap between persecution and justice is finally bridged, Job serves notice that he will have played a role, which is at yet beyond his full comprehension, in pleading for it, believing in it, and working for it.

2 Looking for Job's Redeemer through the Eyes of the Artist: Gilding the Metaphor of Resurrection with "the Edge of Felt Conjecture"

Early Christian artists viewed Job as a prophet of resurrection and thus as a model for those who endure suffering heroically and with patient faith. Such a view would have been available to them in a variety of sources. The LXX translation of Job 19:25–26, for example, reads as follows: "For I know that He is eternal; the One who will dissolve me on earth will raise anew my skin." In the first century Clement of Rome appropriated this translation as a witness to the hope for resurrection (1 Clem 25:1; 26:1). The *Testament of Job* (first century BCE–first century CE) offers an even more explicit interpretation. When Job learns of the calamities about to befall him an angel reassures him with these words: "If you are patient, I will make your name renowned in all generations ... *And you shall be raised up in the resurrection*" (4:6, 8). The penultimate scene in the Testament describes the fulfillment of the angel's words. At his death Job's soul was carried off by a heavenly chariot to the east, there to be reunited with his former children (*T. Job* 52:10; cf. 40:3).

Such a view of Job made him an important figure for early Christians who were themselves often the subject of severe persecution, especially in Rome during the third and fourth centuries. Job's place in early Christian piety is confirmed by the fact that his image is found more than twenty times throughout the Roman catacombs.[8] These frescoes typically depict Job not as a victim or

---

8 For discussion and illustrations, see Samuel Terrien, *The Iconography of Job Through the Centuries: Artists as Biblical Interpreters* (University Park, PA: The Pennsylvania State University Press, 1996), 17–23.

WHO WILL BE JOB'S REDEEMER? 39

even a lamenter but instead as a virile, heroic figure who seems serenely confident of his ultimate return to former glory.[9]

At least from the seventh century, if not before, Christian liturgies looked
to Job as a witness to the promise of resurrection.[10] Until the middle of the
twentieth century, when Vatican II initiated significant changes, the Roman
liturgy included a full range of Joban texts, including those bearing witness to
his persistent questioning and protest of God's treatment. The Matins for the
Dead, for example, appropriated nine readings from Job, which were recited in
the following order: Job 7:16–21; 10:1–7; 10:8–12; 13:22–28; 14:1–6; 14:13–16; 17:1–3,
11–15; 19:20–27; 10:18–23.[11] The sequence of these readings is striking, because
they both begin and end with the same testimony to Job's abject despair:
"I loathe my life; I would not live forever. Let me alone, for my days are but
a breath" (7:16); "Why did you bring me forth from the womb? Would that I
had died before any eye had seen me … Are not the days of my life few? Let
me alone, that I may find a little comfort" (10:18, 20). It is only in the penultimate reading from 19:20–27 that the liturgy recognizes Job's astonishing move
toward a conflicted hope for some more positive outcome in his life. Yet having glimpsed that possibility, the liturgy then returns the reader to the world
of Job's unrequited suffering, there to linger imaginatively in the silence of
his unanswered question "Why?" In this respect the liturgy is consonant with
the tensive connection between reality and hope that defines Job's speech in
19:21–29.

After Vatican II the Roman liturgy breaks with what had been a thousand-
year old tradition. In the revised Liturgy for the Dead the nine readings from Job
are reduced to one primary text – 19:25–27. This text is in turn repositioned as
a response to three readings from the Epistle to the Corinthians, each of which
proclaims the resurrection of Christ as the hope for Christians.[12] Concerning

---

9   For a striking example see the depiction of Job in the Cemetery of Apronianus, which
    Terrien (Ibid.) provides in Color Plate II.

10 See Philippe Rouillard, "The Figure of Job in the Liturgy: Indignation, Resignation, or
    Silence," in *Job and the Silence of God* [*Concilium* 169, 9/1983], eds. C. Duquoc, C. Floristan
    (New York: Seabury, 1983), 8–12.

11 Ibid., 9.

12 Ibid., 10. A similar practice exists in other ecclesiastical traditions, as is evident for
    example in the following Episcopal liturgy for the Burial of the Dead ("The Burial of the
    Dead: Rite One," in *The Book of Common Prayer and Administration of the Sacraments and
    Other Rites of the Church According to the Use of the Episcopal Church* [New York: Seabury,
    1977], 469):
    "I am the resurrection and the life, saith the Lord, he that believeth in me, though he
    were dead, yet shall he live, and whosoever liveth and believeth in me shall never die."
    (John 11: 25)

40   CHAPTER 2

this deletion from the liturgy of Job's anguished voice, P. Rouillard offers the
following observation:

> It is true that the Missal permits Job 19: 25–27a to be read at Masses for
> the Dead: "For I know that my Redeemer lives ..." *But this overcatechised
> Job is no longer the Job of the Bible.*[13]

There can be little doubt that the popular hold on the Christian community
of this "over-catechised Job" owes much to Handel's glorious "exegesis" in the
Messiah, first performed in Dublin in 1742.[14] The text for the first part of the
soprano aria is the King James Version of Job 19:25–26:

> I know that my Redeemer liveth, and that he shall stand at the latter day
> upon the earth. And though worms destroy this body, yet in my flesh shall
> I see God.

The second part of the aria comes from 1 Corinthians 15, the chapter that provides Paul's most comprehensive discussion of Christ's resurrection: "For now
is Christ risen from the dead, the first fruits of them that sleep" (1 Cor 15:20).

In terms of both its tonality and its lyrics the aria signals that the believer
has reached a new and higher level of understanding. The key shifts from the D
of the preceding Hallelujah Chorus to the E of the soprano's enlightened affirmation. The linkage of the redeemer who will appear "at the latter day" with
Christ who is "now" risen proclaims that though one may die, a resurrected life
in Christ is the assured hope of all believers.

The assurance that believers will be resurrected like Christ is then immediately fortified by a sequence of five additional recitations from 1 Corinthians 15:

Bass Recitative
Behold, I tell you a mystery, we shall not all sleep, but we shall be chang'd,
in a moment, in the twinkling of an eye, at the last trumpet.
        1 Cor 15: 51–52

"I know that my Redeemer liveth, and that he shall stand at the latter day on earth, and
though this body be destroyed, yet shall I see God, whom I shall see for myself and mine
eyes behold, and not as a stranger." (Job 19:25–27)

"For none of us liveth to himself, and no man dieth to himself. For if we live, we live
unto the Lord, and if we die, we die unto the Lord. Whether we live, therefore, or die, we
are the Lord's." (Rom 14:7–8)

13   Rouillard, "The Figure of Job in the Liturgy," 10 (emphasis added).

14   See further Roger G. Bullard, *Messiah: The Gospel According to Handel's Oratorio* (Grand
Rapids, MI: Eerdmans, 1993).

Bass Aria

The trumpet shall sound, and the dead shall be rais'd incorruptible, and we shall be chang'd. For this corruptible must put on incorruption, and this mortal must put on immortality.

1 Cor 15: 52–53

Alto Recitative

Then shall be brought to pass the saying that is written, Death is swallow'd up in victory.

1 Cor 15: 54b

Alto and Tenor Duet

O Death, where is thy sting? O grave, where is thy victory? The sting of death is sin, and the strength of sin is the law.

1 Cor 15: 55–56

Chorus

But thanks be to God, who giveth us the victory through our Lord Jesus Christ.

1 Cor 15: 57

Images of the heroic Job depicted in the catacombs and of the selectively censored Job who foreshadows resurrection in much Christian liturgy and music remain a staple in the history of art from the Early Christian to the modern period. Here and there, however, artists have yielded to the "felt conjecture"[15] that Job should not only be portrayed as simply a willing victim, what R. Rubenstein has called a "new kind of Isaac,"[16] whose suffering is summarily cancelled out by the promise of resurrection. Two examples may be singled out for brief comment.[17]

(1). Vittore Carpaccio (1450–1525) was born m Venice, where he studied for a time with Giovanni Bellini. His *Meditation on the Passion of Christ* (c. 1495) is now located in the Metropolitan Museum of Art in New York.

In the foreground of this painting Carpaccio places three figures. Seated on the left is Jerome. Opposite him on the right is Job. Like his counterpart Job

---

15 For this way of describing the artist's capacity to "enchant" us with ideas that constitute the most "ingressive, transformative summons available to human experiencing," see George Steiner, *Real Presences* (Chicago: The University of Chicago Press, 1989), 137–146. The citation is from p. 141.

16 Richard Rubenstein, "Job and Auschwitz," USQR 25 (1970), 425, 427.

17 The comments that follow rely on Terrien's discussion in *The Iconography of Job Through the Centuries*, 135–139, 261–263.

FIGURE 2.1   Vittore Carpaccio (c. 1455–1523/26). *Meditation on the Passion of Christ* (c. 1490) Oil and tempera on wood. John Stewart Kennedy Fund, 1911
COURTESY OF THE METROPOLITAN MUSEUM OF ART, NEW YORK

is seated. His posture indicates his meditation on the central figure of Christ, who slumps in Job's direction as he awaits the coming resurrection. The background provides two contrasting views of the landscape. To the left, just above Christ's throne, is a dead tree, crooked toward a deserted mountain trail where a leopard is about to devour a doe. The imagery suggests a world of death, unrestrained force, and hapless victims. To the right the imagery suggests just the opposite: the trees and plants are full with foliage; walled villages are safe and secure; a leopard walks peacefully behind a doe; a bird sits unafraid on the ground.

For my purposes here it is the figure of Job that deserves attention. Carpaccio places Job on the side where life and peace and promise define the landscape. Job's hope of being restored as a full participant in this world is further indicated by the fragmented Hebrew from Job 19:25–27 that is inscribed across the front of the block on which he sits. Yet there are also signs that death remains a very real presence for Job. A shattered human skull along with dried out bone pieces lie on the ground beneath his feet. A piece of the granite-like block that

WHO WILL BE JOB'S REDEEMER? 43

supports him and bears his words of hope is broken off. And most suggestively, Job supports a weary head in the palm of his left hand while pointing with his right finger to the sandals on his feet. Terrien suggests that Carpaccio seeks to call attention to Job's diseased feet. Even in a world that promises resurrection, Job's feet must be protected by sandals; his journey still picks its way through the hurtful debris of life.[18]

The imagery of Job pointing to his feet provides a suggestive parallel to Luke's account of Jesus post-resurrection appearance to the disciples on the road to Emmaus (Luke 24). *After* the disciples had recognized him, *after* they had broken bread with him, *after* they had proclaimed the post-easter hallelujah – "The Lord has risen indeed!" (24:35) – Jesus came and stood in their midst to speak one further word of instruction: "Look at my hands and my feet. Touch me and see" (24.39). It seems a rather odd thing to say to those who have already experienced his resurrection and have already begun to proclaim its promise for others, *unless* perhaps Jesus is concerned to remind them one last time that even in the afterglow of resurrection it is imperative that those who proclaim the gospel be able to touch and feel the raw hurt of brokenness and loss. Job points to his feet, much like Jesus may have done with the disciples. The evocative difference here is that it is *Job who directs Jesus* to take one last look before resurrection becomes a reality. Perhaps Carpaccio does indeed portray Job as a prophet of Christ the Redeemer.[19] Perhaps Carpaccio also wishes to suggest that Job is the teacher who provides Jesus the lessons about what it means to walk where he has walked.

(2). A second example is Marc Chagall's *Job With Background of Geometricized Christ 'a la Cimabuë*.

This oil on canvas was painted in 1975, when Chagall was eighty-eight, and first exhibited at the Louvre. It is now in a private collection. The setting suggests a typical Jewish village in Eastern Europe. Chagall places Job prominently in the right foreground. His body is arced like a bow, as if he is levitating leftwards toward the distant image of the crucified Christ. Job's eyes are downcast, with a single red tear-drop like stain streaking his cheek. His right hand is clasped over his heart. He appears to be contemplating the not yet complete journey from death to whatever lies beyond. His head rests on the arm of his wife, who supports him in his journey. She offers a jar (of sweet spices?)[20] to the crowd that gathers around. Her dress is the same red color that marks Job's cheek.

---

18 Ibid., 137.
19 Ibid., 135.
20 Ibid., 261.

FIGURE 2.2   Marc Chagall, "Job with Background of Geometricized Christ á la Cimabué"
COURTESY OF ARTISTS RIGHTS SOCIETY

Opposite Job, in the upper-left corner, is the smaller Christ on the cross. He is covered with the same thigh-length garment as Job, and like Job his cross leans him toward the left. Three-quarters of his still dead body is shadowed by the dark clouds that swirl across the upper part of the canvas. To Christ's right an angel flies down from heaven. Its feet are supported by a white, unrolled

WHO WILL BE JOB'S REDEEMER? 45

Torah scroll; its hands extend in the direction of Job and his wife; in its mouth a shofar-like instrument appears to blast forth a message from God. At the base of the cross, between Christ and Job, a crowd of mothers, fathers, children, goats, and lambs move about. The focus of the crowd is about equally divided, half lifting their hands toward Christ, the others toward Job. In contrast with the darkness that covers the top portion of the picture, Chagall places the crowd in the same light that envelopes Job.

The title Chagall has chosen for this painting suggests that he has modeled it in some way after the *Crucifix* by Giovanni Cimabuë (1240?–1302?), which is in the Church of Santa Croce in Florence.[21] The idea that Christ "geometricizes" likely alludes to Chagall's use of geometric shapes to show cosmic correspondences, a stylistic device associated with Paul Cezanne, Cubism, and Postimpressionism. Chagall may also be suggesting that there are correspondences between the suffering of Job and the suffering of Jesus: both are deeply rooted in Jewish history; both are innocent victims caught in the vortex of darkness and light; both are authentic exemplars of what it means to cry out "My God, why?" Such correspondences hint that Job's suffering changes the geometry of Christ. Perhaps Chagall also invites us to imagine that the suffering of Job, no less than that of Jesus, changes the plane of human history against which the mercy of God must be sought, embraced, and proclaimed before resurrection becomes a reality.

In the biblical text Job states emphatically that he knows his redeemer lives. The grammar that conveys this assertion is clear enough. Inside Job's story, however, the extremities of pain rob words of their conventional meanings. There are no more straight-line connections between life and hope, despair and restoration. This is not to deny that Job (or the poet) may have said more than he knew, nor is it to dismiss the creative genius that sees beyond what Job could have seen. One has only to yield to Handel's marvelous aria or to the liturgy's Pauline assurances or to the painter's intuitive construction of the hews and angles in Job's life to realize that even when we have done our best to read Job, his words continue to read us. Even so, when Job's interpreters see clearly enough to recognize that what he "knows" is hard to determine exactly, they stay mindful of the truth that the journey from "redeemer" to "Redeemer" is long and complex.

---

21   Ibid., 262.

46   CHAPTER 2

3   The Theodicists' Perspective: Remembering or "Dismembering" Job?

James L. Crenshaw, arguably the most insightful of contemporary biblical scholars who have addressed the issue of theodicy in ancient Israel, has offered a base-line definition of what theodicists seek to achieve. The principle objective, he argues, is "to pronounce a verdict of 'Not Guilty' over God for whatever seems to destroy the order of society and the universe."[22] The intractable problem with this objective, as Crenshaw notes, is that "every effort at theodicy represents a substantial loss of human dignity."[23] In Job's case, for example, a verdict of "Not Guilty" for God requires that Job's innocence be denied or rationalized, that Job's honor be subsumed under God's sovereignty, that Job's protests against divine justice be silenced or dismissed for the greater gain of affirming God's mysterious providence.

A review of the way theodicists typically deal with the Book of Job indicates that Crenshaw's assessment is accurate. One particularly instructive example comes from A. S. Peake, whose 1905 commentary commends to the reader three lessons that Job learned from his ordeal.[24] First, Job learns that he must "come to a humbler view of his own importance."[25] God alone governs the universe; God alone has the prerogative to say whether the governance of the universe is for good or ill. Job therefore must learn that there is much he cannot know or properly assess. Second, Job learns that he cannot dictate the terms on which God must respond to him. He must set aside his presumptuous claim on God and assume the required posture of contrition and submission before the Almighty.[26] Third, Job learns that he must trust God, even if he cannot understand God. When he learns to be "ignorant yet trustful," when he becomes "penitent and self-loathing," when he "knows himself to have nothing and deserve nothing," then Job is ready for the relationship with God that God intends.[27] Peake concludes that when Job's readers learn his lessons, then they may rightly embrace him as "a model and a help to all who are confronted by

---

22   James L. Crenshaw, "Introduction: The Shift from Theodicy to Anthropodicy," in *Theodicy in the Old Testament*, ed. James L. Crenshaw (Philadelphia: Fortress, 1983), 1.

23   Ibid., 7.

24   A. S. Peake, *Job*, Century Bible (New York: Henry Frowde, 1905), 9–21. This portion of Peake's commentary is reprinted as "Job: The Problem of the Book" in *Theodicy in the Old Testament*, 100–108. All citations are from the reprinted text.

25   Peake, "Job The Problem of the Book," 106.

26   Ibid.

27   Ibid., 107, 108.

WHO WILL BE JOB'S REDEEMER? 47

the insoluble mystery of their own or the world's pain."[28] When we no longer wish to know why we suffer, then we, like Job, can escape "into a region where such problems exist no longer."[29]

It is surely the case that Peake's recommendation of an "ignorant yet trustful" Job has long been an important and instructive theodicean model of piety for the community of faith. It is also patently clear that such a model is highly problematic for all but those who have the theodicist's luxury of viewing innocent suffering *abstractly* and *from a distance*. Those who *live* the pain symbolized in Job's consignment to the ash heap are more likely to shake their heads in bewilderment and disbelief. When encouraged to think that being crushed and broken for no reason is the key to escaping into some imagined place where such problems no longer exist, the Jobs of the world may be expected to respond with words not unlike those George Eliot's narrator attributes to Adam Bede: "Evil's evil, and sorrow's sorrow, and you can't alter its nature by wrapping it up in other words."[30]

Terrence Tilley has made a strong case for the argument that theodicists have typically silenced Job's perspective of "evil's evil and sorrow's sorrow." The conventional strategy has not been to "remember" the totality of Job's witness but instead to selectively "dismember" this text by offering theories that wrap partial perspectives in the cloak of final truth.[31] By employing such a tactic theodicists in effect take their stand on the side of Job's friends. Like the friends, theodicists endeavor to explain, rationalize, contextualize, and otherwise minimize the suffering and sorrow that Job insists defines the world of the ash heap. From Job's perspective all such efforts run the risk of whitewashing the truth with lies (cf. Job 13:4). The problem is stated succinctly by Iris Murdoch: "It is very difficult to concentrate attention upon suffering and sin, in others or in oneself, without falsifying the picture in some way while making it bearable."[32]

---

28   Ibid., 107.

29   Ibid.

30   George Eliot, *Adam Bede. Edited with an Introduction by Stephen Gill* (New York: Penguin Books, 1985), 529. I am indebted to Terrence Tilley (*The Evils of Theodicy*, 189–216), whose discussion of this book has called to my attention its importance for understanding Job's plight.

31   E.g., the perspective of the "patient" Job in the Prologue, the conventionally "repentant" Job in Job 42:6, the ultimately "restored" Job in the Epilogue. Tilley is particularly concerned to critique the multiple possibilities for rendering Job 42: 5–6, *The Evils of Theodicy*, 96-l 02.

32   Iris Murdoch, *The Sovereignty of Good* (New York: Routledge, 1989; original publication, 1970), 73. See further the discussion in Tilley, *The Evils of Theodicy*, 219–225.

Tilley argues that theodicists falsify Job's claim on God by evacuating his persistent protests and cries for help in the dialogues of any real significance. By doing so, theodicists not only *shape* the interpretive context in which readers appropriate the story of this legendary biblical figure. They also *construct* a world of discourse in which reflection on the abiding problem of suffering and God is carefully channeled into the shallow waters of conventional orthodoxy.[33] In the world Job sees from the ash heap innocent suffering, abandonment by friends, and the absence of God are central and real. In this world the cry for help and the demand for justice are urgent and authentic. In the world theodicists endeavor to build God alone is central and victims like Job are marginalized. In this world the only acceptable currency of faith is embossed with the slogan "In God We Trust." In this constructed world brokenness and loss can be imagined out of existence for the right price. The price for such detachment from the evils of the world is high indeed. Tilley makes the case with the following citation:

> A theodicist who, intentionally or inadvertently, formulates doctrines which occlude the radical and ruthless particularity of evil is, by implication, mediating a social and political practice which averts its gaze from the cruelties that exist in the world. The theodicist ... cannot propound views that promote serenity in a heartless world.[34]

Job warns his friends – and with them all theodicists who would sustain their arguments – that there must be a central place in their worlds for him. They must look closely at his besieged "tent" (19:12). They must listen carefully for the truth about suffering that legitimates his anguished questions "How long?" and "Why?" (19:2, 12). They must see with his eyes the *hope* that sustains what he "knows" about God and the world (19:6, 29) and the *weary despair* that threatens to erase this hope. Like Dinah, the Methodist preacher who ministers to the imprisoned Hetty in *Adam Bede*, theodicists who would comfort Job must know that "tears must come before words."[35]

Job's longing for a redeemer in 19:21–29 invites us to sharpen these general comments with more specific observations. Job is centered by a hope for redemption (19:23–27) that theodicists share and endeavor to authenticate.

---

33   For discussion of how theodicists both "shape" a tradition and "participate" in a tradition, see Tilley, *The Evils of Theodicy*, 86.

34   Tilley, *The Evils of Theodicy*, 231. The citation is from K. Surin, *Theology and the Problem of Evil* (Oxford: Basil Blackwell, 1986), 51.

35   Eliot, *Adam Bede*, 455.

WHO WILL BE JOB'S REDEEMER?

With his interpreters through the ages, Job sustains this hope with a verve and imagination that enables him to search for confirmation well beyond the borders of anything in his world. Nevertheless, Job's hope is doggedly framed by pained realities that do not yield to easy affirmations or simple explanations (19:21–22, 28–29). Inside this hemmed-in life, Job insists that being "ignorant yet trustful" is neither possible nor honest. If the future promises "there is a judgment" (19:29) that can redeem him, he determines that his role is to stand in the void between now and then. There he will stake his claim with imperatives, questions, challenges, and warnings. Given the history of the interpretation of Job 19:25, we should not be surprised to find that there has been a consistent effort, especially within the Christian tradition, to rescue Job with the promise of resurrection. If we have sat with him on the ash heap, however, we should not be surprised if we also hear Job respond to all such efforts with words like those of Eva in Doris Betts' short story "The Astronomer:" "I'm not ready for Jesus yet. Not nearly ready. Don't they write any books at all for people who are where I am?"[36]

4 Who Then Will Be Job's Redeemer?

In the midst of a life defined by persecution Job dares to assert that there is something more to believe in than injustice. That "something more" is expressed in terms of the *gōʾēl*. Job knows that somewhere, at some undisclosed future time, his redeemer will appear. When that happens what is wrong will be put right, what is unjust will be rectified, what is broken will be healed. The critical interpretive question is, who will be Job's *gōʾēl*?

Given the context of his complaints and protests throughout the dialogues it is likely that Job looks to some third party who will stand in between himself and God and secure his vindication. The more traditional view is that God will be Job's redeemer. In Christian piety this view invites the understanding that the agent of God's redemption of Job will be Christ. Both answers may be argued with integrity and passion, and both are open to challenge and correction. The issue is too complex and too confessionally freighted to be resolved by any single interpretive strategy. But one observation may provide a useful point of departure for further reflection. Whether Job's redeemer is a third party or God, his expectation is that he will have to *wait* until some future time for the full realization of the vindication he seeks. Given the immediate realties that

---

36 Doris Betts, "The Astronomer," in *The Astronomer and Other Stones* (Baton Rouge and London: Louisiana State University Press, 1995), 224.

bear down upon him, Job urgently needs some way to fight for his redemption in the present. He needs some means to keep alive his hope on earth not only in heaven. He needs justice not only later but now. The provocative suggestion of chapter 19 is that in the hard interim between *what is* and *what might be* Job resolves not to be a passive victim of injustice.

Job dares to believe, against all evidence to the contrary, that "there is a judgment" (19:29). Moreover, he determines to play a role in calling for that judgment and in working to make it a reality in the here and now. What that role looks like may be deduced from verses 21–22 and 28–29. It consists of *demanding* a different response to those who are unjustly accused, of *addressing hard questions* to those who believe persecuting innocent victims is ordained by God, of *challenging* the assumption that the root cause of all suffering is the sufferer's own sin, of *warning* that a certain judgment awaits those who will not stand on the side of the victim. Still more provocative is the idea that Job's demands, questions, challenges, and warnings provide a model for justice that may instruct *both* God *and* the friends. If God condemns an innocent person, then Job's enactment of justice would dare to effect an indictment: "God has put me in the wrong" (v. 6). If the friends persist in acting "like God" (v. 22), then they too will be judged guilty: "If you say, 'How we will persecute him!' ... you may know that there is a judgment" (vv. 28, 29).

To claim responsibility for holding both God and God's spokespersons accountable to justice is of course a dangerous move. All creaturely judgments will be necessarily flawed and incomplete. On this point the biblical witness is clear: in the vast arena of the cosmic domain, only God can know the full measure of what justice means. If Job is justified in challenging the narrow application of the friends' retributive justice, then he must expect that his own estimate of corrective justice may also be skewed and inadequate. But there is one major difference between Job and his theodicist friends that endows his quest for justice with a moral imperative they cannot match. Job speaks as a *victim* of injustice; they speak only as *onlookers*. He cannot survive if the system that sustains his affliction is not changed; they will not question a system that sustains their place within its certainties. Of course, Job may be wrong to contend *with* the friends and *against* God for justice. If he is, then he errs on the side of hoping too much, expecting too much, believing too much. Of course, the friends may be right to argue that Job has no claim on *their theology* or on *God's justice*. But if they are, then their "comfort" offers Job too little to give life meaning in the midst of suffering like his.

Job's resolve to fight for justice invites the understanding that faith may require more than trust in a redeemer who will make all things right in the end. Suffering sometimes so widens the gap between what is and what will be that long term assurances alone are not enough to sustain one's passion for the journey. What is needed in the interim is a way to pull the future into the present by the sheer strength of commitment. Job determines that crying out "Violence!" (19:7) makes a down payment on the final purchase of justice. He believes that his redeemer will ultimately honor this commitment and complete its objectives. In the meanwhile he fights alone, acting on a conviction that yearns to be validated.

The issue theodicists face at the edge of a new millennium is of course much larger than simply adjudicating the biblical Job's place on the spectrum of their theories. In *J.B.*, Archibald MacLeish's contemporary recreation of the Joban story, Mr. Zuss and Nickles debate whether there is sufficient interest in Job to stage the drama. Zuss, the God-character, decides the matter by observing "Oh, there's always Someone playing Job."[37] The measure of the shadows that hang over the horizon of the twenty-first century is that Zuss's observation seems even more apt today than it did in 1956 when MacLeish wrote this play. It is not only the unfathomable horror of the Holocaust that compels us to ask why "the *sovereignty of evil* has become more real and immediate and familiar than God."[38] It is also the heavy burden of knowing that we live in a world where such unparalleled evil repeatedly assaults our creeds with new barbarisms. As I write this essay ethnic cleansing continues to tear apart the Balkans ... and the NATO alliance debates its response. Should we intervene to stop the killing? Is it in our national interest? If we get in, can we get out? In the meanwhile, the innocent blood of thousands of Jobs in Kosovo continues to cry out from mass graves for someone to bear witness to its truth (cf. Job 16:18–19).

It is both Job's resolve to fight for justice and his yearning to have this resolve validated that invites the community of faith to become an active participant in this drama. Inside the trenches, where the hard work of crying for justice goes on, the Jobs of this world await the one who will fulfill the responsibilities of the *gōʾēl*. If Job's readers are satisfied to leave that role to God or some other third party, then they may be content to look on the struggles of the unjustly accused from a distance, confident that the final outcome is not really in doubt. But if it is the commitment to work for justice that somehow hastens its arrival, then readers may want to think again about whether simply looking on is an adequate expression of faith. The critical question that remains to be answered is, who will be Job's *gōʾēl*? How we respond to this question will be an important indication of whether we believe and hope *too much* for the claims of justice on God and the human community or *too little*.

---

37   Archibald MacLeish, *J.B.* (Boston: Houghton Mifflin Company, 1956), 12.

38   Arthur Cohen, *The Tremendum: A Theological Interpretation of the Holocaust* (New York: Crossroad, 1988), 34 (emphasis added).

CHAPTER 3

"Let Love Clasp Grief Lest Both Be Drowned"

The Book of Job is about friendship.* For all its heavy hitting on such important theological topics as innocent suffering and the justice or injustice of God,
it is the theology of friendship that provides the frame for the book's central
concerns. At the beginning of the book, Job sits on an ash heap of suffering,
surrounded by three friends who come to "console" and "comfort" him, only
to find they have no words, at least at the outset (!), equal to the challenge his
suffering presents. They sit with him in silence for seven days and seven nights
(Job 2: 11–13). At the end of the book, Job is once more surrounded by friends,
"brothers and sisters and all who had known him before." They share a meal of
communion with him, they "console" and "comfort" him, and they bring him
tangible gifts – "a sizeable amount of money and a gold ring" – that contribute
to his blessing and his restoration (Job 42:11–12). In between the beginning and
ending of the book, the twists and turns of Job's painful journey tracks through
the dialogues with various "friends" – Eliphaz, Bildad, Zophar, Elihu, ... and
God – who make their way to his ash heap with words meant to make a difference in his situation. Indeed, of the forty-two chapters that comprise the Book
of Job, no less than thirty-eight of them, roughly ninety percent of the entire
story, are forged in the crucible of a lingering, but never articulated question:
Who will be Job's friend?

Let me stretch the imagination by suggesting that we read Job as the Old
Testament's version of the Good Samaritan story (Luke 10:29–37). When the
lawyer asks Jesus, "What shall I do to inherit eternal life?" Jesus points him to
the abiding summons of Deut 6:4–5: "You shall love the Lord your God with all
your heart, and with all your soul, and with all your strength, and with all your
mind; *and your neighbor as yourself*." The lawyer presses for more clarity by
asking a follow-up question: "And *who is my neighbor*?" Jesus responds by telling a story about "a certain man" who was traveling the dangerous road from
Jerusalem to Jericho. Through no fault of his own, he fell victim to random
acts of violence and brutality and was left for dead. Three travelers, a priest,
a Levite, and a Samaritan, each would-be friends, journey on the same road.
The priest and the Levite pass by without offering assistance. The Samaritan,

---

* In memoriam D. N. D. (1950–2000). An earlier version of this essay was presented as one of
two Nils W. Lund Memorial Lectures at North Park Theological Seminary in Chicago, Illinois.
Many thanks to the friends, colleagues, and students for their warm and gracious hospitality.

© SAMUEL E. BALENTINE, 2021 | DOI:10.1163/9789004459212_004

"moved with compassion," stops and pours oil on the beaten man's wounds, bandages him up, and then carries him to an inn, where he pays for his care and safekeeping. When Jesus finishes this story, he asks the lawyer to think about what it means for him: "Which of the three, do you think, was a neighbor to the man?" For the remainder of this paper, I invite you to reflect on the meaning of this story, if the name of the beaten man in the ditch were Job.

1 Models of Friendship

In Jesus' story, neither the three travelers on the road to Jericho nor the beaten man in the ditch speaks a word. We do not know what reason the priest and the Levite may have given for neglecting the man, or why the Samaritan was moved with compassion to care for him. By the same token, we do not know what the man may have said to the two passers-by who left him there to die, or how he might have responded to the one who bandaged his wounds and carried him to safety. If his name were Job, however, and if the priest and the Levite traveled in the company of Job's "friends," Eliphaz, Bildad, and Zophar, then we have a rich deposit of references to friendship from which we may reconstruct the dialogue Luke does not provide.

1.1 The "Friends'" View of Friendship

Let me set the table for a survey of the friendship offered Job by Eliphaz, Bildad, and Zophar with a scene from Edward Albee's Pulitzer Prize-winning play *A Delicate Balance*.[1] One night, while Agnes and her husband Tobias were idling away their time in their comfortable suburban home, Edna and Harry, two life-long friends, showed up uninvited at their door. Something was clearly wrong, although Edna and Harry could say nothing more than "We got frightened." "We got scared" (Act I, 49). Only gradually did it become clear to Agnes and Tobias that their friends had come to seek refuge in their home. When that realization sunk in, another quickly followed. Agnes and Tobias had become ensnared in something that threatened to undo their world. One morning, after Tobias had stayed up all night pondering how to help these friends, Agnes offered her own assessment of the situation:

> [T]hey've brought the plague with them, and that's another matter. Let me tell you something about disease ... mortal illness; you are either immune to it ... or you fight it. If you are immune, you wade in, you treat

---

1 E. Albee, *A Delicate Balance* (New York: Penguin Books, 1966).

54 CHAPTER 3

the patient, until he either lives, or dies of it. But if you are *not* immune, you risk infection. Ten centuries ago – and even less – the treatment was quite simple ... burn them. Burn their bodies, burn their houses, burn their clothes – and move to another town, if you were enlightened. But now, with modern medicine, we merely isolate; we quarantine, we ostracize – if we are not immune ourselves, or unless we are saints. So your night-long vigil, darling, your reasoning in the cold, pure hours, has been over the patient, and not the illness. It is not Edna and Harry who have come to us – our friends – it is a disease.

> Act III, 157

"If you are not immune, you risk infection." This might well be the credo of Job's friends, Eliphaz, Bildad, and Zophar, as they contemplate how to respond to the unexpected intrusion of his angry curses into their world of settled convictions. As long as Job was pious and patient, they were content to "console" and "comfort" him with their silent, sympathetic presence (2:11–13). But when Job begins to curse and complain (Job 3), the friends cock and reload. They have a secure place in their theology for befriending those who bless God. But when Job moves from blessing the God on whom their convictions rest to cursing God, the foundations of their world begin to shake, and they run to shore them up lest everything collapse around them. Now Job is a threat, his words are horrifying. Like a virus bug loosed in the world, Job is now targeted as a disease. For the health and well-being of the world, his poison must be eradicated; at the very least, he must be isolated, quarantined, ostracized. Like Agnes, when Job's friends hear him knocking at their door, they turn to one another and say, "It is not Job – our friend – who has come to us, it is a disease."

We may visualize the friends' transition from silent support for Job to caustic rebuke by placing two of William Blake's etchings side by side. In the first, Job sits on a mound of straw, his head resting on his wife's breast. His hands, palms downward, extend by his side.

His wife kneels behind him, her body providing a pillar of support, her uplifted hands gesturing the prayer Job himself seems now too exhausted to offer. The six uplifted hands of the friends mimic the wife, although their reach heavenward is more extended and their facial expressions convey more intensity and emotion. It is as if by the force of their gestures they wish to lift Job safely out of his distress and into the arms of God. At the top and bottom of the frame Blake has inscribed the words from Job 2:12: "When they lifted up their eyes afar off and knew him not they lifted up their voices and wept." To these words Blake adds a quotation from James 5:11, which provides the catchword – "patience" – that captures not only the popular understanding of

FIGURE 3.1   William Blake, "Job's Comforters"
NATIONAL GALLERY OF ART/WIKIMEDIA COMMONS

Job's exemplary faith but also the reason for the friends' sympathetic support: "Ye have heard of the patience of Job and have seen the end of the Lord, that the Lord is very pitiful, and of tender mercy" (AV).

In the second etching, Blake's Job has moved from the ash heap to a kneeling position.

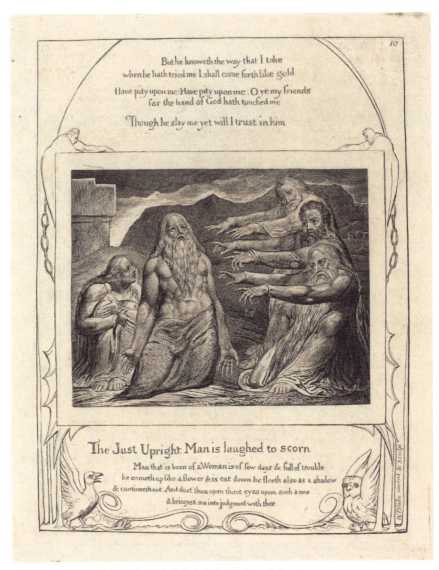

FIGURE 3.2 William Blake, "Job Rebuked By His Friends"
NATIONAL GALLERY OF ART/WIKIMEDIA COMMONS

No longer leaning backward, Job now holds himself upright, his stomach muscles taut, as if flexed in anticipation of a negative response to the curses he has just hurled into the silence of his world. His spotted torso is wrapped from the waist down with the traditional sackcloth. His head is tilted backward. His tear-stained eyes are fixed on the God above whom he cannot see but will not cease

"LET LOVE CLASP GRIEF LEST BOTH BE DROWNED"

to trust. Job's solemn misery is suggested by the three citations of Scripture at the top of the frame:

> But he knoweth the way I take
> when he hath tried me I shall come forth like gold
> > Job 23:10

> Have pity upon me! Have pity upon me! O ye my friends
> for the hand of God hath touched me
> > Job 19:21

> Though he slay me yet will I trust in him
> > Job 13:15

But the friends have ceased to play the role of comforter. They are now Job's inquisitors. With outstretched hands they point fingers of ridicule in Job's direction. Their gesture may have been modeled after Henri Fuseli's (1741–1825) depiction of the ghastly finger-pointing women in *The Three Witches*.[2] In contrast with Job, the friends' expressions are cold and hard, as is particularly clear in the face of the friend to the fore, presumably Eliphaz. Job's wife, whose right hand is also partially extended, seems now to have joined in the reproach. Two further citations in the bottom of the frame from Job's last speech in the first cycle indicate what has drawn the friends' ire:

> The Just Upright man is laughed to scorn
> > Job 12:4

> Man that is born of a Woman is of few days & full of trouble
> he cometh up like a flower & is cut down, he fleeth also as a shadow
> & continueth not. And dost thou open thine eyes upon such a one
> & bringest me into judgment with thee
> > Job 14:1–3

The figures in the border add to the bleakness of Job's situation from the friends' perspective. Two angels, each weighed down with chains, appear to be holding on with some difficulty to the picture of Job. In the bottom left-hand

---

2   M. Cormack, *William Blake: Illustrations of the Book of Job* (Richmond VA: Virginia Museum of Fine Arts, 1997), 45.

corner a bird (a raven? a cuckoo?), perhaps symbolic of slander, steps on a serpent. In the bottom right-hand corner an owl, perhaps symbolic of false wisdom, grasps a helpless mouse in its talons. The cumulative effect of the scene puts a face on the famous speech of Marcus Antonius in *Julius Caesar*. These friends have come "to bury [Job], not to praise him" (*Julius Caesar*, III, ii, 79).

The friends make their case against Job in three cycles of speeches (4–14, 15–21, 22–27). The general theme in the first cycle (4–14) is God's moral governance of the world, especially as this is manifest in God's unfailing care for the righteous and God's equally unfailing punishment of the wicked (4:7–11; 8:8–19; 11:11). The friends' initial approach to Job suggests that they have read the required text for Pastoral Care 101. Like kind and sympathetic counselors they each gently raise a series of rhetorical questions, questions they trust will nudge Job to answers they already know. Eliphaz, always the lead spokesman, sets the tone the others will follow with his first questions:

> If one ventures a word with you, will you be offended?
>   Forgive me, but who can keep from speaking?
>   4:2

> Is not your fear of God your confidence,
>   and the integrity of your ways your hope?
> Think now, who that was innocent ever perished?
>   Or where were the upright cut off?
>   4:6–7

With equal measures of comfort and encouragement, the friends are confident that Job will see things the way they do. If he will heed their counsel, they have no doubt he too will discover that God can always be trusted to reward the righteous and punish the wicked. But when Job looks at the same world and claims that even the birds and the plants know things are more complicated than this (12:7–10), Eliphaz and his friends know they are in for a long day.

In the second round (15–21) the friends reduce their argument to the one truth they are certain Job will not dispute: the wicked (read Job) are always punished (15:17–35; 18:5–21; 20:4–9). From this point on they will dispense with any pretense of claiming that God always prospers the righteous. Their tone is now noticeably much sharper, a signal that they have stiffened their resolve to wrench a confession of guilt from Job. They offer no word of encouragement, hope, or promise to Job. Instead, they increase their warnings, double their rebukes, and up the ante he must pay if he continues to challenge the Judge of all the world. Once again, Eliphaz leads the way:

"LET LOVE CLASP GRIEF LEST BOTH BE DROWNED" 59

> You [Job] are doing away with the fear of God and hindering
>   meditation before God.
> For your iniquity teaches your mouth,
>   and you choose the tongue of the crafty,
> Your own mouth condemns you, not I,
>   your own lips testify against you.
>   15:4–6

When Job counters with a question, one of many, that directly disputes their assertions – "How often then is the lamp of the wicked put out? How often then does calamity come upon them?" (21:1) – the friends know it is time to take off the gloves.

In the third round of speeches (22–27), the friends give up their efforts to coerce a confession from Job. Now they simply pronounce him guilty. Their notion of an orderly trial, with evidence so strong the defendant can only yield and agree to guilt, has not worked. But inasmuch as the friends claim the right to be both judge and jury in the case of God v. Job, they can still secure the desired outcome by simply ruling from the bench that Job is guilty beyond any reasonable doubt. Eliphaz takes the point for the last time: "Is not your wickedness great? There is no end to your iniquities" (22:5). Job has but one option, Eliphaz insists: "Agree with God, and be at peace" (22:21). Eliphaz's counsel bears a close resemblance to the advice Sam offers Berish in E. Wiesel's *The Trial of God*. Berish insists on bringing God to trial for the massacre of Jews in Shamgorod in 1649. Sam, who plays the role of God's defense attorney, warns Berish that God's justice is not subject to human critique.

> Why murder-why death? Pertinent questions. But we have some more: Why evil – why ugliness? If God chooses not to answer, He must have his reasons. God is God, and His will is independent of ours – as is His reasoning.

Berish has one choice, Sam says, and one choice only: "Endure. Accept. And say Amen."[3]

The friends' presumption of Job's guilt effectively leaves him in the ditch with the beaten man on the road to Jericho. They will help him out only if he accepts their terms, unconditional surrender to their theology: to wit, he is suffering, therefore he has sinned; he is guilty, therefore he must repent. This theology inscribes a rejection that recalls a painful scene from Wallace Stegner's short story, "Impasse." Having witnessed the rebuff of his beloved but homely

---

3   E. Wiesel, *The Trial of God* (New York: Schocken Books, 1979), 132.

60   CHAPTER 3

daughter Margaret by yet another potential suitor, her father Louis muses to himself about the advice he might offer her.

> [W]hat had happened so dramatically was forever beyond talk. He could never say to [Margaret], "I saw you invite him, and I saw him take one good look and pass." Could you say to your daughter, "Accept your looks for what they are?" Could you tell her, "You were born struck out, and it won't help to stand in the batter's box demanding that the pitcher throw you a fourth strike?"

Margaret's father cannot bring himself to tell his daughter that God determined willy-nilly before she saw the first light of day that she was "born struck out." "My God," he says, "she has *hope*.... Everybody young has hope."[4]

Eliphaz and his friends look on Job with no such panged restraints. Once the strategy to love Job into conformity with their theology has failed, they are left with but two options. They can rethink their definition of friendship. Could it be that Job deserves their loyalty, no matter his guilt or innocence? Or they can decide that their theology is more important than his friendship. When friends run afoul of theological orthodoxy, one must either convert them or condemn them. Eliphaz and his friends choose the latter course. To be charitable, we might imagine that they simply get tired of "being with" Job. Perhaps, as M. Marty observes, sharing the grief of another, taking into oneself the "agony of the nerves exposed, the plotlessness of pain that never stops," is too much to ask of anyone. Most of those who wear the label of "friend," Marty suggests, will be "tempted to turn their backs" and retreat at some point.[5] Whether charitably viewed or not, we are left with the report that Job's "friends" have condemned him as guilty. Charged and convicted, Job now awaits whatever comes next alone.

1.2   *Job's Theology of Friendship*

In *A Delicate Balance*, Agnes and Tobias look on the arrival of their troubled and needy friends as a threat. They take preemptive measures to isolate, quarantine, and ostracize Edna and Harry, lest they themselves become infected by friendship now become dangerous. To set the table for Job's theology of friendship, I offer you a different model.

---

4 W. Stegner, "Impasse," in *Collected Stories of Wallace Stegner* (New York: Penguin Books, 1991), 291.
5 M. Marty, *A Cry of Absence* (San Francisco: Harper and Row, 1983), 128.

"LET LOVE CLASP GRIEF LEST BOTH BE DROWNED"

Alfred Lord Tennyson's (1809–1892) poem "In Memoriam A. H. H." describes the loss he experienced upon the sudden and tragic death of his best friend Arthur Hallam on September 15, 1833, at the age of 22. Hallam had befriended Tennyson at Cambridge. He had introduced Tennyson to the undergraduate literary group, the Apostles, helped him with his first publications of poetry, traveled with him to the Pyrenees and the Rhineland, and counseled him through difficult periods of loneliness and despair. At the time of his death, Hallam was engaged to marry Tennyson's sister, Emily. They were best friends, brothers in the deepest sense of the word. When Tennyson learned of Hallam's death, he began almost immediately to compose the words of this poem. They had shared a friendship for but five years. He worked on this poem, trying to find the words that matched what he had lost, for sixteen years. His hope, as he put it in the line that I have used for the title of this paper, was to "Let love clasp Grief lest both be drown'd."[6] His lyrics make his loss of Hallam's friendship almost palpable. They are not Scripture, but they may be sacred nonetheless:

> One writes that "other friends remain,"
> That "loss is common to the race" –
> And common is the commonplace,
> And vacant chaff well meant for grain.
>
> That loss is common would not make
> My own loss less bitter, rather more.
> Too common! Never morning wore
> To evening, but some heart did break
> 6, 1–8
>
> I know that this was Life, – the track
> Whereon with equal feet we fared;
> And then, as now, the day prepared
> The daily burden for the back.
>
> But this it was that made me move
> As light as carrier-birds in air;
> *I loved the weight I had to bear,*
> *Because it needed help of Love;*

---

6 Alfred Lord Tennyson, "In Memoriam A. H. H." in *Tennyson's Poetry* (ed. R. Hill; New York, London: W. W. Norton, 1971), 1, 10, p. 121.

62   CHAPTER 3

Nor could I weary, heart or limb,
  When mighty love would cleave us twain
  The lading of a single pain,
And part it, giving half to him.
      25, 1–12; emphasis added

And then these words, written during the holidays of the first Christmas after
Hallam's death, which I trust you will recognize:

I hold it true, whate'er befall;
  I feel it when I sorrow most;
  'T is better to have loved and lost
Than never to have loved at all.
      27, 13–16

I submit to you that Job's theology of friendship provides an enormously
instructive model for the cords that bind us, or should, to one another. When
he looks to his friends, he yearns for love that will clasp grief, "lest both be
drown'd." Of the many texts that disclose Job's theology of friendship, I single
out two for your consideration. The first, Job 6:14–30, is perhaps the clearest
expression of the friendship Job expects and needs. The second, Job 29, is a
poignant witness to the friendship Job himself extends to others.

1.2.1   Job 6:14–30

Job 6:14–30 is part of Job's response to Eliphaz's first speech (Job 4–5). Now
that Eliphaz has spoken, there are three parties who have a stake in this drama:
Job, the sufferer, the friends who would "console" and "comfort" him, and God,
whose presence is as yet undefined. Job's words in chapters 6–7 reflect this
triangulation. Driven by suffering to an existence where there is no "ease,"
no "rest," no "quiet" (3:26), Job now finds himself in a world where would-be
friends are disloyal and a would-be God is silent and much too distant. As far
as he can see, he is caught in the middle of failed relationships, both human
and divine. His words at the close of the first pericope in chapter 6 set the
woeful scene: "In truth I have no help in me, and any resource is driven from
me" (6:13).

Because he can draw nothing more from his own resources, Job now looks to
the friends for the strength that he cannot provide for himself. He sets forth his
expectations concerning true friendship in verse 14. The text is unfortunately
difficult, and scholars have proposed a variety of emendations and syntactical

rearrangements. I propose the following as a plausible translation of the text as it stands:

> The despairing (*lammas*) needs loyalty (*ḥesed*) from a friend,
> even if (perhaps "when") they forsake the fear of the Almighty.

Despite the ambiguity in the text, the major emphasis of the first line is relatively clear. Job expects *ḥesed* from a friend. The conventional translation of this word is "kindness" or "steadfast love." A better rendering is "loyalty." *Ḥesed* describes both an attitude and an action that binds two parties together in an unbreakable partnership. Its fullest meaning is exemplified by God, for whom "loyalty and faithfulness" (*ḥesed wĕʾemet*) are constant attributes (e.g., Pss 25:10; 57:3; 89:14; 138:2). God's loyalty is enacted; it is a disposition that is demonstrated. God "does" (*ʿasah*) *ḥesed* (e.g., Gen 24:12, 14; Exod 20:6 [= Deut 5:10]; 2 Sam 2:6; 1 Kgs 3:6; Jer 9:24 [MT 9:23]), the most tangible evidence of which is God's commitment to "keeping covenant and steadfast love" (*šōmer habbĕrît wĕhaḥesed*; Deut 7:9, 12; 1 Kgs 8:23 [= 2 Chr 6:14]; Neh 1:5; 9:32; Dan 9:4). When humans fail God and break the covenant partnership, it is "loyalty and faithfulness" that motivates God to restore it (Exod 34:6).

God's loyalty is the perfect model of the relentless love that pursues relationship with others, even when they fail. Created in the image of God, humans aspire to this ideal of "loyalty and faithfulness" in their relationships with each other (e.g., Gen 24:49; 32:11; Josh 2:14; Prov 3: 3), even though they cannot fully attain it. Even when human relationships fall short of the ideal, the goal remains the same: "deal loyally and compassionately with one another" (*wehesed wĕraḥămîm ʿásû*; Zech 7:9 [NJPS]). As H. J. Stoebe has put it, *ḥesed* expresses a "magnanimity," which enacts a "sacrificial, humane willingness to be there for the other." It is a commitment to relationship that "surpasses the obligatory."[7]

What Job hopes for from his friends is a loyalty that will not let go of him, even if suffering pushes him beyond the boundaries of conventional piety ("the fear of the Almighty"). What he receives from them is quite different (6:15–21). His friends are "treacherous" (*bāgĕdû*). The imagery suggests "deceit." They are "brothers" (*ʾaḥîm*), which implies they are connected to him by a familial affection and solidarity, but they have abandoned him. They are inconsistent and unreliable. Job compares them to the seasonal wadis of Palestine. In the rainy season when water is plentiful, they are full to overflowing. But when

---

7   H. J. Stoebe, "*Hesed* 'Kindness'," *TLOT* 2:456.

64   CHAPTER 3

the heat of summer arrives, and water is needed and scarce, they dry up and disappear (6:15–17). Job compares his own disappointment at their failure to provide what he needs to that of parched caravaneers who spy out the promise of water in the desert but upon arrival find it to be only a mirage (6:18–20). Like these dried up, empty waterbeds, the friends have become for Job a non-existent resource. The Hebrew of v. 21 says, literally, "you have become nothing (*lōʾ*)." With a final play on words, Job adds, "you see (*tirʾû*) a calamity, and you are afraid (*tîrāû*). If we listen carefully, we will hear the echo of Agnes's words: "It is not Edna and Harry who have come to us – our friends – it is a disease ... *terror sitting in the room upstairs*" (Act III, 158; emphasis added).

1.2.2   Job 29
The second text I offer for your consideration is Job 29, which introduces Job's final summation (Job 29–31) before God comes center stage in Job 38–41. Job closes the dialogues as he began them, with internal musings and reflections. But much has changed since Job's opening soliloquy. In chapter 3 his pain had driven him to curse life and to long for the relief of a death that would not come. In these closing chapters, Job refuses to relinquish the truth about either his integrity (Job 29) or his pain (Job 30). Integrity and pain are now forged into a renewed oath of innocence (Job 31; cf. 27:1–6), which Job hopes will compel his accuser, God, to confront him in court.

My focus here is on Job 29, for when Job speaks of the things that have given his life meaning and value, at least until his suffering changed everything, he places the quality of the relationships he has enjoyed at the top of his list. He begins by remembering how good life used to be (29:1–10). He remembers the days when he enjoyed the intimate "friendship (*sôd*) of God" (29:4; cf. Ps 25:14), a time he wistfully associates with the memory of his children playing joyfully around him (29:5). He remembers how it used to be when he took his place in the community, sitting at the city gate with his peers. He remembers the honor they accorded him as they looked to him to settle their disputes and resolve their conflicts. Whenever he spoke, they would rise in recognition of the fair-minded wisdom he brought to their lives (29:7–10).

It would be a mistake to understand Job's ruminations as merely an exercise in self-flattery. Job enjoyed the friendship of others because he embodied and acted upon the virtues of friendship himself. His concern and compassion is nowhere more evident than in his unfailing response to the cries for help from those who are vulnerable to abuse. The poor, the orphans, the wretched, the widows, the blind, the lame, and even strangers he does not know – all trust Job to stand by their side with a protective rage that shelters them against victimization (29:11–16). Like a shepherd keeping watch over his flock, Job would risk his own life to snatch a helpless victim from the jaws of a wanton predator (29:17).

With good reason, therefore, the community understands Job's friendship as the key to their security and welfare (29:21–25). They wait for him with the same urgent expectancy they have for the spring rains. Even when they cannot believe, their doubt cannot extinguish the guiding light of his countenance (29:24). Like Moses, the mediator of the covenant, Job's radiance keeps hope alive (cf. Exod 34:29–35). Like Aaron, the mediator of the cult, Job's "rituals" of friendship embody the benediction that sustains them (cf. Num 6:25–26). Rather than abandon them to their own depleted resources, Job lives among them as a king, marshaling his troops on their behalf whenever they are needed (29:25a). The final image in Job's ruminations may be the most telling of all: he lives among them as one "who comforts mourners" (29:25b). In other words, he offers the friendship of loyal compassion that he now needs from his own friends but has not received.

When we examine closely the images Job uses for his theology of friendship, we should not fail to notice that the friendship he needs, the friendship he himself offers to others, challenges not only Eliphaz and his associates but also God. In 6:14 he states his need of the *hesed*, the loyalty, that God models and humans who would be friends to others should aspire to demonstrate. Now, in his final summation, he declares that he has done his best to be this kind of friend himself. Like God, he has been a champion for the oppressed (Deut 24:17; Prov 23:10–11), a father to the orphan and a protector of widows (Ps 68:5), and a shepherd who delivers his flocks from the jaws of the wicked (Ps 3:7; cf. Ps 23:1). Like God, Job has clothed himself with "righteousness" and "justice" (Ps 89:14).[8] Still more revealing, and more incriminating, is Job's thinly veiled charge that the friendship he enacts, the justice he embodies, is what sustains creation itself (31:38–40; cf. Gen 3:17; 4:10).[9] If God is listening, and Job trusts that this is so, then Job wants God to hear him saying that he has faithfully comforted the mourners who have been entrusted to his care. Can God claim to have offered the same fidelity to Job, who now sits on the ash heap of destruction, bereft of friends and submerged in divine silence?

I submit to you that Job was in effect a Tennyson to the Hallams of his world. He knew and embodied the truth of friendship that dared to clasp love and grief in an indissoluble bond of commitment. I know of no more telling

---

8   Cf. C. Newsom, "The Book of Job," in *NIB* (Nashville: Abingdon Press, 1996), 4:539.

9   Cf. L. Perdue, *Wisdom in Revolt: Metaphorical Theology in the Book of Job* (Sheffield: JSOT Press, 1991), 187–189; Perdue, *Wisdom and Creation: The Theology of Wisdom Literature* (Nashville: Abingdon Press, 1994), 167–168.

66   CHAPTER 3

confirmation that this theology of friendship is Job's abiding legacy than the
eulogy he receives from the "poor and the orphans and all the helpless" in the
Testament of Job, which is most likely the first commentary (first century BCE–
first century CE) on the book that bears his name:

> Woe to us today! A double woe!
> Gone today is the strength of the helpless!
> Gone is the light of the blind!
> Gone is the father of the orphans!
> Gone is the host of strangers!
> Gone is the clothing of the widows!
> Who then will not weep over the man of God?
>> *T. Job* 53:2–4

2 And Jesus Said, "Which of These Three, Do You Think Was a Neighbor to the Man?"

From Job's perspective the only friendship worthy of the name is that which
proves itself in the crucible of suffering. Those whose suffering pushes them
into despair need "loyalty" (*ḥesed*) from a friend (6:14). Job understands this
to mean that friends will not let go of friends no matter what. In good times
and bad, in success and failure, in joy and in sorrow, friends should be present
with equal commitment and passion. Job's criticism of Eliphaz and his cohorts
offers a graphic description of what we might call "fair-weather friends." They
are present when it does not cost them anything and their resources are not
needed, but when the stakes are high and the cost could be dear they retreat
and wait for better times to appear.

What is particularly intriguing is the suggestion that friendship is most
severely tested in matters of faith. When despair pushes one beyond the
boundaries of conventional piety, what Job calls "forsaking the fear of the
Almighty," then what it takes to be a true friend may be costly indeed. Sufferers
like Job are threatening. Their hurt and brokenness remind the unafflicted of
what may be lurking for them around the next comer. Their cry for help dis-
turbs the serenity of safe and predictable discourse, insisting that life's grammar is punctuated with screams of pain that cannot be ignored and will not
be silenced. Job doubts that he has the strength to endure what God ordains
(6:11–12); he doubts that life is either meaningful or just (7:1–6); he doubts his
identity, his self-worth, his very status as a human being in the world God creates (7:17–21). Honest doubt always threatens belief. When expressed by the

truly "blameless and upright," such doubt can be not only dangerous but also contagious. When Job asks "What is my strength?" those who sit with him must wonder about their own reserves. When he asks "What are human beings?" those who sit with him know that the question is not abstract. Now it is personal: "What am I?"

What if Job's wonderments about these questions are right? This is the constant, if unspoken, anxiety that strikes fear in those who would befriend Job. Perhaps to identify too closely with Job's questions renders one more susceptible to his uncertainties. Perhaps to enter too deeply into his pain leaves us more vulnerable to the brokenness and loss we pray will pass by without leaving its scars on us. Anyone who has ever encountered someone whose suffering is extreme and seemingly irreversible knows the fear of sitting with Job. The temptation is first to ignore, then to silence through arguments, explanations, answers, and finally, if all else fails, to retreat in self-defense and abandon the suffering to suffering. In short, the temptation for those who would be Job's friends is to act like Eliphaz and his companions.

Job expects and hopes for something more from his friends ... and from God. He is not closed to honest advice and sound instruction, but what he most needs is companionship, not so much to ease the pain, but to improve the quality of suffering. In *A Whole New Life*, Reynolds Price offers personal reflections that speak to those who would befriend the Jobs of this world. He writes about his mid-life war with the cancer that invaded his body and grew up his spine like an eel. He survived, although with a paralysis that bears witness to the battle, and from the "far side of catastrophe," what he calls "the dim other side of that high wall that effectively shuts disaster off from the unfazed world," he articulates the sufferer's need:

> In that deep trough I needed companions more than prayers or potions that had worked for another.[10]

Too often what he received from those who wanted to care was something very different. Some of his friends provided "would-be helpful books" that explained why he had cancer – perhaps his own unhealthy habits? – how some new treatment might miraculously cure it – had he tried "moon-rock dust and beetle-wing ointment"? – and, as a last resort, what kind of deal he might cut with God to salvage any life he could – if I give You all the feeling in my legs, and all the control of my upper body, will You permit me a few extra years? His physicians, highly skilled professionals who were trained to

---

10   R. Price, *A Whole New Life* (New York: Atheneum, 1994), 180.

68   CHAPTER 3

treat cancer patients, sometimes offered little or no real comfort. His oncologist turned away from him when he attempted casual conversation in the halls. He seemed unable to offer an unscripted word of encouragement or a spontaneous expression of comradeship. Price's wonderment about such treatment places him in the company of Job:

> Did he think I was brewing my grievance against him, some costly revenge in the crowded market of malpractice suits? Did he shy from involvement with one more face that was hungry for life though already stamped *Dead?* My best guess from here is, he didn't know how to act otherwise; and he hadn't tried to learn. It's often said by way of excuse that doctors are insufficiently trained for humane relations. For complex long-range interaction with damaged creatures, they may well need a kind of training they never receive; but what I wanted and needed badly, from that man then, was the frank exchange of decent concern. When did such a basic transaction between two mammals require postgraduate instruction beyond our mother's breast?[11]

Perhaps there is no adequate training for long-range, complex friendships with "damaged creatures" like Job. It is true that such friendship is never easy and may be costly. The more intimate we become with those who hurt, the more their pain becomes our own. But Job would insist that when such friendship is lacking everyone is diminished, not just the afflicted. Friends who do not hold on to friends who suffer, whether because of fear or indifference, forsake the summons and the opportunity to image God by dealing "loyally and compassionately with one another" (Zech 7:9). The summons and what is at stake when we fail to heed it is not different in the New Testament:

> Beloved, let us love one another, because love is from God; everyone who loves is born of God and knows God.
>
> Those who say, "I love God," and hate their brothers and sisters, are liars; for those who do not love a brother or a sister whom they have seen, cannot love God whom they have not seen.
>
> 1 John 4:7, 20

---

11   Ibid., 56.

"LET LOVE CLASP GRIEF LEST BOTH BE DROWNED"

At the end of the book, Job's friends – Eliphaz, Bildad, Zophar, and Elihu – are gone. To paraphrase Auden, each has retreated to his own mistakes.[12] Center stage is now empty. Job and his readers now wait for the one speaker who may still have something to contribute. God has not spoken a word since saying to the satan, "Very well, he is in your power" (2:6). With these words, to our ears spoken much too casually, God handed Job over to an unimaginable test of piety. Will Job love God for nothing? (1:9). Since then, God has stood on the sidelines, watching and listening. Since then, Job has challenged God with a test of his own: Will God love Job for nothing? Will God come to him, care for him, stay by him through thick and thin, even when Job curses and laments and accuses God?

What was God thinking during those thirty-six chapters of silence? What was going through God's mind and heart when Job's children were laid in their tombs? When Job sat alone on the ash heap, deadened himself to anything beyond grief and despair? Did God feel any sense of loss when the one God called affectionately "my servant" (1:8; 2:3) pleaded for a friend who would be loyal, then yielded in despondency to an existence defined more by death than life?

My mind goes to a scene near the end of the movie "Four Weddings and a Funeral." The film is a raucous and often irreverent portrayal of the friendships shared by Charles, Tom, Scarlet, Matthew, and Garreth. Each of the friends brings a unique zaniness to the relationship, but it is the unbounded joy for life of middle-aged Garreth that sets the bar for their happiness. When he suddenly drops dead of a heart attack while gamboling at a wedding, the bubble of their unfazed happiness burst. One can almost hear the air leaving the room.

Garreth's loss is heavy, especially for his most intimate friend Matthew, who shared a flat with him. At Garreth's funeral, Matthew was asked to give the eulogy. He offered these words from W. H. Auden:

> Stop all the clocks, cut off the telephone,
> Prevent the dog from barking with a juicy bone,
> Silence the pianos and with muffled drum
> Bring out the coffin, let the mourners come.
>
> Let aeroplanes circle moaning overhead
> Scribbling on the sky the message He is Dead,

---

12 W. H. Auden, "The Quest," in *W. H. Auden: Collected Poems* (ed. E. Mendelson; New York: Vintage International, 1991), 286. The full citation is: "Two friends who met here and embraced are gone / Each to his own mistake."

70   CHAPTER 3

Put crepe bows round the white necks of the public doves,
Let the traffic policemen wear black cotton gloves.

He was my North, my South, my East and West,
My working week and my Sunday rest,
My noon, my midnight, my talk, my song;
I thought that love would last for ever: I was wrong.

The stars are not wanted now: put out every one;
Pack up the moon and dismantle the sun;
Pour away the ocean and sweep up the wood;
For nothing now can ever come to any good.[13]

I wonder if God felt a loss comparable to this when God looked on the suffering of Job. I concede that it may be stretching our imaginations too far, perhaps
beyond all boundaries of orthodoxy, to think of God speaking some of these
lines. And yet, having recently experienced the loss of my best friend, I confess to you that I find it more comforting than unsettling to imagine that God
values friendship, that God grieves the loss of a good friend at least as much as
I grieve the loss of mine. Is it really too much to imagine that God might listen
knowingly, perhaps might even join me in speaking these words. "Stop all the
clocks, cut off the telephone." "Put crepe bows round the white necks of the
public doves, / Let the traffic policeman wear black cotton gloves." "He was my
North, my South, my East and West, / My working week and my Sunday rest, /
My noon, my midnight, my talk, my song."

At the end of the book, God speaks at last (Job 38–41). I would exceed the
limits of this paper if I attempted to unravel the complexities of what God
says. Even so, I cannot help but wonder out loud about those animals God calls
to Job's attention (38:39–39:30; 40:15–24). What a strange and diverse assortment of creatures: some wild and threatening, others domestic and timid;
some swift, others slow; some smart, others apparently helplessly stupid. They
are all presented as pairs – lion/raven, goat/deer, ass/ox, ostrich/horse, hawk/
eagle, Behemoth/Leviathan – as if they are created to depend on each other
and together on God, whose constant delight is to care for them, each and
every one. Are their pairings, with each other and with God, the zoological
equivalent of friendship?

---

13   Auden, "Twelve Songs, IX," in *W. H. Auden: Collected Poems*, 141. Used by permission of
      Random House, Inc.

Of one thing I think we can be fairly certain. At the end of the book the silence that has hovered over the story for thirty-six chapters has ended. The conversation *about* Job that dominated the Prologue has now been replaced by conversation *with* Job. God has responded to Job. Job has listened to God and responded. To be sure, the conversation is vexed and very uneven – God speaks for 123 verses, Job for only 9 – but there is nonetheless an "I" and a "You," and in the soil between these two poles a dialogue can take root. Both parties, I suspect, bring something to the dialogue that was not there before. Job concedes this when he says, "I had heard of you by the hearing of the ear, but now my eye sees you" (42:5). God only hints at what may have changed in the divine realm by conceding that when Job prays for his friends, God will not execute the punishment they deserve: "I will accept his [Job's] prayer not to deal with you according to your folly" (42:8).[14] One thing has remained constant from the beginning to the end of this story, despite the silence that has intervened. At the end of the book as at the beginning, God calls Job "my servant" (42:7–8). Even though this servant displays fidelity in ways that would fracture most any "ordinary" friendship, God continues to claim him, to speak to him and listen to him, and to respond to what he says.

When Jesus finished his story about those who did and did not care for the beaten man on the road to Jericho, he asked the lawyer, "Which of these three persons, do you think, was a neighbor to the man who fell into the hands of robbers?" The lawyer said, "The one who showed him mercy." And the God who was in Jesus said to him, "Go and do likewise," to which we might add, I suggest, "even when, especially when, his name is Job."

---

14   On the possibility that Job's prayer changes God, see S. E. Balentine, "My Servant Job Shall Pray For You," *ThTo* 58 (2002), 502–518.

CHAPTER 4

"What Are Human Beings That You Make So Much of Them?" Responses and Counter-Responses from Job, Prometheus, and Frankenstein

The question as posed comes from inter-textual ruminations in Job 7:17 and Ps 8:4 (cf. Ps 144:3), with echoes of Genesis 1.* Hebraic texts and traditions typically address the question by using theology to define and limit anthropological considerations: God is God; human beings are mortal; God's knowledge and capacities surpass anything human might question; thus, the proper role of humans is to accept, submit, and conform themselves to forbidden knowledge and limited participation in the affairs of God and the world.[1] There are of course dissonant, even scandalously defiant, voices in the Hebrew Bible, but perhaps none speaks so loudly and so persistently as Job. From his opening curses in Job 3 ("Damn the day on which I was born; damn the night on which I was conceived; and, by inference, damn the Creator who is responsible for life") to his relentless laments about a God who inflicts suffering "for no reason" (Job 2:3), Job presses a singular question, multiply phrased (cf. 3:11; 6:11; 10:18), but reduced to its essence in 7:17: "What are human beings that you [God] make so much of them, that you set your mind on them?" Job's friends convey the default answer: human beings are "loathsome and foul, beings that drink wrongdoing like water" (15:16; cf. 4:17–21; 25:4–6).

Both the Septuagint and the *Testament of Job* effectively censor Job's defiance. It may be argued that the biblical account encourages such censoring, that by framing Job's story with a prose account of his submission to God and his ultimate reward for doing so, it neutralizes the portrait of defiance that dominates the poetic center of the book. Or does it? Cynthia Ozick, who describes herself as an "ordinary reader" of Job, asks the question I propose to track in this paper:

---

* Presented at the national meeting of the Society of Biblical Literature, Chicago, IL, 2012.

1 Cf. C. Newsom ("Models of the Moral Self: Hebrew Bible and Second Temple Judaism," JBL 131 [2012], 12), who notes that "submission to external authority" constitutes part of "the fundamental grammar of the moral self in the Hebrew Bible." See further, R. Di Vito, "Old Testament Anthropology and the Construction of Personal Identity," CBQ 61 (1999), 234–236.

© SAMUEL E. BALENTINE, 2021 | DOI:10.1163/9789004459212_005

"WHAT ARE HUMAN BEINGS THAT YOU MAKE SO MUCH OF THEM?" 73

> So the poet ... stills Job.
>
> But can the poet still the Job who lives in us? ...
>
> [I]f we are to take the close of the tale as given, it is not only Job's pro-
> tests that are stilled; it is also his inmost moral urge. What has become of
> raging conscience? ... Prosperity is restored by twice the number of boys,
> and by girls exceedingly comely. But where now is the father's bitter grief
> over the loss of those earlier sons and daughters, on whose account he
> once indicted God? Cushioned again by good fortune, does Job remem-
> ber nothing, feel nothing, see nothing, beyond his own renewed honor?
> Is Job's lesson ... finally no more than the learning of difference?
>
> So much for the naked text.[2]

My proposal is this. The Job who defies the default anthropological model in
the Hebrew Bible, however his words may have been muted, remains a cultural
touchstone for those whose aspirations for justice have moved them to "rebel
passion."[3]

1   "Job Is the Prometheus of the World"[4]

The evocation of Job as a tragic, Promethean figure, is deeply embedded in the
Greek tragedians (Aeschylus, Sophocles, and Euripides). The essential features
of the Promethean myth originate with Hesiod (eighth century BCE), who
describes Prometheus as a Titan who stole fire from the heavens and gave it
to humans, against the wishes of the gods, thus provoking Zeus to punish him
by chaining him to a pillar, where he endured the daily torture of an eagle
consuming his liver. Some two centuries later, Aeschylus (525–426 BCE), wrote
what became the most influential version of the myth, *Prometheus Bound*. The
plotline of *Prometheus Bound* comprises seven scenes. Time permits no more
than a passing reference to a seminal line in this work, which resonates with

---

2   C. Ozick, "The Impious Impatience of Job," in *Quarrel & Quandary* (New York: Alfred A. Knopf,
    2000), 72.

3   G. Murray, "Prometheus and Job," in *Twentieth Century Interpretations of the Book of Job*, 58.

4   A. de Lamartine, *Cours familer de literature*, cited in N. Sarna, *The Dimensions of Job: A Study
    and Selected Readings* (New York: Schocken Books, 1969), 43. The full citation reads: "*Job is the
    Prometheus of the world*, raised to the heavens shrieking, still bleeding, in the very claws of
    the vulture gnawing at his heart. He is the victim become judge, by the sublime impersonal-
    ity of reason, celebrating his own torture, like the Roman Brutus, casting up to heaven the
    drops of his blood, not as an insult, but as a libation to a just God."

74   CHAPTER 4

the counsel of Job's friends: fear Zeus "the dispenser of all things" and never transgress what he decrees (II, 527, 550–551; cf. Job 22:21).

Prometheus and Job are literary characters linked by a common struggle. Both endure suffering that exceeds explanation; both must decide whether silent acquiescence or defiant resistance is the faithful response to divine decree; both debate the options with visitors, would-be comforters all, who advise first caution, then compliance with the deity's inscrutable decision; both refuse such counsel by insisting that the deity can be converted to the cause of the righteous; and both complete their journeys with a vexed combination of reward and consequence: for Job, the loss of seven daughters and three sons, coupled with the ultimate restoration of his family; for Prometheus, his savage overthrow by Zeus, coupled with the support of the cosmos. There are differences between the two accounts, to be sure – Prometheus is a god, Job a mere mortal – but at the core of both accounts is an audacious quest for justice, sustained by the conviction that the deity cannot be absolved of responsibility for the suffering of the righteous. Prometheus, like Job, refuses the conventional counsel that when it comes to questioning the deity's wisdom, "mortals must be mortal-minded."[5] This Prometheus refuses to do:

> Worship, adore, and fawn upon whoever is thy love. But I care for Zeus less than nought. Let him do his will, let him hold his power for his little day – since not for long shall he bear sway over the gods.
>
> II, 937–940[6]

Goethe's "Prometheus" (1775) renders Aeschylus's play in eight stanzas that track Prometheus's growth from childhood to maturity, a poetic parallel to

---

5 A. C. Yu, "New Gods and Old Order: Tragic Theology in the *Prometheus Bound*," JAAR 39 (1971), 37.

6 When mortals like Job or Titans like Prometheus refuse to be "mortal-minded" when it comes to divine authority, then we may be sure that their defiance has "cultural-critical implications" (H. Blumenberg, *Work on Myth*, [Cambridge, MS, London: MIT Press, 1990], 307). Georges Méautis, for example, makes a strong case for understanding Aeschylus's depiction of Zeus as a tyrant and Prometheus's defiance of such tyranny as an indictment of the subversion of democracy that he witnessed first-hand during his sojourn in Sicily at the court of Hiero of Syracuse (478–467 BCE) during the Persian wars (G. Méautis, L'Authenticité et la date du Prométhée [Neuchatel: University of Neuchatel, 1960], 46–47). Scholars debate whether there is one specific historical character or one identifiable political era that underlies Aeschylus's critique of regnant political theories. For a review of different theories, see A. J. Podlecki, "Prometheus Bound," in *The Political Background of Aeschylean Tragedy* (Ann Arbor: University of Michigan Press, 1966), 101–122, and "Appendix B: The Date of Prometheus Bound," 142–147.

"WHAT ARE HUMAN BEINGS THAT YOU MAKE SO MUCH OF THEM?"

the Enlightenment's view of humanity's progress from tyranny to freedom. Having indicted Zeus and the gods for wretchedly nourishing themselves on the sacrifices, prayers, and false hopes of children and beggars (Stanzas I–II), Prometheus directs his lament to a silent heaven:

> Who helped me
> Against the Titans' wanton insolence
> Who rescued me from death,
> from slavery? ...
>
> I honor you? For what?
> Have you ever eased the suffering
> of the oppressed?
> Have you ever stilled the tears
> of the frightened?[7]

With a final question, Prometheus chides Zeus for believing that suffering would cause him to retreat ("Did you fancy perchance/that I should hate life/ and fly to the desert/because not all my blossom dreams ripened?"). Stanza VIII conveys the verdict by evoking, then subverting, the *imago dei* affirmation in Gen 1:27.

> Here I sit, forming men
> in my own image,
> a race to be like me,
> to suffer, to weep,
> to delight and to rejoice,
> and to defy you,
> as I do.

Within a decade after its publication, Goethe's "Prometheus" ignited a controversy that extended far beyond eighteenth German philosophical thought. Goethe's denial of divine providence, his affirmation of human beings as independent creators who suffer, rejoice, and refuse homage to religious authority became part of the Pantheism Controversy, out of which emerged the word "nihilism." Regnant philosophical, political, and religious orthodoxies were subjected to severe scrutiny, as thinkers such as Heinrich Heine, Immanuel

---

7 Translations from W. Kaufmann, *Twenty German Poets: A Bilingual Collection* (New York: Random House, 1962), 8–11.

76 CHAPTER 4

Kant, Friedrich Schelling, G. W. F. Hegel, Karl Marx, and Friedrich Nietzsche pushed Goethe's unorthodoxies one way and another. As Hans Blumenberg notes in his assessment of Goethe's impact on the eighteenth century, "his fundamental idea is that God would have had to arrange the world differently if he had been concerned about man."[8] Goethe himself seems to have anticipated that his poem would be "the priming power for an explosion," because it "revealed and brought into discussion the most secret relations of estimable men: [relations] unknown ... and slumbering in an otherwise highly enlightened society."[9]

Goethe's "priming powder for an explosion," which triggers the Romantic interest in a more humanistic depiction of Promethean defiance, is also manifest in Lord Byron's poem, "Prometheus" (1816).[10] The first stanza equates Prometheus's suffering with the "suffocating sense of woe" that comes to all whose pain is "echoless." In the second stanza, Prometheus denounces the gods' "deaf tyranny of fate" and their "ruling principle of hate." In the third and final stanza, Prometheus declares the lesson mortals must learn from the "sum of human wretchedness."

> A mighty lesson we inherit:
> To mortals of their fate and force;
> Like thee, Man is in part divine,
> A troubled stream from a pure source; ...
>
> And his sad unallied existence ...
>
> Triumphant where it dares defy,
> And making Death a Victory.

Even as Goethe, Byron, and other Romantic poets[11] viewed Prometheus as an heroic champion who inspires human beings to defy authority, they were engaging, and stretching, lingering Joban-type questions. Is it noble or scandalous for mortals, even if they are "part divine," to contest the will of the gods? Is it an act of courage to claim that mortals can convert the gods to justice, or

---

8   Blumenberg, *Work on Myth*, 556.

9   Goethe, *Dichtung und Wahrheit*, cited in Blumenberg, *Work on Myth*, 413.

10   G. Byron, "Prometheus," in *The Poetical Works of Byron*, ed., R. F. Gleckner (Boston: Houghton Mifflin, 1975), 191.

11   E.g., Samuel Taylor Coleridge, "On the Prometheus of Aeschylus" (1825); Elizabeth Barrett Browning, "Prometheus Bound" (1833); Henry Wadsworth Longfellow, "Prometheus, the Poet's Forethought" (1858).

is this merely hubris cloaked in poetic imagination? What is the line between being created "in the image" of the gods and being "mortal-minded"? No one exploited such questions more than Milton in *Paradise Lost* (1667), where Prometheus is Satan writ large.[12]

The debate concerning whether Prometheus should be condemned as a blasphemous Satan (Milton) or praised as a champion (Goethe, Byron) is manifest in the work, quite literally the marriage, of Mary Wollstonecraft Godwin and Percy Bysshe Shelley in 1816. Mary Shelley's *Frankenstein* (1818) is subtitled "The Modern Prometheus." The protagonist of the novel, Victor Frankenstein, is a well-intentioned but tragically misdirected Promethean figure who creates life in his own image. The creature he animates from discarded human body parts is strong and eloquent, but his appearance is so extraordinarily horrifying that Victor abandons him immediately. The creature in turn wanders about, seeking revenge on his creator by killing his brother, his best friend, and his wife. One night, while scavenging in the woods for food, the creature discovers a cache of books, among them Milton's *Paradise Lost*, likely intentionally left for him by Victor. From reading Milton, the creature identifies himself with Satan, "wretched, helpless, alone" and filled with "the bitter gall of envy" (92).[13] Of the two major characters, however, the monster, rather than Victor, is more human, despite his murderous ways, and he elicits compassion and sympathy. In trying to convince Victor to let go his rage and hatred and listen to his story, the creature says,

> I am thy creature, and I will be even mild and docile to my natural lord and king, if thou wilt also perform thy part, the which thou owest me. Oh, Frankenstein, be not equitable to every other and trample upon me alone, to whom thy justice, and even thy clemency and affection, is most due. Remember, that I am thy creature: I ought to be thy Adam, but I am rather the fallen angel, whom thou drivest from joy for no misdeed. (69)

Shelley turns the Aeschylean tragedy on its head by exploiting the implications of its romanticized view of human creativity. Victor, the Promethean figure, is a god-like Zeus who creates life only to destroy it "for no misdeed." The creature created in the image of his creator accepts the master-slave relationship,

---

12   Cf. R. J. Zwi Werblowsky, *Lucifer and Prometheus: A Study of Milton's Satan* (London: Oliphants, 1952), 47–66.

13   Citations and parenthetical page references from M. Shelley, *Frankenstein* (New York: Dover, 1994).

78 CHAPTER 4

which consigns him to a life of malignant opprobrium from which there can be no redemption.

Two years after the publication of *Frankenstein*, Percy Shelley's "Prometheus Unbound" (1820) returns to a more "conventional" Romantic rendering of the hero. He singles out Milton's equation of Lucifer and Prometheus in *Paradise Lost* for particular criticism. Milton's Lucifer is tainted by "ambition, envy, revenge, and a desire for personal aggrandizement;" Shelley's Prometheus, by contrast, is a "type of the highest perfection of moral and intellectual nature, impelled by the purest and the truest motives to the best and noblest ends" (133).[14]

In Act I, Prometheus repents of the curse Jupiter has placed on him (I, 303–305), but refuses submission, "that fatal word, The death-seal of mankind's captivity" (I, 396–397). In Act II, Pantheia and Asia descend to the realm of Demogorgon, offspring of Jupiter and Thetis. When Asia questions Jupiter's "Omnipotent but friendless" reign (II, 48–49), Demogorgon explains that the hour is coming when he will dethrone Jupiter, because "All things are subject but eternal love" (II, 120). Act III shifts to heaven, where Jupiter boasts to the gods that his omnipotence prevails over all but Prometheus, whose insurrection, like "unextinguished fire," threatens to make "our antique empire insecure" (III, 5, 9). Demogorgon drags Jupiter into the abyss of chaos; Hercules releases Prometheus; and the "thrones, altars, judgment seats and prisons" that once fated human beings to wretched existence become "the ghosts of a no more remembered fame" (III, 164, 170). Act IV comprises a hymn of rejoicing, which ends with Demogoron's final assessment of the moral of the play.

> To suffer woes which Hope thinks infinite;
> To forgive wrongs darker than Death or Night;
> To defy Power which seems Omnipotent;
> To love, and bear; to hope, till Hope creates
> From its own wreck the thing it contemplates;
> Neither to change nor falter nor repent:
> This, like thy glory, Titan! Is to be
> Good, great and joyous, beautiful and free;
> This is alone Life, Joy, Empire and Victory.
>
> IV, 570–578

---

14 "Prometheus Unbound," in *Shelley's Poetry and Prose, Authoritative Texts and Criticism*. Selected and edited by D. H. Reiman, S. B. Powers (New York, London: W. W. Norton, 1977), 130–210. Internal citations are from this edition.

2   The End of the Promethean Myth?

By the end of the nineteenth century, the myth of Prometheus, generative of "indefatigable explication,"[15] seems to reach its end in satire. André Gide's *Prometheus Misbound* (1899) transforms the poetic account into a burlesque narrative.[16] Zeus is a "Meglionaire" banker in Paris, who gratuitously gives a five-hundred-franc note to a stranger, Cocles, whom he encounters on the street. Zeus explains that his passion is gambling, specifically lending money to strangers as an experiment in proving that those who become rich for no reason cannot help but inflict suffering on others. The "other" in this case is named, suggestively, Damocles. Prometheus is a modern Parisian, who, having once been chained to a rock in Caucasus, became uncomfortable, simply stretched out his arm, and freed himself. "Between four and five o'clock on an autumn afternoon, [he] walked down the boulevard which leads from the Madeleine to the Opéra" and ordered a beer in a sidewalk café (105). There he meets Cocles and Damocles. When he tells them his name, Damocles says, "Excuse me, sir, but it seems to me that this name has already ..." Prometheus interrupts him, "Oh! ... that is of no importance whatsoever" (119). As far as Prometheus is concerned, he has no history, no identity, and nothing to contribute to the conversation with Cocles and Damocles, save for the fact that his sole possession is an eagle that survives by eating his flesh.

These essentials contribute to the absurdity of the narrative, which ends with Prometheus offering a "totem meal"[17] to Cocles and other mourners at Damocles's funeral. The entré is the eagle, fattened by its feeding on Prometheus. The narrative concludes with these words from Prometheus, written, as he says, with a pen made from one of the eagle's feathers.

> Its flesh has nourished us.... I eat it with no animosity; if it had made me suffer less, it would have been less plump; if it had been less plump, it would not have been delectable. (173)

Blumenberg argues, I believe correctly, that by turning the tragedy into a "grotesque" deformation of itself, Gide signals that the myth of Prometheus has reached its hermeneutical end.[18] The realties that generated it are now

---

15   P. A. Bertagnoli, *Prometheus in Music: Representations of the Myth in the Romantic Era* (Aldershot, UK: Burlington, VT: Ashgate, 2007), 3.

16   A. Gide, *Marshlands and Prometheus Misbound* (Trans. G. D. Painter; New York, Toronto: McGraw-Hill, 1965). Internal citations are from this edition.

17   Blumenberg, *Work on Myth*, 627.

18   Ibid., 627–633.

80   CHAPTER 4

forgotten; like the name "Prometheus," they no longer have any importance. In a "brief moment of culinary enjoyment," the "old seriousness" of the myth has been, literally, consumed.[19] Zeus, Prometheus, and those who visit with him, have become little more than aesthetic caricatures in a story of benign entertainment.[20]

What happens, Blumenberg asks, when "Myth can no longer take place, because 'too little' happens?"[21] If the "substratum of truth" that gives rise to the myth is forgotten by all, if the search for its meaning becomes "wearying" to all, if the inexplicable no longer compels a search for the meaning of the inexplicable, then what more is there left to say? If all that remains of the Promethean myth is at the most aesthetic enjoyment, at the least "eschatological melancholy," then "why," Blumenberg goes on to ask, "should the world have to continue in existence if there is nothing more to say?"[22]

Similar questions may be asked of Job's anthropology. If the substratum of truth that grounds righteous defiance and the refusal to bless the world God has created becomes a forgotten footnote to a story that is simply a good read, then why bother to wrestle with inexplicable questions like "Why?" If mortal-minded human beings are no more than "foul and loathsome" creatures who must "be lessoned" into silence before the deity, as Kratos (Power) says to Prometheus (ll. 10–11), then why bother to ask the question, "What are human beings that you make so much of them?" If there is nothing more to say about the Joban story than what can be summed up in a Brothers Grimm truism – "In the beginning ... and they all lived happily ever after" – then defiance may remain an aesthetic curiosity, but it will not likely translate into a culture-critical consciousness.

Early Joban interpreters and commentators, as noted above, move in the direction of muting, minimizing, or omitting Job's scandalous voice of defiance. Septuagint translators soften Job's complaints and denude his indictments of God. The *Testament of Job* omits altogether Job's curses and transfers his doubts and questions about innocent suffering to the friends, whose sins God exposes. The structure of the Book of Job itself no doubt provides some

---

19   Ibid., 628, 633.
20   Blumenberg (Ibid., 633–636) cites Kafka's "Prometheus" (1918; in *Franz Kafka: The Complete Stories*, ed., N. Glatzer [New York: Schocken, 1995], 432), which comprises less than a page, to buttress his argument. Prometheus's story has been forgotten by all over the course of thousands of years, Kafka says. In the end, "Everyone grew weary of the meaningless affair. The gods grew weary, the eagles grew weary, the wound closed wearily." All interpretive options, Kafka concludes, end "in the explicable."
21   Blumenberg, *Work on Myth*, 630.
22   Ibid.

license for such interpretive moves. It frames and rhetorically neutralizes Job's seven curses in 3:1–10 with seven occurrences of "bless" in the Prologue and Epilogue (Job 1:5, 10, 11, 21; 2:5, 9; 42:12). Further, the New Testament reduces the complexity of the Joban story to a single maxim, the "patience of Job" (Jas 5:11), which may not be the equivalent of burlesque but is nonetheless vulnerable to being fossilized as little more than cliché. Moreover, although biblical scholars and others have often compared Job and Prometheus,[23] the usual approach has been to accent the differences between the two, not the similarities. The assessment of H. G. May is representative: "In contrast with the Promethean myth, the solution of the [Joban] drama is found not in a change of mind and heart on the part of the deity, but in the unquestioned submission of man to One with power and knowledge greater than his own."[24] In short, the reception history of Job as a Promethean model for whatever may go by the name of "biblical/theological anthropology" might appear to have been forgotten, by God, by Job himself, and by his readers. To paraphrase Jas 5:11, all that we see and remember of the Joban story is its affirmation of a merciful and compassionate God.

The concluding line of Blumenberg's magisterial study of the Promethean myth ends with a final question: "But what if there were still something to say, after all?"[25] The question returns readers to Blumenberg's first chapter, where

---

23 There is a long trajectory of work connecting Job and the Greek tragedians, beginning with Theodore of Mopsuestia (d. 428; see J.-P. Migne, *Patrolgiae Cursus Completus, Series Graeca* [Paris, 1864], Vol. LXVI, 697–698). On the connections between Job and Greek tragedy, see further, for example, H. M. Kallen, *The Book of Job as Greek Tragedy* (New York: Moffat, Yard, and Company, 1918) [excerpts reprinted as H. M. Kallen, "Job the Humanist," in N. Glatzer, *The Dimensions of Job: A Study and Selected Readings* (New York: Schocken Books, 1969), 175–180]; G. Montefiore, "The Book of Job as Greek Tragedy Restored," HTR 12 (1919), 219–224 [excerpts reprinted in G. Murray, "Beyond Good and Evil," in Glatzer, *The Dimensions of Job*, 194–197]; D. D. Raphael, "Tragedy and Religion," in *Twentieth Century Interpretations of the Book of Job*, ed., P. S. Sanders (Englewood Cliffs, NJ: Prentice Hall, 1968); R. Sewall, "The Book of Job," in *The Vision of Tragedy* (New Haven, London: Yale University Press, 1959), 9–24; U. M. Kaufmann, "Expostulation with the Divine: A Note on Contrasting Attitudes in Greek and Hebrew Piety," in *Twentieth Century Interpretations of the Book of Job*, 66–77. On the connections between Job and Prometheus, see, for example, J. Lindblom, *Job and Prometheus: A Comparative Study* (Lund, 1939); W. A. Irvin, "Job and Prometheus," JR 30 (1950), 90–108; G. Murray, "Prometheus and Job," in *Twentieth Century Interpretations of the Book of Job*, 56–65 [excerpted from G. Murray, "Aeschylus As a Poet of Ideas: The Mystical Plays, *Prometheus* and *Supplices*," in *Aeschylus: The Creator of Tragedy* (Oxford: Clarendon Press, 1940), 87–110].

24 H. G. May, "Prometheus and Job: The Problem of the God of Power and the Man of Worth," *Anglican Theological Review* 34 (1952), 246. See also the citation from Lamartine above, n. 4.

25 Blumenberg, *Work on Myth*, 636.

82   CHAPTER 4

he lays out his argument that myths never simply evaporate into thin air. Even when jettisoned to aesthetic imagination or simply forgotten, myths linger and against all odds demand ongoing work because they are "indispensable aspects of the comprehensive efforts that make human existence possible." As Blumenberg puts it, "Cultures that have not yet achieved mastery of their reality continue to dream the dream and would snatch its realization away from those who think they have already awakened from it."[26]

Is there still something more to say about Joban defiance of the friends' default anthropological model? I submit that there is. The first clue is that Job's words from the ash heap do not end with curses. They reach beyond defiance to lament (Job 3:11–26), which presses the "Why?" question to and perhaps beyond Hebraic convention into litigious argumentation. Unlike Aeschylus's Prometheus, the biblical Job does not simply quake at the god's thunder and lightning and vanish from sight. Instead, he presses his case, demanding that when it comes to seven daughters and three sons who die by God's admission "for no reason," it is God's injustice, not human sin, that merits indictment.

I end with words from Aeschylus's Prometheus. When the Chorus implores Prometheus to tell them his story (ll. 196–198), he concedes, because it is too "painful to keep silent" (ll. 199–200). His account of his response to Zeus's tyranny begins with these words:

> Against this purpose none dared make stand save I myself – I only had the courage; I saved mortals so that they did not descend, blasted utterly, unto the House of Death. Therefore am I bent by so grievous tortures, painful to suffer, piteous to behold. I that gave mortals first place in my pity, I am deemed unworthy to win this pity for myself, but am mercilessly disciplined, *a spectacle that shames the face of Zeus.*
>
> ll. 236–243; emphasis added

I leave you with this question: Does Job's "theological anthropology" honor or shame the face of God?

---

26   Ibid., viii (Translator's Introduction).

CHAPTER 5

"What Provokes You That You Keep on Talking?"

The question posed in my title for this address comes from Job 16:3, which provides Job's response to Eliphaz at the beginning of the second round of dialogues with the friends (Job 15–22).* The translation offered by Eugene Peterson is rather loose, but it is close enough to the gist of what Job is saying to set the table for our reflections:

> Then Job answered his friends by saying:
> I've had all I can take of your talk.
> What a bunch of miserable comforters!
> Is there no end to your windbag speeches?
> What's your problem that you go on and on like this?
> Job 16:1–3[1]

"Miserable comforters"? Why do you keep on talking like this? What's your problem? Job's assessment of the friends' words should give us pause, because they are spokespersons for the religious establishment. Like those of us gathered here, they represent the pastors and teachers, the educators and the pastoral counselors, ones who know themselves called of God to minister to the Jobs of this world. If we are flinching already at this proposed linkage between Job's friends and us clergy types, then the witness of this slice of Holy Scripture is likely to do little to comfort us. More than one-third of the book, roughly 35% (376 verses of a 1069 total) is given to the "windbag speeches" of Job's friends. Their words take up more space than any other character in this drama, including God, who, upon taking center stage in the whirlwind speeches in Job 38–41, gets only 123 verses. In the end, God dismisses the sum total of what the friends say with one chilling sentence, twice repeated to drive home the point: "My wrath is kindled against you [friends], because you have not spoken of me what is right" (42:7, 8). Now we may be not only flinching at the thought of entering into this book; we may also be looking for the exit signs. I'm reminded of the assessment of Virginia Woolf, which I alter ever so slightly for this occasion:

---

* Originally presented at the Montreat Conference Center in Montreat NC in May, 2007. The theme of the conference was "Pushing the Boundaries in Preaching: Text and Context."

1 Eugene H. Peterson, *Job: Led By Suffering to the Heart of God* (Colorado Springs, Colorado: NavPress, 1996), 45.

© SAMUEL E. BALENTINE, 2021 | DOI:10.1163/9789004459212_006

84   CHAPTER 5

"I read the Book of Job last night. I don't think [the friends] come well out of it."[2] (Woolf actually says, "I don't think *God* comes well out of it," but this demands a whole other presentation, which no doubt would be still more unsettling – and so, I leave it to the side for now.)

1   Pastoral Care 101

We may be reasonably confident that the friends did not set out either to speak wrongly about God or to hurt Job with the words they offered him. Indeed, when they first step into this story, these friends are the epitome of wise and skillful pastoral counselors. According to the Prologue, when they learned of Job's misfortunes, they came immediately from their respective homes to "console" and "comfort" him (2:11–13). Perhaps they came hoping to "console" and "comfort" with words "fitly" or "rightly spoken," as Prov. 25:11 commends the truly wise to do. But, when they looked at their friend, they saw, even from a distance, that "his suffering was very great," and they wisely scrapped their speeches. Instead, they adopt the traditional gestures of sympathetic mourning – they weep, tear their garments, and throw dust over their heads – then, they sit with their friend in silence, for seven days and seven nights. Confronted with suffering like Job's – seven sons and three daughters, dead "for no reason" (2:3) – they respond by following the first lesson of Pastoral Care 101: the first and most important act of pastoral ministry is simply to be present. Words are not necessary and often do more harm than good.

Two artistic representations help us to visualize this initial response. The first is from William Blake (1757–1827), the English engraver, painter, and poet, who worked on various versions of his twenty-one *Illustrations of the Book of Job* for most of his life. [See Figure 3.1 William Blake, Job's Comforters] In number seven of the final edition, Blake depicts Job sitting on a mound of straw, his head resting on his wife's breast. Job's hands, palms downward, extend by his side. His wife kneels behind him, her body providing a pillar of support, her uplifted hands gesturing the prayer Job himself seems now too exhausted to offer. The six uplifted hands of the friends mimic the wife, although their reach heavenward is more extended and their facial expressions convey more intensity and emotion. It is as if by the force of their gestures they hope to lift Job safely out of his distress and into the arms of God. At the top and bottom

---

2 *The Letters of Virginia Woolf, Vol. II: 1912–1922*, ed. N. Nicholson (New York: Harcourt Brace Jovanovich, 1976), 585.

"WHAT PROVOKES YOU THAT YOU KEEP ON TALKING?" 85

of the frame Blake has inscribed the words from Job 2:12: "When they lifted up their eyes afar off and knew him not they lifted up their voices and wept ..." To these words Blake adds a quotation from Jas. 5:11, which provides the catchword – "patience" – that captures not only the popular understanding of Job's exemplary faith but also the reason for the friends' sympathetic support: "Ye have heard of the *patience of Job* and have seen the end of the Lord, that the Lord is very pitiful, and of tender mercy" (AV).

As we ponder the truth in this representation, along with our instinctive and by now traditioned-honed inclination toward embracing the proverbial "patience of Job," I offer one caution, which anticipates where this story is about to take us. The words are spoken by Jenny, one of the characters in Henry Fielding's novel, *The History of Tom Jones*: "Patience is a virtue very apt to be fatigued by exercise."[3]

The second visual is Jean Fouquet's depiction of "Job on the Dung Heap."

Fouquet depicts Job, lying forlorn on a pile of manure, as one of the oppressed and famished outcasts in fifteenth century French society. His place is outside the walled city, where the Tower of Vincennes (outside Paris) stands opulent and secure. On the manicured grounds just beyond the walls, people go about their normal affairs: a person on horseback sits tall and erect, perhaps surveying his land; two workers amble along in tranquil conversation. Three "friends," dressed in the regalia that identifies their positions of power and privilege, have traveled the long and winding road that leads outside the city to Job. The person to Job's right wears the scarlet that symbolizes the parliament; the person to his left, the royal blue of the monarchy. The figure in the middle, standing before him with hands uplifted to bless, is robed in the white of the church.

Once again, a word of caution is in order, lest we miss the subtlety of Fouquet's exegesis. On first sight, these three "comforters" appear to model genuine concern and sympathy for Job. On closer inspection, we see that the priest who extends the church's blessing does so with eyes closed. Fouquet subtly suggests that the leaders of France's institutional structures, at the center of which stands the church, feign attentiveness to one their own policies have pushed to the margins of society. If these persons are custodians of the policies that are meant to provide for those who have been robbed of the resources for life, then why do they continue to support a system that drives those who suffer like Job outside the city walls?

---

3 H. Fielding, *The History of Tom Jones, A Foundling*, vol. 1 (New York: P. F. Collier & Son, 1917), 19.

FIGURE 5.1   Jean Fouquet (c. 1415–1481). "Job and His Comforters." *The Hours of Etienne Chevalier, Office of the Dead.* Musée Condé, Chantilly, France
CREDIT: SAIKO, WIKIMEDIA COMMONS, CCA-SA 3.0

After seven days and nights of silence, Job, who had not "sinned with his lips" (2:10) by "charging God with wrongdoing" (1:22), "opened his mouth and cursed God" (3:1). A rough paraphrase of what he says in chapter 3 is this: "Damn the day on which I was born; damn the night on which I was conceived; and (by implication), damn the Creator who brings a life such as this into being." To these curses he adds a series of anguished and freighted "Why?" questions. With each thunderous charge, Job inches one step closer to naming – and indicting – God as the One responsible for these "crimes against humanity":

"WHAT PROVOKES YOU THAT YOU KEEP ON TALKING?" 87

> Why did I not die at birth,
> > come forth from the womb and expire?
>
> Why were there knees to receive me,
> > or breasts for me to suck?
> >
> > 3:11–12
>
> [Why] was I not buried like a stillborn child,
> > like an infant that never sees the light?
> >
> > 3:16
>
> Why is light given to one in misery,
> > and life to the bitter in soul?
> >
> > 3:20

This last question merits careful scrutiny. Most English translations obscure the move Job is making with a passive and impersonal rendering of the verb "give:" "Why is light *given* to one in misery?" (NRSV; cf. REB, NIV, NAB). The Hebrew form of the verb, however, is active, not passive. NJPS captures both the sense and the implication with its translation: "Why does *He give* light to the sufferer?" Job does not explicitly identify God as the one he holds accountable for his plight, but the tone of his language indicates that he understands there is an active agent somewhere behind his suffering. Someone or something "gives" what has happened to him; it is not merely "given." Job's finger is pointing, ever so obliquely, at God.

As soon as Job "opens his mouth and curses," the burden of being his friend – or minister – becomes greater. As long as Job remained pious and patient, the friends were content to "console" and "comfort" him with their silent, sympathetic presence. But when he begins to curse and complain, Job crosses the line between submission and revolt. The friends can affirm blessing God, because they have a secure place in their theology for those who conform to their expectations: whatever happens in life, the proper response is, "Blessed be the name of the Lord" (1:22). But when Job moves from blessing the God on whom their convictions rest to cursing God, he shakes the foundations of their world, and they run to shore them up lest everything collapse around them.

A scene from Edward Albee's Pulitzer Prize-winning play *A Delicate Balance* may help us conceptualize what Job's friends are thinking.[4] One night while Agnes and her husband Tobias were idling away their time in their comfortable

---

4 E. Albee, *A Delicate Balance* (New York: Penguin, 1966). Internal references are to this publication.

suburban home, Edna and Harry, two life-long friends, show up uninvited at their door. Something was clearly wrong, although Edna and Harry could say nothing more than, "We got ... frightened." "We got scared" (Act I, 49). Only gradually did it become clear to Agnes and Tobias that their friends had come to seek refuge in their home. When that realization sunk in, another quickly followed. Agnes and Tobias had become ensnared in something that threatened to disrupt the "delicate balance" of their world. One morning, after Tobias had stayed up all night pondering how to help these friends, Agnes offered her own assessment of the situation:

> ... they've brought the plague with them, and that's another matter. Let me tell you something about disease ... mortal illness; you are either immune to it ... or you fight it. If you are immune, you wade in, you treat the patient, until he either lives, or dies of it. But if you are *not* immune, you risk infection. Ten centuries ago – and even less – the treatment was quite simple ... burn them. Burn their bodies, burn their houses, burn their clothes – and move to another town, if you were enlightened. But now, with modern medicine, we merely isolate; we quarantine, we ostracize – if we are not immune ourselves, or unless we are saints. So your night-long vigil, darling, your reasoning in the cold, pure hours, has been over the patient, and not the illness. *It is not Edna and Harry* who have come to us – our friends – *it is a disease.*
>
> Act III, 157; emphasis added

"If you are not immune, you risk infection." This might well be the credo of Job's friends, Eliphaz, Bildad, and Zophar, as they contemplate how to respond to the unexpected intrusion of his angry curses into the world of their settled convictions. He is a threat; his words are horrifying. Like a virus bug loosed in the world, Job is now targeted as a disease. For the health and well-being of the world, his poison must be eradicated; at the very least he must be isolated, quarantined, ostracized. As Agnes puts it, "If you are not immune, you risk infection."

We may visualize the friends' transition from silent support for Job to caustic rebuke by placing a second etching from William Blake alongside the first one we have already considered. In the second etching, Blake's Job has moved from the ash heap to a kneeling position. [See Figure 3.2. William Blake. Job Rebuked by His Friends] No longer leaning backward, Job now holds himself upright, his stomach muscles taut, as if flexed in anticipation of a negative response to the curses he has just hurled into the silence of his world. His spotted torso is wrapped from the waist down with the traditional sackcloth. His head is tilted backward. His tear-stained eyes are fixed on the God above whom

"WHAT PROVOKES YOU THAT YOU KEEP ON TALKING?" 89

he cannot see but will not cease to trust. Job's solemn misery is suggested by
the three citations of scripture at the top of the frame:

> But he knoweth the way I take
> when he hath tried me I shall come forth like gold
>> Job 23:10

> Have pity upon me! Have pity upon me! O ye my friends
> for the hand of God hath touched me
>> Job 19:21

> Though he slay me yet will I trust in him
>> Job13:15

As the second of these citations reminds us, Job hopes for "pity," for "compassion" from his "friends." We may pause briefly to reflect on Job's definition of friendship, which he articulates most succinctly in 6:14:

> The despairing need loyalty (*hesed*) from a friend,
> even if they forsake the fear of the Almighty.

Or as Peterson paraphrases it,

> When desperate people give up on God Almighty,
> their friends, at least, should stick with them.[5]

Job expects *hesed* from a friend. The conventional translation of this word
is "kindness" or "steadfast love." A better rendering is "loyalty." *Hesed* describes
both an attitude and an action that binds two parties together in an unbreakable partnership. Its fullest meaning is exemplified by God, for whom "loyalty and faithfulness" (*hesed wĕ'emet*) are constant attributes (e.g., Pss. 25:10;
57:3; 89:14; 138:2). God's loyalty is enacted; it is a disposition that is demonstrated. God "does" (*'asah*) *hesed* (e.g., Gen. 24:12, 14; Exod. 20:6 [= Deut. 5:10];
II Sam. 2:6; I Kgs. 3:6; Jer. 9:24 [MT 9:23]), the most tangible evidence of which
is God's commitment to "keeping covenant and steadfast love" (*šōmer habberît
wĕhahesed*; Deut. 7:9, 12; I Kgs. 8:23 [= II Chr. 6:14]; Neh. 1:5; 9:32; Dan. 9:4).

---

5 Peterson, *Job*, 23. Cf. Robert Alter's translation: "The blighted man's friend owes him kindness, / though the fear of Shaddai he forsake" (R. Alter, *The Hebrew Bible. Vol 3: The Writings/
Ketuvim. A Translation with Commentary* (New York, London: W. W. Norton & Co., 2019), 480).

When humans fail God and break the covenant partnership, it is "loyalty and faithfulness" that motivates God to restore it (Exod. 34:6).

God's loyalty is the perfect model of the relentless love that pursues relationship with others, even when they fail. As one commentator puts it, it is a commitment to relationship that "surpasses the obligatory."[6] What Job hopes for from his God, and from his friends who presume to speak for God, is this kind of loyalty, a loyalty that will not let go of him, even if suffering pushes him beyond the boundaries of conventional piety ("the fear of the Almighty"). "Have pity upon me! Have pity upon me! O ye my *friends*...."

But, as Blake's depiction makes painfully clear here, Job's friends have ceased to play the role of comforter. They are now Job's inquisitors. With outstretched hands they point fingers of ridicule in Job's direction. In contrast with Job, the friends' expressions are cold and hard, as is particularly clear in the face of the friend to the fore, presumably Eliphaz. Job's wife, whose right hand is also partially extended, seems now to have joined in the reproach. Two further citations in the bottom of the frame invite reflection on what it feels like, from Job's perspective, to be treated this way by those who claim to be friends.

> The Just Upright man is laughed to scorn
> Job 12:4

> Man that is born of a Woman is of few days & full of trouble
> he cometh up like a flower & is cut down, he fleeth also as a shadow
> & continueth not. And dost thou open thine eyes upon such a one
> & bringest me into judgment with thee
> Job 14:1–3

The figures in the border add to the bleakness of Job's situation from the friends' perspective. Two angels, each weighed down with chains, appear to be holding on with some difficulty to the picture of Job. In the bottom left-hand corner a bird (a raven? a cuckoo?), perhaps symbolic of slander, steps on a serpent. In the bottom right-hand corner an owl, perhaps symbolic of false wisdom, grasps a helpless mouse in its talons. The cumulative effect of the scene puts a face on the famous speech of Marcus Antonius in *Julius Caesar*. These friends have come "to bury [Job], not to praise him" (*Julius Caesar*, III, ii, 79). Or, as we might say today, "With friends like these, who needs enemies?"

---

6   H. J. Stoebe, "*Hesed*, Kindness," TLOT, vol. 2, 456.

"WHAT PROVOKES YOU THAT YOU KEEP ON TALKING?" 91

2 "What a Bunch of Miserable Comforters!"

In Job 16:2, Job describes his friends as "a bunch of miserable comforters." Elsewhere he refers to them as "treacherous" (6:15), "stupid" (cf. 12:2–3; 13:2), "whitewashers of the truth" (13:4a), and "quack doctors" (13:4b). How and why do Job's friends – and ministers – deserve this critique? If we are to "reclaim" this text, then we must pay careful attention to what these spokespersons for orthodoxy say, even if to do so "pushes us beyond the boundaries" of our settled ways of thinking.

The friends make their case against Job in three cycles of speeches (4–14, 15–21, 22–27). In each cycle their approach follows a similar pattern. They always begin with a series of rhetorical questions that attempt to lead Job to answers they already know. For example, when Bildad asks, "Does God pervert justice? Or does the Almighty pervert the truth?" (8:3), the only legitimate answer, the only answer he will accept from Job, is an unequivocal "No." When Eliphaz asks whether one who claims to be wise, as Job insists he is, should argue with God in "unprofitable talk" (15:3), the only answer he can imagine Job considering is "No, of course not." Once the friends are confident their questions have moved Job into their corner, then they begin to spell out the consequent truths of their observations. If *God* never perverts justice, then it stands to reason that when justice is perverted the culprits are necessarily *human beings*. If it is never wise to *argue* with God, then surely the wiser course is to *agree* with God and accept without question God's way of doing things.

The problem, of course, is that rhetorical questions only work when both the speaker and the addressee agree that the right answers are so obvious they need not even be spoken. At the most fundamental level, such questions require both silent consent and willing submission. When either of these conditions is lacking, the questions may spin out of control, inviting unexpected answers and unwanted detours from the argument they are meant to enforce. As any courtroom attorney knows, you never ask a witness a question without already knowing the answer yourself; otherwise, you run the risk of being blindsided with new testimony you never intended the jury to hear. Such is the problem Job presents for his friends. He does not accept the answers they assume. He does not come to the conclusions they believe are unassailable.

Because Job is so stubborn, so intractable, the friends feel compelled to trim their arguments in order to hem Job in. In the first cycle (4–14) their focus is on God's moral governance of the world, especially as this is manifest in God's unfailing care for the righteous and God's equally unfailing punishment of the wicked. Thus, for example, Eliphaz:

> Think now, who that was innocent ever perished?
>   Or where were the upright cut off?
> As I have seen, those who plow iniquity
>   and sow trouble reap the same.
> By the breath of God they perish,
>   and by the blast of his anger they perish.
>
>   4:7–9; cf. 8:8–19; 11:11

But when Job looks at the same world and claims that even the birds and the plants know things are more complicated than this (12:7–10), the friends know they are in for a long day.

In the second round (15–21), the friends reduce their argument to the one truth they are certain Job will not dispute: the wicked are always punished (15:17–35; 18:5–21; 20:4–9). From this point on they will dispense with any pretense of claiming that God always prospers the righteous. Their tone is now noticeably much sharper, a signal that they have stiffened their resolve to nullify Job's complaints. They offer no word of encouragement, hope, or promise to Job. Instead, they increase their warnings, double their rebukes, and up the ante Job must pay if he continues to challenge the Judge of all the world. When Job counters with yet another question that directly disputes their assertions – "How often then is the lamp of the wicked put out? How often then does calamity come upon them?" (21:17) – the friends know it is time to take off the gloves.

In the third round of speeches (22–27), the friends give up all efforts to coerce a confession from Job. Now they simply pronounce him guilty. Their notion of an orderly trial, with evidence so strong the defendant can only yield and agree to guilt, has not worked. But inasmuch as the friends claim the right to be both judge and jury in the case of God v. Job, they can still produce the desired outcome by simply ruling from the bench that Job is guilty beyond any reasonable doubt. Eliphaz reads out the verdict:

> You know that your wickedness is great,
> And that your iniquities have no limit.
>
>   22:5; NJPS

Their approach to Job is not unlike that which confronts Joseph K. in Kafka's novel *The Trial*. When K., a well-placed bank official, a man of reason, sanity, and logic, is arrested "without having done anything wrong," he seeks redress in the court. Much to his despair, however, he discovers that the law, "an unknown system of jurisprudence," has an Alice-in-Wonderland kind of arbitrariness about it. As his lawyer's maidservant warns him when he asks for advice on how to prepare his defense, "You can't defend yourself against this court, all you can do is confess."

In sum, Job has but one option. As Eliphaz puts it, "Agree with God, and be at peace; in this way good will come to you" (22:21). His presumption of Job's guilt recalls a painful scene from Wallace Stegner's short story, "Impasse." Having witnessed the rejection of his beloved but comely daughter by yet another potential, Louis, her father, muses to himself about the counsel he might offer her. Should he say, "Accept your looks for what they are?" Should he tell her, "You were born struck out, and it won't help to stand in the batter's box demanding that the pitcher throw you a fourth strike?"[7] Eliphaz looks on Job with no such panged restraints. Now that the strategy to love Job into conformity with his theology has failed, he and his friends are left with but two options. They can rethink their own assumptions about Job's guilt – could it be that Job is innocent after all? – or they can find in their own theology the justification to condemn Job without evidence. Eliphaz and the friends choose the latter course. Convinced beyond any doubt that they are right, they equate their theology with divine law, which must be implemented, even if it means falsifying the truth in order to convert or convict those who disagree. They authenticate coercion to their belief with passion more inflamed than informed. They model for us clergy types one of the most dangerously seductive temptations we face. As the Welsh priest and poet R. S. Thomas reminds us,

> A preacher's temptation
> is the voice persuading
> he is own message.[8]

3   "Look at Me and Be Appalled, and Lay Your Hand on Your Mouth"

What is required of us if we are to minister to the Jobs of this world? If we are to move beyond theories that try to explain suffering to comforting and consoling and loving those whom life has consigned to the ash heap? I am struck by the fact that Job repeatedly asks his friends to *look* at him and *listen carefully* to his words:

---

7 W. Stegner, "Impasse," in *Collected Stories of Wallace Stegner* (New York: Penguin Books, 1991), 291.

8 R. S. Thomas, "Incarnations," in *No Truce with the Furies* (Newcastle upon Tyne: Bloodaxe Books, 1995), 35.

94 CHAPTER 5

Be pleased to look at me
Job 6:28

Listen carefully to my words
Job 13:17; 21:2

Look at me and be appalled, and lay your hand on your mouth
Job 21:5

Perhaps we should add this last citation to the lessons we take from Pastoral Care 101. First, "Look at me and be appalled;" second, "lay your hand on your mouth." I want to try to exegete this text with the help of two visuals.

The first is Vittore Carpaccio's *Meditation on the Passion of Christ* (c. 1495). [See Figure 2.1. Vittore Carpaccio: *Meditation on the Passion of Christ*] Carpaccio (1450–1525) was born in Venice, where he studied for a time with Giovanni Bellini. His *Meditation on the Passion of Christ* is now located in the Metropolitan Museum of Art in New York. In the foreground of this painting, Carpaccio places three figures. Seated on the left is Jerome. Opposite him on the right is Job. Like his counterpart, Job is seated. His posture indicates his meditation on the central figure of Christ, who slumps in Job's direction as he awaits the coming resurrection. The background provides two contrasting views of the landscape. To the left, just above Christ's throne, is a dead tree, crooked toward a deserted mountain trail where a leopard is about to devour a doe. The imagery suggests a world of death, unrestrained force, and hapless victims. To the right the imagery suggests just the opposite: the trees and plants are full with foliage; walled villages are safe and secure; a leopard walks peacefully behind a doe; a red bird sits unafraid on the ground.

It is the figure of Job that deserves attention, for Carpaccio suggests that he is among the saints who commune with Jesus during his time between life and death. Carpaccio places Job on the side where life and peace and promise define the landscape. Yet there are also signs that death remains a very real presence for Job. Job's body is frail and withered. He supports his weary head in the palm of his left hand, while pointing with his right finger to the sandals on his feet. The sandals seem flimsy, as if to suggest they are thin protection for one who has walked through a life filled with as much hurt as he has experienced. Lying on the ground at the bottom of his feet are a shattered skull with empty eye sockets that can no longer see, a severed jaw with a mouth that can no longer speak, a dried out and severed leg bone that can no longer walk or run – all symbolic reminders of how much death Job experienced in life. Job is pointing to his feet, as if directing Jesus to take one last look at him before

"WHAT PROVOKES YOU THAT YOU KEEP ON TALKING?" 95

Jesus' resurrection becomes reality. "Please look at me," he seems to be saying, "Please listen carefully to what I am saying about what it feels like to me. Please look at me and be appalled."

Job is sitting on a piece of granite-like block. If we look closely we will see that it bears a Hebrew inscription. The words are from Job 19:25, perhaps the most famous sentence in the book that preserves his story: "I know that my Redeemed lives." But the inscription, like the hope it voices, is broken off. Like Job, it needs repairing. These words of broken hope beg a question: Who will be Job's redeemer?

The Hebrew word for "redeemer" is *gōʾēl*. The word comes from the field of family law. It designates the nearest male relative – brother, paternal uncle, cousin – who is duty-bound to protect and preserve the family when his kinsman is unable to do so. The responsibilities of the *gōʾēl* include buying back family property that has fallen into the hands of outsiders (Lev. 25:28; Ruth 4:3–6), redeeming a relative sold into slavery (Lev. 25:47–49), and marrying a widow to provide an heir for her dead husband (as in the famous case of Ruth; Ruth 3:12–13; 4:5). In religious usage, God is described as the *gōʾēl* of those who have fallen into distress or bondage (as, for example, those who are slaves in Egypt: Exod. 6:6; 15:13; Ps. 74:2). We may take special note of the affirmation that God acts as *gōʾēl*, "redeemer," for those who are too helpless or too vulnerable to fend for themselves (Ps. 119:154; Prov. 23:11; Jer. 50:34; Lam. 3:58).

So who is the redeemer Job looks for? If we stay focused on the Old Testament's story of Job, then we may suspect that Job hopes a family member might come to his aid. But the tragedy of his story is that his family is dead. We may expect that he hopes a friend will come to comfort and console him. But the credentials of his friends – Eliphaz, Bildad, and Zophar – hardly give him any reason to believe that they are willing to be his redeemer. We may expect that he longs for God to be his redeemer. But the Book of Job causes us to wonder about this, because according to the text, Job searches in vain for some assurance of God's presence, through thirty-five chapters. At every step along this painful journey, God is silent. From Job's perspective, it appears that his hopes for a redeemer are dashed, no matter where he looks, like this broken piece of inscription in Carpaccio's painting.

If we shift our thoughts to the New Testament, we may take some comfort in the promise of the resurrection, for we hold it true that Christ offers eternal life, even to those who have died in faith. Perhaps we may think of Job as the Old Testament's version of Jesus' parable about the rich man and Lazarus (Luke 16:19–31). Ignored and abandoned in life, the poor, sore-covered man named Lazarus (read Job), will be carried away in death, there to be comforted in the bosom of Abraham, until Jesus comes to make all things right. As a

Christian, I affirm with you the promise of resurrection. Like you, I am brought to the edge of my seat when I hear the stirring words of the Hallelujah Chorus in Handel's *Messiah* (first performed in Dublin in 1742). When Handel responds to Job's words, "I know that my Redeemer liveth," by citing by Paul's words from I Corinthians, "Thanks be to God who gives us the victory through our Lord Jesus Christ" (I Cor. 15:57), I want to step up and applaud.

But I want to press us to think carefully about what the promise of resurrection offers to the Jobs of the world. If in life, the Jobs of the world are abandoned and ignored. If in life they yearn for a presence that does not come until they die. If they cry out for comfort in a world that seems oblivious to their pain, the hope of justice and redemption in death notwithstanding, is that what God wants? Is that what the journey of faith requires of us? If you and I are content to leave the role of comforting the suffering to Jesus, confident that in his hands the final outcome is not really in doubt, then perhaps we need not bother too much with God's condemnation of Job's friends, for in the end, as Paul assures us in Romans, "We know that all things work together for good for those who love God" (Rom. 8:28). But Carpaccio's rendering of this scene should give us pause before settling for this promise of resurrection for the Jobs of this world. Why must the Jobs of this world suffer a virtual (or real) death before someone comes to "console and comfort" them? Why must the Jobs of this world live, and often die, as persons abandoned and ignored? Why must their fight for justice and redemption be only a post-mortem victory? These words from Tennyson itch at my ears:

> Come not when I am dead,
>> To drop thy foolish tears upon my grave,
> To trample round my fallen head,
>> And vex the unhappy dust thou wouldst not save.
> There let the wind sweep and the plover cry;
>> But thou go by.[9]

"Come not when I am dead." I'm struck by Carpaccio's suggestion that while Jesus was between Friday's death on the cross and Sunday's resurrection, during what George Steiner has described as the "long day's journey of the Saturday"[10] in between, Job was giving Jesus some last minute instructions

---

9   Alfred Lord Tennyson, "Come Not When I Am Dead," in *The Works of Alfred Lord Tennyson with an Introduction and Bibliography* (Wordsworth Poetry Library; New York: NTC/ Contemporary Publishing Company, 1998), 369.

10   G. Steiner, *Real Presences* (Chicago: The University of Chicago Press, 1989), 232.

"WHAT PROVOKES YOU THAT YOU KEEP ON TALKING?" 97

about what to teach his disciples about life on the other side of death. To get our bearings on the anticipated next scene, the day after resurrection, when the resurrected Jesus will appear to his disciples, I turn to Luke's account of the journey to Emmaus (Luke 24:13–35).

Luke reports that it had been three days since the disciples had been together with Jesus in Jerusalem. They had celebrated the Passover meal with him. They had watched him pray at Gethsemane, at least until Jesus found them "sleeping because of grief," as Luke so tenderly puts it (22:45). They had watched him die at Golgotha, although they stood at a distance for fear someone might recognize them (23:49). They had seen the tomb where Joseph of Arimathea buried him. Now it was the first day of a new week; it was to be their first try at life on the other side of death. It was, we might say today, the first day of the rest of their lives. What were they to do now? How were they to live now, now that the one they had followed lay dead in a "rock-hewn tomb where no one had ever been laid before" (Luke 23:53)?

So it was, Luke tells us, that they came to the tomb at early dawn on the first day of this new week. When they arrived, they saw that the stone had been rolled away. Two men in dazzling clothes told them that Jesus was not there. "He has risen," the men said. Mary Magdalene, and Mary the mother of Jesus, and Joanna ran to tell the others, but they could not believe the news. It seemed to them "an idle tale;" it sounded like nonsense. Even Peter, who had to look for himself, could not believe what he saw. He saw the linen clothes, he found no body, and he went home "amazed at what had happened" (24:12).

Later on that same day, two of them were going to Emmaus, a small village about seven miles northwest of Jerusalem. It was an ordinary place, a place that held no particular attraction, a place that promised nothing special. Its precise location on the map is uncertain, although the proposed sites lie along a road that runs generally northwest from Jerusalem. Wherever it may be on the map, Emmaus likely represented a place the disciples headed toward in the hope of getting away from the terrible things they had witnessed in Jerusalem. Frederick Buechner describes such a place this way:

> The place we go in order to escape – a bar, a movie, wherever it is we throw up our hands and say, "Let the whole damned thing go hang. It makes no difference anyway." ... Emmaus may be buying a new suit or a new car or smoking more cigarettes than you really want, or reading a second-rate novel or even writing one. Emmaus may be going to church on Sunday. Emmaus is whatever we do or wherever we go to make ourselves forget that the world holds nothing sacred: that even the wisest and bravest and loveliest decay and die; that even the noblest ideas that

98   CHAPTER 5

men have had – ideas about love and freedom and justice – have always
in time been twisted out of shape by selfish men for selfish ends.[11]

Whatever the reason, they went to Emmaus, and on the way they were talking about all the things that had happened over the last three days. In the midst
of their conversations Jesus appeared, but they did not recognize him. "What
are you talking about?" Jesus asked them. They simply stared at him, too sad at
first to respond. Finally, one named Cleopas answered him: "Are you the only
one in Jerusalem who does not know what has happened?" (24:18). Jesus was of
course the only one who *did know* what had happened, but they could not yet
know this. They were under the impression that they knew more about what
had happened than this Jesus who spoke to them from the other side of death.
So they journeyed on toward Emmaus, talking to this stranger, telling him *their
version* of the story.

In their version (vv. 19–24), they tell about the Jesus "of Nazareth" they had
known and followed. They had known him to be a "prophet mighty in deed
and word before God," but "all (the rest of) the people" had refused to accept
him and had handed him over to be crucified. They conveniently overlook or
try to forget their own complicity in calling for Jesus' death (23:18–21). In their
minds, they were guilty of nothing more than misplaced trust: "We had hoped
that he was the one to redeem Israel," but now he was dead. This "stranger"
Jesus who was listening to their story responds by asking them about what
Scripture says about prophets. Did not Scripture say, "beginning with Moses
and all the prophets," that it was necessary for the Messiah to suffer? That "suffering," even unto death, was part of God's chosen plan for all those who would
follow the Messiah and "enter into his glory"? Still, the two disciples were convinced they had been wrong – about Scripture, about Jesus, about God, about
their discipleship – and so they journeyed on, disappointed, sad, confused.

When they came close to the village, this stranger walked on ahead, as if
he was preparing to leave them behind. They urged him to stay. It was almost
evening, at least he could stay long enough to share a meal with them. Jesus
agreed, and they gathered round the table. Then something truly miraculous
happened. Jesus took some bread, blessed it, broke it in two, and gave it to
them. Suddenly they were back at that Passover table, where they had shared
their last meal with him three days ago. Now "their eyes were opened, and they
recognized him" (24:31). And then just as suddenly, he vanished.

Luke continues the story by reporting that once the disciples recognized
Jesus, their hearts burned within them. Now they sensed that they understood
everything he had taught them before he died. Luke says that at that very hour

---

11   F. Buechner, *The Magnificent Defeat* (New York: Seabury, 1966), 85–86.

they got up and returned to Jerusalem. They found the rest of the disciples, and they told them what had happened on the road to Emmaus, how he had been made known to them in the breaking of the bread. Now they were all ready to share in the post-resurrection Hallelujah that we too have heard and proclaimed as our own: "The Lord has risen indeed!" (24:35).

"Hallelujah. The Lord has risen indeed." It seems like just the right ending for the story doesn't it? They thought Jesus was dead; now they knew he was alive. They had not recognized him at first; now their eyes were opened, and they saw him. They had been sad over their loss; now their hearts burned with a new-found fervor. They had left the holy city on a journey to nowhere; now they were back in Jerusalem, ready to spread the good news far and wide. They seem to be at the same place we all are on Easter morning, when we gather with Christians round the world to sing and celebrate the good news of the resurrection. Such a perfect ending to the story. And so we prime ourselves to respond to their affirmation: "Hallelujah, Christ is risen. He is risen indeed!"

In fact, this seems like such a good place to end the story that I wonder why Luke does not put just put a period after verse 35 and close the book on his gospel. Once the disciples can make the confession that Christ has risen from the grave, what is there left to say? What more do they need to know than this? Perhaps the disciples were just as surprised as we are to learn that there is more to the gospel story than the affirmation that Christ is risen. Luke seems to be saying that Easter morning praise, if it is to be authentic, must stretch past Sunday. It must spill into the rest of our lives. If it does not translate into concrete deeds, day by day, that mirror Jesus' compassion for the outcasts, "the poor, the crippled, the lame, and the blind" (Luke 14:13), who must always be welcome at Jesus' table, then it counts for nothing.

The rest of Luke's story about what happened on the other side of that first Easter is recorded in Luke 24:36–53. I cite a critical portion of this text:

> While they were talking about this, Jesus himself stood among them and said to them, "Peace be with you." They were startled and terrified, and thought that they were seeing a ghost. He said to them, "Why are you frightened, and why do doubts arise in your hearts? *Look at my hands and my feet*; see that it is I myself. *Touch me and see*; for a ghost does not have flesh and bones as you see that I have." And when he had said this, *he showed them his hands and his feet.* While in their joy they were disbelieving and still wondering, he said to them, *"Have you anything here to eat?"* They gave him a piece of broiled fish, and he took it and ate in their presence.
>
> Luke 24:36–43; emphasis added

While the disciples were in Jerusalem, still talking about these things, presumably while the words "The Lord has risen indeed" were still ringing in the air, Luke reports that Jesus came and stood in their presence yet one more time. He greeted them with familiar words that should have put them at ease – "Peace be with you" – but they were "startled and terrified." After all they had shared with Jesus on this long day's journey to Emmaus, now they could not recognize the one who spoke to them. Just moments before they had recognized and acclaimed him as the risen Lord; now they thought they were seeing a ghost. For the second time this day Jesus does something truly remarkable. He says to all of them, "Look at my hand and my feet ... Touch me and see that it is I myself." (24:39). And then, while they were "disbelieving and still wondering" (24:41) about what it all meant, he asked them if they had any food to offer him. *He* had just given *them* bread, blessed and broken. Now he asked *them* to feed *him*. They gave him a piece of fish, the same kind of food they had once seen him use to feed the five thousand who had followed him into a deserted place outside Bethsaida (Luke 9:10–17). He took the fish and ate in their presence. Luke pauses just at this point to allow us to take a close look at this scene: Jesus with scarred hands and feet, asking for food; disciples, disbelieving and wondering, offering him the only thing they have.

I am struck by those words, "Look at my hands and feet." Why did Jesus think it important for the disciples to look at his hands and his feet? Commentators usually suggest that Jesus wants to show them that he is not a ghost. He is real; he is tangibly present with them; he is indeed truly alive. Surely this must be part of the reason for what he does. But is there more to it than this? They seem to have already recognized that he is real. When they saw him breaking the bread, they knew he was Jesus, the same one who had shared Passover with them. And had they not already seen his hands and feet? After all they were at Golgotha. They saw him being crucified. Even though they stood at a safe distance, surely the disciples knew what kind of scars the spikes would have left when they were nailed to their target.

"Look at my hands and feet. Touch me and see." What a strange command for Jesus to give to disciples on that first Easter morning, especially after they clearly already understood enough to shout to the heavens, "The Lord is risen indeed!" Why ever would Jesus want them to look at his wounds and scars again? What are they supposed to *see* and *feel* on this side of Easter that they didn't see and feel before?

My musings on this question lead me to Wallace Stegner's novel *Crossing to Safety*. A scene from near the end of the book describes the vacation Sally and her husband took to Italy, along with another couple with whom they had shared years of friendship. They visited the tiny village of San Sepolchro in

FIGURE 5.2   Pierro della Francesca, "The Resurrection," c. 1462–1464. Palazzo Communale, San Sepolchro. Full view
CREDIT: WIKIMEDIA COMMONS, PD-OLD

southern Tuscany. There they happened upon Pierro della Francesca's fifteenth century fresco of the resurrected Christ.

On the left, the painting depicts a barren landscape with naked trees reaching toward a darkening sky. To the right, the landscape is alive with foliage, human dwellings, and bursts of sunlight. Between these scenes of life and death, della Francesca places the resurrected Christ, with one foot still in the tomb, as if he is still in the act of stepping out of the grave. In Christ's right hand is a staff holding a flag of victory. On his left hand and foot we can see the crucifixion scars. His side shows the wound from the soldier's spear, still dripping drops of blood.

Sally's husband and their friends have stopped casually to look at the painting, as tourists often do, and then they have moved on. Sally, however, lingers behind. She is fixed on the face of Francesca's Christ.

FIGURE 5.3   Pierro della Francesca, "The Resurrection," detail of Christ's face
CREDIT: WIKIMEDIA COMMONS, PD-OLD

Despite the golden halo over Christ's head and the flag of victory in his hand, she notices that his eyes are staring into the foreground with a look that seems to be remembering the pain of crucifixion, as if to suggest that "if resurrection had taken place, it had not yet been comprehended."[12] Sally's husband notices her staring at the painting. He wonders what has so captured her interest and imagination. He looks at her intently. She is standing there, propped up on the crutches she has needed to walk since a childhood bout with polio crippled her with a lasting lesson about what pain and loss means. His eyes returned to the painting and gradually, but with increasing clarity, he understands what Sally sees in the eyes of this one who until moments ago had been horribly dead. The truth and the promise of resurrection, he now sees, is that "those who have been dead understand things that will never be understood by those who have only lived."[13]

"Those who have been dead understand things that will never be understood by those who have only lived." I wonder, could it be that what Sally saw in this painting is what Luke suggests the Christ, who is ever defined by compassion for the broken and the bruised, wants every disciple to see during these "ordinary days" this side of Easter. "Look at my hands and feet. Touch me and see." Could it be that on this side of the empty tomb we are supposed to know more about pain and suffering, more about hurt and brokenness than we did before? Could it be that we need to look again at his wounded hands and his

---

12   W. Stegner, *Crossing to Safety* (New York: Random House, 1987), 221.
13   Ibid., 222.

"WHAT PROVOKES YOU THAT YOU KEEP ON TALKING?" 103

feet, look again at those eyes that teach us what it means to hang on a cross of affliction, suspended between darkness and despair? Could it be that we are not ready to shout the good news of life everlasting until we have learned to listen to the screams of those who like Jesus – and like Job – are trapped in a world that seems to be empty of God? "Look at my hands and feet. Touch me and see."

"Look at me and be appalled," Job says to his friends, "and lay your hand on your mouth" (Job 21:5). "Look at my feet," Job seems to be saying to Jesus in Carpaccio's "Meditation on the Passion of Christ," "and be sure you speak the truth about the suffering they have experienced when you go back to the living." On the other side of the grave, Jesus says to his disciples, "Look at my hands and feet ... Touch me and see." Why? Because if we have eyes to see, then someone right around the corner, some Job who has been consigned to the ash heap of suffering "for no reason," is about to ask us the same question Jesus asked his disciples on the road to Emmaus: "Do you have anything to eat?" (Luke 24:31). Note well that Jesus' question is *not*, "Do you have any *words* for me?" but "Do you have anything tangible to offer to someone like me?" Jesus expects his disciples, all those who have touched and felt and seen what suffering means, to be able to set a table and say, "Yes, I do."

A final word returns us to the Book of Job and once more to the title that has set the compass for this presentation. By the time we reach the end of this story, the first friends who sought to "console and comfort" Job with their "windbag speeches" have been dismissed by God, because they "have not spoken of me [God] what is right" (42:7, 8). In the words of W. H. Auden,

> [The] friends who met here and embraced are gone,
> Each to his own mistake.[14]

The Epilogue reports that a new community of friends now gather round, "all his brothers and sisters and all who had known him before" (42:11). It is they who offer the "consolation" and "comfort" (42:11b; the same words as in 2:11) that Eliphaz, Bildad, and Zophar would not, or could not, provide Job. They offer fellowship through the sharing of a meal, and they demonstrate compassion with tangible gifts – a modest amount of money and a gold ring (42:11) – that contribute to his material needs. We note that these friends comfort Job

---

14   W. H. Auden, "The Quest," in *W. H. Auden: Collected Poems*, ed. E. Mendelson (New York: Vintage International, 1991), 286.

with active communion, not with theology or with words. Indeed, the Epilogue records no spoken words at all during the Joban version of this "last meal."

Perhaps we should leave it at that. Silence in the face of suffering like Job's may be, as I have indicated already, the first and most faithful act of pastoral ministry we can offer. And yet, having done my fair share of preaching and teaching in the church, I am seared by the summons to speak a word from God that will be true without being glib. What might that word be? I take my cue on this from the Duke of Albany, who has the last word in Shakespeare's gut-wrenching tragedy, *King Lear*. Having witnessed the last scene of the play, the Duke speaks these words:

> The weight of this sad time we must obey;
> Speak what we feel, not what we ought to say.
> *King Lear*, v, iii, ll. 322–323

These words are not scripture, but they may be sacred nonetheless.

PART 3

Job and the Priests: "Look at Me and Be Appalled"

∵

CHAPTER 6

Job as Priest to the Priests

Sometimes you want to go
Where everybody knows your name,
And they're always glad you came;
You want to be where you can see,
Our troubles are all the same;
You want to be where everybody knows your name.

Theme song from "Cheers"

∴

People of faith will surely agree that a pub, however winsomely portrayed on television, should not be the only place where people may find sanctuary from the troubles of the world.* Week in and week out we gather in other sanctuaries, each time bringing baggage stuffed with an assortment of hurts and hopes into a place our faith marks off as sacred. We come because we yearn for a word from God that will make a difference. The strong and the weak come with their victories and defeats. The loved and the lonely come, each seeking a place in the fellowship of God. Those whose faith is undaunted sit side by side with those whose doubts and fears seem unassailable. We all come hoping to find a place where we are known and recognized, a place where someone will call our name and invite us, baggage and all, into the very presence of God.

Whatever else we may strive for in our spiritual formation, surely we know that we must tune ourselves to God's compassion for the broken and bruised persons with whom we share this world. In ancient Israel, the responsibility for this ministry fell primarily to the priests, who were specially charged with the responsibility of sustaining the connection between God and humankind. The early church recognized the importance of the ministry of priesthood and anchored it to the work and ministry of Jesus, the "great high priest" who is "able to sympathize with our weaknesses," because he "has been tested as we

---

* This essay was originally presented at the Symposium on Theological Interpretation of Scripture (Theme: "Spiritual Formation") at North Park Theological Seminary, Chicago, Illinois, September 26–28, 2002.

© SAMUEL E. BALENTINE, 2021 | DOI:10.1163/9789004459212_007

are" (Heb. 4:14–15). Moreover, the New Testament affirms that Christ's model for priestly ministry is the compass that charts the course for the collective ministry of the Christian community, which is called, like its forebears in ancient Israel, to become a "royal priesthood, a holy nation" (1 Peter 2:9; cf. Exod. 19:6).

Among the issues this symposium will address, I have selected one that I hope and trust will receive careful consideration. My focus may be initially framed as a question: How can we learn to be faithful priests, ministers one and all, who are able to sympathize with the weaknesses of sisters and brothers yearning to find a place where everybody knows their name? The question summons us, because we know Christian scripture teaches us that our fidelity to God must be measured by our love for one another. I John states the matter with undiminishable clarity: Those who say, 'I love God,' and hate their brothers and sisters, are liars; for those who do not love a brother and sister whom they have seen, cannot love God whom they have not seen" (1 John 4:20). The question also summons us, I believe, because Hebrew scripture insists that we share this journey toward God with sisters and brothers who have walked in the footsteps of Job. If we are to be priests to the Jobs of this world, his story must be part of the spiritual formation that prepares us for the journey. I invite you to consider the possibility that Job may become a priest to all who seek to be priests to one another.

In the long and instructive history of Job's representation in art and iconography he has often been depicted as a priest. As witness to this trajectory of interpretation, Samuel Terrien notes that more than forty statues of "Saint Job the Priest" have been preserved in Belgium, Luxembourg, and the Netherlands.[1] Included among Terrien's examples is this sixteenth century wood sculpture located in the Church of Saint Martin, Wezemaal, Belgium.[2]

The sculptor portrays a seated Job, dressed in a full-length priestly robe. On his head is a cap with earflaps, which Terrien suggests resembles the Phrygian headgear worn by priests of the ancient Persian god of light and wisdom, Mithras, opponent of darkness and evil. This attire has been suggestively appropriated to call attention to the sacerdotal role of Job, a role here explicitly

---

1 S. Terrien, *The Iconography of Job Through the Centuries: Artists as Biblical Interpreters* (University Park, PA: The Pennsylvania State University Press, 1996), 149–158.

2 Ibid., 149–150. Since the publication of my article, Barry Huff has extended and refined the discussion of this Wezemaal sculpture; see B. Huff, "Job the Priest: From Scripture to Sculpture," in B. R. Huff, P. Vesely, eds., *Seeking Wisdom's Depths and Torah's Heights. Essays in Honor of Samuel E. Balentine* (Macon, GA: Smyth & Helwys Publishing Company, 2020), 327–353.

FIGURE 6.1　"Saint Job as Priest," Church of Saint Martin, Wezemaal
CREDIT: BARRY HUFF, PERSONAL PHOTOGRAPH

reinforced by the depiction of his hands. In his right hand – the priestly "blessing hand" – Job holds a sign with a partial inscription in Flemish from Job 1:21: "The Lord gave, and the Lord has taken away; blessed be the name of the Lord." The object in the left hand, although partially damaged, may reasonably be identified as the Host or the chalice of the Eucharist.

The use of both ancient Near Eastern and Christian symbolism to interpret Job's priestly role is worthy of an article in its own right, for it is a link to Job's common importance for religions that in other respects may espouse

110   CHAPTER 6

quite different affirmations. Christianity, for example, draws a sharp distinction between the priestly ministries of Aaron, its Jewish forebear, and Christ (see Hebrews 9–10). Too often overlooked is the fact that this distinction is only meaningful when interpreted against the backdrop of Israel's high priestly model. Without a sympathetic comprehension of the priest's role on the Day of Atonement in Leviticus 16, the statement in Heb. 9:11 – "But when Christ came as a high priest of the good things that have come …" – is fundamentally unintelligible. Both grammatically and theologically it is a fragment, an incomplete thought suspended in ethereal abstraction, where subjects, verbs, and objects have lost their reference points. More to the point for the purposes of this article, as the Wezemaal sculpture so evocatively suggests, perhaps neither Aaron nor Christ's ministries as priests can be fully understood apart from the witness of Job. In the rich and variegated history of Joban interpretation, Job is the model for the priest who offers to the sick of heart and wounded of faith what Terrien aptly describes as "a sacramental Communion with the crucified and risen Lord."[3]

In what follows, I propose to explore the possibility that the Book of Job presents Job as a "priest to the priests." Toward this end, I will examine 1) the priestly imagery that comprises Job's profile in the Prologue and Epilogue; 2) the image of Job as an *afflicted (and contentious) priest* inside the ritual system, specifically his affliction with and response to "loathsome sores" (Job 2:7), which defines him as one who *should be* addressed by the priestly rituals prescribed in Leviticus 13–14; and 3) Job's challenge to the priestly system, which on theological grounds may be compared to that of Henri Nouwen's model of the "wounded healer."

1   Priestly Imagery in the Prologue and Epilogue of Job

The priestly imagery that provides Job's profile in the Prologue and Epilogue is oblique and elusive. Indeed, most commentators, even when they recognize the telltale signs, treat them as incidental, not definitive, for Job's story. As David Clines puts it, "the story's setting in time and place lies beyond the horizon of the priestly law."[4] Clines' discernment provides an important caution, which requires a preliminary caveat at the outset. The objective here is not to argue for a direct connection between the author(s) of the Book of Job and the tradents responsible for what we call the Priestly literature in the Old

---

3   Ibid., 149.
4   D. J. A. Clines, *Job 1–20*. Word Biblical Commentary (Dallas, TX: Word Books, 1989), 16.

Testament. The Book of Job is notoriously difficult to date. Absent any explicit indications of the date for composition within the book itself, scholars have proposed a variety of possibilities ranging from the early seventh century to the fourth-third centuries, that is, deep into the Second Temple period. Most would be content with a general location in the early post-exilic period, sixth-fifth centuries BCE. The date for the Priestly literature has proved to be similarly contentious. Until recently the conventional view assigned most if not all of this literature to the post-exilic period. Serious arguments have now been raised in support of a pre-exilic date for both an early recension of the Priestly material (mid eighth century) and a later internal redaction (end of the eighth century) by the so-called "holiness school" that produced the bulk of the "Priestly Torah."[5] Given these uncertainties, it is both unwise and unwarranted to suggest any straight-line connection between Job and Priestly literature.

Even so, I do not wish to rule out completely this possibility, for there are a number of intriguing clues that suggest the issue merits further reflection. At least two prominent recent studies of the Priestly literature have opened a door of invitation. Mary Douglas has noted, almost in passing, that the treatment of the law of talion in Leviticus (Leviticus 24), and more broadly its general reflections on God's justice, possibly makes an "opening ... for the complex view of retribution celebrated in the Book of Job." In her words, Leviticus "reaches forward to the book of Job."[6] From a different perspective, Israel Knohl has called attention to a similar theological trajectory in Job and the "Priestly Torah." In his judgment, both collections of texts depict a "dynamic process" that moves from the level of elementary faith, which places humanity at the center of the universe, where piety is securely grounded in moral laws of reward and punishment, to an "exalted faith consciousness" grounded in the centrality of God, whose justice is necessarily beyond the grasp of human insight.[7] I do not propose to pursue directly these two tantalizing suggestions. Whether Leviticus (and the Priestly literature) "reaches forward" to Job, as Douglas suggests, or more intriguingly, Job's priestly profile is perhaps responsive to and influential for the priestly model in Leviticus and elsewhere must remain for now an open question. I am persuaded, however, that the priestly images identified below should not be dismissed as irrelevant or unimportant for understanding the biblical portrait of Job.

---

5   See especially I. Knohl, *The Sanctuary of Silence: The Priestly Torah and the Holiness School* (Minneapolis: Fortress Press, 1995), 199–230; J. Milgrom, *Leviticus 1–16*. The Anchor Bible (New York: Doubleday, 1991), 3–35.

6   M. Douglas, *Leviticus as Literature* (Oxford: Oxford University Press, 1999), 212, 250.

7   Knohl, *The Sanctuary of Silence*, 165–167.

At the outset of Job's story, the Prologue identifies him as "blameless" (*tām*). The word occurs in a variety of contexts and thus cannot be simply equated with any one particular setting. Because Job's blamelessness is coupled with three other attributes – he is also "upright, one who feared God and turned away from evil" (Job 1:1) – it is likely that the narrator simply intends to call attention, albeit in an extraordinary way, to Job's unparalleled moral and ethical piety. He is, as the narrator informs us, "the greatest of all the people of the east" (1:3). Given the story that is about to unfold, however, especially Job's complaint that God intends to "slash open" his body and pour out his blood (e.g., Job 16:13, 18), it is hard to overlook the fact that one of the principal referents for the word *tāmîm*, which derives from the same root as *tām*, is the sacrificial animal that must be "unblemished" when presented on the altar.[8] The drama of Job's story rests on the presenting report that his "blamelessness" – morally, ethically, and perhaps also ritually construed – inexplicably targets him as a victim suitable for sacrifice.[9]

The Prologue and Epilogue frame the story of Job with the report that he offers sacrifice. Job 1:5 describes his presentation of "burnt offerings" (*ʿōlôt*) on behalf of his children as a preemptive propitiation for any inadvertent sins they may have committed. Job 42:8 reports that Job receives the "burnt offering" (*ʿōlāh*) presented by the friends, who require his prayer of intercession if God is to forgive their wrongdoings. To be sure, these accounts do not envision Job as a cultic official in a formal ritual setting; he acts instead, in accord with conventional patriarchal practice, as head of the family (cf. Gen. 8:20; 22:2, 13; 31:54; 46:1). N. Habel has noted, however, that in his role as devout mediator for the household Job "plays the part of the perfect priest."[10]

This priestly frame for the book, admittedly only obliquely described, is highly suggestive. It is conventionally accepted that the Prologue and Epilogue present an idyllic but simplistic view of the doctrine of retribution, typically associated with Israel's wisdom traditions: God can be trusted to prosper the righteous and punish the wicked. It is precisely this doctrine that the dialogues at the heart of the book put to the test. The framing images of Job as a priest may be understood as fine tuning what is being tested in this story. It is not only wisdom's retribution doctrine that is at stake. It is also, and perhaps primarily,

---

8   The word *tāmîm*, "unblemished," occurs approximately 40x in priestly texts, e.g., Lev. 22:19, 21; Num. 19:2; Ezek. 43:22–23.

9   A related term, *tummāh* ("integrity"), is also important in the description of Job's character (Job 2:3, 9; 27:5; 31:6).

10   N. Habel, *The Book of Job*. Old Testament Library (Philadelphia: Westminster Press, 1985), 88; cf. J. Hartley, *The Book of Job*. The New International Commentary on the Old Testament (Grand Rapids, MI: William B. Eerdmans, 1988), 69–70.

JOB AS PRIEST TO THE PRIESTS   113

the Priestly tradition's advocacy for the effectiveness of the entire ritual system. In this connection, it is instructive to consider J. Milgrom's contention that the sacrificial system "constitutes the priestly theodicy."[11] In his judgment, one of the pillars of Priestly theology, built upon Israel's staunch monotheism, is the belief that humans need have no fear of autonomous and competing demonic deities. There is but one creature in the world with "demonic" power, and that is the human being, whose God-given free will has the capacity for evil that not only defies God but potentially also drives God out of the sanctuary.[12] The proposed Priestly remedy for this situation are the cultic procedures, specifically the sacrificial offerings that atone for people's sinful behavior and ritually cleanse the sanctuary.

The setting for Job's diligent offering of his own priestly sacrifices is the paradisiacal land of Uz, where initially everything seems to be in place for a near perfect recapitulation of the "very good" world first enjoyed in the garden of Eden. By all accounts Job's reliance upon the sacrificial system works, for there is no sign of evil's intrusion anywhere in his world. By the end of the Prologue, however, this one who always "turned away from evil" (*rāʿ*; 1:1) has been overwhelmed by "evil" (*rāʿāh*, 2:11; NRSV: "troubles") that has come to him, by God's own admission, "for no reason (*ḥinnām*)" (2:3).[13] Against this backdrop, the satan's question – "Does Job fear God for nothing (*ḥinnām*)?" (1:9) – is freighted in ways that have typically gone unnoticed.

Lurking ominously behind the general query about whether religion can ever be truly disinterested is perhaps a more specific and unsettling challenge that threatens the core of Priestly theology. Are the priestly rituals, especially the sacrifices that address evil's calamitous effects, of any real use in a world where *God, not humans*, unleashes evil "for no reason"? The answer to this question depends on how we interpret Job's complaints on the other side of the ash heap. For the moment, we must take seriously the Prologue's report that Job responds to this dilemma with a question that strains to remain merely rhetorical: "Shall we receive the good at the hand of God, and not the evil (*rāʿ*; NRSV: "bad")?" (2:10). If he goes beyond this, as we know he is about to do, he

---

11   Milgrom, *Leviticus 1–16*, 260.

12   Ibid., 43.

13   The syntax of the sentence containing the phrase "for no reason" (*ḥinnām*; Job 2:3) may invite different readings. In my judgment, however, all readings leave painfully little hermeneutical space for interpretations that explain or exonerate God's behavior. At the end of the struggle to understand, the Prologue to Job's story reports that his seven sons and three daughters are dead, and it still insists that the relationship between the words "God," "evil," and "for no reason" must be reckoned with. For further discussion of this unsettling text, see S. E. Balentine, "For No Reason," *Interpretation* 57 (2003), 349–369.

114   CHAPTER 6

will perforce reintroduce the idea of the demonic into a theology that claims already to have dismissed it. When this happens, the "priestly theodicy" must either respond effectively or collapse like a house of cards.

The Prologue reports that "one day the heavenly beings came to present themselves before the Lord" (1:6; 2:1). The reference to "one day" is nonspecific, like all the chronological markers in Job, and so readers may easily skip over it as incidental to the major concerns of the story. It is worth noting, however, that rabbinic texts pay attention to this detail and speculate on what it means. The Targum of Job from Qumran (11QtgJob) identifies the reference to "one day" in Job 1:6 with "the day of judgment at the beginning of the year" and the "one day" in Job 2:1 with the next day, which is the Day of Atonement.[14] The suggestion that God's deliberations in the heavenly council concerning Job's destiny took place on the Day of Atonement is inviting, for Priestly theology holds that on this day, once a year, the high priest was empowered to *purge the sanctuary* completely – inner sanctum, outer sanctum, and outer altar – and *the people* of sins that violated the sancta and compromised God's presence in Israel (cf. Lev. 16:11–28). According to the requirements of preparation for this auspicious ceremony, Aaron must assemble the necessary sacrificial animals, ritually purify himself by bathing in water, and clothe himself with linen garments – tunic, breeches, sash, and turban – that are reserved exclusively for this Day of Atonement (Lev. 16:1–10).

The instructions pertaining to the Day of Atonement in Leviticus 16 appear primarily intended to inform the laity. They omit important details, for example, any instructions concerning Aaron's spiritual preparation, which would seem to be necessary if they were meant to be a complete guide for the priests. On this point, however, it is instructive to note once again that the rabbis have been alert to the issue. The Talmud stipulates a seven-day preparation period for the priest before the rituals for the Day of Atonement begin. Included among the spiritual exercises required during this period are readings from the biblical books of Job, Daniel, Ezra, and Nehemiah (*m. Yoma* 1:6). The rabbis do not explain their selection of this lectionary of texts, but we may speculate that the legendary story of Job, the priest who suffered the ineffective ministries of friends who would not or could not deal honestly with his questions about God's justice, was understood to be particularly apt for every high priest who was preparing himself to represent *all* of his congregation before God.

The connection of Job to the priestly rituals of the Day of Atonement may of course confirm nothing more than the imaginative theological exegesis of the rabbis. Then again, who can doubt that the image of the high priest immersed

---

14   Cf. Clines, *Job 1–20*, 19.

JOB AS PRIEST TO THE PRIESTS

in the story of Job on the day before he offers the sacrifices that secure God's presence in the world is an appropriate spiritual discipline?

The Prologue describes two scenes in the heavenly council that involve conversations between God and the satan (*haśśaṭān*) concerning Job's fate (1:6–12; 2:1–6). The satan, one of God's intimates in the heavenly council, serves as a kind of prosecuting attorney. His responsibility, which is delegated to him by God, is to investigate the claims of those who profess fidelity to God and bring a report to the council for adjudication.[15] In the first scene, the satan responds to God's boast about Job's piety (1:8) with two questions. The first – "Does Job fear God for nothing?" (1:9) – is a general probe of *Job's motives*. The second – "Have you not put a fence around him and all that he has, on every side?" (1:10) – is a more specific challenge to *God's management of life's blessings*. Is it not the case, the satan asks, that God has so defined Job's world and so protected his life that God can be assured of Job's unmitigated devotion? If, however, God removed this protective border and permitted affliction to enter Job's world, would not Job's piety change? It is clear that Job blesses God when God blesses him. But the satan now wagers that if Job were cursed with brokenness and loss, he would respond to God in kind: "he will curse you to your face" (1:11).

The second round of dialogue between God and the satan (2:1–6) begins by replicating what has been said in the first meeting. The repetition provides a sense of narrative calm in the aftermath of the calamities that have just been reported (1:13–19). In spite of all that has transpired, God's assessment of Job remains the same as before. One new detail emerges, however, and it sends the story spinning in a new direction. God candidly admits to the satan that the destruction Job has experienced thus far has occurred "for no reason" (2:3). The admission effectively puts the satan's original question in 1:9 back on the table for further inspection. If, as God concedes, there is no connection between Job's conduct and God's treatment of him, if God is willing to bring him to ruin for no reason, and if, as God boasts yet again, Job still clings to his rituals of faith despite everything, does this not confirm that his fidelity is indeed truly unconditional? The satan responds by inviting God to permit an escalation of Job's suffering to another level of intensity. Once more the satan challenges God to "stretch out" the hand (2:5; cf. 1:11), this time extending Job's affliction to his bone and flesh. The wager is that if God exacts the

---

15   Clines offers an analogy that is especially instructive when considering Job's priestly role. He suggests a comparison of the satan figure with the *advocatus diaboli*, the functionary in Christendom, "whose task is to raise objections to the canonization of a saint: his office and his appointment owe their existence to the body that actively supports the canonization, and his role is to ensure that no potential criticism of the candidate remains unheard and unanswered" (*Job 1–20*, 25).

price of physical pain and suffering in exchange for Job's love, Job will refuse to pay. Echoing the aphorism attributed to Oscar Wilde, Job might be expected to plead, "God spare me physical pain and I'll take care of the moral pain myself."[16] If his plea goes unanswered, the satan wagers once more that Job will curse God (2:5).

The sequel to this second scene reports that the satan departs the heavenly council, and with God's permission he inflicts upon Job "loathsome sores" that cover his body head to toe (2:7). The term for Job's condition is *šeḥîn*, which is one of the generic words Leviticus uses to describe the various skin diseases the priest is empowered to address (Lev. 13:18–23). Job's affliction suggestively places him among those whose uncleanness compels them to look to priestly rituals for relief and restoration. What those rituals offer, and how Job might be expected to respond to them, will be addressed in the next section of this essay.

Another window for reflection on the import of these heavenly council scenes may be suggested. The Hebrew Bible records one other occasion when the satan dialogues with God concerning the assessment of a person's righteousness. The fourth of Zechariah's heavenly visions, Zech. 3:1–10, is set against the backdrop of Israel's exile and eventual subjugation to Persian rule, specifically the reign of Darius I (522–486 BCE). Although I do not suggest a direct linkage between this text and Job, the thematic concerns they share invite us to bring them into conversation with one another.[17]

When Zechariah looks into the heavenly council he sees three figures, an angel of the Lord, the satan, and Joshua, the high priest. Joshua's presence signifies that on this occasion it is not *Job's piety* that will come under scrutiny, it is the *priest's*. The satan has evidently already raised some charges against the priest. The charges are not recorded here, but we may speculate that they concern Joshua's fitness as a priest. Two interrelated reasons could perhaps justify the challenge. First, Joshua's genealogy makes him vulnerable to the charge, frequently articulated by Israel's prophets (e.g., Isa. 1:10–15; Hos. 4:4–17; Mic. 3:9–12; cf. Lam. 4:11–13), that he and his priestly colleagues bear responsibility for the judgment that resulted in Israel's exile. Joshua's grandfather, Seraiah, was the chief priest when Jerusalem was destroyed in 586; the Babylonians executed him at Riblah (II Kngs. 25:18–21; I Chron. 6:14–15; Jer. 52:24–27). Seraiah's son, Jehozadak, was exiled to Babylon, where Joshua was born and presumably

---

16 Cited in E. Scarry, *The Body in Pain. The Making and Unmaking of the World* (Oxford: Oxford University Press, 1985), 33.

17 On the conceptual relationship between the visions in Zechariah 3 and Job 1–2, see N. Tidwell, "*Wa' omar* (Zech 3:5) and the Genre of Zechariah's Fourth Vision," JBL 94 (1975), 343–355.

JOB AS PRIEST TO THE PRIESTS 117

remained until he returned to Jerusalem with Zerubbabel in 520, when both were commissioned by Darius to reorganize the secular and religious institutions of the Persian province Yehud. Second, the satan may have charged that because Joshua had been born in an unclean land, had lived in an unclean land, and had become a priest in an unclean land, he was unclean himself and thus was unworthy of administering the priestly rituals.[18] The report that Joshua stands in the council "dressed with filthy clothes" (3:3) clearly indicates that whatever the cause, he is now associated with uncleanness.

God's response to the satan's charges against Joshua stands in marked contrast with the scenes in Job. God does not consider the charges worthy and will not permit any further disparagements to be leveled against the priest. God rebukes the accuser by making it unequivocally clear that Joshua is and will remain the priest God has chosen. Joshua's guilt is removed; in keeping with Priestly theology, even a priest may be forgiven for his transgressions or those he bears on behalf of others (cf. Exod. 28:36–38). Joshua's filthy garments are removed and replaced with rich, ornate robes that are reminiscent of the regalia worn by the high priest in the ordination ceremony (see Exodus 29 and Leviticus 8) and on the Day of Atonement (Leviticus 16).

One item of apparel, a clean turban, is singled out for special attention. The word is *ṣānîp*, which is not the usual term for the high priestly turban (*miṣnepet*; Exod. 39:28; Lev. 8:9), although it clearly is related to this garment. Perhaps more instructive is the recognition that this term is used elsewhere in the Hebrew Bible of only one other person, Job (cf. Isa. 62:3, with reference to Zion). In his final speech before God appears, Job once again protests his innocence and defends his "integrity" (cf. *tummāh* in Job 27:5, 31:6) by calling attention to how he has faithfully responded to the cries for help from the poor and afflicted: "I put on righteousness, and it clothed me, my justice was like a robe and turban" (*ṣānîp*; Job 29:14). Apart from the thematic parallels, only this one thin linguistic thread ties Zechariah's vision of Joshua's priestly role specifically to Job. It is inviting nonetheless to consider whether God's affirmation of Joshua is in some sense a vindication of Job's defense of his own "priestly" ministry to others. The succeeding oracle in Zech. 3:6–7, even if it does not belong to the original vision, seems to point in this direction by placing a freighted, Joban-like condition on Joshua's priestly role. If Joshua walks in God's ways and keeps God's requirements, he will be permitted to stand in the very council of God. There, we may speculate, this priest, robed in the priestly/Joban garments

---

18   Cf. D. L. Petersen, *Haggai and Zechariah 1–8*. Old Testament Library (Philadelphia: Westminster Press, 1984), 195.

118   CHAPTER 6

of righteousness and justice, will be prepared to respond to any and all charges the satan may bring against those who have been accused "for no reason."

2   Inside the Priestly Rituals: Job's Affliction and Contention

The Prologue and Epilogue frame the story as a test of *Job's* piety. The dialogues between Job and his friends at the center of the book insist, however, that the one on trial is *God*. Moreover, inasmuch as Job is portrayed at the beginning and end of the story as having passed the test by clinging to his faith *and to the rituals* by which he enacts it, the debate with the friends centers on whether this faith and these rituals can pass muster when tested by affliction that comes "for no reason." In short, the dialogues turn the table. The priestly Job who diligently performs the rituals for his family and friends in the book's frame becomes the one who stands in need of the rituals that other ministrants may offer him. Lear-like, Job now holds a mirror up to his comforters: "If thou wilt weep my fortunes, take my eyes" (*King Lear*, IV, vi). Simply put, the priest has become the layperson. Eliphaz signals the shift in his opening words to Job:

> See, you have instructed many;
>   you have strengthened the weak hands.
> Your words have supported those
>   who were stumbling,
>   and you have made firm the feeble knees.
> But now it has come to you,
>   and you are impatient;
>   it touches you, and you are dismayed.
>   Job 4:3–5

Eliphaz and his cohorts are spokespersons for religious orthodoxy. Given the priestly images that frame the story, they may be viewed as speaking for the priestly establishment. Their advice to Job is of course multifaceted, but it is fair to say they take different routes to what is essentially the same end. Their objective is nicely captured in a scene described by Gail Godwin in *Father Melancholy's Daughter*. Father Gower, Rector of St. Cuthbert's, a small parish in rural Virginia, struggled with his faith but took comfort in the sacraments. "The thing about a ritual," he always said, "is that it brings containment and acceptance to people. The sacramental life is a sort of sanity filter against the onslaughts of existence." Father Adrian, his friend and colleague,

JOB AS PRIEST TO THE PRIESTS

recognizes the wisdom in this approach to ministry and confirms it with a personal anecdote:

> There was a Jesuit studying with me in Zurich, at the Institute. I once asked him, "What if you as a priest stopped believing? What would you do then?" "Make a fist in my pocket," he said, "and go on with the ritual."

Such is the gist of the friends' advice to Job: when in doubt, make a fist in your pocket and persevere with the prescribed rituals. How will Job response to such counsel? Father Gower's response to Adrian hints at what we may expect to hear from Job.

> "Exactly!" ... "Although my problem as a priest these last decades has been keeping my fist in my pocket when they keep diminishing and degrading the rituals *I* still believe in as much as ever."[19]

One inroad to what the priestly rituals might require of Job is suggested by the report that he has been afflicted with "loathsome sores" (2:7). His condition is described with the term *šĕhîn*, which is one of the words used to identify the skin diseases (Lev. 13:18–23) that make a person unclean and needful of the priestly rituals spelled out in Leviticus 13–14.[20] From a thematic standpoint these two chapters may be read as a microcosm of Job's story. At the beginning and end the focus is on the priest's responsibilities, first to diagnose the various skin diseases that render a person unclean and therefore unable to come near God's holy presence (Lev. 13:1–44), and then to administer the purification ritual for persons who have recovered from a skin disease and may therefore resume their normal activities within the community (Lev. 14:1–32). Our effort to tease out the possible connections with Job suggests that we read these priestly instructions with an ear cocked toward the advice of his friends: "make a fist in your pocket and trust the ritual." Inside the frame of these priestly instructions there is a brief but important description of the behavior prescribed for persons afflicted with skin diseases (Lev. 13:45–46). Here is where we may look to see if Job's fist remains resolutely clenched in trust, or if he determines the rituals have now become so "diminished and degraded" he can no longer believe in them.

---

19   G. Godwin, *Father Melancholy's Daughter* (New York: Avon Books, 1991), 274.
20   I have explored the connections between Leviticus 13–14 and Job in more detail in *Leviticus* (Interpretation; Atlanta: John Knox Press, 2002).

The Framing Rituals (Lev. 13:1–44; 14:1–32). Leviticus 13 begins the pericope with instructions concerning seven skin diseases (ṣārāʿat) that make a person ritually unclean. The instructions are detailed and complex, as we expect from the Priestly tradition, but for my purpose here it is sufficient to note the following salient features. Any person who suffers an irritation, swelling, or eruption on the skin must be brought to a priest for an examination. The priest will examine the coloration of the lesion and the degree to which it has spread on the body. If the examination suggests uncleanness, the priest will order a period of quarantine outside the camp, following which there will be a reexamination and a final disposition. If the priest determines that the presenting symptoms have passed, he will pronounce the person "clean" and restore him to normalcy. If he determines that the symptoms persist, he will pronounce the person "unclean" and confine him to isolation until such time as a change merits further review.

One particular issue requires careful consideration. The words "clean" (ṭāhēr) and "unclean" (ṭāmēʾ) occur in Leviticus 13–14 more than sixty times. There can be no doubt that the Priestly tradition understands the integrity of the body to be vitally connected to the wholeness and holiness of the community. To be clean is to be whole; to be whole, without blemish, is to be holy and acceptable for communion with God. By the same token, it is instructive that these chapters do not use the word "sin" to define the body's physical blemishes, nor do they require a confession of sin from the afflicted person. It is true that outside Leviticus the Hebrew Bible does associate skin disease (ṣārāʿat) with God's wrath and punishment. The cases of Miriam (Num. 12:1–5), Gehazi (II Kngs. 5:25–27), and Uzziah (II Chr. 26:16–21) are perhaps the parade examples. Such examples likely reflect a widespread popular belief that skin disease could indeed be a telling sign that God was punishing a sinful person. Nevertheless, the absence of sin words in Leviticus 13–14 makes it plausible to suggest that the priests sought to reframe the popular connection between sin and suffering within a ritual context that permitted a different assessment. Skin disease *may* be a sign of divine judgment, *but it is not necessarily so.* Sometimes, perhaps even most of the time, disease is caused by nothing other than a breakdown of the body's defense mechanisms against foreign invasion. In such cases, the priestly purification rituals provide a non-accusatory way for society to recognize, protect, and provide for the possible restoration of innocent victims.[21]

---

21 On the possibility that the priestly purification rituals in Leviticus 11–15 mandate that what is unclean is to be protected because it is vulnerable to abuse, not because it is evil, see M. Douglas, "The Forbidden Animals in Leviticus," JSOT 59 (1993), 3–23; idem., *Leviticus as Literature*, 166–169, 176–194.

JOB AS PRIEST TO THE PRIESTS 121

We may pause here to note that Job's friends champion the popular view of the connection between skin disease and sin, which suggests that if they knew themselves to be charged with implementing the guidelines in Leviticus 13, they might well have argued for a more rigid interpretation. Bildad, for example, gives Job a lengthy lecture on the certain judgment that God exacts on the wicked (Job 18:5–21), part of which is the warning that disease will devour their skin like a beast consuming its prey (18:11–13). In addition to the precedent cases of Miriam, Gehazi, and Uzziah cited above, the friends might be expected to share the anxiety, widespread in the ancient Near East and in Israel, that even if there is no obvious linkage between affliction and sin, one must be ever anxious about the possibility that some inadvertent sin is lurking in the background. Job himself is attentive to this possibility, as his preemptory sacrifices for his children make clear (1:5). He both presses his friends to teach him how he might have erred without knowing it (6:24) and protests that even if he has (19:4), his punishment – seven sons and three daughters dead, for no reason – is cruelly disproportionate to any sin he may have committed.[22]

Leviticus 14 closes the pericope on skin disease with a description of the purification ritual the priest performs for those who have recovered from their affliction. The provision of this ritual is significant, because it serves notice that the ultimate objective of these instructions is not to banish persons as outcasts but to anticipate the day when they may be restored to a full and normal life within the community. The case of Miriam is particularly instructive for understanding both the *fear* and the *compassion* that inform this ritual. When Aaron saw that Miriam had been stricken with leprosy (ṣārāʿat), he said to Moses, "Let her not be like something stillborn, whose flesh is half eaten away when it comes from the womb" (Num. 12:12; REB). In response to this plea, Moses cries, "Lord, not this! Heal her, I pray!" (Num. 12:13). God's response is telling. Miriam must remain outside the camp for seven days, during which time the people must not advance any farther on the journey toward the promised land. They may continue only when Miriam's quarantine is over, and she is brought back into the camp to be part of the journey (Num. 12:15–16).

---

22   The verb for "err" in both Job 6:24 and 19:4 is *šāgāh*, which in Priestly theology signifies unintentional or inadvertent sin, that is, the offender has erred either through negligence or ignorance. In either case, he is unaware of both what he has done and why it is wrong. Priestly sacrifices offer expiation for all accidental sins through the *ḥaṭṭaʾt*, "purification offering" (Lev. 4:1–5:13), and the *ʾāšam*, "reparation offering" (Lev. 5:14–6:7 [MT 5:14–26]). It is interesting, but beyond the scope of this essay, to speculate on how Job's case may have contributed to the Priestly incentive to address the problem of inadvertent sin. See further, J. Milgrom, "The Cultic *Segaga* and Its Influence in Psalms and Job," JQR 58 (1967), 73–79.

122   CHAPTER 6

According to Leviticus 14, the journey from affliction to healing and from banishment to restoration is ritually enacted through an eight-day process (day one, vv. 2–8; day two, v. 9; day eight, vv. 10–32). Each day's rituals are carefully spelled out. A variety of sacrificial offerings are required, but it is the reparation offering (*'āšām*, Lev. 14:12–18; NRSV: "guilt offering") that provides the key for understanding the ritual. The priest takes some of the blood from the lamb of the reparation offering and some of the ritual oil and places it on the person's right earlobe, right thumb, and right big toe. He dips his right finger in another portion of the oil and sprinkles it seven times before the Lord. The remainder of the oil the priest places on the head of the one being cleansed. Once these acts have been completed, the person is free to reenter the sanctuary and to resume full participation in the rituals and the shared activities that are part of every Israelite's life in community. This restoration ritual *for the person healed of skin disease* parallels the ritual administered *to the priests in their ordination ceremony* (Lev. 8:22–30), which as will be suggested below, invites reflection on whether there might be a peculiar connection between the preparation for priesthood and the compassion required to minister to the afflicted.

It is instructive to note once more that the restoration rituals do not presume sin and do not require confession or repentance. Here too, Job's friends, vigorous defenders of religion's requirements, if not always its imperative to compassion, may well have found themselves at odds with the Priestly theology they speak for. On the one hand, they may be expected to endorse with little hesitation the idea that Job should be banished for the sake of protecting the community from his uncleanness. Eliphaz, for example, commends to Job the truth that the wicked (read Job) are consigned by God to live in darkness from which there is no escape; they live, as they must, in "desolate cities ... that no one should inhabit" (Job 15:22, 28). Bildad adds that the ungodly (read Job) are (and should be) "driven out of the world," leaving behind no memory that they ever existed (Job 18:17–18). On the other hand, the friends put no trust in any restoration ritual that does not require the penalty of confession. Because they read affliction as a metaphor for sin and divine judgment, they promulgate an "if-then" theology that always begins with confession of sin:

> *If* you will seek God
>   and make supplication to the Almighty,
> *if* you are pure and upright,
> *surely then* he will rouse himself for you
>   and restore to you your rightful place.
>   Job 8:5–6

JOB AS PRIEST TO THE PRIESTS

If you direct your heart rightly ...
Surely then he will lift up your face without blemish (*mûm*);[23]
   you will be secure, and will not fear.

>   Job 11:13, 15

If you return to the Almighty,
   you will be restored, ...
and if the Almighty is your gold
   and your precious silver,
then you will delight yourself in the Almighty,
   and lift your face to God.
You will pray to him, and he will hear you.

>   Job 22:23, 25–27

Inside the Framing Rituals (Lev. 13:45–46). Two brief verses provide the only description of what diseased persons should do in the painful interim between affliction and restoration. Persons with certified cases of *ṣārāʿat* must tear their clothes, dishevel their hair, cover their mouth, and cry out "Unclean, unclean!" This symbolic enactment of affliction confirms that they know themselves to have become repugnant to the community. They must cry out a warning, lest others inadvertently come too close to their impurity, and they must banish themselves from the community by living alone outside the camp for the duration of their affliction (cf. Num. 5:1–4). Isolated from the community, where the observance of holy statutes and ordinances define the fullness of life God enjoins (cf. Lev. 18:5), they now reside in a place where deprivation, shame, and abandonment mark them as the living dead. The only thing that stands between them and a final dismissal to the grave of the forgotten is the very ritual that has required their exclusion. One day, perhaps, the priest will say, "He is clean" (13:17; cf. vv. 6, 13, 23, 28, 34, 35, 37, 38, 40). Until then, the afflicted wait, and cry, and hope. John Updike, who writes of his life-long battle with psoriasis, a non-contagious condition that has the "volatility of a disease," offers a firsthand account of the mental anguish experienced by those whom society treats as lepers. They are forced to eke an existence under the heavy hand of "another presence coöcupying [their] body and singling [them] out from the happy herds of healthy, normal mankind."[24]

---

23   The word *mûm* is also used to describe the physical blemishes that disqualify animals (Lev. 22:25) and priests (Lev. 21:17–23) from rituals at the altar.

24   J. Updike, "At War with My Skin," in *Self-Consciousness* (New York: Alfred A. Knopf, 1989), 42.

124 CHAPTER 6

How might Job respond to the behavior prescribed by the priestly restoration ritual? Like the afflicted person addressed by the instructions in Leviticus 13–14, Job is in limbo, waiting inside a gaping chasm of divine silence. On one side, there are the old affirmations, the once trusted rituals, now clouded by God's painfully dismissive address to the satan: "Very, well, he is in your power" (Job 2:6). On the other side, there is God's blustery but enigmatic response from the whirlwind (Job 38–41). Between relinquishment and revelation, Job is surrounded by little more than God's "ontological stammer."[25] He has, of course, the "comfort" of his friends, who like the priest addressed in Leviticus will make repeated visits to his ash heap outside the city. They come, however, not to see if he is healed but to press him relentlessly for an admission of guilt. Because they are trained to read disease as a sure sign of sin, they urge him to repent so that God can be present for him once more. In the words of Eliphaz, there is but one viable choice for Job, "Agree with God and be at peace, in this way good will come to you" (Job 22:21).

Job is not persuaded. Against the assumption that affliction is a metaphor for sin, Job insists that the reality, the very physicality of his pain, shatters every attempt to give suffering a name that belongs to something else. "*Look at me, and be appalled*," he says to the friends, "and lay your hand on your mouth" (Job 21:5; cf. 6:28). If they would but look into his eyes, red-raw with weeping, if they would but touch his body and feel the hurt that has been stitched like sackcloth into his very skin (Job 16:15–16), then they would know that moralisms, even ones reinforced by priestly rituals, can never bandage physical pain. Against the assumption that God requires his confession of guilt for sins he did not commit, he insists instead that God is guilty of shamefully mocking his affliction (Job 9:23), refusing his pleas for intervention even though there is "no violence" in his behavior and his prayers are "pure" (Job 16:17), and perverting his innocence (Job 19:6). Although he knows himself to have become someone the community regards as "unclean" and too repugnant for inclusion in their company (cf. 17:2, 6;19:13–20; 30:1–15), Job persists in believing, against all evidence to the contrary, that neither his suffering nor God's silence can be permanent if God is God. What the friends claim to be God's benevolently mysterious transcendence, Job insists is instead a sinister ruse (10:13–17) for God's malignant abandonment of good to evil and justice to injustice (10:1–17; 16:6–17; 19:6–12; 27:7–12; and especially 24:1–17). Like Salieri, the musician in Peter Shaffer's play *Amadeus*, whose career was derailed by Mozart's brilliant but disrespectful talent, Job takes his stand against any God (and any ritual)

---

25   For this evocative phrase, see S. Sontag, "The Aesthetics of Silence," in *The Susan Sontag Reader* (New York: Farrar, Straus, and Giroux, 1982), 199.

that is indifferent to the wrongfully accused. In Salieri's words, "They say the spirit bloweth where it listeth: I tell you NO! It must list to virtue or not blow at all."[26]

Leviticus 13–14 offers a ritual for identifying, addressing, reviewing, and potentially restoring those whose afflictions make them society's outcasts. Outside the gate, these persons cry out "Unclean, unclean!" and wait for a word from God's priests that will remove the barriers between them and the life they once enjoyed. The *ritual promises* that the religious establishment will not let first discernments concerning affliction be the last; all persons who are cut off from God's presence deserve a second chance to have their case reviewed and their situation reversed. At the same time, Job's case argues that the *ritual is limited*, even short sighted; it contemplates no response from the afflicted other than patient submission. In the end, following God's first speech from the whirlwind, Job will in fact place his hand on his mouth (Job 40:4), a sure sign that he is indeed tempted to yield in despair to the paltry truth that "Life-under-God ..." is nothing more than "pointlessness posing as a purpose."[27]

And yet, it is none other than God who presses Job to move beyond silent acquiescence. With a second speech, God repeats once more the summons that has already been issued but apparently not yet satisfactorily answered: "Gird up your loins like a man; I will question you, and you declare to me" (Job 40:7; cf. 38:2). God now reshapes the first revelation with a provocative imperative that puts on the table for the first time the issue of justice (cf. Job 40:8: *mišpaṭ*) that has so vexed Job: "Deck yourself with majesty and dignity; clothe yourself with glory and splendor" (Job 40:10). Is there perhaps here a distant, still lingering echo of God's decision in the heavenly council before which Joshua the high priest stood falsely charged as guilty? "Take off his filthy clothes ... Let them put a clean turban on his head" (Zech. 3:4–5). Might it be that when Joshua takes up the challenge of restoring the religious institution that will sustain the community in the aftermath of Jerusalem's destruction, there will no longer be rituals requiring those whose affliction consigns them to the ash heap "for no reason" to cry out "Unclean, unclean"? Might it be that priests will now know truth demands a place in the ritual for the words "Injustice, injustice"?

The biblical portraits of both Joshua and Job are reminders that priestly rituals, like all social behavior that becomes institutionalized and ensconced in

---

26 P. Shaffer, *Amadeus* (New York: Signet Books, 1984), 74.

27 For this phrase, see J. Woods, "The Broken Estate: The Legacy of Ernest Renan and Matthew Arnold," in *The Broken Estate: Essays on Literature and Belief* (New York: Random House, 1999), 254.

tradition, are in constant need of systemic review. Jean Fouquet (1416?–1480), court painter to both Charles VII and Louis XI, was in many respects the voice of "loyal opposition" to his royal patrons. One example, which appropriates Job's story, is this fifteenth century illumination.[28] [See Figure 5.1. Jean Fouquet, "Job on the Heap of Refuse and His Three Comforters"]

Fouquet depicts Job, lying forlorn on a pile of manure, as one of the oppressed and famished outcasts in French society. His place is outside the walled city, where the Tower of Vincennes stands opulent and secure. On the manicured grounds just beyond the walls, people go about their normal affairs: a person on horseback sits tall and erect, perhaps surveying his land; two workers amble along in tranquil conversation. Three "friends," dressed in the regalia that attests their positions of power and privilege, have traveled the long and winding road that leads to Job. The person to Job's right wears the scarlet that symbolizes the parliament; the person to his left, the royal blue of the monarchy. The figure in the middle, standing before him with hands uplifted to bless, is robed in the gold and white of the church. On first sight, the scene suggests concern and sympathy for Job. On closer inspection, one notices that the priestly figure who extends the church's blessing does so with eyes closed. Fouquet has subtly but certainly suggested that the leaders of France's institutional structures, at the center of which stands the church, feign attentiveness to one their own policies have made invisible at the margins of society.

3 Job's Challenge to the Priestly System

Job's challenge to the Priestly system of rituals may be introduced by reflecting on a scene from Ian McEwan's novel, appropriately titled *Atonement*. McEwan describes an island temple that sits on the far side of the grounds of the Tallis family's nineteenth century English country home. The temple had once been a grand structure, but its maintenance has been long neglected. "The temple was the orphan of a grand society lady, and now, with no one to care for it, no one to look up to, the child had grown old before its time, and let itself go." But the temple had also been witness to a grievous loss, the burning of the original Adam house that had stood on these grounds in the century before. When Briony Tallis, the novel's main character, looks at the temple now, she imagines that its lamentable condition is its way of grieving for the burned down mansion. McEwan discloses Briony's thoughts with a sentence that might just as well describe the promise for any temple – in Vincennes, Wezemaal,

---

28   See the discussion in Terrien, *The Iconography of Job*, 102–104.

JOB AS PRIEST TO THE PRIESTS

or Jerusalem – where priests do more than feign an interest in the Jobs of this world: "Tragedy had rescued the temple from being entirely a fake."[29]

The Jobs of this world know that tragedy is never fictional. Any ritual that promises them atonement must heed Job's warning: "Those at ease have contempt for misfortune" (Job 12:5). Until and unless those who administer the rituals of faith look square in the eye of this truth, all rituals run the risk of being entirely a fake. When Job is placed inside the priestly rituals of Leviticus, his challenge portends either a collapse of the entire structure of levitical religion or a reformation that tunes it to larger and fuller truths. In either case, the rituals of atonement and reconciliation cannot survive in any meaningful way if Job's challenge is ignored.

William Scott Green has suggested that the Book of Job "stretches" Judaism's three most critical and distinguishing traits: monotheism, covenant, and cult.[30] Although the presence of the satan figure in Job 1–2 certainly clouds the issue of monotheism, Green notes that the greater stress comes from Job's challenge to the cult, where the primary goal of the ritual complex is the maintenance of the covenant relationship between God and Israel. The fundamental assumption of the cult is that "humans can take concrete action – through repentance and ritual – to maintain and reconstitute their relationship with God."[31] This assumption rests on the belief that it is *human transgression*, not *divine caprice*, which jeopardizes the covenant. The Prologue stands this belief on its head by insisting that God has afflicted Job both willfully and gratuitously. Green spells out the consequences as follows:

> ... from a cultic or halakhic perspective, there is nothing concrete Job can do to repair his relationship with God. Sacrifice, repentance, and any religious behaviors that develop from them are nugatory under these circumstances. Job cannot atone for a transgression he did not commit. No offering, no change of heart, can appease divine caprice or undo an affliction that happens for no reason.... It is probably no accident that Job's speeches nowhere explore a cultic option as a solution to his miseries.[32]

If Job's story undermines the very basis of the covenant relationship with its witness to divine caprice, and if all rituals to repair the covenant "are nugatory

---

29 I. McEwan, *Atonement* (New York: Doubleday, 2001), 69.

30 William Scott Green, "Stretching the Covenant: Job and Judaism," *Review and Expositor* 99 (2002), 569–577.

31 Ibid., 573–574.

32 Ibid.

under these circumstances," then it is not only Job's personal piety but also the entire religious structure by which he comprehends the world that is threatened with oblivion. With so much at stake, one may wonder not only how but also why Job is included in Israel's sacred scriptures. Perhaps Coleridge was right. The very existence of the Book of Job proves that the Bible is a human production, because God would never have written such a powerful argument against himself!

Coleridge's quip notwithstanding, the Book of Job is surely remarkable. For all the threat to priestly religion that Job represents, his story does not end with the cult in shambles. Following God's long awaited address to Job, the Epilogue (Job 42:7–17) returns the focus to Job's priestly profile. The one who had offered sacrifices on behalf of his children is instructed by God to administer the sacrifices brought by his now chastened friends and to add to them his prayer for their forgiveness.[33] With a terseness that raises at least as many issues as it resolves, the text simply reports that Job complies with God's instructions. Job asks no questions, he offers no explanation, he provides no insight into why he returns to the very rituals that before had left him and his family so utterly vulnerable to evil. There has been a revelation from God, and Job states that it has enabled him to hear and see things in a new way (Job 41:5). Yet even as the story reaches for this all's-well-that-ends-well conclusion, it does not decode the connection between revelation and response. *Something* has changed between Job and God, although it seems to have little to do with God's "answers" to Job's questions. At the end of the book, Job's complaints about God's injustice are still on the table. His seven sons and three daughters are still dead. No restoration of family, however satisfying, can erase the words "for no reason." No restoration of fortune, however substantive, can replace what he has lost.

Green has provocatively suggested that *whatever* has changed between God and Job, *whatever* constitutes Job's new understanding, has been "absorbed almost immediately into the cultic system."[34] Once again, Job offers sacrifices, now for persons who had wrongfully accused Job himself. Once again, the sacrifices are said to be effective. The friends are forgiven, although forgiveness seems not to have been God's first plan for them. And Job is restored, although no reason has ever been established for why God should have afflicted him to begin with. In a world that both Job and the friends now know is less

---

33   On Job's prayer, see S. E. Balentine, "My Servant Job Shall Pray for You," *Theology Today* 58 (2002), 502–518.

34   Green, "Stretching the Covenant."

JOB AS PRIEST TO THE PRIESTS   129

predictable, a world where God's covenant with those who strive for fidelity is now far more complicated than they ever dreamed, where misconceptions and incomplete knowledge seem the norm, not the exception, the old rituals of faith remain, stretched but not broken. The administrator of these rituals is still Job, but he now exercises his priestly role on the other side of the ash heap, where faith is measured not by calculable possessions but by incalculable losses. The *conviction* and the *sadness* that defines Job's priestly role at the end of his story stands at a far remove from what Thomas Lynch, mortician qua theologian, describes as the steady diet of "Tragedy-cam" and "Grief TV" that too often provide our rituals of caring for the afflicted:

> Tragedy-cam and Grief TV give couch potatoes easy access to the "therapies" of "national mourning" for people they have no acquaintance with or knowledge of or interest in except as covers on the magazines in waiting rooms and checkout lines. With round-the-clock coverage on three cable channels and network news magazines and special reports, no one need change their schedule, put on a suit, order flowers, bake a casserole, go to the funeral home or church, try to find something of comfort to say or endure the difficult quiet of genuine grief when words fail, when nothing can be said. Nor need they see a body or help carry one or pay for anything, or perpetually care. They needn't budge. The catharsis is user-friendly, the "healing" home delivered. "Being there" for perfect strangers has never been easier. When they've had enough they can grab a DoveBar, flick to The Movie Channel or the Home Shopping Network and wait until the helicopters locate another outrage to zoom in on.
>
> Whatever they have experienced, it is not grief. Grief is the tax we pay on our attachments, not on our interests or diversions or entertainments. We grieve in keeping with the table stakes of our relationships, according to the emotional capital we invest in the lives and times of others, that portion of ourselves we ante up before the cards are dealt. We might be curious about our losses when we play to kill time, or interested when we play for fun, or even obsessed a little if we find the game compelling. But we grieve for losses only in games we play for keeps – real love, real hate, real attachments broken.[35]

---

35   T. Lynch, *Bodies in Motion and at Rest: On Metaphor and Mortality* (New York, London: W. W. Norton and Co., 2000), 193–194.

130   CHAPTER 6

There is a suggestive hint in Leviticus 14 that the model for the priest who would come to Job on the ash heap, the model for the priestly role Job himself resumes at the end of the book, is in fact defined by the "tax paid on the heart's attachments."[36] The restoration ritual prescribed in Lev. 14:1–32 instructs the priest to daub blood and oil on the healed person's right earlobe, right thumb, and right big toe. The only other ritual in which this daubing of the extremities occurs is the priestly ordination ceremony (Lev. 8:22–30), where it constitutes the final endowment that confirms the priest is now ready to take up his responsibilities. Because the priest and the "leper" are the only persons who receive this daubing, we may be permitted to wonder if the ritual recognizes a peculiar connection between priesthood and suffering. Is it the case, perhaps, that only those who have traveled the life-scarring road from being condemned and ridiculed to being restored and embraced can really know what it means to be a priest to the afflicted? Is it the case, perhaps, that priests who stand inside the rituals that bind a fragile world to a holy God are most attuned to their tasks when they know themselves vulnerable to the wounds of this world? To be sure, the restoration ritual in Leviticus 14 appears to be focused on matters far more immediate and practical than such abstract theological ruminations. Even so, the image of a priest daubed from head to toe with holy oil administering the same rite to a leper invites a wonderment about why and how our rituals bless or curse the afflicted to whom we minister.

Included among Terrien's visual representations of Job as priest is this sixteenth century wood sculpture located in the Mayer van der Bergh Museum in Antwerp.[37]

The ecclesiastical hat, the right hand raised in blessing, and the chalice offered with the left hand are all conventional symbols for the priest. One distinctive feature, however, focuses the viewer's attention. The sacramental cup of blood Job offers flames with fire that appears to have burned a gaping hole in his very heart. The image may suggest, as Terrien notes, that the blood offered in the chalice has poured from Job's own wounds.[38] In any case, there is no mistaking the sculptor's connection of the wounds that define Job's priestly ministry and those the church identifies with Christ, the eternal High Priest.

The artist might well have titled this wood sculpture with Henri Nouwen's suggestive phrase, "the wounded healer." "If the ministry is meant to hold the

---

36   Ibid., 88.
37   See the discussion in Terrien, *The Iconography of Job*, 149–151. For a comprehensive discussion of this sculpture and its significance for understanding the reception history of Job as priest, see now Huff, "Job the Priest: From Scripture to Sculpture," 330–338.
38   Ibid., 149.

FIGURE 6.2 "Saint Job as Priest," Mayer van der Bergh Museum, Antwerp
CREDIT: BARRY HUFF, PERSONAL PHOTOGRAPH

promise of the Messiah," Nouwen says, then "whatever we can learn of His coming will give us a deeper understanding of what is called for in ministry today." How does the Messiah come? Nouwen says the beginning of the answer may be found in the following rabbinic legend:

> Rabbi Yoshua ben Levi came upon Elijah the prophet while he was standing at the entrance of Rabbi Simeron ben Yohai's cave … He asked Elijah, "When will the Messiah come?"

132   CHAPTER 6

> Elijah replied, "Go and ask him yourself."
>
> "Where is he?"
>
> "Sitting at the gates of the city."
>
> "How shall I know him?"
>
> "He is sitting among the poor covered with wounds. The others unbind all their wounds at the same time and then bind them up again. But he unbinds one at a time and binds it up again, saying to himself, 'Perhaps I shall be needed: if so I must always be ready so as not to delay for a moment'."[39]

If priests are to take their cue from the One who sits outside the gates of the city, from the One who offers sacred rituals with wounded-bandaged-still wounded hands, they may expect to find themselves in the company of Job, the prototypical model of the "wounded healer" for both Aaron and Christ. With his sacrifices Job keeps us mindful that priestly rituals are enormously important gifts of grace; they help us mediate the gaps that explicably and inexplicably threaten to undo our world and subvert our trust in God. With his wounds Job reminds us of another truth, which we should also receive as a gift of enormous importance: unless the steady rhythms of priestly ceremony can be interrupted in mid-rite by the unscripted shrieks of the Jobs of the world, they risk becoming vapid gestures that offer nothing more than sacramental nonsense.

Perhaps the journey towards the model for priestly ministry begins with a story that predates the one Nouwen references. Perhaps it begins with the very story the rabbis commended to ancient Israel's high priest before he entered the Holy of Holies on the Day of Atonement. That story begins with the words, "There once was a man in the land of Uz whose name was Job." It ends with a divine discernment that lingers and beckons:

> My servant Job has spoken of me what is right; now therefore, take seven bulls and seven rams and go to my servant Job, and offer up for yourselves a burnt offering; and my servant Job shall pray for you.
>
> Job 42:7–8

---

39   H. Nouwen, *The Wounded Healer* (Garden City, NY: Image Books, 1972), 81–82.

CHAPTER 7

Job and the Priests: "He Leads Priests Away Stripped" (Job 12:19)

The title for this essay references the only occurrence of the word "priest(s)" (*kōhēn*) in Job or in any other wisdom book in the Old Testament. The context for this occurrence conveys a negative assessment. In this last response to the friends in the first cycle of dialogues (Job 4–14), Job argues that priests and temple officials, along with other leaders – "counselors," "judges," "kings," "elders," and "princes" – have lost their status and power in society (12:17–21). The image of priests being lead away naked underscores the humiliation that comes with the loss of their authority. In short, as David Clines notes, the priests' "cultic office has lost its efficacy."[1]

This lone reference to "priests" in Job invites several questions:

– What was the Joban author's understanding of the priests and the priestly traditions that convey their roles in society?[2] Are priests only part of a generic list of once powerful but now diminished political and religious leaders in communal life, or does their inclusion in this list have import for understanding the complex Joban story?

– Why does the author attribute the diminishment of the priests and other leaders to God (the implied referent for the pronoun "he")? Is there some specific reason God divests priests of authority, some real or imagined failure on their part in relation to Job that merits God's ire? Or, is the author's objective simply to demonstrate that, from Job's perspective at least, God has incomprehensible "wisdom" and incontestable "strength" to tear down what God wills (Job 12:13–14, 16), in sum, to "strip understanding from the leaders of the earth" (12:24)?

– These and other such questions invite reflection on the relative dating of the book of Job in relation to Old Testament Priestly traditions. For the purpose of this essay the question can be sharpened by asking whether possible connections between Job and Priestly traditions are the result of the Joban

---

1 David J. A. Clines, *Job 1–20* (Word Biblical Commentary; Dallas, TX: Word Books), 301.

2 For the purpose of this essay, the term "priestly traditions" refers broadly and primarily to the following corpus of Pentateuchal texts: Gen 1:1–2:4a; Exod 25–31; 35–40; Leviticus; and Num 1–10; 26–36. Other texts clearly identified with priestly traditions, for example, Ezekiel, also contribute to this corpus.

© SAMUEL E. BALENTINE, 2021 | DOI:10.1163/9789004459212_008

134   CHAPTER 7

author reading backwards, from Job to Priestly traditions, which assumes the chronological priority of the Priestly traditions, or whether the connections result from readers who place Job and Priestly writings in conversation with each other, irrespective of their chronological relationship.

From a methodological perspective, the two approaches may be categorized as "diachronic"/"author-oriented" or "synchronic"/"reader-oriented." The former typically relies on authorial intent, which may be demonstrated by the density of identifiable lexical and thematic parallels that are shared by two or more texts. As such, one may argue that "an author has intentionally borrowed from other texts" for the purposes of either revision or polemic. The latter typically relies on a synchronic approach to texts, in which readers, not authors, recognize the inherent dialogical nature of all texts and thus construct connections that are meaningful. "If a reader recognizes a link between two or more texts, then that link is legitimate *ipso facto*."[3]

I concede at the outset that these questions currently exceed definitive answers. Critical assessment of the possible connections between Job and Priestly traditions has only just begun. Most scholars who have addressed this issue thus far have either assumed or simply asserted the chronological priority of Priestly traditions, and thus, concomitantly, attribute any connections with Job to authorial intent.[4] My own work to date falls broadly within the limitations of

---

3 For a cogent summary and critique of the two methodological approaches, see G. D. Miller, "Intertextuality in Old Testament Research," *Currents in Biblical Research* 9 (2011); for the citations here, see 285, 294, respectively.

4 In addition to mostly random observations in commentaries on Job, the following studies should be singled out. In a seminal study, Leo Perdue (*Wisdom and Cult: A Critical Analysis of the Views of Cult in the Wisdom Literatures of Ancient Israel and the Ancient Neat East* [Missoula, MT: Scholars Press, 1977]) demonstrates that Job, and wisdom literature in general, both embraces and adapts cultic genres and priestly rituals. Commenting on numerous connections between Job and Leviticus, especially their respective views of retribution, Mary Douglas (*Leviticus as Literature* [Oxford: Oxford University Press, 1999], 212) suggests that "Leviticus' general reflection on God's justice *reaches forward* to the Book of Job" (emphasis added). Similarly, William Scott Green and Israel Knohl have argued, from different perspectives, that Job either "stretches" or "transforms" conventional Priestly understandings of retributive justice (Wm. S. Green, "Stretching the Covenant: Job and Judaism," *Review and Expositor* 99, 2002, 569–577; I. Knohl, *The Sanctuary of Silence: The Priestly Torah and the Holiness School* [Minneapolis, MN: Fortress, 1995], 165–67; 2003, 115–22). Konrad Schmid argues that Job's attitude toward conventional Priestly representations of sacrifice confirms that "the Book of Job does not repudiate Priestly theology, but rather takes an ambivalent position towards its fundamental precepts" (K. Schmid, "The Authors of Job and Their Historical Setting," in L. Perdue, ed., *Scribes, Sages, and Seers: The Sage in the Eastern*

the current discussion.[5] In thinking about the trajectory of my work, however, I find it instructive that my first probes into Job and the priests were the unexpected result of colliding deadlines that forced me to work on two seemingly very different texts at the same time. Approximately halfway through writing a book-length commentary on Job, I had to suspend the work in order to write a commentary on Leviticus.[6] I have no doubt that my simultaneous immersion in both Job and Leviticus heightened my awareness of the ways in which they are connected, but it is also the case that my first discernments were mostly synchronic. In retrospect, I did assume that the Joban writer was dependent on and reacting to an existent Priestly tradition. While I still suspect this is highly likely, it is now clear to me that in the absence of a full-scale investigation of the demonstrable use of specifically Priestly language in the book of the Job, the question of the chronological relationship between Job and Priestly traditions must remain open. To date, no such study has been done, although with good reason we may expect this situation will be corrected in the future.[7] If it could be demonstrated that the Joban author was intentionally employing specifically Priestly language and themes, then a solid foundation could be laid for arguing that he was deliberately responding to and critiquing an existing Priestly tradition. Without a thorough analysis of Priestly language and themes in Job, however, the question of "provenance, influence, and authorial intent"[8] cannot be resolved.

Mediterranean World [FRLANT 219: Göttingen: Vandenhoeck & Ruprecht, 2008], 147; cf. idem., *"Innerbiblische Schriftdiskussion im Hiobbuch,"* in T. Krüger, et al., eds., *Das Buch Hiob und seine Interpretationen: Beiträge zum Hiob-Symposium auf den Monte Verità vom 14–19. August 2005* [Zurich: Theologischer Verlag, 2007], 241–61).

5   S. E. Balentine, "My Servant Job Shall Pray for You," *Theology Today* 58 (2002), 29–52; idem., *Leviticus* (Interpretation; Louisville: John Knox, 2002), 502–18; idem., "For No Reason," *Interpretation* 57 (2003), 349–69; idem., *Job* (Smyth and Helwys Bible Commentary Series; Macon, GA, 2006); idem., "Inside the Sanctuary of Silence: The Moral and Ethical Demands of Suffering," in M. D. Carroll R., J. Lapsley, eds., *Character Ethics and the Old Testament: Moral Dimensions of Scripture* (Louisville, Westminster John Knox, 2007), 63–79.

6   Balentine, "Job as Priest to the Priests."

7   See now, Barry R. Huff, "Dipped in Filth and Clothed in Glory: Job's Transformation of Priestly Terms, Themes, Texts, and Theologies," (Ph.D. dissertation, Union Presbyterian Seminary, 2017).

8   Cf. Miller, "Intertextuality in Old Testament Research," 286–87. The issue could be explicated in terms of Benjamin Sommer's delineation of four types/categories of intertextuality: exegetical function, influence (revisionary or polemical), allusion, and echo (*A Prophet Reads Scripture: Allusion in Isaiah 40–66* [Stanford, CA: Stanford University Press, 1998]).

1   A Framing Perspective: The Priestly Profile of Job in the Prologue and Epilogue

An overview of scholarly work to date indicates that readers have seen connections with Priestly traditions in all major sections of the book of Job. The narrative construal of Job and his world in the Prologue–Epilogue (Job 1–2 + 42:7–17), which provides the structural frame for the book, has evoked comparison with the Priestly creation account in Gen 1, with the primordial couple in the Garden of Eden recast as Job and his wife in the "garden of Uz."[9] The poetic dialogues between Job and his friends, which comprise the middle of the book (Job 3–31), have invited reflection on the efficacy of cultic remedies for affliction and suffering. The friends advocate Job's submission to conventional expectations – confession, sacrifice, and repentance (e.g. Job 8:5–7; 11:13–20; 22:21–27; 33:23–28). Job counters that cultic options provide no remedy for those whom God wounds "for no reason" (*ḥinnām*, Job 9:17; cf. 1:9; 2:3).[10] God's speeches (Job 38:1–41:34), which seem intended to resolve the debate between Job and his friends, evoke consideration of Priestly construals of both creation (Gen 1) and the tabernacle/temple (Exod 25–31, 35–40),[11] now transposed to convince Job that the administration of divine justice is a cosmic matter that exceeds every spatially limited conception, whether tied to memories of Sinai or Jerusalem.

Of these proposed connections, the profile of a "priestly Job" in the Prologue – Epilogue is perhaps the most intriguing, and, from the perspective of reception history, clearly the most influential.[12] The opening of the book locates Job in "the land of Uz," an indefinable place somewhere in "the east" (1:1, 3) where, according to Hebraic geography, the primeval Garden of Eden was planted (Gen 2:8). Readers are thereby invited to imagine that when we enter into the world of Uz, we are simultaneously entering into a distinctly theological conception of primordial beginnings that marks the first place on earth where human beings were introduced to God's cosmic design and

---

9   E.g. S. Meier, "Job I–II: A Reflection on Genesis I–III," *VT* 39 (1989), 184–185; Balentine, *Job*, 41–78.

10   E.g. Green, "Stretching the Covenant," 574–75; cf. Balentine, "For No Reason," 358–363; idem., "Inside the Sanctuary," 66–67; *Job*, 58–60; idem., "Traumatizing Job," *RevExp* 105 (2008), 213–28.

11   E.g. Wm. P. Brown, *The Ethos of the Cosmos: The Genesis of Moral Imagination* (Grand Rapids, MI/Cambridge, UK: Eerdmans, 1999), 341–42; Balentine, *Job*, 645–49.

12   In what follows, I reprise and expand my observations in Balentine, "My Servant Job Shall Pray for You," and *Job*, 41–78.

JOB AND THE PRIESTS

charged with the responsibility to "till it and keep it" (Gen 2:15). In Eden, God's summons is directed to Adam and Eve; in Uz, it is directed to Job and his wife. Read as "The Creation Story: Part Two," the Joban prologue invites consideration of this question: How will Job's life in the "Garden of Uz" compare to life in Eden's paradise?

The ensuing drama in Uz unfolds in six narrative scenes, replete with creation imagery that alternates between heaven and earth, which invites a comparison between the "genesis" of Job and the "genesis" of the world.

Gen 1:1–2:4a	*Job 1–2*	
(Day 1)	1:1–5	On *Earth*: Job's unparalleled piety
(Day 2)	1:6–12	In *Heaven*: God's first dialogue with the satan
(Day 3)	1:13–22	On *Earth*: The destruction of Job's family and possessions
(Day 4)	2:1–7a	In *Heaven*: God's second dialogue with the satan
(Day 5)	2:7b–10	On *Earth*: Job's personal affliction
(Day 6)	2:11–13	On *Earth*: The friends arrive to "console" and "comfort" Job
(Day 7)		[No parallel]

These structural parallels call attention to the absence in Job 1–2 of a seventh scene. In the Priestly creation account, God "blesses" (*bārak*, Gen 2:3) the seventh day and calls it holy. The Joban Prologue ends instead in a protracted seven days and seven nights of silence. No one can speak a word it seems, not Job, not the friends, and not God, "for they saw that [Job's] suffering was very great" (Job 2:13). The silence serves to heighten the drama by raising the reader's expectations. When the seven days and nights of silence end, will Job image God by declaring that his world is "very good" (Gen 1:31)? Will Job punctuate his last words to this point – "Should we accept only good from God and not accept evil?" (Job 2:10 NJPS) – by blessing the Creator for the life he has been given?

Two hermeneutical moves may be considered when thinking about these questions. The first is to follow the conventional understanding of the compositional history of the book of Job, which treats the Prologue–Epilogue as originally a set prose piece, now fragmented by a later insertion of the poetic dialogues in the middle. From this perspective, the Epilogue provides the missing seventh scene; it is God who breaks the silence that ends the sixth scene by "blessing" Job and restoring his fortunes. There are seven total occurrences

138 CHAPTER 7

of the verb "bless" (*bārak*) in Job. Six are located in the Prologue (1:5, 10, 11, 21; 2:5, 9); the seventh occurs in the Epilogue (42:12). The six Prologue occurrences are widely understood as intentionally ambiguous; two are routinely understood with the normal meaning "bless" (1:10, 21); four are widely taken as a scribal substitute for "curse" (presumably the verb *qālal*; cf. Job 3:1; Job 1:5, 11; 2:5, 9), on the assumption that the author considered it unacceptable to transmit a text that mentioned cursing God. Whether or not this argument can be sustained,[13] what "blessing" God or being "blessed by" God means in the Prologue is unclear, until, perhaps, the Epilogue provides the seventh and final occurrence of the term, which indicates unequivocally that "God blessed the latter days of Job more than the beginning" (42:12). Lest there be any doubt, the narrator quantifies the blessing by reporting that God doubled the possessions Job had lost.

A second option is to read the final form of the text sequentially, moving directly from the end of ch. 2 to the beginning of ch. 3. This places the prose and poetry in immediate and tensive juxtaposition, irrespective of the compositional history. From this perspective, Job 3 "completes" the Prologue by attributing the first words that break the sabbactical silence that hovers over the ash heap to Job, not God. With this reading, the seventh scene reports that instead of blessing his "very good" world (*ṭôb měʾōd*, Gen 1:31), despite undeserved suffering that was "very great" (*hakkěʾēb měʾōd*, Job 2:13), Job "curses" his life (3:1–10; note the use of *qālal* in 3:1) and laments his destiny (3:11–26) in a world where God consigns him to nothing more than "trouble" and "turmoil" (*rogez*, 3:26). Beyond the clear parallels with Jer 20:14–18, multiple commentators have noted that Job's seven curses in 3:1–10 can be read as a "counter-cosmic incantation"[14] that has the rhetorical effect of nullifying the hopes and promises attached to each day of the Priestly seven-day creation schema. The clearest example is Job's opening curse of "that day" when he was born – "let that day be darkness" (*yěhî ḥōšek*, 3:4) – which rhetorically reverses God's first creative act, "let there be light" (*yěhî ʾôr*, Gen 1:3). The remaining parallels are not exact, as indicated below, but they are sufficient to suggest that Job's first words from the ash heap offer a direct challenge to each aspect of God's primordial design for human life:

---

13 T. Linafelt, "The Undecidability of *brk* in the Prologue to Job," *Biblical Interpretation* 4 (1996). For my assessment of this argument, see Balentine, *Job*, 49.

14 M. Fishbane, "Jeremiah IV 23–26 and Job III 3–13: A Recovered Use of the Creation Pattern," *VT* 21(1971), 153.

JOB AND THE PRIESTS

Genesis 1: "And God said ..."		*Job 3: And Job said*	
v. 3	Let there be light	v. 3	Let there be darkness
v. 7	[Let there be] waters *above* the firmament	v. 4	Let not God *above* seek it ...
v. 2	darkness was upon the face	v. 5	Let gloom and deep darkness claim it
v. 14	[Let there be] lights to separate day and night ... for seasons and for years	vv. 6–7	Let thick darkness seize that night Let it not rejoice among the days of the year Let it not come into the number of months Let that night be barren
v. 21	[Let there be] great sea monsters	v. 8	Let those who curse it curse the Sea those who are skilled to raise up Leviathan
v. 15	[Let there be] lights to give light upon the earth	v. 9	Let the stars of the dawn be dark Let it hope for light, but have none
		v. 15	Let it not see the eyelids of the morning[15]

Both hermeneutical options discussed above underscore the importance of reading the narrative frame of Job (Job 1–2 + 42:7–17) not only as a set piece that advocates an uncontested all's-well-that-ends-well conclusion but also as presenting an issue, framed in terms of Priestly theology, that invites serious dissent. Are Priestly assertions of God's primordial design for a "very good" world that is worthy of blessing vulnerable to a different assessment? When canonized texts like the final form of the book of Job suggest that God is complicit in suffering that happens "for no reason," when such texts advocate that the faithful respond to God's primordial designs with curses and laments rather

---

15   The generative work on this issue has been done by Fishbane, "Jeremiah IV 23–26 and Job III 3–13." Others have appropriated and expanded Fishbane's observations; see especially, L. Perdue, "Job's Assault on Creation," *Hebrew Annual Review* 10 (1987), 295–315; idem, *Wisdom in Revolt: Metaphorical Theology in the Book of Job* (JSOTSup 112; Sheffield: Almond Press, 1991), 96–98; *Wisdom and Creation: The Theology of Wisdom Literature* (Nashville: Abingdon, 1994), 131–37. The parallels above are adapted from Balentine, *Job*, 84.

140   CHAPTER 7

than blessing and praise, what should readers conclude? Such is the drama created by the structural frame of the book of Job.

The structural connections between Job 1–2 + 42:7–17 and Priestly affirmations of God's designs for a "very good" world are augmented by close attention to specific linguistic links between the two. The Prologue identifies Job as "blameless" (*tām*, 1:1, 8; 2:3; cf. 8:20; 9:20, 21, 22). The word occurs in a variety of contexts, but given the story that unfolds, especially Job's complaint that God intends to "slash open" his body and pour out his blood (16:13, 18), it is hard to overlook the fact that one of the principal referents for *tāmîm*, a derivative from the same root as *tām*, is the sacrificial victim that must be "unblemished" when presented on the altar.[16] The drama of the story rests on the presenting report that Job's "blamelessness" – morally, ethically, and perhaps also ritually construed – inexplicably targets him as a victim suitable for sacrifice.

The Prologue and Epilogue frame the story by reporting that Job offers sacrifice. Job 1:5 describes his presentation of "burnt offerings" (*'ōlôt*) as a preemptive propitiation for any inadvertent sins his children may have committed. Job 42:8 reports that Job receives the "burnt offering" (*'ōlâ*) presented by his friends, who require his prayer of intercession, if God is to forgive their wrongdoings.[17] Commentators rightly note that these reports of sacrifice do not envision Job as a cultic official in a formal ritual setting;[18] he acts instead in accord with conventional patriarchal practice as head of the family (cf. Gen 8:20; 22:2, 13; 31:54; 46:1). N. Habel, has noted, however, that in his role as a devout mediator for the household, Job "plays the part of the perfect priest."[19] The Prologue describes two scenes in the heavenly council that involve

---

16   The word *tāmîm*, "unblemished," occurs approximately 40 times in Priestly texts, predominantly in cultic regulations concerning sacrifices (e.g. Lev 22:19; Num 19:2; Ezek 43:22–23). I am instructed and cautioned by D. R. Magary's observation that the semantic association between *tām* and *tāmîm* is more suggestive than exact (D. R. Magary, "Response to Balentine," *Ex Aud* 18 (2002)), 54.

17   On the Priestly regulations for the "burnt offering" (*'ōlâ*) see Lev 1:1–17.

18   Note, e.g., Clines (*Job 1–20*, 16): "the story's setting in time and place lies beyond the horizon of priestly law." For a more categorical dismissal of any connection between Job and Priestly rituals, see the comment of J. Fichtner (*Die Altorientalische Weisheit in iher Israelitisch-Jüdischen Ausprägung* [Giessen: Töpelmann, 1933], 42): "Der Kult spielt [...] für das Hiobbuch keine Rolle."

19   N. Habel, *The Book of Job* (Old Testament Library; Philadelphia: Westminster, 1985), 88; cf. J. Hartley, *The Book of Job* (New International Commentary on the Old Testament; Grand Rapids, MI: Eerdmans, 1988), 69–70. The *Testament of Job* embellishes Job's concern for proper sacrifice. *T. Job* 2–5 reports that Job was concerned about the burnt offerings being offered at a near-by "idol's temple." When he learns from an angel that the temple belongs to Satan, Job asks for permission to destroy it. The angel grants permission but warns Job in advance that if he does so, then he will have to endure Satan's wrath as the price for his

JOB AND THE PRIESTS 141

conversations between God and the satan concerning Job's fate (1:6–12; 2:1–6).[20] The first scene, which reports the destruction of Job's property and his children, segues to Job's initial response. He tears his clothes and shaves his head (1:20), the latter, especially, a ritual gesture of mourning[21] (cf. Isa 15:2; 22:12; Jer 7:29; 16:6; Ezek 7:18; Amos 8:10; Mic 1:16), then gives audible expression to his worship by using a conventional liturgical formula of blessing: "Blessed be the name of the Lord" (1:21; cf. Ps 113:2).[22] Job's friends enact similar rituals

---

     ultimate victory. According to this account, Job's afflictions are a direct result of his having put an end to idolatrous sacrifice.

20   The dialogue between God and the Satan in Job 1–2 is the only recorded conversation between these two in the Old Testament. The report in Zech 3:1–10 invites close comparison (for the conceptual parallels with Job 1–2, see N. Tidwell, "Wa'omar (Zech 3:5) and the Genre of Zechariah's Fourth Vision," JBL 94 (1975), 343–55). When Zechariah looks into the heavenly council, he sees three figures: an angel of the Lord, the satan, and Joshua, the high priest. Joshua's presence indicates that on this occasion it is *the priest's* piety that merits scrutiny. The Satan has evidently raised charges against the priest. The charges are not recorded here, but we may speculate that they concern Joshua's fitness as a priest, perhaps including the accusation that because Joshua was born and has lived in an unclean land (Babylon), he is unclean, thus unworthy of administering priestly rituals (cf. D. Petersen, *Haggai and Zechariah 1–8* [Old Testament Library; Philadelphia: Westminster, 1984], 195). That Joshua stands in the council "dressed with filthy clothes" (Zech 3:3), suggests that whatever the specific cause of concern, he is associated with uncleanness.

     God rejects the satan's allegations against Joshua and replaces his filthy clothes with ornate robes that evoke the regalia won by the high priest in his ordination ceremony (see Exod 29 and Lev 8) and on the Day of Atonement (Lev 16). One term of Joshua's apparel – his turban (*ṣānîp*) – is singled out for special mention. The term is not the usual one for a priestly turban (*miṣnepet*; e.g., Exod 34:28; Lev 8:9), although it comes from the same root and is clearly related to this garment. It is instructive to consider that the only other occurrence of this term is with reference to Job. In his final speech before God appears, Job reasserts his "integrity" (*tummātî*, 31:6; cf. Job 2:3, 9; 27:5) by claiming that he has faithfully responded to the cries for help from the poor and afflicted by clothing himself with righteousness and justice, "like a robe and turban" (*ṣānîp*, Job 29:14). For the details in support of this argument, see Balentine, "My Servant Job Will Pray for You," 34–35, 37–38; *Job*, 441–42.

21   See, e.g., G. A. Anderson, *A Time to Mourn, a Time to Dance: The Experience of Grief and Joy in Israelite Religion* (University Park, PA: Pennsylvania State University Press, 1991); Xuan Huong Thi Pham, *Mourning in the Ancient Near East and the Hebrew Bible* (JSOTSup 302; Sheffield: Sheffield Academic Press, 1999); S. Olyan, *Biblical Mourning: Ritual and Social Dimensions* (Oxford: Oxford University Press, 2004). In an unpublished paper ("The Meaning of Mourning in the Book of Job," presented at the Society of Biblical Literature International Meeting 2011, London), H. Thomas suggests that understanding the function of mourning rituals is an important hermeneutical lens for interpreting all major sections of the book of Job. I am grateful to Professor Thomas for sharing with me a copy of this paper.

22   Clines, *Job 1–20*, 39.

in Job 2:12, although in this case the seven days and seven nights of silence evoke the traditional time for mourning the dead, not the living (cf. Gen 50:10; 1 Sam 31:3; Sir 22:12).

The second heavenly council scene concludes with God permitting the satan to afflict Job with "loathsome sores" (2:7) that cover his body from head to toe. The term that describes Job's condition is *šĕhîn*, one of the terms Leviticus uses to describe the seven skin diseases the priest is empowered to address (Lev 13:18–23). Job's affliction thus suggestively identifies him with those whose uncleanness requires priestly rituals for relief and restoration. Levitical instructions for the priest are typically quite detailed and complex (Lev 13–14), but one salient issue merits attention. Leviticus 13–14 repeatedly locates skin disease on a spectrum of what makes a person ritually "clean" (*ṭāher*) or "unclean" (*ṭāmē*). To be "clean" is to be whole, without bodily blemish, thus to be holy and acceptable for communion with God. To be "unclean" is to be ritually unfit for participating in the cult. Leviticus 13–14 does not, however, use the word "sin" to describe physical blemishes, nor does it stipulate confession of sin as a prerequisite for the afflicted person's restoration to full participation in the cultic activities of the community. Instead, Lev 14 outlines an eight-day process by which the afflicted can be ritually cleansed and declared ready to reenter the sanctuary. Outside Leviticus, it is true that skin disease is associated with God's wrath and punishment. The parade examples are Miriam (Num 12:1–5), Gehazi (2 Kgs 5:25–27), and Uzziah (2 Chr 26:16–21), which likely reflect the view, widespread in the ancient Near East and in Israel, that skin disease can be a telling indicator that God is punishing a sinful person. Given the entrenchment of this perspective, it is reasonable to speculate that the author of the Joban dialogues (Job 4–31) strategically portrays Job's friends as staunch advocates of the view that disease equates to divine punishment. Zophar's counsel in Job 11:13–20 is but one telling case in point. *If* Job repents of his iniquity, *then*, Zophar assures him, he "will lift up [his] face [to God] without blemish" (11:15). The word "blemish" (*mum*) occurs only here in Job. Elsewhere, it is predominantly a Priestly term for physical defects that render a priest unfit for approaching the altar (Lev 21:17, 18, 21, 23) or an animal unsuitable for sacrifice (Lev 20:20, 21, 25). One might argue that Zophar uses the term "blemish" in the general sense of moral "shame" or "disgrace" (note Zophar's emphasis on "sin" words, "iniquity" (*ʾawen*) and "wickedness" (*ʿawlâ*) in Job 11:14); nonetheless, his use of this distinctively Priestly term for "blemish" invites reflection on the possibility that he understands Job's putative "sin" to have disfigured him both morally and physically, thus rendering him unfit for entry into the presence of God.

JOB AND THE PRIESTS

Intertextual studies do not typically concern themselves with reception history issues. In this case, however, it is instructive to note that Job has often been depicted as a priest in art and iconography. S. Terrien notes that more than forty statues of "Saint Job the Priest" have been preserved in Belgium, Luxembourg, and the Netherlands.[23] One sixteenth-century statue in the Mayer van der Bergh Museum in Antwerp, for example, shows a seated Job wearing the four-cornered biretta of Roman Catholic priests. Job's right hand is raised in blessing; in his left hand, he holds a chalice, perhaps representing the offering of the Eucharist (see Figure 6.2, "Saint Job as Priest").[24] A fourteenth-century statue located in the Church of Saint Martin in Wezemaal, a small village in the former duchy of Brabant that became the center for the "Cult of Saint Job," merits special attention (See Figure 6.1, "Saint Job as Priest"). From the mid-fifteenth to the mid-sixteenth centuries, pilgrims made the journey to the Church of Saint Martin, where the main object of devotion was a statue depicting Job, dressed in a full-length robe and wearing a hat with earflaps, perhaps, as Terrien speculates, resembling the Phrygian cap worn by the priests of Mithras, the Persian god of light and wisdom.[25] In his right hand, Job holds a placard that says in Flemish "The Lord gives and the Lord takes away" (Job 1:21); in his left hand, he holds what appears to be a fiery chalice or the Host of the Eucharist.[26] From 1450–1550 pilgrim badges were struck for those making the journey to Wezemaal. Of the 25 extant badges, the oldest (c. 1450) represents a priestly Job offering the sacrament of communion by which all those afflicted may be healed and reunited in the fellowship of the saints.

---

23   S. Terrien, *The Iconography of Job Through the Centuries* (University Park, PA: Pennsylvania State University Press, 1996), 149–56.

24   For the image and discussion, see ibid., 149–50, 151 Fig. 82.

25   Ibid., 149. For the image, see 150 Fig. 81.

26   B. Minnen, "Le Cult de Saint Job à Wezemaal aus XV et XVI Siècles," in *Actes des VII Congrès l'Association des Circles Francophones D'Histoire et de Belgique et LIV Congrès de la Féderation des Circles d'Archéologie et d'Histoire de Belgigue* (2007), 603–9. A comprehensive, two-volume, multidisciplinary study of the "Cult of Saint Job" at Wezemaal is forthcoming (B. Minnen, *De Sint-Martinuskerk van Wezemaal en de cultus van Sint Job 1000–2000* (Averbode: Altiora), including an English summary by Minnen ("'Den heyligen Sant al in Brabant.' The Church of St. Martin in Wezemaal and the Devotion to St. Job 1000–2000. Retrospective: The Fluctuations of Devotion"). I am grateful to be able to draw upon personal correspondence with Bart Minnen over many years and to have been able to review an advance copy of his contributions to this publication.

144   CHAPTER 7

2   Concluding Reflections: "He Leads Priests Away Stripped"

I linger over Job's complaint, referenced at the beginning of this essay
(Job 12:19). Setting aside the question of whether the Joban author is intentionally engaging with antecedent Priestly traditions, which I argue must be
suspended until further evidence is available, important hermeneutical issues
continue to press my thinking. On a first reading, Job is clearly protesting God's
banishment of the priests from his world. A world stripped of the understanding and wisdom conveyed by its leaders is a world in which a "just and blameless man" becomes a "laughing-stock" (12:4). It is a world where chaos reigns,
where the wise are mocked, and the innocent condemned; where the strong
become weak and the weak become weaker. In short, it is a world where there
is no difference between light and darkness (Job 12:22). Worst still, from Job's
perspective, the agent of such caprice in his world is none other than God. For
reasons beyond Job's comprehension, God has decided that the priests no longer serve a sufficiently useful purpose to remain in his world. On a first reading,
Job laments and protests the removal of the priests, presumably because he
believes his world is the poorer without them.

On second reading, one may wonder whether the priests in Job's world have
in fact failed, not only in God's estimation but also perhaps in Job's, and thus
have brought their demise upon themselves. The "priestly" Job in the Prologue–
Epilogue seems resolutely committed to the efficacy of the sacrifices, prayers,
and rituals that define religious behavior from a cultic perspective. The Job of
the dialogues, however, seems equally resolute in rejecting the counsel of his
friends, erstwhile advocates for the cultic system that has now failed him, and
perhaps, also betrayed God. On this reading, one wonders if Job's words in 12:19
are freighted with irony. Job's protests against God's abusive power, here and
throughout the dialogues, cannot be effectively muted; nonetheless, it is fair to
say that the friends are portrayed, minimally, as exceedingly poor representatives of a Priestly system that may, nonetheless, be worth saving. The intertextual connections between Job and Priestly traditions accentuate these issues
by complicating them.

Whether reading backwards from Job to Priestly antecedents, reading Job
and Priestly traditions synchronically, or reading forward, toward post-biblical
interpretation by "common" readers,[27] such as artists, there are substantial

---

27   I borrow the term "common" reader from C. Ozick ("The Impious Impatience of Job," in
      C. Ozick, *Quarrel and Quandary* [New York: Alfred A. Knopf, 2000], 59–73). She writes:
      "[T]he striking discoveries of scholars – whether through philological evidences or
      through the detection of infusion from surrounding cultures – will not deeply unsettle

JOB AND THE PRIESTS

reasons for considering Job's priestly profile. The cumulative evidence, based not only on the Prologue – Epilogue, which has been accented here, but also on the emerging work on the poetic dialogues and the divine speeches, suggests that investigation of the book of Job's interaction with, its critique and transformation of, "the Priestly theodicy"[28] is a project awaiting full exposition.

the common reader. We are driven – we common readers – to approach Job's story with tremulous palms held upward and unladen" (59).

28 J. Milgrom (*Leviticus 1–16* [Anchor Bible; New York: Doubleday, 1991], 260) argues that one of the pillars of "Priestly theodicy" is the belief that humans need have no fear of demonic deities that create evil. There is but one creature in the world with "demonic" power, and that is the human being, whose God-given free will has the capacity for evil that not only defies God but also potentially drives God out of the sanctuary. The proposed Priestly remedy for this situation is the cultic procedure, specifically the sacrificial offerings that atone for people's sinful behavior. A cultic remedy for suffering that God permits "for no reason" is unavailable to Job. Whether sacrifice, repentance, or other cultic remedies can be stretched or sufficiently transformed to address innocent suffering, or whether the entire Priestly system of thought will collapse like a house of cards under its weight, is a major question raised by an intertextual reading of Job and Priestly traditions.

CHAPTER 8

"My Servant Job Shall Pray for You"

After forty-two chapters and 1,059 verses, the epilogue brings the book of Job to a vexed and vexing conclusion with these words:

> After the Lord had spoken these words to Job, the Lord said to Eliphaz the Temanite: "My wrath is kindled against you and your two friends; for you have not spoken of me what is right, as my servant Job has. Now therefore take seven bulls and seven rams, and go to my servant Job, and offer for yourselves a burnt offering; and my servant Job shall pray for you, for I will accept his prayer not to deal with you according to your folly; for you have not spoken of me what is right, as my servant Job has done." So Eliphaz the Temanite and Bildad the Shuhite and Zophar the Naamathite went and did what the Lord had told them; and the Lord accepted Job's prayer. And the Lord restored the fortunes of Job when he had prayed for his friends; and the Lord gave Job twice as much as he had before.
>
> Job 42:7–10

"My servant Job shall pray for you." The question I wish to pose for this essay is: What does Job say when he prays? The text does not record the words of Job's prayer. Instead, it leads up to the edge of the prayer then skips over it to report that "when he had prayed" the Lord restores Job's fortunes. My objective is to go inside the gaps of this report and reflect on what the narrator has not provided. When Job addresses the Almighty in prayer, what does he say?

At first blush, this question may seem unnecessary, even unworthy. The epilogue actually seems pretty straightforward. The friends *have not* spoken the truth about God, and God is angry. Job *has* spoken the truth about God, and it will take Job's prayer to make things right for the friends with God. All the signs indicate that Job prays a conventional prayer of intercession for his friends, perhaps something like this: "O Lord, forgive the friends, do not deal with them according to their foolishness."[1]

I find this conventional interpretation plausible, even instructive, but ultimately unsatisfying. For the last several years, I have been writing a commentary on the book of Job, hence I have been living in Job's world. The longer I

---

1   See, for example, J. Gerald Janzen, *Job* (Atlanta: John Knox, 1985), 266; James A. Wharton, *Job* (Louisville: Westminster John Knox, 1999), 179.

© SAMUEL E. BALENTINE, 2021 | DOI:10.1163/9789004459212_009

sit with Job on the ash heap, the more difficult it becomes for me to believe that there is anything conventional about what he thinks and says about God. I share the suspicions of Virginia Wolff, who wrote in 1922 to her friend Lady Robert Cecil saying, "I read the Book of Job last night. I don't think God comes well out of it." Even if Job prayed for the forgiveness of his friends, and even if God accepted Job's prayer, I am not sure this offers an unqualified commendation of the One who targeted Job for destruction "for no reason" (Job 2:3; compare 1:9).

I find myself wondering if Job's prayer has more than a conventional meaning in the book of Job. Could it be that, in his role as intercessor, Job might be praying *for God* as much as *for the friends*? From Job's perspective – at least as presented through much of the book we now have – both the friends and God seem to need someone to pray for them, for none of them seems able or willing to understand what Job is saying. Perhaps when Job stands in the gap between God and these misguided comforters he is implicitly modeling for them all the fundamental prerequisite of loyal companionship that he has relentlessly sought but not found for himself. As Job puts it in his first response to Eliphaz, "The despairing need loyalty from a friend, even if they forsake the fear of the Almighty" (6:14). Could it be that both God and the friends need the loyalty of one like Job if they are to live fully into their true identities? The epilogue suggests that if Job does not pray the friends will be doomed. And if Job does not pray, the epilogue hints that God might exact a judgment that is incongruent with divine justice and mercy. In short, the friends are wrong, but they are worth praying for. God is angry, but God can be persuaded to check the anger, *if* someone like Job prays. God, too, it seems is worth praying for.

To make my case, I begin with the conventional view of Job's intercession, which I judge to be both true to the text and heuristic for the community of faith. Indeed, it is only when we take this reading seriously that we begin to sense that Job's prayer may invite different possibilities. It is these other, nonconventional possibilities that I examine in the second part of the essay. By juxtaposing the conventional and the nonconventional, we may be able to draw some tentative conclusions about what it means when this vexing text ends by saying, "My servant Job shall pray for you."

1 The Conventional and Salutary View of Job as Intercessor

The epilogue (Job 42:7–17) clearly intends to return us to the prologue (Job 1–2) and to the idyllic, preholocaust world of Uz described by the narrator of the book. In that world, Job is an unparalleled exemplar of virtue and faith. By

148   CHAPTER 8

God's own assessment, "there is no one like him in all the earth" (1:8). This assessment is justified by the threefold affirmation of Job (once by the narrator [1:1] and twice by God [1:8; 2:3]) as a "blameless and upright man who fears God and turns away from evil." Job's exemplary status is confirmed by his full family and his contingent of servants and possessions (1:2–3). Moreover, we learn that it was Job's custom to offer preemptory sacrifices on behalf of his children, just in case they had unwittingly sinned and "cursed God in their hearts" (1:4–5). In all these ways, the prologue depicts Job as a unique human being. Not since Adam has there been one who has so fully received and so fully realized the creational commission to "be fruitful and multiply" and to have "dominion" over that which has been entrusted to him (compare Gen 1:22, 28).

When the bottom falls out of Job's world, and he suffers the loss of his wealth, his possessions, and his family, Job heroically maintains his devotion to God. He raises no questions; he offers no resistance or protest; he admits no doubt or uncertainty. Instead, he remains persistently reverent before and submissive to the inscrutable will of God. He appropriates a traditional theological assertion – "The Lord gave and the Lord has taken away; blessed be the name of the Lord" (1:21) – and when urged by his wife to curse God, he dismisses her and her suggestion as foolish and unworthy of him and his God (2:9–10).

In the prologue's last frame (2:11–13), the three friends come to "comfort and console" Job. In the original folktale, what the friends say has been displaced by what now constitutes the poetic dialogues in Chapters 3–27. God's rebuke of the friends in the epilogue – "[Y]ou have not spoken of me what is right" (42:7, 8) – suggests that the friends spoke disparagingly of God and urged Job to curse God, counsel that Job steadfastly refused to follow.

The epilogue provides a reasonable and faith-affirming conclusion. Once again, the narrator invites us to focus on Job, now identified no less than four times as God's "servant" (42:7–9; compare 1:8; 2:3). Once again, we see Job acting out his piety on behalf of others. Whereas in the prologue Job offers preemptory sacrifices that spare his children from the consequences of inadvertent sin, now he offers a preemptory prayer upon the receipt of his friends' sacrifice (42:8) that spares them from God's judgment.

In the aftermath of his prayer, Job is restored and blessed by God. He leaves the ash heap (2:8) and returns to his "house" (42:11). He leaves behind the alienation imposed by suffering and resumes the joyful fellowship with family and acquaintances (42:11). His possessions are returned to him twofold (42:12; compare 1:3). His family is restored with the birth of ten children, seven sons, and three daughters (42:13–15). Job's doubly blessed life enables him to see four generations of his progeny. After 140 years of postcatastrophe life (42:16), twice the normal lifespan (compare Ps 90:10), Job dies "old and full of days" (42:17), an

"MY SERVANT JOB SHALL PRAY FOR YOU"

epitaph that links him with the memory of some of Israel's revered ancestors, most notably Abraham (Gen 25:8) and Isaac (Gen 25:29; compare 1 Chr 29:28 [David] and 2 Chr 24:15 [Jehoiada the priest]).

There can be little doubt that the Job of the prologue and epilogue – the selfless intercessor who prays for the forgiveness of those who wrongfully abuse him – is deeply rooted in both Jewish and Christian piety.[2] Moreover, we may suppose that this portrait of Job has played a (largely) positive role both socially and religiously in societies that tell this story.[3] On religious grounds, the conventional view of the saintly Job endorses a simple piety, an unquestioning belief in God's control of the world, and, by extension, a satisfying and full participation in the religious establishment that promotes itself as the institutional incarnation of God's will on earth. For Christians, the image of the saintly Job has the added attraction of positioning Job as a forerunner of Christ, whose prayer from the cross – "Father, forgive them; for they do not know what they are doing" (Luke 23:34; compare Stephen's prayer in Acts 7:60) – offers the ultimate Joban model for how to be faithful and forgiving in the midst of undeserved adversity.

On social grounds, the saintly Job promotes obedience over rebellion, conformity over agitation, tolerance over rigid adherence to nonnegotiable principles of justice. In short, this story promotes and encourages a stable society, where God is in the heavens and all is well, or at least tolerable, on earth. The governing principle behind this theology/ideology is famously articulated in the interchange between Shakespeare's widow of Florence and Helena:

> Widow: Lord, how we lose our pains!
> Helena: All's well that ends well yet,
>   Though time seem so adverse and means unfit.
> *All's Well That Ends Well*, Act 5, Scene 1, 24–26

We may also note that artists have added their own imaginative "exegesis" to this portrait of Job as a saintly, Christlike intercessor. By way of example, I offer one image for consideration.

Taddeo Gaddi (1300–1366) was perhaps the most distinguished pupil of the Florentine painter Giotto. This fresco of Job praying for his friends, painted

---

2   For a brief survey of the interpretation of the Joban folk tale in Jewish, Christian, and Muslim literary traditions, see Nahum N. Glatzer, ed., *The Dimensions of Job* (New York: Schocken, 1969), 12–16.

3   Cf. David Penchansky, *The Betrayal of God: Ideological Conflict in Job* (Louisville: Westminster/ John Knox, 1990), 30–34.

FIGURE 8.1 Taddeo Gaddi (1300–1366). "Job Intercedes for his Friends," (1355). Fresco Camposanto Monumentali di Pisa Archivio Fotographico Opera Primaziale Pisana
CREDIT: SAMUEL E. BALENTINE, PERSONAL PHOTOGRAPH

circa 1355, is one of a dozen panels depicting scenes from the book of Job that once adorned the peristyle of the Camposanto in Pisa.[4]

---

4 The Camposanto Monumentale (Monumental Churchyard), along with the Cathedral, the Baptistry, and the Bell Tower (more popularly known as the "Leaning Tower") comprise the four grand structures of the famous cathedral square in Pisa. Begun in 1278 under the direction of Giovanni di Simoni, the Camposanto was designed to gather in one place all the graves scattered around the cathedral. Until it was badly damaged in the bombing raids of 1944, it also provided one of Italy's richest galleries of medieval painting and sculpture. Of Gaddi's Joban frescoes, this one, now partially restored and relocated, is one of three still available for viewing. For discussion, see Samuel L. Terrien, *The Iconography of Job Through*

"MY SERVANT JOB SHALL PRAY FOR YOU" 151

Gaddi depicts a restored Job, kneeling in prayer before his friends. Consonant with the account in the *Testament of Job*, which identifies the biblical hero with Jobab, "the king of all Egypt" (28:7; compare LXX Job 42:17b–e), Gaddi paints Job as a royal figure. Behind him is an ornate chair, canopied with a palatial edifice that calls to mind a royal chamber. At the base of the throne, to Job's right, is his royal crown. But for Gaddi, as for many artists of the Middle Ages, Job is no ordinary king, and his righteousness is far from commonplace. Painted into this scene are a number of symbols that link Job to the royalty and righteousness of Christ. To Job's left, resting on the folds of his garment, is a skull, an allegorical reminder of the skull of Adam, which, according to medieval legend, was buried at the foot of the cross of Christ. In front of Job is a crown of thorns alongside what appears to be an instrument of torture, both symbols of Jesus in his passion. Combining sacred Scripture and artistic imagination, Gaddi has created a Job who is no longer defined solely by the words of holy writ. When this Job prays for his friends, he steps off the pages of Scripture and into the lives of those who now stand before his uplifted hands.

When Gaddi painted this Job in the fourteenth century, the world of Pisa and Tuscany had been turned upside down.[5] In its own way, Pisa was an analogue for Uz, the setting for the biblical Job's story. In the first half of the century, Pisa and the cities of Tuscany had enjoyed unprecedented prosperity. But in 1346 and 1347, bad weather conditions began to reduce harvest and produce famines. In 1348, a bubonic plague known as the Black Death arrived in Sicily and quickly spread inland, ultimately killing between a third and a half of the population in many urban areas, including the Tuscany cities of Florence and Siena. As personal incomes plummeted and tax revenues grew increasingly scarce, marauding mercenaries began to harass survivors by raiding their homes and destroying their families. In such a world as this, where prosperity had vanished for reasons beyond control and the graveyards were full of righteous victims, Gaddi saw Job's Christlike intercession as reason to hope that the future might be redeemed.

---

the Centuries: Artists as Biblical Interpreters (University Park: Pennsylvania State University Press, 1996), 92–6, Figures 45–48. See further, Mario Bucci, "Storie di Giobbe: Taddeo Gaddi," in *Camposanto monumentale di Pisa* (Pisa: Opera della Primaziale, 1970), 93–102, Plates 85–98.

5   For discussion of the relationship between Italian art produced between 1350 and 1500 and the religious, political, and social culture, see Evelyn S. Welch, *Art and Society in Italy, 1350–1500* (Oxford: Oxford University Press, 1997).

152   CHAPTER 8

2   The Nonconventional and Salutary View of Job as Intercessor

Athalya Brenner speaks for many commentators when she observes that although the Job of the prologue and epilogue is "positively saintly," his conduct forces us to wonder if he is altogether "human."[6] Once Job loses everything "for no reason," we would expect a normal person, regardless of piety and devotion, to protest and complain, to despair and grow weary of faith affirmations that seem so utterly disconnected to life's experiences. The Job of the prologue and epilogue does none of these things.

The Job who speaks from the ash heap in Chapters 3–31 models a very different kind of piety. This Job curses and laments. He protests the injustice of his plight and the injustice of the God who sanctions and sustains it "for no reason." He rejects his friends' suggestion that he is guilty, insisting instead that his innocence shifts the burden of guilt to God. If we take the portrait of this Job seriously, we might well restate Brenner's concern by saying that he is indeed fully human, *but is he saintly*? It is, of course, this portrait of Job as rebel that the epilogue seems to dismiss or correct. Or does it? I submit that a number of clues invite a different understanding.

First, the epilogue begins by referring not to Job's but to God's last words.[7] No matter who has supplied this epilogue, whether it is the same author of the poetic dialogues or a different one, the statement "After *the Lord* had spoken these words to Job" (42:7) directs us not to Job's so-called confession in 42:1–6 but instead to God's beguiling revelation in 38:1–40:34. In the whirlwind speeches, God twice challenges Job to gird up his loins like a *geber* (38:3; 40:7), to prepare himself, like a "mighty man" or "warrior," for a valiant encounter with a strong opponent. In the first speech, God offers Job a vision of the cosmic boundaries of creation (38:4–18: earth, sea, heaven, underworld), coupled with a discourse on five groups of paired animals (38:39–39:30). God makes no reference in this survey of the animals to human beings, a telling omission that may be interpreted as a strategic subversion of Job's presumptive claim to a special place of importance in creation's order. When Job initially responds by placing his hand over his mouth and withdrawing in silence (40:3–5), it appears that God's speech has accomplished its objective. Job will not continue to contest the God whose creational design renders his personal misfortune comparatively insignificant.

---

6   Athalya Brenner, "Job the Pious? The Characterization of Job in the Narrative Framework of the Book," *JSOT* 43 (1989), 44.

7   So also Edwin M. Good, *In Turns of Tempest: A Reading of Job, with a Translation* (Stanford: Stanford University Press, 1990), 380.

"MY SERVANT JOB SHALL PRAY FOR YOU" 153

When God presses on with a second speech (40:6–41:34; MT 40:6–41: 26), however, and again challenges Job to act like a *geber*, it appears that God desires something more than silence from his servant. God now challenges Job to act like a king. He is to put on the regalia of "glory and honor" (40:10: *hôd wĕhādār*) and participate in a governance of the world that joins him by commitment and practice to a dominion that images God's own.[8] On the heels of this challenge, God summons Job to focus specifically on a sixth and final pair of animals: Behemoth and Leviathan.

The presentation here is intricate and finely nuanced.[9] For my purposes, it is sufficient simply to note that from God's perspective Behemoth and Leviathan are figures of strength, pride, and dominion. They are *celebrated – not condemned* – as creatures that are the near equals of God. Both are subject to confrontation and assault, and both are vulnerable to God's control, but neither will relinquish its identity or abandon its creaturely responsibilities. If the river Jordan should burst forth against Behemoth, it will trust that its own resources are sufficient to withstand the assault (40:23). If Leviathan should ever be captured and forcibly domesticated, it would not make a "covenant" with its master that required it to plead for mercy or speak "soft words" (41:3–4; MT 40:27–28). In short, Behemoth and Leviathan show Job something important about God's design for creaturely existence. The "poetic logic" of the book hints that Job is to gird his loins with the strength, pride, and fearless dominion of a Behemoth and Leviathan.

I seem to have at least one kindred spirit in the artist who painted this suggestive miniature for an eighth-century Greek codex of the book of Job, which has been preserved in the Saint John Monastery on Patmos.[10]

---

8   Compare the similar and suggestive celebration by the psalmist of being "crowned with glory and honor" that enables a dominion comparable to God's own:

"Yet you have made them [human beings] a little lower than God,
    and crowned them with glory and honor (*kābōd wĕhādār*).
You have given them dominion of the works of your hand;
    you have put all things under their feet." (Ps 8:5–6; MT 8:6–7)

On the rhetorical links between Job and Psalm 8, see Michael Fishbane, *Biblical Interpretation in Ancient Israel* (Oxford: Clarendon, 1985), 285–286; idem, "The Book of Job and Inner-biblical Discourse," in *The Voice from the Whirlwind: Interpreting the Book of Job*, eds. Leo G. Perdue and W. Clark Gilpin (Nashville: Abingdon, 1992), 87–90. I have explored these connections in more depth in "'What Are Human Beings, That You Make So Much of Them?' Divine Disclosure From the Whirlwind: 'Look at Behemoth,'" in *God in the Fray: A Tribute to Walter Brueggemann*, eds. Tod Linafelt and Timothy K. Beal (Minneapolis: Fortress, 1998), 259–278.

9   For further discussion, see Balentine, "'What Are Human Beings?'" especially pp. 264–274.

10   For discussion, see Terrien, *Iconography of Job*, 37–40.

FIGURE 8.2
"Job Prepares to Fight." 9th c. Illumination.
Saint John Monastery, Patmos
CREDIT: BIBILOTHEQUE DU
MONASTERE ST. JEAN LE THEOLOGIEN,
PATMOS

Dressed in ceremonial robes, Job takes his stand before the God who has twice summoned him to "gird up his loins." The force with which God confronts Job is symbolized by the cords of his belt and the drapes of his robe, both blown sideways by the hurricane-like speech of God. Job's head and neck are twisted backward, and the profile of his face, which has been partially damaged, signals that he is contemplating either a voluntary or forced retreat. But we may also note a hint of defiance in his posture. His feet are firmly planted. His knees are flexed, as if he is bracing himself to lean into the very power that threatens to blow him away. His hands are clasped firmly on his belt. This dramatic rendering nicely captures the moment of decision for Job at the end of God's second speech. Will Job advance or retreat? Will he contend with God or submit to God? This Job contemplates both alternatives, but his posture invites us to imagine that with his next move he will take a combative and dangerous step in God's direction.

Second, the epilogue suggests that God instructs Job to act as an *intercessor* for his friends, that is, he is to stand between them and God and arbitrate the different perspectives they represent. Because intercessors are third-party mediators, God's instructions to Job invite reflection on other places in the Joban drama where the idea of intercession or mediation occurs. Four such occurrences merit consideration. In 9:33, Job, recognizing that God is no ordinary litigant who can be summoned to trial by a mere mortal (v. 32), imagines that there might be an impartial "arbiter" (*môkîaḥ*; NRSV: "umpire") who can negate the inequalities between him and God.[11] At this point in the drama,

---

11   Elsewhere in the Hebrew Bible, the *môkîaḥ* is often a third-party mediator who listens to disputes between two persons and offers a judgment that both accept as appropriate (compare Gen 31:37) For the full range of usage, see *The Dictionary of Classical Hebrew*, eds. David J. A. Clines and John Elwolde (Sheffield: Sheffield Academic Press, 1998), 4: 209–210.

"MY SERVANT JOB SHALL PRAY FOR YOU"   155

Job despairs that there is no such *môkîaḥ* for him, and he dismisses the idea as impossible.

In 16:19, Job hopes for a heavenly "witness" (*'ēd*) who would take his side in God's court and give testimony to the truth of his claim.[12] On this occasion, Job summons the earth not to cover up the evidence of his blood, which cries out for justice with the same claim on God as Abel's blood after his murder by Cain (Job 16:18; compare Gen 4:8–10), and he states emphatically his purchase on that claim, "[E]ven now, in fact, my witness is in heaven." Yet here, too, Job despairs that there is no such witness for him.

In 19:25, Job returns for a third time to the idea that someone, a "redeemer," a *gō'ēl*, will come to his defense against God and the friends. Job "knows" that his redeemer lives, and he knows that at some future time "he will stand upon the earth." Job's defense attorney is no more precisely defined than is the *śāṭān* who serves as God's prosecutor in the prologue. What is clear, however, is that for the first time Job does not dismiss the idea out of hand or express it with caution. What is of most concern to Job is *when* his *gō'ēl* will appear. He lives in the tensive interim between the present, when he concedes that "there is no justice" (19:7), and some undisclosed future time, when "at the last" (19:25) "there is a judgment" (19:29). In between *what is* and *what must be*, Job clings to the desperate belief that someday, somebody will stand in the breach between him and God and be his redeemer.[13]

A fourth occurrence, in 40:2, may be the most telling of all, for here God applies the term *môkîaḥ*, "arbiter," the same word that Job uses in 9:33, to Job himself.[14] Stephen Mitchell deftly captures the sense of God's query to Job: "Has God's accuser resigned? Has my critic [that is, my *môkîaḥ*] swallowed his tongue?"[15] It is common to interpret God's question as a rebuke of Job, but the logic of the divine speeches argues against this.[16] If God seeks to dismiss Job's role as *môkîaḥ* and to compel him to submissive silence instead, then why does God press on past Job's apparent concession in 40:3–5? Moreover, if all God wants Job to understand is that creation's design is too complex and too

---

12   Compare the similar figure in Zech 3:1, described as the "angel of the Lord," who stands at the side of Joshua, the high priest, and successfully defends him before the heavenly court against the baseless charges of the satan (*haśśāṭān*).

13   For further discussion of this famously vexed passage, see Samuel E. Balentine, "Who Will Be Job's Redeemer?" *Perspectives in Religious Studies* 26 (1999), 269–89.

14   Cf. Good, *In Turns of Tempest*, 349; J. William Whedbee, *The Bible and the Comic Vision* (Cambridge: Cambridge University Press, 1998), 240–1.

15   *The Book of Job* (New York: HarperCollins, 1992), 84.

16   For an example of such an interpretation, see the translation proposed by Marvin H. Pope: "Will the contender with Shaddai *yield*? He who reproves God, let him answer for it" (*Job* [Garden City, NY: Doubleday, 1965], 316 [emphasis added]).

156   CHAPTER 8

mysterious for any mortal to contest, then why does God proceed to single out
and celebrate Behemoth and Leviathan as creatures who proudly stand their
ground against creation's forces? Could it be that God actually invites Job to
be a *môkîaḥ*? Could it be that God is challenging Job to be for himself and for
others the *môkîaḥ*, the witness, the *gōʾēl*, that he has longed for but despaired
of finding? I return to the first curiosity that the epilogue presents to us: The
narrator hints that it is *God's* questions to Job, *not Job's* answers to God, that
deserve a response.

There remains, of course, the thorny question of what to do with Job's second response in 42:6, which virtually all commentators understand as the crux
of the book. If, as the conventional interpretation goes, Job ends up saying,
"I despise myself, and repent in dust and ashes" (NRSV), how can this possibly be construed as consonant with the model for the *môkîaḥ* that God has
invited? Conversely, if Job does not repent and conform himself to God's
inscrutable will, how can he be a pray-er whose petitions God will hear and
accept? I believe the key to this conundrum lies in 42:6b.[17] The syntax of the
Hebrew is relatively clear: Job "repents" or "changes his mind *concerning*" dust
and ashes. Job's repentance signifies a reversal or a retraction of a previous
decision or position. It is the meaning of the phrase "dust and ashes" that discloses the object of Job's changed mind.

The phrase "dust and ashes" occurs only three times in biblical Hebrew:
Gen 18:27; Job 30:19; and Job 42:6. In each case, it signifies something about the
human condition in relation to God. In Job 30:19, Job laments that being "dust
and ashes" means that afflicted human beings are consigned to live in a world
where they cry out to God for justice, and God does not answer (30:20). In
Gen 18:27, Abraham, who dares to argue with God concerning justice in Sodom
and Gomorrah, concedes that as a mere creature of "dust and ashes" he has
embarked on a dangerous mission. Abraham's recognition of his status before
God is not dissimilar to Job's, *except that* Abraham persists in questioning God,
and God answers.[18]

These two images of "dust and ashes" lay the foundation for understanding
the third occurrence of the phrase in 42:6. Job has previously concluded that

---

17   For a fuller treatment of this passage, see Balentine, "'What Are Human Beings?'" 274–278.
18   On the postexilic provenance of Gen 18:22–33 and its connections with Job, see Ludwig
      Schmidt, *"De Deo": Studien zur Literarkritik und Theologie des Buches Jona, des Gesprachs
      zwischen Abraham und Jahwe in Gen 18, 22ff. und von Hi I* (Berlin: Walter de Gruyter, 1976),
      131–164. See further, Joseph Blenkinsopp, who notes that these connections were already
      noticed by medieval Jewish commentators ("Abraham and the Righteous of Sodom,"
      Journal of Jewish Studies 33 [1982], 126–127; idem, "The Judge of All the Earth: Theodicy in
      the Midrash on Genesis 18:22–33," *Journal of Jewish Studies* 41 [1990], 1–12).

innocent suffering rendered him mute and submissive before a God who permits neither question nor confrontation. God's disclosures, however, require of Job a new understanding of "dust and ashes." While creaturely existence may entail undeserved suffering, it does not mandate silence and submission. By instructing Job to learn from Behemoth and Leviathan, God discloses that human beings are divinely endowed with power and responsibility for their domains. They are and must be fierce, unbridled contenders for justice, sometimes with God and sometimes against God. As near equals of God, they live in the dangerous intersection between the merely human and the supremely divine. When humans dare to stand with and against God as "dust and ashes," they claim their heritage as faithful descendants of Abraham. Like Abraham, everyone who risks pressing the "Judge of all the earth to do justice" (Gen 18:25) may know that God will not be indifferent to their pleas.

In 42:5, the verse just before his last words in the book, Job says to God, "[N]ow my eye sees you." I suggest that Job's new vision is informed by a new understanding of what it means to be fully and dangerously human. He has learned that human beings may image God not by acquiescing to innocent suffering but by protesting it, contending with the powers that permit or sustain it, and, when necessary, by taking the fight directly to God. Job has learned well the lessons that God gave him in Behemoth and Leviathan. He has despaired that he has no *môkîaḥ*, God has challenged him to act like a *môkîaḥ*. Now he becomes what God has already declared he is. He has found his *môkîaḥ*, and his name is Job.

Artists are often less reticent to defy conventional interpretations than biblical scholars. One example is this twelfth-century illumination from another Greek codex of the book of Job.[19]

Job is standing face-to-face with God. His head is not turned away; instead he fixes his eyes on God's, and the two square off before each other. Job's hands are not raised in the traditional gesture of prayer; instead he raises his right hand and gestures in God's direction with an upturned index finger. Regrettably, the illumination is damaged and does not allow us to see whether Job's mouth is closed or open, but all the signs indicate that he is in the act of speaking directly to God. Job's posture invites reflection on the observation

---

19   Gr. 1231, fol. 419v. Library, Biblioteca Vaticana, Rome. A copy of this manuscript is preserved in the Index of Christian Art. There are four complete copies of the Index: in the Dumbarton Oaks Research Library, Washington, DC (established 1940); in the Biblioteca Vaticana, Rome (established 1951); in the Kunsthistorisch Institut of the Rijksuniversisteit, Utrecht (established 1962); and in the University of California, Los Angeles (established 1964). I am grateful to Dr. Natalia Teteriatnikov of the Dumbarton Oaks Research Library for her conversations with me concerning this manuscript.

FIGURE 8.3
"Job Interrupts God." Vatican Museum, Rome
© BIBLIOTECA APOSTOLICA VATICANA. GR 1231, FOL 19V/WIKIMEDIA COMMONS

by the Hasidic teacher Rabbi Bunam: "A man should carry two stones in his pocket. On one should be inscribed 'I am but dust and ashes.' On the other, 'For my sake the world was created.' And he should use each stone as needed."[20] Job's gestures suggest that he has chosen his stone, and he is prepared now to use it (or hurl it) in a confrontation with God about the justice on which the world depends.

After Job prays, the epilogue turns to the matter of restoration. Job's prayer is the key to discerning who and what is restored and why. First, it is apparent that Job's prayer restores the friends. They have been wrong in what they have said about God, and presumably about Job as well. After they bring their sacrifices to Job, and after he prays for them, the threat of judgment that hangs over their heads is lifted. Although the text provides no details, it leads us to think that the *friends' relationship with God* is different after Job prays.[21]

The text also daringly invites us to think that, after Job prays, *God's relationship with the friends* is different. Before Job prays, God is angry and, according to the text, intent on doing "foolishness" (*nĕbālāh*) with the friends (42:8). The word *nĕbālāh* normally refers to reprehensible acts of shame that subvert accepted ethical norms and bring dishonor and judgment on the perpetrator.[22] The occurrence in 42:8 is the only time in the Old Testament where God is

---

20 Cited in Robert Gordis, *The Book of God and Man: A Study of Job* (Chicago: University of Chicago Press, 1965), 131.
21 Cf. *Testament of Job* 42: 8: "And I took them [the friends' sacrifices] and made an offering on their behalf, and the Lord received it favorably and forgave their sin."
22 Cf. Magne Saebo, "*nabal* fool," in *TLOT*, ed. Ernst Jenni and Claus Westermann (Peabody, MA: Hendrickson, 1997), 2: 712. See further the comments of Samuel Rolles Driver and George Buchanan Gray "[T]he fault of the *nabhal* was not weakness of reason, but moral and religious sensibility, an invincible lack of sense or perception, for the claims of either God or man" (*A Critical and Exegetical Commentary on the Book of Job* [Edinburgh T & T Clark, 1977], 26).

said to be the one doing *nĕbālāh*. The conventional view (for example, in the NRSV) is that the *friends'* foolishness, not *God's*, needs changing or forgiving. A straightforward reading, however, suggests that Job may be praying words like these: "O Lord, do not do anything foolish when you deal with the friends."[23] To judge the friends according to the conventional standards of retributive justice would, in Job's view, subvert and dishonor God's commitment to and passion for forgiveness. Job prays, at God's invitation, and on the other side of his prayer God does not deal foolishly with the friends. In sum, Job's intercession restores *both* the friends *and* God to a relationship that is different than that which existed before Job stepped into the breach between them.[24]

Second, after Job prays, he and his family are also restored, but here too there are at least two subtle clues that Job's restoration is more than simply a return to the status quo for either him or God. Job's possessions are not only restored, they are doubled: "[T]he Lord gave Job twice as much as he had before" (v. 10; compare v. 12). Perhaps the doubling is only a rhetorical flourish designed to bring the epilogue into conformity with the prologue, which lists Job's possessions as evidence for his unparalleled wealth *and* his exemplary character. But it is hard to overlook the connection elsewhere in the Old Testament between double compensation and (at least) a tacit admission of guilt. As Francis I. Andersen observes, calling attention to the legislation in Exod 22:4, "It is a wry touch that the Lord, like any thief who has been found

---

23   Cf. Pope, *Job*, 347, 350–1; Janzen, *Job*, 266; Good, *In Turns of Tempest*, 383. There is a suggestive echo here of Job's rebuke of his wife in 2:10 for "talking like a shameless fool (*hannĕbālôt*)" by urging him to curse God. Just as Job dismisses his wife's counsel as foolishness, so now he appears to be unwilling to accept God's "foolish anger" toward the friends.

24   Robert Frost ("A Masque of Reason," in *The Poetry of Robert Frost*, ed. Edward Connery Lathem [New York: Henry Holt, 1969], 475–476) has imagined that if there had been a post-epilogue Chapter 43 to the book of Job, God might have thanked Job for saving God from "moral bondage" to bad theology:

> "My thanks are to you for releasing me
> From moral bondage to the human race.
> The only free will there was at first was man's,
> Who could do good or evil as he chose.
> I had no choice but I must follow him
> With forfeits and rewards he understood –
> Unless I liked to suffer the loss of worship.
> I had to prosper good and punish evil.
> You changed all that. You set me free to reign,
> You are the Emancipator of your God,
> And as such, I promote you to saint."

160   CHAPTER 8

out (Ex. 22:4), repays Job double what He took from him."[25] We may think of *Job's restoration*, then, as coinciding with, if not effecting, *God's restoration*.

Job is also given a new family of seven sons and three daughters (42:13–15). Again, we might simply take this as another example of the way the epilogue returns the drama to its beginnings. However, the narrator names the daughters, not the sons, and informs us that Job gave them an inheritance along with their brothers. In the conventional world of biblical patriarchy, daughters inherited only when there was no son (Num 26:33; compare 27:1–11; 36:1–12). In the aftermath of his prayer, Job's legacy to his daughters hints that social conventions in the world of Uz will be turned on their end.[26]

3   Concluding Discernments: to Pray ("As My Servant Job Has") or Not to Pray?

If the conventional view of Job's prayer invites the Shakespearean motto "All's well that ends well," the nonconventional view might well resonate with a paraphrase of Hamlet's famous soliloquy:

> To [pray] or not to [pray]. That is the question:
> Whether tis nobler in the mind to suffer
> The slings and arrows of outrageous fortune,

---

25   *Job: An Introduction and Commentary* (Downers Grove, IL: InterVarsity, 1976), 293; cf. Roland E. Murphy, *The Book of Job: A Short Reading* (New York: Paulist, 1999), 102.

26   On the biblical world of patriarchy, which the book of Job assumes and tests, see Carol A. Newsom, "Job," in *The Women's Bible Commentary*, eds. Carol A. Newsom and Sharon H. Ringe (Louisville: Westminster/John Knox, 1992), 133–135. Scholars are divided on whether the inheritance of Job's daughters is truly subversive of patriarchal convention or merely representative of it. See, for example, the contrasting viewpoints on Job 42:10–17 of Dianne Bergant, *Israel's Wisdom Literature: A Liberation-Critical Reading* (Minneapolis: Fortress, 1997); Joan Chittister, *Job's Daughters: Women and Power* (New York: Paulist, 1990); and Ilana Pardes, *Countertraditions in the Bible: A Feminist Approach* (Cambridge: Harvard University Press, 1994), 145–156. I am particularly indebted to the cogent observations of Peter Machinist concerning the prominence given the inheritance of Job's daughters in the *Testament of Job* (Chapters 46–53). He concludes that the *Testament's* explication of the biblical concept of inheritance is an example of the "scripturalization" that characterized concerted efforts made during the Second Temple and later rabbinic periods "to meet the demands of changing social preferences" ("Job's Daughters and Their Inheritance in the Testament of Job and Its Biblical Congeners," in *The Echoes of Many Texts: Reflections on Jewish and Christian Traditions: Essays in Honor of Lou H. Silberman*, eds. William G. Dever and J. Edward Wright [Atlanta: Scholars Press, 1997], 67–80; the quotation is from p. 80).

"MY SERVANT JOB SHALL PRAY FOR YOU"

> Or to take arms against a sea of troubles,
> And by opposing end them?
>> *Hamlet*, Act 3, Scene 1, 56–60

I have suggested that the conventional view of Job's intercession is deeply rooted and positively instructive in Jewish and Christian piety. The question that must be addressed now is: Can the same be said for the nonconventional view? Is there some gain for the community of faith and for the world in which it bears its witness of modeling a Joban way of contending with God on matters of justice? I suggest that there is something not only important but perhaps imperative – for the world *and* for God – in having someone like Job who risks praying like a *môkîaḥ* for a restoration of the afflicted that transforms heaven and earth.

In this connection, I have been mulling over the observation by Jack Miles that after God directs Job's attention to Behemoth and Leviathan, God never again speaks directly to anyone in book of Job.[27] Indeed, after this, God never again speaks directly to anyone in the Tanakh.[28] Why does God not speak again after Job? Might it be that after Job rises up to pray for his friends and for a restoration that goes beyond all the conventional limitations of justice, God is free not to speak, not to intervene? Might it be that God finds in Job someone who images the best of God's hopes and expectations, even when, for whatever inexplicable reasons, God does not or cannot actualize them directly? Might it be that God has in effect staked God's own reputation for justice and righteousness on the possibility that Job will pray as the *môkîaḥ* that God has challenged him to be?[29]

In the wake of Job's prayer, the epilogue invites the reader to return to the prologue, thus to reenter the land of Uz. The landscape is now no longer so

---

27 Jack Miles, *God: A Biography* (New York: Knopf, 1995), 314. Miles neither justifies nor defends this assessment. He presumably regards God's speaking to Eliphaz in the epilogue (42:7–9) as a third-person-narrated report of what God said. In any event, the observation that God speaks for the last time in Job is a provocative beginning point for reflection.

28 Miles draws a fairly negative conclusion from this observation. In his judgment, God does not speak again, because Job has exposed God's own ambiguity, God's "fiend-susceptible side." In his words, "the world still seems more just than unjust, and God still seems more good than bad; yet the pervasive mood, as this extraordinary work ends, is one not of redemption but of [God's] reprieve" (ibid., 328).

29 Cf. Wharton, *Job*, 182: "If God's justice, righteousness, and compassion are evident nowhere else in a morally formless universe, God's own reputation is staked on the possibility that they will nevertheless come to expression in the outraged speech of God's servant Job." From a different perspective, Miles makes a similar probe: "Job turns out to be a more perfect self-image of the Lord than the Lord had planned" (*God*, 404).

idyllic, and the world of Joban faith can now no longer be so simply expressed in the conventional language of piety. With a second-level naïveté, we hear again God's freighted question: "Have you considered my servant Job?" Now we hear words that we may not have been ready for at the beginning: "My servant Job shall pray for you." Now we may dare to imagine that when Job prays everything changes – for all the Jobs of the world, for all the misguided "friends" of Job, and for God, who started the whole drama in the first place.

Elie Wiesel concludes his essay "Job: Our Contemporary" by suggesting that the ending of the book is only an invitation to a new beginning. His way of reading between the lines of this ancient text to find a way to its present claim on us offers a fitting conclusion to this essay:

> Once upon a time, in a faraway land, there lived a legendary man, a just and righteous man who, in his solitude and despair, found the courage to stand up to God. And to force Him to look at His creation. And to speak to those men who sometimes succeed, in spite of Him and of themselves, in achieving triumphs over Him, triumphs that are grave and disquieting.
>
> What remains of Job? A fable? A shadow? Not even a shadow of a shadow. An example, perhaps?[30]

An example. Perhaps? Much depends on whether we are willing to pray with Job and with Job-honed poets like Emily Dickinson, who dare to stand before God and say, "We thank thee, Father, for these strange minds that enamor us *against* thee."[31]

Of course, I could be wrong about Job's prayer. Nevertheless, I take encouragement from T. S. Eliot who, in appraising the incomparable Shakespeare, concluded, "About anyone so great it is probable that we can never be right; and if we are never right, it is better from time to time that we should change our way of being wrong."[32]

---

30   In *Messengers of God: Biblical Portraits and Legends* (New York: Touchstone, 1976), 235.

31   For this quotation, along with discussion of its reflection of Dickinson's poetic penchant for wrestling with God, see Alfred Kazin, *God and the American Writer* (New York: Knopf, 1997), 142–160. The quotation (emphasis added) is from p. 153.

32   Cited in Tryggve N. D. Mettinger, "The God of Job: Avenger, Tyrant, or Victor?" in *The Voice from the Whirlwind: Interpreting the Book of Job*, eds. Leo G. Perdue and W. Clark Gilpin (Nashville: Abingdon, 1992), 39.

PART 4

Traumatizing Job: "God Has Worn Me Out"

∴

CHAPTER 9

"Ask the Animals, and They Will Teach You"

From his opening lament in chapter 3, Job complains that suffering like his must make some claim on God's moral governance of creation. Throughout the first cycle of dialogues, Job's friends evoke the witness of creation, both its evident (8:11–19) and its mysterious truths (11:7–9), in an effort to teach Job that the world is reliably tuned to God's moral sensibilities. Job is not persuaded.

> [A]sk the animals, and they will teach you;
>> the birds of the air, and they will tell you;
> ask the plants of the earth, and they will teach you;
>> and the fish of the sea will declare to you.
> Who among these does not know
>> that the hand of the Lord has done this?
>
>> 12:7–9

Job's rebuttal begs a critical question. Why should he or his friends assume that animals can teach humans anything important about living in God's world?

There is broad consensus that Job extensively appropriates creation imagery, especially in the Prologue–Epilogue, which effectively frames the book as a sequel to the primordial creation accounts in Genesis, and in God's hymnic survey of the cosmos (38:1–40:2; 40:6–41:34), which responds to Job's complaints about creation's injustice in ways both profound and baffling.[1] Less often factored into the discussion, however, are the numerous appeals to the animal world in chapters 3–37 by both Job and his friends.

A survey of these occurrences indicates that the objective is not to produce a comprehensive or systematic taxonomy – as, for example, in Lev 11:2–23 and Deut 14:3–20 – but rather a more random (but not necessarily arbitrary) evocation of various animals that contribute by way of metaphor or suggestive allusion to larger arguments about the world's moral order.[2] Thus, the friends

---

1 For a survey of creation imagery in Job, see Leo G. Perdue, *Wisdom and Creation: The Theology of Wisdom Literature* (Nashville: Abingdon, 1994), 123–192.

2 For discussions focusing primarily on taxonomy, see J. Feliks, *The Animal World of the Bible* (Tel Aviv: Sinai, 1962); Edwin Firmage, "Zoology (Animal Profiles)," *The Anchor Bible Dictionary*, ed. David Noel Freedman, 6 vols. (New York, London: Doubleday, 1992), 6:1119–1167; Richard Whitekettle, "Where the Wild Things Are: Primary Level Taxa in Israelite Zoological Thought," JSOT 93 (2001), 17–37; idem, "All Creatures Great and Small: Intermediate Taxa in Israelite

---

© SAMUEL E. BALENTINE, 2021 | DOI:10.1163/9789004459212_010

166   CHAPTER 9

repeatedly use animals as anecdotal proofs for their claims that God has inscribed the world with the principles of retribution theology, which resolutely affirms that the wicked will be punished (e.g., 4:10–11; 8:14; 11:12; 18:8–10; 20:14, 16; 25:6). Job evokes animals to refute the friends' exegesis of the justice creation promises the innocent (e.g., 7:5, 12; 9:26; 10:16; 13:28; 16:9; 19:6; 21:10–11; 24:2–8; 30:1–8, 29). In sum, both the friends and Job use animals as ciphers for creation's moral order, but in doing so they arrive at very different conclusions. The appeal to creation in 12:7–12 is case in point.

1   Creation's Ambiguous Truths

Job's lesson on creation in 12:7–12 sounds much like the counsel the friends have already offered him (e.g., 8:8–10; 11:8–9).[3] Although he may be simply quoting his friends, it is more likely that he is parodying their conventional thinking, in effect, setting a rhetorical trap by inviting the friends to listen to *his* words and hear how silly *they* sound. The effectiveness of parody depends on its proximity to truth. In this case, both Job and the friends skirt along the edges of two truths that neither has as yet fully discerned.

First, does creation *reveal* truth about God or *conceal* it? Zophar appeals to the farthest boundaries of the cosmos – the heights of the heavens, the depths of Sheol, the width of the earth, the breadth of the sea – in order to teach Job that God's wisdom is beyond every creature's grasp (11:7–9). Job appeals to animals that inhabit the same general boundaries to argue that the truth about God is accessible to all creatures. Both are right, but neither has full clarity on these matters. When Zophar claims that mere mortals can never fully comprehend the mysterious ways by which God governs the universe, he can appeal to a truth widely attested in biblical traditions (e.g., Isa 40:12–14; Prov 30:4;

Zoological Thought," SJOT 16 (2002) 163–183; idem, "Of Mice and Wren: Terminal Level Taxa in Israelite Thought," SJOT 17 (2003), 163–182. For the use of animals in religion and literature, see, E. J. Schochet, *Animal Life in Jewish Traditon: Attitudes and Relationships* (New York: KTAV, 1984); Marie Louise Henry, "Das Tier im religiösen Bewusstsein des alttestamentlichen Menschen," in *Gefährten und Feinde des Menschen: Das Tier in der Lebenwelt des alten Israel*, ed. Bernd Janowski (Neukirchen-Vluyn: Neukirchener, 1993), 20–61; Katherine Dell, "The Use of Animal Imagery in the Psalms and Wisdom Literature of Ancient Israel," SJT 53 (2000) 275–291; Oded Borowski, "Animals in the Literatures of Syria-Palestine," in *A History of the Animal World in the Ancient Near East*, ed. Billie Jean Collins (Leiden: Brill, 2002), 289–306; idem, "Animals in the Religions of Syria-Palestine," in *A History of the Animal World*, 405–424.

3   My discussion of this and other Job texts in this essay draws upon my commentary, *Job* (Smyth and Helwys Bible Commentary; Macon, GA: Smyth and Helwys, 2006).

see also Job 28:21–22). Indeed, God will employ a similar rhetorical strategy when questioning Job's knowledge of creation (38:1–39:40). At the same time, Zophar does not do justice to Job's truth, the supporting evidence for which is also widely attested: God has purposefully created animals as witnesses to the "vital order" of nature (e.g., Isa 1:3; Jer 8:7; Prov 6:6; 27:8; 30:24–28).[4] But if Job is right to argue that even the animals know the truth about creation, he is wrong to assume that what they disclose is clear and simple. The tell-tale clue is the ambiguity encoded in the word *běhēmôt* (12:7). In the present context, this term is a generic reference to large land animals, usually cattle. However, when God subsequently instructs Job to pay special attention to the creature called Behemoth, "which I made just as I made you" (40:15), then Job will discover, presumably, that the animals have more to teach him than he has yet understood.

Second, *what* does creation teach about God? Job's answer is straightforward but oblique: "the hand of the Lord has done this" (v. 9). If the "life" and "breath" of every living creature is in the hand of God (v. 10), is this a good thing or a bad thing? The wisdom tradition recognizes that one cannot always be sure of God's intentions. Both the righteous and the wicked may be in the hand of God, as Qohelet says, but "whether it is for love or hate one does not know" (Eccl 9:1). Job has good reason to agree, since his afflictions are the result of God's having stretched out the "hand" to test his piety (1:11; 2:5). Job hints, however, at a larger truth than he can presently see. His words in 12:9 are a verbatim repetition of Isa. 41:20b. Perhaps he is once again only mouthing a frayed affirmation, but his words stretch toward a far-reaching promise: "Do not fear ... do not be afraid, for I am your God; I will strengthen you, I will help you, I will uphold you by my victorious right hand" (Isa 41:10). Even so, for Job, as for the exiles in Babylon, God's promise of something more than a world of inexplicable suffering remains more hope than reality, more "then" than "now."

2   Conflicting Discernments

Job explores the painful gap between his "then" and his "now" in the summarizing speech of chapters 29–30. The threefold repetition of the phrase "but now"

---

4   For the distinction between the "vital order" of nature, which animals instinctively obey, and the "moral order" of the world, which humans are free to obey or disobey, see E. Kohák, *The Embers and the Stars: A Philosophical Inquiry Into the Moral Sense of Nature* (Chicago: University of Chicago Press, 1984), 70–73, 89–93.

(*wĕʿattâ*; vv. 1, 9, 16) that punctuates the first half of Job 30 reads like a "before and after" advertisement for faith that has gone horribly wrong. "Before" suffering wrecked his world, Job's life was blessed by unmarred relationships with his family, friends, and God (for his reflection on these times past, see Job 29). "After" his world fell apart, the respect he enjoyed turned to scorn (30:2–8), society's admiration for him turned to hostile aggression (30:9–15), and God, whom Job once knew to be unquestionably gracious and compassionate, became inexplicably cruel (30:16–19). Although much has changed between Job's "then" and "now", one thing remains constant: his resolute "cry" to God for help (30:20, 24, 28). This one certainty, however, only adds to Job's confusion. How can any world inhabited by primal screams and a cruel God be called "very good"?

Job's description of the world may be pictured as a series of carefully structured concentric circles, each one defined by the moral values that determine his "lived reality."[5]

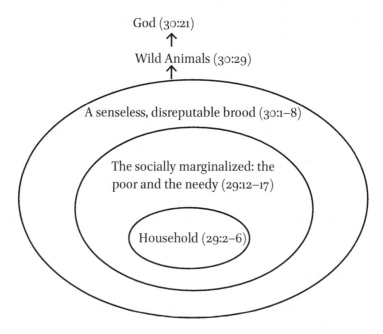

---

[5] On the moral world inscribed in Job 29–31 and its relations to Job's "lived social reality," see Carol Newsom, *The Book of Job: A Contest of Moral Imaginations* (Oxford: Oxford University Press, 2003), 183–199.

At the center of Job's once "very good" world is the memory of relation-ships cemented by "righteousness" and "justice" (29:14): first and most inti-mately, with his family, which had been graced by the presence of God and the laughter of his children (29:2–6); next, with the elders, who gathered at the city gate to discuss the social, economic, and legal matters on which the entire community depended (29:7–11); and then, with persons vulnerable to neglect and abuse, who directed their cries for help to Job (29:12–17). At the outer edge are those who laugh at Job and mock his values (30:1–8). They are contemptible in his eyes and deserve to be "driven out from society" (30:5), yet clearly their presence in his world remains close enough for their insults to wound him.

Two categories of creatures/persons are beyond even the outer boundaries of any civilized world Job can imagine. First among these banished equals are the wild animals, exemplified by the "jackal" and the "ostrich" (30:29). The Old Testament associates jackals with the piercing shrieks that give voice to the desolateness of their wilderness domain (Isa 13:22; Jer 9:10–11; 10:22). Ostriches, which also make eerie screeches (Mic 1:8), are routinely described as ungainly and stupid creatures that are ritually unclean (Lev 11:16; Deut 14:15) and utterly shunned, even by nomads and shepherds (Isa 13:21; 34:13; Jer 50:39). Beyond (*more* than? *less* than?) these creatures is God (30:21), whose cruelty seems more animal-like than divine.[6] In an upside down world, where justice and righteousness seems no longer a virtue, Job concludes that his unanswered cries for help resonate only with the jackals and the ostriches, which means that he has been consigned to eke out his pained existence on the backside of nowhere, out of sight, out of ear, out of mind ... unless, perhaps, even jackals and ostriches have a place in God's world.[7]

When the debate between Job and his three friends ends in a stalemate (31:40), a redactor inserts Elihu (32–37), a "belated" commentator, who pro-ceeds to "answer" (32:1, 3, 5, 6, 12, 17, 20) the questions that have been raised but thus far not resolved.[8] In his last and longest speech (36–37), Elihu summons

---

6 The word for "cruel" in 30:21 (*'akzār*) elsewhere describes the mercilessness of military foes (Jer 6:23; 50:42; cf. Jer 30:14), the "cruel mercy" of the wicked (Prov12:10; cf. Prov 11:17), the venom of snakes (Deut 32:33), and the heartlessness of wild animals that refuse to nurse their young (Lam 4:3; cf. Job 39:16).

7 Cf. Isa 43:20, which envisions a future day when the wild animals, including the jackal and the ostrich, will change their cries to praise, because God has transformed the wilderness into a garden paradise.

8 On Elihu as a "belated" reader/commentator, see Newsom, *The Book of Job*, 204–205. Newsom appropriates the term from Harold Bloom, who argues that every reader comes belatedly to

both the friends and Job to "behold/see" (*hen*; 36:5, 22, 26, 30) the majesty of God's world as he sees it and to "listen, listen" (*šimʿû šamôʿa*; 37:2) to what he hears when God speaks through nature. Lightening punctuates the corners of the earth with dazzling illumination (37:3, 11b). Thunder bespeaks the unfathomable mysteries of God's power (37:4–5). Winter storms bear witness to God's miraculous transformation of rain into ice and snow (37:6–7, 10). Clouds laden with moisture move across the sky, constantly changing shape at God's command (37:11–12). In every instance, God uses nature to "govern" and "command" (36:31–32), and in every instance, nature responds to God's directives with unfailing fidelity. Job should praise the Lord of nature, because like the rain, the lightening, and the thunder, he too has been created to serve the Creator. And like nature itself, Job becomes most fully who God has created him to be when he joyfully joins his voice to the collective praise of all who see what Elihu sees (36:24–25).

In Elihu's view, God's mastery of nature is not only powerful; it is also morally purposeful. When governing and commanding nature, God chooses from two options. The first is "correction" or "punishment," the second, "love" (37:13). This sequencing of God's priorities echoes Elihu's own message concerning God's use of suffering to warn those who, like Job, need the chastening of pain in order to learn what God requires of them (33:14–30; 36:5–15). The syntax of 37:13 permits a third option. The words "for his land (*ʾereṣ*)" may be emended to "for his pleasure/acceptance (*rāṣâ*)." What the emendation gives with one hand, however, it may take back with the other. Elihu interprets God's acceptance (*rāṣâ*; 33:26) as requiring a confession of sin, which throughout the dialogues Job has steadfastly refused to give.

The template for the way Elihu reads creation is the sapiential nature hymn (e.g., Pss 104, 148; Sir 42:15–43:33).[9] He perceives the world as invoking an overwhelming sense of awe and wonder that displaces or at least neutralizes Job's complaints. Even though the world may not reward Job as he thinks best, it remains essentially good, and its Creator, whose justice Job may not understand, remains worthy of, in fact expects and demands, his unfaltering praise. Elihu's attentiveness to intricate details suggests that he is mesmerized by his own sense of wonder at what God has created. It is for this same reason

---

a text that has already served a previous audience and must now be reinterpreted to serve a later one, if it is to continue to have currency. This reinterpretation necessarily enacts what Bloom calls an interpretive "swerve," whereby present readers effectively usurp the authority of previous readers.

9   For Elihu's appropriation of stock images from the nature hymn, especially from Sirach 42–43, see Newsom, *The Book of Job*, 220–228.

therefore curious that what most evokes Elihu's admiration is a world *essentially emptied of creatures and human beings*. Different words for thunder, rain, lightening, and clouds occur multiple times throughout his speech. By contrast, there are but three references to living creatures, two to human beings (37:7: "everyone" [*kol 'ādām*]; "all [*kol 'anše*] whom he has made") and one to animals (37:8: *ḥayyâ*; cf. 36:33). Textual difficulties obscure the meaning of verse 7; about all that is clear is that God uses nature to "seal" or "close up" (*ḥātam*) human beings. NIV's translation stays relatively close to the Hebrew: "he [God] *stops* every man from his labor." Verse 8, likely a parallel statement with reference to animals, provides some clarification. Just as animals seek shelter in their dens when the winter storms arrive, so human beings retreat to the sanctuary of their homes when the weather becomes too severe to continue with their normal labor. Perhaps, given Elihu's reading of creation as God's agent of retribution (cf. 34:21–25), all creatures should be glad to have at least a place to hide. And perhaps in Elihu's world, cowering praise is better than no praise at all (cf. 37:21–24). But is a world in which animals and humans instinctively run and hide from God the world that God desires?[10]

Elihu's "ode to creation" provides a strategic segue to God's own hymnic summons to Job to look at the world (38:1–42:6). Unlike Elihu's world, which has almost no place for creatures, animals or human, God's world is full of animals (38:39–39:30; 40:15–24; 41:1–34 [MT 40:25–41:26]), which God describes with such attentive detail they seem near enough to touch. But what is God's objective? Creation imagery provides the beginnings of an answer. God does not bring the *animals to Job* so that he can name them and thus define their existence in relation to himself, as in Gen 2:19–20. Instead, God brings *Job to the animals*, presumably so that they can teach him something about his own creaturely existence in God's world.[11]

---

10   To the extent that nature hymns describe creation as interacting with or relating to God, they typically do so with master-servant imagery: what God gives or takes, creation dutifully and *happily* accepts (e.g., Ps 104:27–30). Similarly, nature hymns typically summon or *command* creation to use its voice only to praise God (e.g., Ps 148; Sir 43:27–30). Such appeals to creation may evoke terror, not praise, from the Jobs of the world, as Newsom has suggested (*The Book of Job*, 232). Can Elihu's world "be properly urged upon a person in pain"? Can it "properly be spoken by a person in pain"? Is the displacement of everything save a sense of wonder and a response of praise ever "adequate to the moral demand posed by the presence of Job in his pain"?

11   Cf. William P. Brown, *The Ethos of the Cosmos: The Genesis of Moral Imagination in the Bible* (Grand Rapids, MI: Wm. B. Eerdmans, 1999), 365.

3   The Celebration of "Un*man*-aged Freedom"[12]

The drawing below attempts to visualize God's rhetoric in Job 38–41.

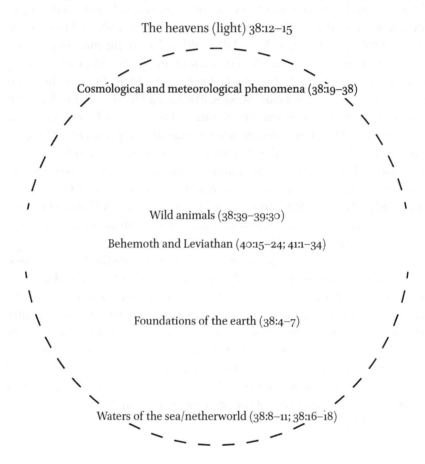

The far reaches of the cosmos (38:4–18) overhang (and undergird) cosmological and meteorological phenomena (38:19–38), which provide a sacred canopy under which five pairs of animals – all but one (the horse) numbered among the wild (38:39–39:30) – frolic in the freedom of being exactly who they are. At the epicenter of God's world is a sixth pair of animals – Behemoth and

---

12   I take this suggestive language from T. Fretheim, whose description of the God speeches exemplifies his keen insights into the world of "God's good creation:" [...] "God does not take Job into the temple or into the depths of his own soul, or insist on some ancient version of C. P. E. God takes him to the zoo, or better, out to 'where the wild things are' [...] whose unman-aged freedom is celebrated" ("God in the Book of Job," *Currents in Theology and Mission* 26 (1999), 89.

Leviathan (40:15–41:34) – conventionally regarded as such a threat to the world that God must defeat them. God, however, sees no cause for opposition and instead celebrates their power, pride, and fierce resistance to domestication, for these are the God-given virtues of creatures that instinctively confront all challenges without fearing defeat. To the extent that there are boundaries or borders in God's canopied world, they are more porous and permeable than what Job has seen. This is especially clear in the contrasting views of God and Job concerning the "waste and desolate land" (30:3b; 38:25–27). Job sees this as a place of punishment, where wild animals and "wild" human beings must scavenge for survival. God looks on the same desolateness and sees promise and potential; barren ground can be watered, and where death seems inevitable, new life may appear.

If Job "asks the animals" that center God's world about the truth of creation's moral order, what will he learn? Most commentators suggest that God asks Job a series of impossible questions – "Do you know?" "Can you?" "Have you?" – in order to silence and rebuke him. Terry Fretheim has challenged this conventional interpretation by arguing that God's objective is not "to set Job up for failure." With a brief but cogent rebuttal, he notes that Job's laments resonate with the wild wailings of those animals that "are embraced by God's care and nurture."[13] Here, as in many other places in my own work, I follow his lead.

Job complains that his cries for justice make him nothing more than a "companion to ostriches" (30:29). Like this shunned creature, Job believes God has banished him to desolate and dangerous places, where his wailings will not disturb or threaten the civility God requires. With the important exception of Behemoth (40:15–24),[14] the ostrich is the only animal that God introduces with affirmations, not questions. God does not ask Job to do or say anything. Job must simply look, listen, and learn what the ostrich has to teach him.

God challenges Job to reconsider the merits of the ostrich in four ways. (1). Job refers to his companions with the conventional name "screechers" (*ya'ănâ*; 30:29). God calls the ostrich by a different name, "cries of joy" (*rĕnānîm*; 39:13; cf. Lam 4:13), which suggests a more positive appraisal of the sounds they contribute to creation's chorus. (2). The ostrich's wings, which are useless for flying, are conventionally regarded as an aberration that singles it out for ridicule. The verb God uses to describe its wild but flightless flapping is

---

13   Ibid., 90, 92.

14   On the importance of Behemoth (and Leviathan) for the argument I make here, see Samuel E. Balentine, "'What Are Human Beings, That You Make So Much of Them?' Divine Disclosure From the Whirlwind: 'Look at Behemoth'," *God In the Fray: A Tribute to Walter Brueggemann*, eds. Todd Linafelt, Timothy K. Beal (Minneapolis: Fortress, 1998), 242–258.

better translated as "to be glad" or "rejoice" (39:13a: *ālas*; cf. NJPS, NIV). (3). The ostrich is alleged to be indifferent to its young by leaving its eggs to hatch on top of the ground, cruelly forgetting that they may be trampled on or devoured by predators (39:14–16). God takes full credit for the ostrich's presumed lack of "wisdom," and "understanding" (39:17), as if celebrating the deficiencies others mock. (4). Lastly, the ostrich is widely regarded as the epitome of stupidity, a trait that no doubt makes it all the more attractive for hunters who enjoy tracking an animal too dumb to elude them. What others take for stupidity, however, God describes as heroic disregard for danger. As the horse and rider draw near for the kill, the ostrich turns and laughs (*śāḥaq*; 39:18) in their face, as if mocking warriors who foolishly underestimate the resources of their opponent.[15]

What conclusions should we draw from God's assessment of where Job and the ostriches belong in creation's moral order? In my judgment, the most constructive answers to this question will come from those who pursue the markers Fretheim has already laid down.

> If all the wild animals are embraced by God's care and nurture, then so also is Job in his disconnectedness ... In the end God is more honored by the impatient probing of Job than by the friends who place certain questions off limits. Job gives voice to those who dare not raise unconventional questions for fear of treading on existing orthodoxies, or being shunned by those who think it improper to explore the edges of faith. Job gives voice to those who indeed experience great suffering, but who cannot find their voices in the midst of a clamor that suggest such questions are impertinent. Job gives voice to those who do not have the courage or the theological moxie or the articulateness to raise their deepest questions.[16]

---

15 Laughter in the face of danger is also exemplified by the wild ass (39:7) and the horse (39:22). The horse is especially instructive, because its fearlessness, here described as "might" (39:19; cf. 12:13), "terror" (39:20b; cf. 9:34; 13:21), "majesty" (39:20b; cf. 37:22), and "thunder" (39:25; cf. 40:9), is God-like.

16 Fretheim, "God in the Book of Job," 92, 93.

CHAPTER 10

Inside the "Sanctuary of Silence": The Moral-Ethical Demands of Suffering

How does the Torah's conceptualization of worship shape character and ethics? The primary custodians of the answer to this question are ancient Israel's priests, whose contribution to the final form of the Torah bears witness to the centrality of the sanctuary – and the ritual activity that takes place within it – in shaping Israel's identity. The sheer volume of material in the Pentateuch that deals with the sanctuary is the first indication of its importance in the priestly perspective. Nearly one-third of the book of Exodus is given to detailed instructions for the building of the tabernacle (Exod. 25–31, 35–40), and the entire book of Leviticus – twenty-seven chapters – deals with the rituals performed within its holy precincts (Lev. 1–16), which in turn seed the requirements for ethical behavior in the everyday world outside the sanctuary (Lev. 17–27). In sum, when a band of refugees gather themselves at Sinai to hear God say, "You shall be to me a priestly kingdom and a holy nation" (Exod. 19:6), the priests insist that worship is the principal means by which they become the Israel of God's hopes and expectations.[1]

This priestly preoccupation with worship begs a further question: What goes on in the complex of rituals inside the sanctuary that is so critically important for shaping the character and ethics of the people of God?

1   Inside the Sanctuary of Silence

In reflecting on this question, I have returned to an observation offered years ago by Y. Kaufmann. Inside the temple, Kaufmann argued, one enters a "sanctuary of silence."[2] Outside the temple, both priests and laity engage in a variety of

---

1   On the theological importance of the Pentateuch's seemingly disproportionate attention to matters relating to worship, see S. E. Balentine, *The Torah's Vision of Worship* (Minneapolis: Fortress, 1999).

2   Y. Kaufmann, *The History of Israelite Religion*, 4 vols. (Tel Aviv: Dvir, 1937–1956; Hebrew), 2:476–77. The first three volumes were abridged and translated by M. Greenberg as *The Religion of Israel* (Chicago: University of Chicago Press, 1960). The fourth volume was translated in its entirety by C. W. Efroymson as *The History of the Religion of Israel: From the Babylonian Captivity to the End of Prophecy* (New York: KTAV, 1977).

© SAMUEL E. BALENTINE, 2021 | DOI:10.1163/9789004459212_011

176   CHAPTER 10

verbal activities, for example, confession, thanksgiving, praise, and blessing.[3] Inside the sanctuary, however, everyone observes a strict code of silence. The priest executes his duties – lighting the lamps, burning incense, dispersing the sacrificial blood, among other things – and the people bring prescribed offerings, but no word is spoken. Kaufmann attributes this silence to "the priestly desire to fashion a non-pagan cult," that is, one that deliberately breaks away from the magical incantations and mythological allusions that characterized cultic activity in Egypt and Mesopotamia.[4]

Kaufmann's assertion has often been taken as axiomatic, although surprisingly little attention has been devoted to examining his explanation, still less to exploring its theological basis in priestly thinking.[5] Israel Knohl has addressed this need in a number of recent publications by building upon Kaufmann's seminal ideas in two important ways.[6] First, Knohl argues that

---

3 Priestly and other texts both within and beyond the Pentateuch refer, albeit obliquely and often negatively, to the use of the spoken or sung word alongside the ritual acts of Israel's worship. Within Priestly texts, see Lev. 5:5; 16:21; Num. 5:21–22; 6:22–26. Elsewhere, see, e.g., Deut. 21:1–9; 26:2–10; 1 Sam. 1:3, 10–15; 1 Kgs. 8:5, 12–64; Amos 5:21–23; Isa. 1:13–15; 38:20; 56:7. Special mention should be made of the various psalms ascribed to Levitical families (cf. 1 Chr. 6:16–34; 15:16–24; 16:4–43), especially the Korahites (Pss. 42, 44–49, 84–85, 87–88) and the Asaphites (Pss. 50, 73–83). The conventional assessment is that such examples attest the use of music and psalmody in the temple courtyards, outside the priestly areas. In other words, the "sanctuary of silence" is strictly limited to the priestly rituals of sacrifice at the altar. Cf. J. Milgrom, *Leviticus 1–16* (AB 3A; Garden City, NY: Doubleday, 1991), 60–61.

4 Kaufmann, *History of the Religion of Israel*, 303. On the division of the central temple personnel in Mesopotamia into cult priests, incantation priests, and diviners, see J. Renger, "Untersuchungen zum Priestertum in der altbabylonischen Zeit," *ZA* 58 (1966): 112–14. Of particular interest here is the role of the so-called lamentation priest (*kalu*) in voicing the congregational and individual responses to a variety of crises that threaten status quo affirmations of divine justice and punishment. For a convenient summary of the texts and their relevance for assessing biblical literature, see W. W. Hallo, "Lamentations and Prayers in Sumer and Akkad," *CANE*, 1871–82.

5 Note, e.g., Milgrom's extension of Kaufmann's argument to the priestly polemic against anthropomorphism, which he judges to be an essential plank in the rejection of all forms of idolatry (Milgrom, *Leviticus 1–16*, 58–61; and *Leviticus 17–22* [AB 3B; Garden City, NY: Doubleday, 2000], 1426–28). Idolatry not only seeks to conform God to human thought, it also seduces human beings into believing that they can influence or control God with human speech, on the assumption that the Deity's will is pliable, just like any other human being. The paradigm for the priestly polemic against human speech in the presence of God, Milgrom argues, is Moses, the putative father of the cult, who is typically silent when performing the signs and wonders God commands and whose verbalized prayers are typically private, never public (e.g., Exod. 5:22; 8:8, 25–26; 9:29, 33; 10:18; 32:11–13; 33:7–11), lest it be thought that his words, not divine prerogative, are the reason for God's response.

6 See I. Knohl, *The Sanctuary of Silence: The Priestly Torah and the Holiness School* (Minneapolis: Fortress, 1995), esp. 124–64; "Between Voice and Silence: The Relationship between Prayer

INSIDE THE "SANCTUARY OF SILENCE" 177

the silence required inside the sanctuary is an expression of the priests' particular conception of the holiness of God.[7] A holy God is beyond any form and personality, indeed, beyond any notion of morality that invites praise or petition. God's holiness exceeds all human comprehension and thus cannot be reduced to such practical functions. If we cannot say anything about God, then "silence is praise," as the psalmist puts it (Ps. 65:2).[8] If there is a dimension of God's majesty that exceeds every expectation that God acts to meet human need, then prayers of lament and petition lose their significance. "The relationship [with God] that exists in the Temple," Knohl says, "is not one of covenant or dependence. Rather, it is a unilateral pact."[9] Confronted with a holy God, humans become aware of their insignificance and necessarily yield to "feelings of guilt and the need for atonement." In the "ideal cultic system," obedience and contrition are nonnegotiable divine commands. As Knohl puts it, "There is no room for the slightest deviation from the divine command even if it is done out of religious enthusiasm."[10]

A second aspect of Knohl's argument is still more intriguing. The requirement of silence inside the sanctuary reflects not only the priestly theology of God's holiness but also bears witness to a priestly inspired "Copernican revolution" in Israel's understanding of the faith God requires.[11] Within priestly thinking, Knohl argues, we can discern a "dynamic process" of maturation, a shift from the "elementary faith" that characterized the Genesis period to the "exalted faith consciousness" that Moses and Israel exemplify.[12] In the pre-Mosaic period, according to the priestly view in Gen. 1, faith consists in believing that God (Elohim) places human beings at the summit of creation,

---

and the Temple Cult," *JBL* 115, no. 1 (1996): 17–30; and *The Divine Symphony: The Bible's Many Voices* (Philadelphia: Jewish Publication Society, 2003), 71–85.

7 Knohl, *Divine Symphony*, 73–74; *Sanctuary of Silence*, 148–52.

8 For this translation, which reflects the rendering of *dumiyyâ* in Jewish tradition, see Knohl, *The Sanctuary of Silence*, 149 n101.

9 Knohl, *Divine Symphony*, 73. He calls attention to the selective use of the terms *běrît*, "covenant," and *'edût*, "commandments, orders," in the Priestly Torah (see *Sanctuary of Silence*, 137–48). The priests typically use the word "covenant," he contends, with reference to the bilateral promises and obligations of God to Noah, Abraham, and their descendants (Gen. 6:18; 9:9–17; 17:2, 4, 9–13, 19, 21; Exod. 2:24). A change takes place with the revelation of the Tetragrammaton (YHWH) to Moses, after which the term *běrît* "disappears" from the Priestly Torah and is replaced by the term *'edût*. The "pact" between YHWH and Israel consists solely of the unilateral demands God imposes on Israel, irrespective of any promise or obligation on God's part that invites the notion of "reciprocal utilitarian relations" (*Sanctuary of Silence*, 149 n103) between God and human beings.

10 Knohl, *Sanctuary of Silence*, 150–51.

11 Ibid., 146.

12 Ibid., 164; cf. Knohl, *Divine Symphony*, 19–23, 71–74.

invests them with responsibility for creation's potential to be "very good," and then tunes the moral order of the world to human behavior. When human beings rightly exercise their God-given stewardship of creation's resources, they may expect God to reward their efforts with abundance and prosperity. Alternatively, when human beings fail to be God's worthy superintendents, not only they but also creation itself pay the price. In sum, the priests recognize that faith *begins* when human beings comprehend that God, "[human]like in his image and his actions," is approachable.[13] But such faith, while foundational and important, is not fully adequate for what God requires.

In the distinctive revelation that comes from God (YHWH) to Moses, the priests discern that faith must ascend to a higher level, for the Tetragrammaton reveals a numinous aspect of divinity that will not be defined by human behavior. A mature awareness of God's centrality requires a recalibration of humanity's place in creation, for God has not created everything in the world to serve the needs of human beings. An increased awareness of the mysterious, intangible, holiness of God requires a recalibration of the world's moral order, for a holy God governs in ways that exceed elementary notions of reward and punishment. In sum, elementary faith, which aspires to a close, personal, and reciprocal relationship with God, is authentic but insufficient and immodest. Inside the sanctuary, one must respond to a fuller revelation from God that requires a higher level of faith. Humility, not self-assertion, silence, not words, convey the worship required by a holy God, who is essentially other and different from human beings. Knohl's assessment of this dynamic process of faith refinement rests largely on close examination of literary details in two independent priestly sources within the Pentateuch: the Priestly Torah and the Holiness School. Although the details of this argument merit close scrutiny, I have chosen not to engage him at this point. I will focus instead on another aspect of his argument. As if trying to put a human face on this literary analysis, Knohl directs us to the book of Job and thus to a specific example of how one's faith can and should mature according to the priestly discernment.[14] In his words, "The book of Job depicts a dynamic process – the refinement of faith consciousness – generally similar to the shift that occurs in PT [Priestly Torah]."[15] The gist of his argument is that the beginning of the book (Job 1–2) echoes the priestly discernment of the faith consciousness depicted in Gen. 1.

---

13   Knohl, *Sanctuary of Silence*, 146.
14   Ibid., 165–67; Knohl, *Divine Symphony*, 115–22. See also M. Douglas, who notes without discussion that "Leviticus' general reflection on God's justice reaches forward to the Book of Job" (*Leviticus as Literature* [Oxford: Oxford University Press, 1999], 252; cf. 212).
15   Knohl, *The Divine Sanctuary*, 165.

INSIDE THE "SANCTUARY OF SILENCE" 179

At the outset, Job believes there is a direct correlation between his behavior and the behavior of the Creator, who tunes the moral order of the whole world to reward his personal righteousness. However, when Job experiences suffering and loss "for no reason" (Job 2:3), this elementary faith leads him to question God's justice. Not until God (YHWH) invites his contemplation of the mysteries of creation does he come to understand his proper place in the world.[16] According to Knohl, Job ascends to "a higher level of faith" when he responds to this revelation first with silence (40:4–5: "I lay my hand on my mouth. I have spoken once but will proceed no further"), then with contrition ("I knew of you only by report, but now I see you with my own eyes. Therefore I yield, repenting in dust and ashes" [42:5–6 NJPS]).[17] At the end of Job's journey he effectively arrives at the "sanctuary of silence," where priestly rituals of sin and atonement, not words of lament, provide the most authentic theodicy any person ever needs.[18]

---

16 A critical component in Knohl's thesis is the distinction between divine revelations from Elohim, El Shaddai, or Eloah, and those from YHWH. The former correlates with Genesis and a first stage in faith consciousness, the latter with the exalted faith of Moses and Israel. The book of Job depicts a dynamic process from the elementary to the mature in a way comparable to the Priestly Torah, with one important difference. According to the priests, an exalted faith consciousness is available only through the complex of rituals inside the sanctuary; it is the legacy of Israel alone. According to the book of Job, an exalted faith consciousness is neither limited to observance of temple rituals nor restricted to Israel. Job, a non-Israelite, gains access to this revelation through reflection on creation, not through the execution of sacrificial worship, which is mentioned "only at the stage of Job's early faith level" (Job 1:4–5). Knohl, *Sanctuary of Silence*, 165–66; and *Divine Symphony*, 120–22.

17 Knohl, *Divine Symphony*, 118.

18 On cultic rituals, especially the sacrifices for sin prescribed in Lev. 4:1–35, as "the priestly theodicy," see Milgrom, *Leviticus 1–16*, 260–61. His explication of the priestly advocacy of collective responsibility for sin merits citation, for it seems to be a response to the questions one might hear from the Jobs of the world: "[The priests] knew full well that the prophet was justified in protesting 'why does the way of the wicked prosper?' (Jer. 12:1 [cf. Job 21:7, 17–19]), and they provided their answer: the sinner may be unscarred by his evil, but the sanctuary bears the scars, and, with its destruction, he too will meet his doom.... That the righteous were engulfed in disaster (i.e., God's retribution) may have been protested by a few biblical voices (e.g., Gen. 18:23; Ezek. 18:1–32), but existential reality and the monotheistic premise make it impossible to conceive God otherwise.... The 'good' people who perish with the evildoers are not innocent. For allowing the evildoers to flourish, to pollute the sanctuary beyond repair, they share the blame. Indeed, they are the inadvertent sinners who contribute to the pollution of the sanctuary. Let a modern – hence, more vivid – example illustrate the point. World War II would have presented no theological quandary for Israel's priests of old. They would have rejected with scorn our contemporary theologians who have proclaimed that 'God is dead.' Instead of bewailing the silence of God, they would have pointed the accusing finger at the human culprits, the

180   CHAPTER 10

2 Job as a "Test Case" for the Sanctuary of Silence

I find Knohl's discussion of the connections between Job and the Priestly Torah instructive, but I question whether his conclusions do them full justice. A number of clues within the book lead me in a different direction. If we imagine Job as among those addressed by the directives of priests, that is, if Job is the "test case" for their view of worship, is there sufficient evidence in the book that records his story to confirm that he in fact silences his complaints and rises to the higher level of faith – obedience and contrition – that Knohl believes the priests require? I address this question in the nine observations that follow.

1. The Prologue uses four terms to establish Job's extraordinary piety. Two adjectives describe his character, "blameless" (*tām*) and "upright" (*yāšar*), and two expressions describe his ethics, "fearing God" (*yirē 'ĕlohîm*) and "turning away from evil" (*sār mēra'*). Both Job's character and his ethics are further profiled by the reports in the Prologue and Epilogue that he offers sacrifice. Job 1:5 describes his presentation of "burnt offerings" (*'ōlôt*) on behalf of his children as a preemptive propitiation for any inadvertent sins they may have committed. Job 42:8 reports that he receives the "burnt offering" (*'ôlâ*) presented by the friends, who require his prayer of intercession if God is to forgive their wrong-doings. While neither of these texts envision Job's sacrificial acts as occurring in a formal cultic setting, they invite us nonetheless to see him as one who "plays the part of the perfect priest" within his household.[19] Moreover, instead of locating Job in a specific time and place in the postexilic period, which most agree is the likely historical setting for the book, the narrator retrojects this story into the patriarchal epoch, which invites us to consider how Job's priestly profile relates to the priestly conceptualization of pre-Mosaic worship.[20]

---

inadvertent sinners, the 'silent majority' – the German people who voted the Nazis into power and the peoples of the free world who acquiesced to the annexation of the Saar, Austria, and Sudetenland while barring their own doors to the refugees who managed to escape. A worldwide cataclysm was thus inevitable. Indeed, Israel's priests would have asked: How long under the circumstances could God have been willing to abide in his earthy sanctuary?"

19 N. Habel, *The Book of Job* (OTL; Philadelphia: Westminster, 1985), 88; cf. J. Hartley, *The Book of Job* (NICOT; Grand Rapids: Eerdmans, 1988), 69–70. I believe this assessment holds, despite D. J. A. Clines's important caution: "The story's setting in time and place lies beyond the horizon of priestly law" (*Job 1–20* [WBC 17; Dallas: Word, 1989], 16).

20 However we assess the historical accuracy of this profile, it is instructive to note that Job has often been depicted as a priest in both ancient Near Eastern and Christian iconography. See S. Terrien, who notes that more than forty statues of "Saint Job the Priest" have been preserved in Belgium, Luxembourg, and the Netherlands (*The Iconography of Job*

INSIDE THE "SANCTUARY OF SILENCE" 181

2. Whereas the prose Prologue-Epilogue frames the book as the story of a priestlike Job who extends the rituals of sacrifice to others, the poetic dialogues inside the frame turn the tables. Now it is Job who stands in need of the rituals of comfort that other ministrants may offer him. In short, the priest now requires a priest.[21] The Prologue subtly anticipates this role reversal by reporting that Job has been afflicted with "loathsome sores" (*šĕḥîn*; 2:7). The same word is used in Lev. 13–14 to identify the skin diseases that make a person unclean and needful of priestly rituals (see 13:18–23). In the midst of two lengthy pericopes detailing the priestly diagnosis of skin diseases (13:1–44) and the requisite purification rituals (14:1–32), two brief verses describe what diseased persons (like Job) should do in the painful interim between affliction and restoration. Until the priest determines that they are "clean," they must live outside the camp, where they tear their clothes, dishevel their hair, cover their mouth, and cry out, "Unclean, unclean!" (13:45–46). The gesture of covering the mouth confirms that they know themselves to have become repugnant to their community. The words "Unclean, unclean!" warn others against coming too close, lest they inadvertently endanger themselves.

3. The Prologue describes affliction as a test of Job's piety, which is to be judged in large part by what does or does not come from his mouth. The *śaṭān* wagers that Job will curse God. God wagers that the *śaṭān* is wrong. By all accounts, God has placed the better bet. Like the diseased person in Lev. 13, Job responds to affliction with a ritual gesture: He tears his clothes, shaves his head, and falls on the ground. Despite his losses, Job speaks words of blessing and "does not charge God with any wrongdoing" (1:21–22). Despite temptations to speak like foolish persons who question God and scorn the rewards of the righteous, Job remains steadfast. Even as he sits alone on his ash heap of suffering, presumably outside the city, where society consigns the rejected and the destitute, Job does not "sin with his lips" (2:10).[22] When the curtain falls on the Prologue, Job's world is submerged in silence (2:13). Whether this silence is sacred, hence comparable to what the priests require inside the sanctuary, is the question that prepares for the next scene in this drama.

4. When the curtain rises on the next scene, Job opens his mouth (3:1) and moves beyond silence. He speaks seven curses – three against the day of his

---

through the Centuries: Artists as Biblical Interpreters [University Park: Pennsylvania State University Press, 1996], 149–58).

21 For a preliminary exploration of these matters, see S. E. Balentine, "Job as Priest to the Priests," *ExAud* 18 (2002), 29–52.

22 The text does not identify Job's location in 2:8. Commentators widely assume that he sits in a place of shame outside the city walls, a judgment that LXX seems to support by translating "ashes" as "the dung heap outside the city."

182   CHAPTER 10

birth (3:3–5), four against the night of his conception (3:6–9) – that mount a
rhetorical assault on the seven days of creation and, by implication, the creator who pronounced the primordial design of the world "very good." To these
curses he couples a string of anguished laments, peppered with the question
"Why?" (3:11, 12, 20; implied in vv. 16, 23), which press the issues that every subsequent speaker in the book, including God, must address. From Job's perspective, there is much at stake, for he contends that suffering like his calls the
whole of the created order into question. If his questions cannot be satisfactorily addressed, then they will continue to rip and tear at the fabric of life until
creation itself is undone.

One by one Job's three friends rise to the challenge of providing the answers
they believe he needs (Job 4–27). They are not priests, but they are clearly
spokespersons for the religious establishment, and much of what they say is
consonant with the priestly *tôrôt* concerning sacrifice and repentance.[23] *If* Job
confesses that he is a sinful mortal in the presence of a holy God, *then* God
will restore him to his rightful place in the world (e.g., 8:5–6; 11:13–15; 22:23–27).
Eliphaz speaks for all when he reduces the *torah* that applies to Job to one
nonnegotiable mandate: "Agree with God and be at peace; in this way good will
come to you" (22:21). Virtually every word of this *torah*, however, only adds to
Job's burden. Given the plotline of the canonical story, *if* Job agrees with God,
then he is innocent and thus cannot atone for a sin he has not committed (1:2,
8; 2:3). *If* religious orthodoxy requires the sacrifice of personal integrity as the
price for peace with God, *then* Job must loathe the person God has created him
to be, which means per force that he is ever at war with himself and with his
creator (e.g., 7:16; 9:20–21, 30–31; 10:1a). Given this conundrum, it is little wonder that Job remains defiant, that he insists his words be preserved for posterity
(19:23–24), that the friends, and God, must listen to his words (6:25–26; 7:11–15;
10:1–2; 13:3, 13–17; 16:18; 21:1–5; 23:1–7; 27:1–6; 31:35–37). What do the rituals of
the cult offer to one such as Job, whose suffering has been willingly inflicted on
him by God? W. Scott Green states the matter bluntly:

> From a cultic or halakhic perspective, there is nothing concrete Job can
> do to repair his relationship with God. Sacrifice, repentance, and any
> religious behaviors that develop from them are nugatory under these

---

23   The instructions in Lev. 1–15 consist of ten *tôrôt* or "commandments." Five *tôrôt* deal
        with sacrifice: burnt offerings (6:2–6), cereal offerings (6:7–16), purification offerings
        (6:17–23), reparation offerings (7:1–7), and well-being offerings (7:11–21). Five *tôrôt* con-
        cern impurity: animal carcasses (11:1–23, 41–42), childbirth (12:1–8), skin diseases (13:1–59),
        purification from skin diseases (14:1–57), and genital discharges (15:1–32). See Milgrom,
        Leviticus 1–16, 2.

INSIDE THE "SANCTUARY OF SILENCE" 183

circumstances.... No offering, no change of heart, can appease divine caprice or undo an affliction that happens for no reason.[24]

5. When Job's words are ended (31:40), a fourth friend, Elihu, steps into the story as the "Answerer" Job seeks but has not yet found (Job 32–37). Drawing upon both forensic and cultic metaphors, Elihu seeks to persuade Job that God uses suffering to save his life, principally by turning him away from misplaced pride and toward a public confession of sin (33:15–28). By inviting Job into both the courtroom and the cult, Elihu seems intent on clarifying the distinctions between these two ways of addressing his issues with God. On closer inspection, Elihu seems only to blur the differences. The trial Job seeks is one in which the accused is presumed innocent, until a fair and impartial jury decides that the evidence requires a different verdict (e.g., Job 9–10). When Elihu invites Job into the courtroom, however, he announces before the first word is spoken that Job is in the wrong (33:12). Similarly, when Elihu summons Job to prayer, he declares that the cult provides him only one option. He must speak the words his angelic counselor tells him. He must confess and say, "I sinned, and perverted what was right" (33:27). Prayer, at least as Elihu defines it, is simply another word for legal language that presumes Job's guilt and God's innocence. In short, whether Job presents his case in the courtroom or the cult, the verdict will be the same.

6. The ultimate answer to Job's situation, once he attains the required humility before God, according to Elihu, is to yield to the Lord of creation, whose unfathomable justice (36:5–15) necessarily commands awe and praise (36:22–37:13). Embedded within Elihu's summons to praise is a subtle but telling clue concerning his assessment of where human beings rank among the wonders of God's creation. For all its attention to the intricate details of nature (note, for example, the multiple words for thunder, rain, lightning, and clouds throughout the speech), Elihu's "Ode to Creation" provides almost no place for living creatures, animal or human. To find them in Elihu's world, one must look for the places where they hide (37:7–8).[25] Retreating to their lairs and homes,

---

24 W. Scott Green, "Stretching the Covenant: Job and Judaism," *RevExp* 99, no. 4 (2002), 574.

25 Elihu's last speech contains but three oblique references to living creatures: two to human beings (37:7) and one to animals (37:8). Textual difficulties obscure the meaning in verse 7; about all that is clear is that God uses nature to "seal" or "close up" (*hātam*) human beings. The NIV's translation is relatively close to the Hebrew: "He [God] *stops* every man from his labor." Verse 8, likely a parallel statement with respect to animals, provides some clarification. Just as animals seek shelter in their dens when the winter storms arrive, so human beings retreat to the sanctuary of their homes when the weather becomes too severe to carry on with their normal labors.

184   CHAPTER 10

both animals and humans cower before God, whose awesome display of power seems far more threatening than inviting. Perhaps, given Elihu's reading of creation's grammar, all creatures should be glad to have at least a place to hide. And perhaps in Elihu's world, cowering praise is better than no praise at all. But we may wonder if Job can accept Elihu's invitation into a world of coerced confession and cowered praise. Carol Newsom's questions are mine as well: Can Elihu's world be properly urged upon an innocent sufferer? Is such a world "adequate to the moral demands posed by the presence of Job in his pain"?[26]

7. Elihu's hymn to creation segues to God's dramatic revelation to Job from the whirlwind, which in turn brings us back to the nub of Knohl's observations. In his view, once God invites reflection on the mysteries of creation, Job at last attains the exalted faith the priests aim for. Knohl argues that Job rises to the level of the modesty required, for now he knows that human beings are not the "crowning glory of Creation. The crown is taken off the human head and placed upon that of a terrible sea monster [Leviathan; 41:25–26]."[27] And he rises to the level of faith consciousness that defines the priestly ideal. Having seen and understood more than before, he bows in silent contrition, for now he knows that the holiness of God comes with one nonnegotiable commandment: obedience. I repeat words from Knohl I have already cited: "There is no room for the slightest deviation from the divine command even if it is done out of religious enthusiasm." Here too, however, other clues in God's revelation to Job invite a different assessment.

8. Unlike Elihu's world, which has almost no place for creatures of any kind, God's world is full of animals, which are described with such attentive detail they seem almost near enough to touch. But what is God's objective? Creation imagery provides the beginning of an answer. God does not bring *the animals to Job* so that he can name them and thus define their existence in relation to himself, as in Gen. 2:19–20. Instead, God brings *Job to the animals*, so that they may teach him something about his own creaturely existence in God's world.[28] The lesson begins with five pairs of animals (38:39–39:30), all but one (the horse) numbered among the wild that frolic in the freedom of being exactly what God has created them to be.[29] When the lesson concludes, God invites Job to say what he has learned (40:1–2). Job responds with the concession "I am

---

26   Carol Newsom, *The Book of Job: A Contest of Moral Imaginations* (New York: Oxford University Press, 2003), 232.

27   Knohl, *Divine Symphony*, 118.

28   Cf. William P. Brown, *The Ethos of the Cosmos: The Genesis of Moral Imagination in the Bible* (Grand Rapids: Eerdmans, 1999), 365.

29   Note especially the wild ass, ostrich, and the horse, each of which "laugh" (39:7, 18, 22) in the face of potential danger. The horse is especially instructive, because its fearlessness,

INSIDE THE "SANCTUARY OF SILENCE" 185

small." Placing his hand on his mouth, he retreats in silence. When he agrees to speak no further (40:3–5), Knohl – along with most interpreters – assumes that Job has arrived at the answer God desires. The logic of the revelation, however, suggests otherwise, for with a second speech God pushes past Job's silence with still another request for his response (40:7). Silence, it seems, is not fully adequate.

God now singles out a sixth and final pair of animals, Behemoth (40:15–24) and Leviathan (41:1–34), which require Job's special attention. The structure of this part of the speech suggests that these two animals exemplify the intent of God's work on the sixth day of creation, when God made "wild animals" (*běhēmâ*), along with human beings (Gen. 1:24–27). "Look at Behemoth," God says to Job, "which I made just as I made you" (40:15). Consider Leviathan, God continues, a creature "made without fear" (40:33 [MT 41:25]). What is the lesson for Job? Most commentators argue that God singles out Behemoth and Leviathan, creatures conventionally regarded as wild and hostile to creation, in order to teach Job that God alone has the power to subjugate them. If Job persists in his own creaturely defiance of God, so this argument goes, then he can expect certain defeat. Once again, I believe the text invites a more nuanced reading.

I cite but one of the clues.[30] A critical part of God's discourse on Leviathan is the description of what does and does not come forth from its mouth. What does not come from this creature's mouth are "soft words" (41:3–4 [MT 40:27–28]). In the unlikely event that anyone should ever successfully capture Leviathan and force it into service, even then it would not conform to any "covenantal" (*běrît*) existence that requires it to do or say only what its master permits. Instead, when it opens its mouth (41:18–21 [MT 41:10–13]) what comes out is fire and light, smoke and flames, phenomena typically associated with the strong and compelling appearance of God (e.g., Pss. 18:7–8, 12–15; 29:7–9). Instinctively godlike, Leviathan announces its presence with an awesome fierceness that commands attention and defies coercion. Contrary to the conventional view, when God looks at Leviathan, God sees no cause for opposition. Instead, God celebrates its power, pride, and fierce resistance to domestication, for these virtues exemplify its God-given creaturely royalty (41:33–34 [MT 41:25–26]: "On earth it has no equal.... It is king"). If Job's piety is to be judged by what

---

described as "might" (39:19; cf. 12:13), "terror" (39:20b; cf. 9:34; 13:21), "majesty" (39:20b; cf. 37:22), and "thunder" (39:25; cf. 40:5) is Godlike.

30   I have explored these matters further in "'What Are Human Beings, That You Make So Much of Them?' Divine Disclosure from the Whirlwind: 'Look at Behemoth,'" in *God in the Fray: A Tribute to Walter Brueggemann* (eds. T. Linafelt and T. K. Beal; Minneapolis: Fortress, 1998), 259–78; and *Job* (SHBC; Macon, GA: Smyth & Helwys, 2006).

186	CHAPTER 10

does and does not come forth from his mouth, then the lesson from Leviathan commends strong words, not soft or gentle ones, speech that demands respect, not silence.[31]

9. According to Knohl, Job rises to the level of faith consciousness God requires when he responds to this revelation not only with silent humility (40:3–5) but also with a verbalized confession of sin. Knohl finds this repentance (with a majority of commentators) in Job's last words in the book: "I despise myself, and repent in dust and ashes" (42:6). Most would agree that these words constitute the crux of the book, so perhaps I may be forgiven for not engaging the ongoing debate about the range of legitimate exegetical possibilities that must be considered. Let me simply invite consideration of one issue that all agree is critical. The words "repent *in* dust and ashes" (*niḥamtî ʿal*) may be more properly translated, "repent *concerning* dust and ashes." Whereas the conventional translation suggests that Job retreats to the traditional ritual of gesturing forth sorrow for wrongdoing by sitting *in* dust and ashes,[32] the syntax may legitimately be taken to mean that Job "repents" or "changes his mind" *about* dust and ashes. If we pursue this option, then we must be open to the possibility that what finally comes forth from Job's mouth is not a confession of sin but instead a (re)affirmation of his creaturely stature before God. If God does not rebuke Abraham, another mere mortal of dust and ashes who dares to challenge God's justice (Gen. 18:27), then perhaps God will not rebuke Job when he dares to follow Abraham's model of faith.[33]

31	J. G. Gammie also notes that what comes from Leviathan's mouth is a major emphasis in the poem. He suggests that the poet uses this emphasis both to caricature Job's verbal defenses and at the same time to affirm his protests. Gammie, "Behemoth and Leviathan: On the Didactic and Theological Significance of Job 40:15–41:26," in *Israelite Wisdom: Theological and Literary Essays in Honor of Samuel Terrien* (ed. J. G. Gammie et al.; Missoula, MT: Scholars Press, 1978), 223, 225.

32	For references and discussion, see, e.g., S. Olyan, *Biblical Mourning: Ritual and Social Dimensions* (New York: Oxford University Press, 2004), 111–23.

33	The phrase "dust and ashes" (*ʿāpār waʾēper*) occurs only three times in the Old Testament: Gen. 18:27; Job 30:19; and Job 42:6. In each case it signifies something about the human condition in relation to God. In Job 30:19, Job laments that God has thrown him into the "mire" (*ḥōmer*; cf. Job 4:19; 10:9; 33:6) of human mortality, where human existence is defined as "dust and ashes." In the context of his suffering, Job understands this to mean that he exemplifies the way afflicted human beings are banished from society (30:1–8), then scorned and terrorized by their peers (30:9–15) and by God (30:16–23). His experience leads him to conclude that as "dust and ashes" he has been consigned to live in a world where he cries out to a cruel God who does not answer (30:20–21). In Gen. 18:27, the phrase "dust and ashes" applies to Abraham. In the context of arguing with God about matters of justice, Abraham acknowledges that he is a mere creature of "dust and ashes" who has entered dangerous territory. Abraham's recognition of his status before

INSIDE THE "SANCTUARY OF SILENCE"   187

3   "Inside the House, an Archaic Rule; Outside, the Facts of Life"?

What then are we to make of the priests' commendation of silence as *the* cri-
terion for the highest expression of faith? On the one hand, Knohl, Kaufmann,
and others are on solid ground when they argue that the "outstanding characteristic of this [priestly] sanctuary is the holy silence within it."[34] On the other,
there is ample evidence, both within and beyond Priestly texts, that worshipers created in "the image of God" are peculiarly empowered for speech. With
mouths opened in the image of the Creator, human beings are birthed into
created life with a capacity not only to receive God's words but also to speak
their own, words not only of praise and thanksgiving but also of complaint
and protest.[35] Indeed, if the "priestly" Job is a reliable script for the words that

---

God is similar to Job's in 30:19, with one important exception: Abraham persists with his
questions, and God answers. Indeed, the Hebrew text of Gen. 18:22 – "YHWH remained
standing before Abraham" – suggests that God, the "Judge of all the earth" (Gen. 18:25),
stands waiting to hear what "dust and ashes" will say on the subject of divine justice. As
E. Ben Zvi has discerned, this picture of Creator and creature locked in dialogue over
matters of mutual concern provides a glimpse of how the creaturely pursuit of justice
enacts what it means to be made in the image of God: "The text underscores the notion
that when the ideal teacher defends the universal order and confronts God with the standards by which God ought to judge the world, *he is in fact fulfilling the role God has chosen
for him to fulfill*" (Ben Zvi, "The Dialogue between Abraham and Yhwh in Gen. 18:23–32:
A Historical- Critical Analysis," *JSOT* 53 [1992], 39; emphasis added).

34   Knohl, *Divine Symphony*, 71. The argument for a silent sanctuary is surely apt when considering Leviticus, which records no direct response, no specific verbal reply, to God from
either Moses or Israel. Moreover, as G. Auld has noted, Leviticus depicts the sanctuary
as both a structural and theological sanctuary in the midst of the wilderness, which is a
prominent theme in Exodus and Numbers. The "wilderness theme" occurs twelve times
in Exodus (*bammidbār*: 3:18; 5:1, 3; 7:16; 8:23, 24; 14:11, 12; 15:22; 16:2, 32; 19:2) and thirty-one
times in Numbers (1:1, 19; 3:4, 14; 9:1, 5; 10:12, 31; 12:16; 14:2, 16, 29, 32, 33, 35; 15:2; 16:13; 21:5, 11,
13; 26:64, 65; 27:3, 14; 32:13, 15; 33:8, 11, 13, 15, 36). By contrast, the wilderness is mentioned
but twice in Leviticus (7:38; 16:22). Auld, "Leviticus: After Exodus and before Numbers," in
The Book of Leviticus: Composition and Reception (eds. R. Rendtorff and R. Kugler; Leiden:
Brill, 2003), 43. Both before and after Leviticus, that is, in the wilderness, the discourse
between God and Israel frequently includes complaint and protest (e.g., in the "murmur-
ing traditions" preserved in Exod. 15–18 and Num. 11–25). Inside the sanctuary, however,
the tabernacle is an oasis of obedience; those who might address God differently in other
places now respond with reverent silence.

35   Space limitations permit no more than a footnote reference to ancient Near Eastern texts
describing the ritual of "washing" (*mis pi*) or "opening" the mouth (*pit mi*) of cultic images
for the deity, which appear to have been in existence throughout Mesopotamia from at
least the eighth to the first centuries BCE. Although no extant text preserves the complete
mis pi or *pit mi* ritual, it seems to involve two essential acts. First, the ritual specialist performs a symbolic act by which the deity opens the mouth of the statue, thereby indicating that it is able to breathe, that is, it has been ritually birthed into the world of created

188   CHAPTER 10

seek a hearing inside the sanctuary, then we have reason to suspect that the latter was a prominent component of cultic speech, even if the priests provided no place for it within the sanctuary itself.[36] But this only accentuates a larger question, which has been lurking at the edges of my ruminations from the outset. If the priests were well aware of the legitimate role of all forms of human speech to God, why then did they insist that its proper place was *outside* the holy sanctuary, not inside? To return to Knohl's observations, why do the priests insist that silence before God is "the most exalted level of faith"? Let me shape the question more specifically to the concerns of this session. How and why should silence before God be understood as the key to character formation?

---

life. Then the ritualist adds incantations, which empower the image to speak and to be spoken to by human beings with whom it now shares its existence. For translation and assessment of the extant texts, see C. Walker and M. B. Dick, "The Introduction of the Cult Image in Ancient Mesopotamia: The Mesopotamian *mis pi* Ritual," in *Born in Heaven, Made on Earth: The Making of the Cult Image in the Ancient Near East* (ed. M. B. Dick; Winona Lake, IN: Eisenbrauns, 1999), 55–121.

   The existence of such precedent rituals in the ancient Near East begs an important question of the priestly insistence that human beings are created "in the image of God" (Gen. 1:26). Despite the polemic against both cultic images and the anthropomorphism they typically conveyed in so-called pagan cults, could Israel's priests have been completely unaware of the implication that human beings, created in the image of the God, whose mouth is open, not closed, are peculiarly shaped for communication both *from* and *to* God? On this question, see the insightful comments of my colleague Andreas Schüle in his essay "Made in the 'Image of God': The Concept of Divine Images in Gen 1–3," *ZAW* 117 (2005), 1–20. Pondering the question, the words of George Steiner may help us to bridge from ancient texts to contemporary discernments: "It is the Hebrew intuition that God is capable of all speech-acts except that of monologue which has generated our arts of reply, of questioning and counter-creation. After the Book of Job there *had* to be, if man was to bear his being, the means of dialogue with God, which are spelt out in our poetics, music, art" (Steiner, *Real Presences* [Chicago: University of Chicago Press, 1989], 225).

36   For all his attention to Job as a model for "exalted faith consciousness," Knohl never quite succeeds in getting him completely inside the sanctuary of silence. Job's role, according to Knohl, remains that of the outsider who speaks truth to truth. As Knohl says, "We can recognize that there is a place for, and significance to, the kind of debate in which the *other* view may also be a reflection of divine truth" (*Divine Symphony*, 146). Moreover, Knohl affirms that the tension between Job's cacophonous words outside the sanctuary and the sublime silence that characterizes the liturgy inside the sanctuary is necessary and should not be blurred. "Inevitably, there was a tension between the silent inner circle and the outer circles, a tension between the Priestly theology concentrated upon the sanctity of God and the popular religion that cared for the satisfaction of everyday human needs. At the same time, the different beliefs gave rise to a single, unified, holy system, where sound and silence found their place in harmony" (Ibid., 74).

INSIDE THE "SANCTUARY OF SILENCE" 189

I confess that I still falter when trying to formulate a persuasive answer to this question. My dis-ease is not unlike that of the narrator in Saul Bellow's short story "Something to Remember Me By." As a schoolboy brought up in an Orthodox Jewish home, he often felt trapped between high-minded religious commandments and the "grimly ordinary" requirements of life on the Chicago streets: "At home, inside the house, an archaic rule; outside, the facts of life. The facts of life were having their turn. Their first effect was ridicule."[37]

I suspect that we do not need Job's witness to convince us that the grimly ordinary facts of life too often ridicule "high-minded" affirmations of faith. We may, however, take real comfort in thinking that, because of Job's witness, when we limp toward the sanctuary with bruises and wounds exceeding any sin we may have committed, no one will block our entrance by saying, "No protesters allowed beyond this point." By the same token, we likely feel more authentically human, more empowered to meet the moral and ethical demands of life, when we can cry aloud to the heavens – inside the sanctuary – for justice. Given the tragic sense that defines so much of life in this world, "the chiefest sanctity of a temple," as M. de Unamuno says, "is that it is a place to which men go to weep in common. A *miserere* sung in common by a multitude tormented by destiny has as much value as a philosophy," or, I would add, as any theology.[38] Such are the moral demands of innocent suffering on the rituals of worship. The Jobs of this world cannot be fully human in the presence of God if religious authorities require them to stay outside the sanctuary yelling "Unclean, unclean!" Religious authorities who ignore or deny this truth only indict themselves. The charge they can expect to be leveled against them, as A. S. Park has discerned, will place them in the company of Job's friends; when challenged to offer comfort to the "sinned-against," they do not speak "what is right" about God:

> The God of Job is angry at this simplistic sin-repentance formula the church has applied to the victims of sin.... It is overdue for us to provide a sensible theology of healing for the victims of sin and tragedy. Our present one-dimensional theology is under God's wrath. Theologians owe burnt offerings to God and our apology to the victims.[39]

---

37 S. Bellow, "Something to Remember Me By," in *Saul Bellow: Collected Stories* (New York: Viking, 2001), 415, 431.

38 M. de Unamuno, *The Tragic Sense of Life* (New York: Dover, 1954), 17.

39 A. S. Park, "The Bible and Han," in *The Other Side of Sin: Woundedness from the Perspective of the Sinned-Against* (eds. A. S. Park and S. L. Nelson; Albany, NY: SUNY Press, 2001), 51.

But surely Israel's priests knew that their rituals must be meaningful not only to sinners but also to the sinned-against. Even if the sanctuary represents only an idealized "island of silence in a sea of hymn and prayer,"[40] as Knohl puts it, the priests' insistence on silence in the presence of God presses us to do more than simply probe for the weaknesses in their view of worship. Might it be that they have discerned a larger truth than we skeptics have been willing to see? Given the modern tendency to view ourselves as the center of the universe, surely there is virtue in a summons to worship that reorients us, in proper humility and contrition, to a God whose fullness surpasses our needs. Private woes are important – indeed, for those trapped in the clutches of affliction they may be all we can feel, all we can say, all we can believe is real. To be invited – no, according to the priests, to be *commanded* – to silence our words and still our souls is to be reminded that there is a divine dimension to life. In the midst of all that is painfully real and constricting in this world, Israel's priests envision a sanctuary in which the "really real" becomes not only palpable but also freeing.[41] On this point, Barbara Brown Taylor's reflections on God's decentering revelation to Job are instructive. When she looks at the vastness of God's creation through the revelation vouchsafed to Job, two things happen to change her perspective:

> First, my ego undergoes radical shrinkage. Even though I know better, I still work so hard to justify my existence on this earth. I teach classes, I write books, I give to good causes, I work out with weights ... but what does the night sky care? "You think you're so big, well take a look at *this!*" I am not even a flea on the back of this universe. I know some of those stars by name, but they do not know mine. They look the same when I am happy as they do when I am sad. As beautiful as they are, they ignore me. They remind me of my true size.
>
> The second thing that happens when I look at them is that I feel deeply reassured. Thank God they ignore me. Can you imagine how awful it would be, if you got into a rage one night and knocked nine or ten stars out of the sky with your wrath? Or if you walked into your back yard for a good cry and toppled your favorite shade tree with grief? Some of us

---

40 Knohl, *Divine Symphony*, 73.

41 On the capacity of religion's sacred symbols to distinguish between the "real" (the realities of everyday life) and the "really real" (wider realities that correct and complete), see C. Geertz, "Religion as a Cultural System," in Geertz, *The Interpretation of Cultures: Selected Essays* (New York: Basic Books, 1973), 110–12.

dream of being that powerful, but it is a great mercy that such dreams do not come true.[42]

Further, we may take it as truth that silence in the presence of God can be not only freeing but also cleansing. Every speech act is in some sense an interference of thought and a corruption of vision. In her essay "The Aesthetics of Silence," Susan Sontag suggests an analogy that may be useful: "A landscape doesn't demand from the spectator his 'understanding,' his imputations of significance, his anxieties and his sympathies; it demands, rather that he does not add anything to it."[43] Just so, when we stand in the presence of the ineffable God, words are not only inadequate and unnecessary, but they also betray the transcendence of the ordinary we so desperately seek. God does not need our words in order to be fully God, and we, perhaps, only counterfeit the moment of revelation by speaking instead of listening. Silence has the salutary effect of cleansing our world of noise and redeeming us from what Sontag calls the "treachery of words" that encumber, compromise, and often adulterate our proximity to the sacred.[44]

Still, rituals that demand silence in the face of innocent suffering and gross injustice may be guilty of the worst kind of evasion. If the highest level of faith requires that we subtract our voices from this world in order to add to God's heavenly chorus, then can the sanctuary of worship be anything more than a retreat from the ethical mandate not only "to walk humbly" with God but also to "do justice" (Mic. 6:8)? The question is of course one frequently addressed to the priests by Israel's prophets. I believe we can be confident that the priests heard it and responded, though perhaps in ways unexpected. Even within Leviticus, Israel's "book of worship," the priests understand that silence inside the sanctuary (Lev. 1–15) is not the sum total of what is required of the faithful. It is but the first and necessary step toward moral and ethical engagement with the world that lies outside (Lev. 17–27). If one is to "be holy" in creaturely ways that image God's holiness (19:2), then silence is merely the preparation for the action that must follow, not the action itself. Just as narrowing the gauge heightens the compression and increases the velocity, so worship that narrows faith to obedience increases the likelihood that we may go out into the world with a passion for ministry that will not be thwarted. We may be confident that what we do and say outside the sanctuary matters, both to God

---

42   B. Brown Taylor, "On Not Being God," *RevExp* 99 (2002), 613.

43   S. Sontag, "The Aesthetics of Silence," in Sontag, *Styles of Radical Will* (New York: Farrar, Straus & Giroux, 1966), 16.

44   Ibid., 5, 15.

192   CHAPTER 10

and to the world. *And* we may take comfort in the truth that our efforts are not all that matters. Relieved of the burden of being God, we are freed to live as God's faithful stewards. In this world, God does not require and we cannot aspire to do more.

I cannot end without acknowledging one further matter that continues to nag at my best efforts to accept the priests' invitation to lay aside all reservations and enter fully into the sanctuary of silence. We may well accept the notion that silent obedience is the better route toward becoming the person God wants us to be. Even so, we cling to the hope that unspoken doubts and worries will not be lost in rituals of silence. In short, we trust that the priest will know our story. Here I take some comfort in a rabbinic clue about the lingering importance of Job for Israel's priests. The Mishnah stipulates a seven-day preparation period for the high priest before administering the rituals for the Day of Atonement, which includes required readings from the books of Daniel, Ezra, Nehemiah, and Job (*Yoma* 1:6). The rabbis do not explain their selection of this lectionary. Daniel, Ezra, and Nehemiah may have been thought appropriate because each contains models of the penitential prayer that the Day of Atonement requires (e.g., Dan. 9; Ezra 9; and Neh. 9). Job may well have been included for the same reason, given the widespread assumption that he too repents in the end. But in the absence of evidence to the contrary, we may wonder if rereading Job's story, the whole of his story and not just selected excerpts, might have sensitized the high priest to the presence of authentically dissonant voices among those he would soon summon to silence.[45]

If so, then I offer one last contemporary reflection on the issue before us. In *Father Melancholy's Daughter*, Gail Godwin describes a scene in which Father Gower, rector of St. Cuthbert's, a small parish in rural Virginia, struggles with the ministry of the sacraments. "The thing about a ritual," he always says, "is that it brings containment and acceptance to people. The sacramental life is a sort of sanity filter against the onslaughts of existence." Father Adrian, his friend a colleague, recognizes the wisdom in this theology and confirms it with a personal anecdote:

---

45   The comment in *Yoma* is frustratingly oblique. Similar references to the reading of Job in connection with Daniel, Ezra, and Nehemiah occur in Tosefta *Kippurim* (4:4) and in relevant discussions of the Talmud to *Yoma* 1:6, but none provide an explanation. I am grateful to Jack Neusner, who graciously responded to my inquiries concerning the rabbinic treatment of Job by pointing out that in reading Job, the rabbis deemed his story kosher, that is, "proper" or "suitable for use according to Jewish law" (see *Dictionary of Judaism in the Biblical Period 450 B.C.E. to 600 C.E.* [J. Neusner, ed. in chief, W. S. Green, ed.; New York: Macmillan, 1996], 374).

INSIDE THE "SANCTUARY OF SILENCE" 193

There was a Jesuit studying with me in Zurich, at the Institute. I once asked him, "What if you as a priest stopped believing? What would you do then?" "Make a fist in my pocket," he said, "and go on with the ritual."[46]

I think the Jobs of this world may well take comfort from the thought that the priest who summons them to submit in silence to the rituals of faith does so with a clinched fist. Might that fist be clinched in anger or protest, as if to say, "I don't really want to do this"? I concede that I would like to believe this is so. Might it be clinched as a deep expression of will and determination, maybe even, as Israel's priests might say, of faith? I am not sure, but I suspect there is always something more to be learned from any priest, ancient or contemporary, who resolves, clinched fists and all, to "go on with the ritual."[47]

As language always points to its own transcendence in silence, silence always points to its own transcendence – to a speech beyond silence.[48]

46   G. Goodwin, *Father Melancholy's Daughter* (New York: Avon, 1991), 274.
47   With deep gratitude, I acknowledge that the shaping of this last paragraph owes much to the comments of Bill Green, one of my most valued conversation partners, who helped me to think deeply about what the image of the priest's clinched fist might convey.
48   Sontag, "Aesthetics of Silence," 18.

CHAPTER 11

Traumatizing Job

The notion of psychological trauma emerged in medical lexicons in the late nineteenth and early twentieth centuries, largely in connection with the mental breakdown of soldiers returning from World War I with what came to be described as "shell-shock." Prolonged exposure to trench warfare fractured foundational beliefs (religious and otherwise) about the meaningfulness of the world. It forced ordinary persons to become philosophers and theologians. It reduced the language of those traumatized by "impacted grief" to one bewildered question, "Why?". Judith Herman offers a verbatim of the "crisis of faith" experienced by a combat veteran of the Vietnam War:

> I could not rationalize in my mind how God let good men die. I had gone to several ... priests. I was sitting there with this one priest and said, "Father, I don't understand this: How can God allow small children to be killed? What is this thing, this war, this bullshit? I got all these friends who are dead." ... That priest, he looked me in the eye and said, "I don't know, son, I've never been in war." I said, "I didn't ask you about war, I asked you about God."[1]

Herman's report of this conversation is revealing. It is the one outside the religious establishment who asks about God. It is the priest who speaks from inside this establishment who fails to understand that whatever wisdom he may impart about the world, about war, about life, his response will not be adequate without saying something about God.

1 The Old Testament's Lexicon of Trauma

The Old Testament has its own lexicon of trauma. We find it primarily in Lamentations, Deutero-Isaiah, portions of Jeremiah and Ezekiel, and in a number of "Jerusalem lament" psalms (e.g., Pss 44, 69, 74, 79, 102, 137). When Judah

---

1 J. Herman, *Trauma and Recovery: The Aftermath of Violence – From Domestic Abuse to Political Terror* (New York: Basic Books, 1992, 1997), 55. Herman quotes M. Norman, *These Good Men: Friendships Forged from War* (New York: Crown, 1989), 24. For the phrase "impacted grief," see Herman, *Trauma and Recovery*, 69.

© SAMUEL E. BALENTINE, 2021 | DOI:10.1163/9789004459212_012

"went away into exile" (586–538 BCE) as II Kngs 25:21 reports, the grand narrative that tracked Israel's pre-exilic "history" with God – from the garden of Eden to the temple in Jerusalem – comes to a punctiliar end. When the dust clears enough for the historical record to continue, some fifty years later, the narrative will resume (in Ezra-Nehemiah and I–II Chronicles). In the interim between what was and what will be, the texts that claw for answers to Israel's "Why?" question are these raw poetic articulations, a cacophony of words seeking a coherent narrative structure that no longer exists.

We may reflect on the intersection between this "Why?" question and its possible answers by considering William Gass's "Exemplum." God's primordial decision to "write the world," Gass suggests, presents an enormous challenge for those who would subsequently "exegete" God's script.

> And God decided to write the world. He wrote the words *round vast empty dark*. They made a line He liked. He wrote the word *vast* in triplicate because He wanted the world to be very, very vast. He wrote the word *empty* twice because He wanted the world to be mostly empty, so that one might turn tens of thousands of its pages and find them all blank and black. The word *dark* He doubled for the same reason.... God appointed one *vast* to accompany the darkness like a friend, and another to confront emptiness like an enemy, for what is it to be vast if your emptiness is for rent?

> *round vast empty dark*
> *vast dark empty vast*

> [I]nstructed by the future, then, God wrote *host of angelic scriveners* in His very long hand. Let them do the writing, which is damnably hard, God silently, inside Himself, said; I'll just publish. These were God's last words, even to Himself, since He wished to remain Omnipotent.

> *round vast empty dark*
> *vast dark empty vast*
> *host of angelic scriveners*

> God's last thought, however, was a bit of rearrangement.

> *round vast empty dark*
> *host of angelic scriveners*
> *vast dark empty vast*

196   CHAPTER 11

He wanted his writers to be in the thick of things.[2]

If God wanted writers "to be in the thick of things," then surely the ancient scribes working during the years 586–538 were well placed, though not by choice, to do the "damnably hard" work of putting the proverbial pen to the paper. For all their different ways of responding to the post-586 crisis of faith, Israel's "theologians of exile" return again and again to one common affirmation. The underlying answer to the question why Israel has experienced such brokenness and loss is human sin, not divine caprice. For the purpose of this essay, we may allow the word from God delivered by Ezekiel to speak for the whole: "They shall realize that it was *not without cause* (*lo' 'el-ḥinnām*; literally, "not for no reason") that I the Lord brought this evil upon them" (Ezek 6:10; cf. 14:23). We should not be surprised that such an answer ricochets throughout Israel's long years in exile, and far beyond, as those summoned to yield to its truth stumble toward comprehension. "Trauma," as A. Berlin has noted, "takes time to find literary expression."[3]

2   "Have You Considered My Servant Job?"

With this is mind, I turn to the Book of Job, perhaps the quintessential text in the biblical lexicon of trauma. The dating of the book is notoriously difficult, and I will not enter into this debate here. Suffice it to say that the final form of the book (excepting the Elihu speeches in Job 32–37 and perhaps the Wisdom poem in Job 28) can be dated between the seventh and fifth centuries BCE. Though there are no concrete references to historical events, including no mention of the fall of the Jerusalem, we can be reasonably confident that the hard questions about the justice of God so acutely connected to this post 586 world are generative in Job as well. Moreover, there are clear affinities between Job and the texts mentioned above – Lamentations, Deutero-Isaiah, Jeremiah, Ezekiel, and the psalms of laments – especially in the poetic "middle" of the book (Job 3:1–42:6), which indicate that the Joban author(s) was deeply engaged with the same or at least a very similar set of issues as these other poetic voices. Indeed, in most cases where the Joban poet appears to be in dialogue with these other exilic poets, he typically goes far beyond them, either

---

2   W. Gass, "Sacred Texts," in *A Temple of Texts: Essays* (New York: Alfred A. Knopf, 2006), 358, 360.

3   A. Berlin, *Lamentations, A Commentary* (OTL; Louisville: Westminster John Knox, 2002), 33.

by accentuating the grief and despair they express or by radicalizing the hope they envision.[4]

My focus here, however, is not on the unresolved poetic dialogue that rages at the center of the book but rather with the apparently settled narrative of the Prologue-Epilogue (Job 1–2; 42:7–17) that frames this debate, specifically the divine assertion recorded in Job 2:3:

> The Lord said to the *satan*, "Have you considered my servant Job? There is no one like him on the earth, a blameless and upright man who fears God and turns away from evil. He still persists in his integrity, although you incited me against him, to destroy him *for no reason*" (*ḥinnām*).

Inside the gap between Ezekiel's affirmation that God's punishment of sin is "not without cause" (Ezek. 6:10; 14:23) and the Joban narrator's affirmation that God can and does punish a righteous person like Job "without cause," biblical exegetes are perforce dragged into the deep waters of what the Hebrew Bible has to say about trauma and theology.[5]

In what follows, I probe two simple but exacting exegetical questions that I believe we must address.[6] First, what do these texts *mean*? When texts lacquered with authority affirm that God executes and/or sanctions the loss of life, possessions, and property *both with and without cause*, what does this mean for those who must respond with real-time commitments? Second, are these texts *true*? Whatever the meaning for ancient readers, is it true – not only then, but also now and always – that "evil," is an irremediable fact of creaturely existence in this world, whether one explains it as human failure or divine judgment?

---

4   A few examples must suffice. Compare the way Job 16 pushes the lament described in Lam 3 toward a radically litigious demand for justice; the way Job 3 pushes the curses of Jer 20 toward a criminal indictment of God; the way Job 9–10 (cf. Job 13, 16, 19, 29–31) expands the legal metaphor in Jer 12:1–4 in order to bring a formal suit against God; the way Job's complaints about innocent suffering critique Deutero-Isaiah's commendation of vicarious suffering; and the way Job 7 subverts the conventional praise exemplified in Psalm 8.

5   Space does not permit a lexical survey of the 32 occurrences in the Old Testament of the adverb *ḥinnām*, "needlessly, without purpose, for nothing." The most pertinent observation is this: of the 32 occurrences, only Ezek 6:10, 14:23 and Job 2:3 (cf. Job 9:17) use this word to describe actions of God that are "with" or "without cause." For further discussion, see S. E. Balentine, "For No Reason," *Interpretation* 57 (2003), 349–369 and *Job* (Macon, GA: Smyth & Helwys, 2006), 41–78.

6   Here I follow the cogent discernments of J. Barton, *The Nature of Biblical Criticism* (Louisville, London: Westminster John Knox, 2007), especially his chapters on "The Plain Sense" (69–116) and "Biblical Criticism and Religious Belief" (137–186).

198 CHAPTER 11

What do these texts mean? The first task is to ask what texts that describe God acting with or without cause mean. This requires that we temporarily bracket the question about whether what they mean is true, that is, whether what they say about God is theologically constructive or productive, in order to examine critically the essential givenness of the text. Three matters require attention: syntax, genre, and context.

(1). The syntax of *ḥinnām*. The word order of Job 2:3 permits different interpretations. The location of *ḥinnām* at the end of the verse is typical, but in this instance it follows two verbal forms, "you incited me" (*wattĕsîtenî*) and the infinitive construct, "to destroy him" (*lĕballĕʿô*), which immediately precedes it. It is possible to take the adverb as modifying the first verb, in which case the sense would be that the *satan, not God*, has acted "without cause" or "vainly," because the test the *satan* proposed has not produced the intended result. Such a reading is not impossible. But, even accepting that the adverb describes the futility of the *satan's* test, we still have to reckon with the admission, attributed here to God, that the *satan* has successfully provoked God to afflict Job, something God presumably would not have considered doing on God's own, which is the clear meaning of the phrase "you [*satan*] *incited* me [God]."[7] It is also possible, and I would argue more likely, that *ḥinnām* modifies the infinitive construct, in which case the text conveys an admission from God that God has acted "to destroy" Job (literally, "to swallow him" [*lĕballĕʿo*]; cf. Prov. 1:10–11) "for no reason." That is, the emphasis is not on the *futility of the satan's test* but rather on *God's gratuitous treatment of Job*. This "plain sense" of the verse, as jarring as it may be to our sensibilities, accords well with the two counter assertions in Ezek 6:10 and 14:23. There, God declares that God will punish Israel because of its sin, thus the exile is "not for no reason." In Job 2:3, God declares, with apparent equanimity, that God has afflicted Job, who has not sinned, "for no reason."

(2). Genre. The Prologue exhibits the typical characteristics of a didactic tale. As Carol Newsom has perceptively argued, the rhetorical strategy of the Joban didactic tale creates a sharp tension with the strategy of the wisdom dialogue that is the generic template for the poetry in Job 3–27.[8] The didactic tale prizes simple assertions, conceptual clarity, and monologic truth, as conveyed by the authoritative narrator who tells the story. The world works

---

7 The construction "incite against" (*swt* [hiphil] + *bĕ*) means to stir up someone to an action against another that would not have occurred without provocation (cf. 1 Sam 26:19; 11 Sam 24:1; Jer 43:3). Job 2:3 is the only place in the Hebrew Bible where this construction is used with God as the subject of the verbal action.

8 C. Newsom, *The Book of Job: A Contest of Moral Imagination* (Oxford: Oxford University Press, 2003), especially 32–89.

TRAUMATIZING JOB 199

this way, the narrator says, and the implied reader of the story is expected to agree and to conform to unambiguous truths. The wisdom dialogue, by contrast, prizes argumentation, debate and dissension, and a skeptical, or at least critically inquisitive, response to monologic assertions of truth buttressed by hierarchical claims to privilege. The world in which we live defies certainty, the wisdom dialogue insists, truth resides in the contradictions between expectation and experience, and the implied reader is thereby instructed to adapt to a life defined more by irresolvable questions than predetermined answers.

Against the backdrop of these different rhetorical strategies, what are we to make of the Prologue's assertion that God acts "for no reason"? It would be easy to dismiss this as a "superfluous detail"[9] that has little effect on the larger truth towards which the Epilogue presses its readers. We might wonder, however, if this assertion, here cast as direct divine speech for the first and only time in Hebrew scripture, is not in fact the primary truth this didactic tale strives to make. The narrative that conveys the truth about God and the world has seemingly dead-ended with Israel's exile. Inside this cul-de-sac, Israel's prophets, priests, and sages offer a variety of responses, sometimes giving voice to anguished "Why?" questions, sometimes countering the questions with assurances that transcend them. These multiple voices continue to speak in the Book of Job; indeed, the poetic dialogues between Job and his friends provide a hyper example of the intertextual debate we see in Lamentations, Deutero-Isaiah, Jeremiah, and Ezekiel. But if the final form of Job sustains this debate, it also locates it within a narrative that now includes a new wrinkle. The story that once insisted that God *does not* act "without cause" now resumes by turning the complaint rumbling throughout the exile that God *does* act "without cause" into a truth that promises reward in exchange for surrender.

(3). Context. The prose narrative commends Job's patient endurance as the exemplary response God expects of those whose piety is tested by suffering. The test is posed in the *satan*'s question, "Will Job fear God *for no reason*? (*hinnām*; 1:9), which hints that the relationship between God and humans is essentially a calculated transaction. When God blesses humans with prosperity, humans bless God with faithful service in return. But do the terms of the

---

9 Newsom notes that didactic literature typically eliminates "superfluous details" that may distract from the message. "This impulse," she says, "is present to a remarkable degree in the prose tale of Job" (*The Book of Job*, 43). But, as she also acknowledges, "One must always keep in mind that stories *participate* in genres rather than *being defined by them*" (Ibid., 38; emphasis added). I would argue that the words "for no reason" in Job 2:3 are one such example. Cf. D. J. A. Clines, who notes that *hinnām*, which occurs in Job 1:9, 2:3, 9:17, and 22:6, "is a leitmotif of the Job story" (*Job 21–37* [WBC; Dallas: Word, 2006], 556), though he does not explain how or why.

transaction change when God's blessings are not forthcoming, when, as in the exile, for example, life is measured out in social dislocation, physical affliction, and economic loss? Is complaint and protest a necessary or legitimate return for God's apparent indifference to the terms of the relationship? The evident answer offered by the narrative is "No."

There is widespread agreement that a later author found this answer unsatisfactory and spliced the narrative with the poetic dialogues, which offer alternative perspectives on how the faithful relate to God in times of crisis. I do not disagree with this assessment, but I question whether we have rightly understood the rhetorical role the Prologue now plays within the context of the final form of the book. My suspicion is that the "test" the narrative addresses is not (or not only) the *satan*'s question in 1:9 about disinterested human piety but God's admission in 2:3 about the gratuitousness of divine justice. The words "for no reason," previously implausible descriptors of divine justice, have now inched their way into a narrative that authorizes – and naturalizes – them as divine assertion. Once "for no reason" becomes part of the "authorized version" of the story, once it is asserted as a "simple truth" articulated with God's moral authority, can there be any dissent, whether from the friends or Job, which can be commended as righteous?

Are these texts true? The second exegetical question asks how or if a text's essential meaning has import for the world in which we live, that is, if it is true in relation to what we already know or believe. We may evaluate a given truth as one that remains not only persuasive but also authoritative, in which case the text can either confirm or correct what we know or believe to be true. We may evaluate a text's given meaning as plausibly true and authoritative in its own context but not automatically or necessarily so in ours. In this case, what we know and believe to be true in our world may require that we reject what the text says is true in its world. In either case, the move from understanding what a text means to evaluating and/or appropriating its truth requires a procedural pause. Between analysis and advocacy, there must be a safe-zone where readers are free to ponder what texts require of them.

The syntax, genre, and context of Job 2:3 indicate that in the wake of the trauma of exile, the words "for no reason" found a place within one narrative that claimed to speak with authority about the truth of innocent suffering, from God's perspective. Is this assertion from and about God true? If the text actually says that God acts "for no reason," is this a theologically constructive or productive assertion?

To get our bearings on the import of such questions, we might imagine ourselves into the role of the priest who sits before a trauma victim like the one Herman describes in the verbatim cited at the beginning of this essay. Better yet, we might imagine ourselves into the role of the narrator who turns to Job's story in order to address those who have lived through the horrors of exile. What can we say about God, if the words "for no reason" are part of the scripture we have received?

3   Traumatizing Job

Is the declaration that God acts "for no reason," a *traumatized concession* to reality, a change forced upon the narrative by a truth that can no longer be erased or manipulated? Or, does this text convey a *traumatizing assertion*, a psychic shot across the bow of all would-be dissenters that is designed to shock them into (in)voluntary compliance? By juxtaposing these questions, I do not suggest that simple "Yes" or "No" answers will be adequate for either. As Barton has wisely cautioned, questions that presume only one answer tend to be no more than "pseudoquestions."[10] I risk the following ruminations.

It seems to me that the shift from Ezekiel's "not for no reason" to the Prologue's "for no reason" could well be a *traumatized concession* to reality. Some experiences of brokenness and loss are simply too devastating, the wounds they open too gaping, the scars they leave too permanent. Existing narratives about what life can be or should be are no longer adequate to tell the story. Absent alteration, they remain authoritative and constructive only for those who have been spared the uninvited wisening that comes from what Tennyson calls the "Dirty Nurse" named "Experience."[11] If our analysis is done, in fact, in a safe-zone, where we are free to contemplate all possibilities without restraint, then might it be that the "dirty nurse, Experience" vandalizes even the Creator, wrenching a concession to reality that was not part of God's primordial hopes and expectations for the world?

How might those who have walked in the footsteps of Job respond to the concession that reality is fungible; that trusted – even divine – truths can be traumatized, forced to bow before larger truths that were previously denied plausibility? Is the concession that God does what God does "for no reason" a truth that comforts because it affirms that life in relation to God is by necessity an ongoing negotiation with the implausible? It is not difficult to imagine that the Jobs of this world would say "Yes," if only because they could be assured that their traumatized truth about life and about God has a legitimate place in

---

10   Barton, *The Nature of Biblical Criticism*, 168.

11   Alfred Lord Tennyson, "Idylls of the King: The Last Tournament," in *Tennyson's Poetry*, selected and edited by R. Hill (New York: W. W. Norton, 1971), ll. 317–318, p. 394.

the lexicon of faith. It is also not difficult to imagine that the Jobs of this world, not to mention those who would be Job's friends and counselors, would wince at the concession that God is complicit in innocent misery, "for no reason." Once the boundary between the plausible and the implausible is breached, once the Creator of the world speaks the words "for no reason," is there any defense against the assault that claims victory by declaring that God is a nonfactor in the outcome?

It seems to me that the declaration that God acts "for no reason" might also be a *traumatizing assertion*. Its rhetorical effect might be likened to the electric shock treatments used during World War I to treat "shell-shock" victims. After prolonged exposure to trench warfare, soldiers who returned home exhibited what the British psychiatrist Lewis Yealland described as the "hideous enemy of negativism."[12] To correct their hysterical behavior, Yealland strapped patients into a chair and applied electric shocks to their *throat*. As that image begins to take shape in our mind, consider what Yealland was saying to the soldiers as the shocks were being applied: "you must behave as the hero I expect you to be.... A man who has gone through so many battles should have better control of himself."[13] The objective of the treatment was to return the soldier to battle as soon as possible, which usually happened within a matter of weeks.

I do not wish to over analogize this method of treatment. But, if we read Job through the lens of trauma theory, it is hard to read the narrator's words in Job 2:10 (cf. 1:22) without making a connection. After God speaks the words "for no reason" (Job 2:3), the narrator confirms that "In all this, Job did not sin *with his lips.*"

Would trauma victims who have walked in Job's footsteps find comfort in God's assertion that there is "no reason" for what they have experienced? Would this be a theologically constructive truth? Would it help victims rebuild shattered values and beliefs? I can imagine that it might be a positive word, even if a traumatizing one, if only because it could address the "Why me?" question that typically dogs the victim. The "answer," such as it is, is that there is no reason that can be traced either to the person who has been traumatized or to the God who has permitted it, sanctioned it, or watched over it. Bad things happen to good people, for no reason. The route to recovery, therefore, will only be stymied by the search for a culprit. Best simply to treat the wound, then get up and return to the fray.

---

12   *Hysterical Disorders of Warfare* (1918), cited in Herman, *Trauma and Recovery*, 21.

13   Herman, *Trauma and Recovery*, 21. Herman quotes E. Showalter, *The Female Malady: Women, Madness, and English Culture, 1830–1980* (New York: Pantheon, 1985), 177.

I can also imagine, and indeed think it far more likely, that trauma victims will not find the truth that God acts for no reason to be theologically constructive. Newsom has argued that the appeal of the didactic tale is also the basis for resistance to it. It offers parental assurance by "infantilizing the reader."[14] "For no reason" is, by God's design, simply a part of life's equation that those who are too immature to comprehend need not question. Not all readers are children, however, and the presumption that they cannot or should not make their own decisions about what to believe, say, or do in times of crisis is flawed. Newsom describes the reader's instinctive resistance to the narrator's assertion as follows: "[D]idactic literature provokes hostile responses from those who find in its excessively sheltered world of meaning the threat of perpetual moral immaturity."[15] Many readers, especially those seared by traumatic experiences, will decide that perpetual moral immaturity is too high a price to pay for the "psychic reassurance" promised in the Joban narrator's words, "for no reason."[16]

One further issue continues to press for a place in my ruminations on whether the words "for no reason" are a traumatized *concession to reality* or a traumatizing assertion that *defies reality*. Herman notes that studies of psychological trauma have both prospered and floundered in direct connection with political support or political indifference or opposition.[17] It is not a new thing to recognize that all texts, including biblical texts, are forged in the crucible of political power. When we read a narrative that seeks to recruit its readers to certain beliefs and their consequent imperatives for shaping attitudes and behavior, we must ask whose political and ideological interests it is serving.

For whom does the Joban narrator speak? When he asserts that God acts "for no reason," does he speak for the religious establishment, for those who may be insulated from the trauma of life's uncertainties by social standing and economic privilege? If so, then whatever authority the narrator claims, it must be credible in the face of those who are vulnerable to questions the narrator may understand only from a safe distance. Does the narrator speak with first-hand knowledge of what it means to be vulnerable to brokenness and loss that happens "for no reason"? If so, then he may speak more for those who have been traumatized by the religious establishment's orthodoxy than for those who wish to defend it.

---

14 Newsom, *Book of Job*, 45. Newsom cites S. Suleiman, *Authoritarian Fiction: The Ideological Novel as a Literary Genre* (Princeton: Princeton University Press, 1983), 10.

15 Newsom, *The Book of Job*, 45.

16 Ibid., 47.

17 Herman, *Trauma and Recovery*, 7–32.

There are clues that the Book of Job emerges from and speaks for a learned scribal culture, one that enjoys the luxury of sophisticated analysis that is not disinterested in shoring up its privileges within power structures that may be under assault. I concede that the evidence that permits us to speak of the social location of the Joban author(s) is largely circumstantial. Nonetheless, there is an itching truth in William Gass's observation that sacred texts "supply the illusions which suit the powers that be, and calm the fears of the general population." In a certain sense, as Gass goes on to say, now focusing more directly on the authors of biblical texts, "that's what theologians are for – [they are] the spin doctors of the sacred."[18]

Have the authors of the Book of Job traumatized this legendary character's contribution to what scripture says about God by inserting the words "for no reason" into the narrative? Is the Book of Job in and of itself a traumatizing witness to what life in relation to God means when the dust settles and the final accounts are tallied? As far as I can see, both questions are legitimate and requisite; neither yields to simple "Yes" or "No" answers, at least none that either the ancient scriveners or we modern guardians of sacred texts have thus far crafted. In the end, there is *this God* who "decided to write the world," and the legacy of *this text*, with the words "for no reason" now intractably etched into "the inky realm of the sacred."[19]

I conclude by returning one last time to Gass's "Exemplum" on sacred texts:

> Such goings-on, God thought, when only **round dark vast empty** were the four words written. Did no one find themselves troubled by the contradictions among all these truths ...?
>
> God had created the scriveners for a not entirely laudable purpose. It made Him less responsible for all the divinely inspired balderdash they'd fill the earth with.... Not all these fellows had Chrysostom's golden throat. He thought about tossing the lot out of heaven and into some fiery pit, but then He remembered in time that there was no heaven in His system, only in theirs, and no Hell in His, either. Hell was their damn doing, as well. He could have cried *erase*, as He had considered crying earlier; however, He remained tied to His vow like a pony to a post, and docile and content in regard to Himself. So He spoke through the forks of the scriveners tongues and wrote them off. Go roast your toes in your own lies, He said, stroking the beard some said He had, letting the no-longer-holy

---

18   Gass, "Sacred Texts," 367.

19   Ibid.

TRAUMATIZING JOB

host be swallowed in the fog of their own illusions. I'll catechize the four I can count on.

> *round*
> *vast*
> *empty*
> *dark*[20]

There is no period at the end of Gass's quote and none at the end of my essay. I cannot speak for Gass, but as for me, the absence of some kind of punctuation that brings satisfying or authoritative closure to the sentence is intentional.

---

20   Ibid., 372, 374.

PART 5

Out of the Whirlwind:
"Can You Thunder with a Voice Like God's?"

∵

CHAPTER 12

"What Are Human Beings, That You Make So Much of Them?" Divine Disclosure from the Whirlwind: "Look at Behemoth"

In his search for a new shape for Old Testament theology, Walter Brueggemann has argued that serious attention must be given to Israel's restless practice of lament, for herein lies "a fresh hunch" about God. In his words, "The hunch is that this God does not want to be an unchallenged structure, but one who can be frontally addressed."[1] A central thesis in Brueggemann's proposal is that lament forces both God and Israel to recalculate the possibilities and the requirements of covenant relationship. It draws God into the fray of human pain and trouble, and as a result God must *do* or *be* something new. In the process Israel learns that obedience is more than "docile submissiveness," it is also "bold protest."[2]

As evidence of Israel's courage and persistence in lament, Brueggemann points specifically to a "countertradition" of approaching God that is represented by Moses, the lament psalms, Jeremiah, and Job.[3] What is most striking about these examples is that in the case of Job, the practice of lament seems to have failed. Here, the single most sustained and harsh lamentation in the Hebrew Bible is coupled to a divine response from the whirlwind that is conventionally interpreted as an unequivocal rebuke of Job. Job dares to address God frontally, so this line of interpretation goes, and he pays a heavy price for his recklessness. With the force of hurricane-like winds, God denies Job's approach and drives him into silence and submission.[4]

With this essay I wish to express my deep appreciation for Brueggemann's passionate insistence that Israel's lament traditions be accorded their rightful

---

1   W. Brueggemann, "A Shape for Old Testament Theology II: Embrace of Pain," CBQ 47 (1983), 401.
2   Ibid.
3   Ibid., 402–406.
4   Brueggemann does not offer extended discussion of the divine speeches in Job in his programmatic essay for Old Testament theology, but his proposal suggests some sympathy with the conventional understanding noted above. He observes, for example, that while Israel's laments had the power to evoke from God a new posture of relationship, they did not always do so. On some occasions, as in Job, the lament is "rejected" or "disregarded" (Brueggemann, "Embrace of Pain," 404, 405).

© SAMUEL E. BALENTINE, 2021 | DOI:10.1163/9789004459212_013

place in the theology of the Old Testament. As one small witness to the influence of Brueggemann's own daring and imaginative reconstrual of Israel's faith traditions, I propose here to reconsider the revelation that Job receives from the whirlwind. I suggest that God's speech may be interpreted not as a rebuke or a denial, but rather as a radical summons to a new understanding of what it means for humankind to be created in the image of God. In this view, it is not silence and submission that God requires; it is steadfast lament and relentless opposition to injustice and innocent suffering, wherever it appears. In this view of the divine speeches, God regards Job not as an aberration within the created order that is to be corrected or eliminated. He is rather a supreme model for humankind that God is committed to nurture and sustain.

The emergence of this model in Job may be traced through three stages (1) the debate within the dialogues about what it means, in Job's world, to be created in the image of God; (2) the importance of the revelation concerning Behemoth and Leviathan in addressing this debate; and (3) Job's final response to God's revelation.

1 Primordial Questions: "What Are Human Beings, That You Make So Much of Them?"

The prologue to the book of Job envisions "the land of Uz" as the setting for a drama that returns imaginatively to the beginnings of creation.[5] Job's world is idyllic, a perfect recapitulation of primordial Eden. Everything is in place for life that is in complete harmony with God's cosmic design. But then Job's

---

5 A number of verbal and thematic parallels sustain the connection between Job 1–2 and Genesis 1–3, of which the following may be singled out. (1) "The land of Uz" orients the story towards the east (cf. Job 1:3), the putative locus for the Garden of Eden (Gen 2:8), thus marking the location where humankind was first prepared for the revelation of God's cosmic design. (2) As the hero of the story, Job is portrayed as a second Adam. His full family and his contingent of servants and possessions (Job 1:2–3) suggest his exemplary fulfilment of the creational commission to "be fruitful and multiply" and to have "dominion" over the created order (Gen 1:28). (3) The story of Job 1–2 is enacted through six scenes alternatively set in heaven and earth (1:1–5; 1:6–12; 1:13–22; 2:1–7a; 2:7b–10; 2:11–13). A seventh scene is introduced with Job's curse (Job 3), which serves as the preface to the poetic dialogues. The structuring of this grand drama in seven scenes recalls the heptadic patterning of the creation story in Genesis 1. On these and other connections, see S. Meir, "Job I–II: A Reflection of Genesis I–III," VT 39 (1989), 183–193. On creation imagery generally in Job, see L. G. Perdue, *Wisdom in Revolt: Metaphorical Theology in the Book of Job* (JSOTSup 112; Sheffield: Almond Press, 1991); idem, *Wisdom and Creation: The Theology of Wisdom Literature* (Nashville: Abingdon, 1994), 123–192.

paradise is shattered, and his story of what it means to live in accordance with God's design for creation takes a radical turn. The loss of his wealth and possessions, the unjust death of his children, and the affliction of horrible physical suffering suggest that the forces of the cosmos, heaven and earth, have been unleashed against this servant of God.[6] Still more unsettling is the report that Job's world has been undone "for no reason" (2:3: *ḥinnām*; cf. 1:9), other than that God has been "provoked" (*swt*) by the satan.

How will Job respond to *this* world of brokenness and loss, where the harmony of creation's design yields to unexpected and unwarranted assault? The prologue wants to insist that Job blesses (*brk*), not curses, God (1:21). But as commentators have noted, the semantics of blessing in Job are unclear. Despite all efforts to resolve the ambiguity, the reader is left with no certain criteria for deciding whether Job blesses or curses God, or offers some other response that moves between these two poles.[7]

The ambiguity of Job's response to God in the prologue is suspended once the dialogues begin. After seven days of quiet suffering in this now afflicted world, Job breaks the silence of pain with words of curse, not blessing (3:1–10), words of lament, not praise (3:11–26). With a series of seven curses against the day (vv. 3a, 4–5) and the night (vv. 6–9) Job speaks a "countercosmic incantation" that parodies the language of Genesis 1.[8] He calls in effect for a negation of creation and a reversal of its orders. The lament in vv. 11–26 tracks Job's steady deterioration, through the repetition of the question "Why?" (vv. 11, 12, 20), into a bitterness of soul marked by rage and agony (v. 26: *rōgez*). These opening words signal that suffering like Job's calls the whole of creation into question and with it the Creator who is responsible for its design. Job's questions will reverberate throughout the rest of the dialogues and will set the agenda for the friends' responses. Whatever answers are proposed, Job will insist that they

---

6   In Job 1:13–22 the agents of the calamities that befall Job are described alternatively from earth and heaven (vv. 13–15: Sabeans; v. 16: "fire of God"; v. 17: Babylonians; vv. 18–19: a "great wind" (*rûaḥ gĕdôlāh*; cf. Gen 1:2).

7   The uncertainty derives from the fact that in the prologue *bārak* seems to convey the normal meaning "bless" in 1:10, 21, but in 1:5, 11, and 2:5, 9 it seems to have an opposite meaning, "curse, blaspheme." Cf. T. Linafelt, "The Undecidability of *brk* in the Prologue to Job and Beyond," *BI* 4 (1996), 154–172.

8   Note esp. the work of L. Perdue, "Job's Assault on Creation," *HAR* 10 (1987), 295–315; "Metaphorical Theology in the Book of Job: Theological Anthropology in the First Cycle of Job's Speeches (Job 3; 6–7; 9–10)," in *The Book of Job* (ed. W. A. M. Beuken; Leuven: University Press, 1994), 142–148; *Wisdom in Revolt*, 91–110; *Wisdom and Creation*, 131–137. On the countercosmic incantation see M. Fishbane, "Jeremiah IV 23–26 and Job III 3–13: A Recovered Use of the Creation Pattern," *VT* 21 (1971), 153.

212   CHAPTER 12

must have meaning not only In the paradisiacal world of Eden/Uz, but also in
the world of innocent sufferers who sit among the ashes.

The ensuing dialogues address a variety of issues and questions, but for the
purpose of this essay, none is more important than the primordial question
about what it means – in Job's world – for humanity to be created in the image
of God. The exploration of this question begins in Job 7:17–21, where Job's critical scrutiny of a traditional vision of humankind subverts praise into a doxology of sarcasm.[9]

The model for Job's doxology is Ps 8:3–5 (MT 4–6).[10] For the psalmist the
hierarchy of the created order, which exalts humankind as a near equal to God
(as in Genesis 1) witnesses to God's wondrous attention and beneficence. In
God's design mere humans are elevated to royal status and given dominion and
responsibility for God's creation. In the world of the psalmist such a design is
occasion for astonished praise: "What are frail mortals [*ĕnôš*] that you should
be mindful of them, human beings, that you should take notice of them?" In
the world of Job, however, these words are laden with vexed ambiguity. They
evoke astonishment, but not praise: What are human beings (*ĕnôš*)? that God
should expend such effort to examine (*pqd*) them and test (*bḥn*) them so
relentlessly (Job 7:18)? Job's perspective from the ashes indicates that the status of the human being before God is that of a powerless victim, not a royal
steward. Through the lens of innocent suffering he concludes that humans are
creatures targeted for destruction, not for special care and exaltation.

It is the nature of the dialogues that virtually no assertion or reflection goes
unchallenged. Job's critique of the theology of Psalm 8 is no exception. Of the
friends, it is Eliphaz who repeatedly takes up the question of what it means
to be a human being before God (cf. Job 4:17–19; 15:7–16; 22:1–11). Especially
pertinent is the speech in 15:7–16 in which Eliphaz responds to Job specifically
by returning to the psalmist's question, this time with a strategic shift of focus:
"What are mortals [*ĕnôš*], that they can be clean [*yizkeh*]?" (v. 14).[11]

---

9   Cf. Perdue (*Wisdom in Revolt*, 153–56), who describes Job's 13:13–25 as a "doxology of ter-
     ror." In this speech Perdue observes that hymnic praise is subverted into a doxology to
     God's destructive power.

10   On the rhetorical links and differences between Job 7 and Psalm 8, see esp. M. Fishbane,
     Biblical Interpretation in Ancient Israel (Oxford: Clarendon, 1985), 285–286; idem, "The
     Book of Job and Inner-biblical Discourse," in *The Voice from the Whirlwind: Interpreting
     the Book of Job* (ed. L. G. Perdue and W. C. Gilpin; Nashville; Abingdon, 1992) 87–90;
     P. E. Dion, "Formulaic Language in the Book of Job: International Background and Ironical
     Distortions," *SR* 16 (1987), 187–193.

11   Cf. Fishbane, "Book of Job and Inner-biblical Discourse," 93.

"WHAT ARE HUMAN BEINGS, THAT YOU MAKE SO MUCH OF THEM?"   213

On the surface the argument by Eliphaz is a simple one: human beings are sinful. They cannot claim to approach God in innocence, as Job repeatedly insists he is doing (9:15, 20–21; 10:15; 12:4), because they are inevitably flawed and imperfect reflections of the Creator (cf. 4:17–21). To insist otherwise is a foolish and risky breach of the boundary established by God between the divine and the human. Eliphaz warns Job that he stands on the verge of violating this boundary by invoking an old creation tradition about "the firstborn [*ri'yšôn*] of the human race" (15:7).[12] Does Job dare to imagine that he was present at creation, privileged by birth and by status to participate in the decisions of the divine council (v. 8)?

It is interesting, however, that as part of the argument against Job's misplaced hubris, Eliphaz challenges him with a question: "Were you brought forth before the hills?" (v. 7). The question is a quotation of Prov 8:25, where it is used with reference to the origins and vocation of personified Wisdom.[13] The context for the verse is Prov 8:22–31, a hymn in which Wisdom exults in being the "first" (v. 22: *rē'šît*) of God's creative acts. The hymn carries no suggestion of hubris, no indication that primal wisdom should be regarded as a figure for rebuke or condemnation. Instead, Wisdom celebrates its role as the firstborn child who works as a cocreator beside YHWH, the divine parent and master architect of the cosmos (vv. 27–29). Indeed, the parent Creator and the begotten cocreator are intimately linked by their mutual delight in one another (vv. 30–31). Joyfully partnered with God in the work of creation, Wisdom invites all who will to take up the life it models: "happy are those who keep my ways. ... For whoever finds me finds life" (vv. 32, 33).

Eliphaz clearly intends his question about the "firstborn" to be a rebuke of Job for misunderstanding his proper place in the hierarchy of creation. But in the tradition from which he draws in order to challenge Job, there is a latent ambiguity. Is it *misguided hubris* or *radical faith* to believe that human beings are created in the image of God and are thereby specially prepared for delightful

---

12   Rooted in ancient Near Eastern mythology, the figure of "the primal human" was used to speak of the origins of kingship. The assumption of the myth is that the king, as the first human created by the gods, was present at creation and participated in the divine decisions that ordered the cosmos. In biblical texts some vestige of the myth may be detected in Genesis 3–11 and in Ezekiel 28, where it takes on a negative connotation in association with the temptation of humans to rebel against divine rule and to arrogate to themselves divine authority and wisdom. On the significance of this myth for Job, see especially, Perdue, *Wisdom in Revolt*, 165–170.

13   The myth about the primal human is no doubt older than both Proverbs and Job. On the question of the relative datings of Proverbs and Job, a good case can be made that the of literary dependence is from the former to the latter; cf. D. J. A. Clines, *Job 1–20* (WBC 17; Dallas: Word, 1989), 350.

214   CHAPTER 12

communion and shared partnership with the deity? Eliphaz asserts the former,
but the evidence he cites ironically invites consideration of the latter. Between
Eliphaz and Job, therefore, the debate about the theology of Psalm 8 produces
no clear affirmation. The primordial question of human identity and vocation
remains contested and unresolved.

In the broken world of Job, where innocent suffering calls every faith assertion into question, what are human beings to be and do? The question is
addressed by other speakers in a variety of ways throughout the dialogues, but
without resolution, and the drama therefore reaches an important juncture
with the divine speeches in Job 38–41. It is highly suggestive, I believe, that the
exploration of Psalm 8 and of the image the firstborn that has so concerned Job
and Eliphaz reappears in God's speech about Behemoth and Leviathan.

2   Divine Disclosure: "Look at Behemoth"

The whirlwind speeches provide God's "answer" to Job; but as Carol Newsom
has aptly observed, they are fraught with "irreducible ambiguities" that invite
and perhaps require more than one interpretation.[14] In what follows I do not
pretend or necessarily desire to resolve these ambiguities. I do wish to suggest,
however, that certain clues in the text invite new ways of thinking about how
this theophany, in both form and substance, serves to unite God and Job in perhaps the most daring and revealing exploration of what it means to be "created
in the image of God" that is found in the Hebrew Bible.[15] Four discernments
inform my own "fresh hunches" about what God is revealing to Job.

---

14   C. Newsom, "The Book of Job," in *NIB* (Nashville: Abingdon, 1996), 4: 595. Newsom
       observes, rightly in my judgment, that the polyvalence of the divine speeches is more
       than a problem to be resolved. It is an invitation to each reader to wrestle imaginatively
       with the meaning of divine disclosure. "The elusiveness of the divine speeches requires
       the reader to assume a more active role in making meaning than does a text in which the
       'message' is simple and transparent" (596).

15   Interpretive efforts often emphasize the incongruity between the *medium* for the divine
       response, theophany, and the *message* that the theophany conveys. Theophanies mark
       a special revelation that brings God into more intimate relationship with human beings
       that is ordinarily evident or possible. Yet God's appearance to Job seems designed to
       rebuke him and to deny his search for intimacy with the one he would embrace. See,
       e.g., J. L. Crenshaw ("When Form and Content Clash: The Theology of Job 38:1–40:5," in
       Creation in the Biblical Traditions [eds. J. J. Collins and R. J. Clifford; CBQMS 24; Washington:
       Catholic Biblical Association of America, 1993], 70–84: "If anything the portrayal of deity
       in the speeches increases the distance between human beings and their maker. This
       distancing takes place, paradoxically, despite a literary form that emphasizes incredible

1. Both the structure and the content of Job 38–41 recall the heptadic vision of creation presented in Genesis 1. At the outset, therefore, the reader may know that the divine speeches return the Joban drama to the prologue and to the primordial questions that have been raised in the land of Eden/Uz. God's "answer" begins with a vision of the cosmic boundaries of creation (38:4–18: earth, sea, heaven, underworld), followed by six strophes describing the meteorological phenomena that are assigned places within creation's domain (38:19–38). A seventh component in this vision is the discourse on the animal world, comprising initially five groups of paired animals (38:39–39:30) and subsequently, after Job's initial response, one additional pair that receives special attention: Behemoth (40:15–24) and Leviathan (41:1–34 [MT 40:25–41:26]).

This review of creation's design – boundaries, objects, and animals – corresponds in part to the sequence in Genesis 1. There is, of course, one often noted exception: the creation of human beings is not presented.[16] This omission is typically interpreted as a strategic subversion of the assumption that humanity occupies a special place of importance in creation's design.[17] Without discounting this view altogether, I suggest that the text also invites consideration of other perspectives. One may understand that Job is a special creature who is *addressed* by God and not simply one of many creatures who can be listed in the divine catalog.[18] Further, within the sequence of the speeches, Behemoth and Leviathan, the sixth and last pair of creatures, recall the creation of humankind on the sixth day as the crown of God's cosmic design. Perhaps God not only addresses humanity, through Job, but also provides a particular model for humanity, in Behemoth and Leviathan, of what it means to occupy this privileged position within creation.

2. God's review of creation's design serves primarily to confront and challenge Job, not to condemn or silence him. A number of clues buttress this observation. Job is challenged to gird up his loins like a *geber* (38:3; 40:7), that is, like a "mighty man" or "warrior" who is preparing for combat. It is often assumed that the image is used negatively with reference to Job, that God

---

closeness. Here form and content clash, with the latter gaining supremacy. Must 'the greater glory of God' always require a belittling of human beings?" (84).

16 On the differences between creation's design in Job and in other traditions see R. Albertz, *Weltschöpfung und Menschenschöpfung: Untersucht bei Deuterojesaja, Hiob und die Psalmen* (Calwer theologische Monographien 3; Stuttgart: Calwer, 1974), 140–46.

17 R. Gordis, *The Book of God and Man* (Chicago: University of Chicago Press, 1965), 118. The comment of J. L. Crenshaw states the position clearly: "The absence of any reference to humans in the entire speech is calculated to teach Job the valuable lesson that the universe can survive without him" (*Old Testament Wisdom: An Introduction* [Atlanta: John Knox, 1981], 110).

18 Cf. J. G. Janzen, *Job* (Interpretation; Atlanta: John Knox, 1985), 229.

either mocks him as a "pretend warrior" or summons him to a battle in which he will certainly be defeated.[19] But the image may just as well be understood positively, as a summons to make the right preparation for a valiant encounter that God intends and desires (cf. Jer 1:17).[20]

Further, Veronika Kubina has shown that there is a form-critical connection between the interrogatory style of the divine speeches and prophetic trial speeches. She calls particular attention to trial speeches in Second Isaiah, which function to challenge false understandings about God.[21] It is worth noting that the function of such speeches in Second Isaiah is not only to counter misunderstandings of God, but also to summon forth fresh articulations of faith from weary and despairing exiles.[22] Such parallels suggest that God also questions Job not only to correct him but also to elicit affirmations that may generate new possibilities in the midst of a broken world.

It is not only the manner in which Job is addressed or the form of his divine interrogation that indicates he is being summoned for a positive encounter with God. The very substance of the created order teaches Job that God designs creation not to silence and subdue all opposition, but to protect it and nurture it as a proper and necessary component in God's master plan. In his opening curse, Job looked inward and found inexplicable suffering to be the unbearable center of his world. In Job 38 God counters with a panoramic vision that affirms creation is teeming with life and vitality.[23] Some of these life forces, like the animals described in 38:39–39:30, are wild and undomesticated. Outside their designated boundaries they may be harmful to human life. Yet God provides for them and sustains them in their wild, potentially threatening freedom. Other life forces, by God's design, fulfill their appointed roles by aggressively challenging the boundaries God imposes on them. The "proud waves" of the sea (*yām*), traditional symbols of primordial chaos, constantly

---

19   E.g., S, Terrien. "The Yahweh Speeches and Job's Response," *RevExp* 58 (1971), 507.

20   Cf. Janzen, *Job*, 232–33.

21   V. Kubina, *Die Gottesreden im Buche Hiob* (Freiburger theologische Studien 115; Freiburg: Herder, 1979), 131–43. See further H. Rowold, "Yahweh's Challenge to Rival: The Form and Function of the Yahweh-Speech in Job 38–39," *CBQ* 47 (1985), 207–9.

22   In the opening disputation of Isa 40:12–31, for example, a series of rhetorical questions resembling those in Job 38–41 climaxes with a ringing affirmation of the Creator's promised empowerment of the weak and the helpless (see esp. vv. 27–31). Such connections between Second Isaiah and Job are often noted. See, e.g., P. D. Hanson, *Isaiah 40–66* (Interpretation; Louisville: Westminster/John Knox, 1995), 26–32.

23   R. Alter has convincingly argued that God's speech in Job 38 constitutes "a brilliantly pointed reversal, in structure, image, and theme," of Job's opening curse. In his view, God's poetry, that is, God's "imagination of the world," transcends the limitations of creaturely modes of perception (*The Art of Biblical Poetry* [New York: Basic Books, 1985], 96–110).

"WHAT ARE HUMAN BEINGS, THAT YOU MAKE SO MUCH OF THEM?"

threaten destruction. Yet God attends them with parental care, wrapping them in "swaddling bands" that both restrain and protect them (38:8–11).[24] Through this review of creation, Job is invited to understand that God intends not to eliminate or banish forces of opposition and challenge but to preserve and direct them, because they are vital elements in the architecture of life.

God's initial review of creation's design ends with a challenge to Job (40:2).[25] Stephen Mitchell has captured the sense of the divine query nicely: "Has God's accuser resigned? Has my critic swallowed his tongue?"[26] Job's initial response in 40:3–5 seems to answer with an unqualified yes. He places his hand over his mouth in an act of deference that may indicate either contempt or shame.[27] In either case he responds with silence, not with a fresh articulation of faith. Some commentators take Job's silence to be the pathetic but normative response that God intends from those who risk confronting the Creator of the world as Job has done.[28] But with the initiation of the second speech from God, both Job and his readers learn that God desires not silence but something more.

3. God's design for humankind's role in creation attains clarity when viewed through the lens of Psalm 8. Once more God summons Job to prepare as a *geber* for an encounter with divinity (Job 40:7). The subject of this second encounter

---

24   Note further that the verb in Job 3S:8a, usually translated "shut in" (e.g., NRSV, NIV, NAB), is *swk*, literally "hedged in." The same verb occurs in Job 1:10 and 3:23. In the prologue the reference is to God's protective hedging in of Job against the afflictions that may beset life. In chap. 3 the reference comes in the form of Job's complaint that God has hedged him in in negative ways that obstruct his discernment of life's meaning. The ambivalence in the imagery conveyed by these occurrences of the term echoes in Job 38. As Alter observes, "What results is a virtual oxymoron, expressing a paradoxical feeling that God's creation involves a necessary holding in check of destructive forces and a sustaining of those same forces because they are also forces of life" (*The Art of Biblical Poetry*, 100).

25   In a most discerning way Janzen has called attention to the parallels between the divine response to Job and that given to Jeremiah in Jer 12:5. Of the latter he suggests that "The point of this divine response is not to put the prophet down with an impossible question, but to express surprise over the quickness with which the prophet succumbs to discouragement and disillusionment and to challenge the prophet to a deeper loyalty and vocational endurance" (*Job*, 242). With Janzen, I suggest that God's question to Job represents a similar challenge to struggle on toward greater vocational clarity.

26   S. Mitchell, *The Book of Job* (New York: HarperCollins, 1992), 84.

27   On Job's gesture as an image of shame, see C. Muenchow, "Dust and Ashes in Job 42:6," JBL 108 (19S9), 608.

28   See, e.g., the conclusion of J. T. Wilcox: "if we assume, as I do, that the theophany is normative, then we must conclude that the book as whole is profoundly skeptical, agnostic; its message is largely a counsel of silence" (*The Bitterness of Job: A Philosophical Reading* [Ann Arbor: University of Michigan Press, 1994], 122).

218   CHAPTER 12

is the "governance" (40:8: *mišpāṭ*) of the world that God has designed.[29] Divine governance is signified through images of the "arm" (v. 9a, *zĕrôaʿ*) and the "voice" (v. 9b, *qôl*) and "glory" (v. 10, "glory and splendor" [*hôd wĕhādār*]). These images are usually understood to convey God's rebuke or denial of Job's presumptuous criticisms of divine governance. According to this interpretation, God's rule is undergirded by sovereign power and majesty that cannot be equalled by Job. Hence Job's charge that God has denied his justice (19:7) and perverted the process through which his justice can be sought (9:32) is more than mere ignorance. It is an impertinent assault on the very nature and character of God.

Although the element of rebuke may be present in Job 40:7–14, there are hints that this is not God's only purpose in addressing Job. The divine challenge is couched in terms that invite Job to offer more than a simple concession that God alone has responsibility for the governance of the cosmos. A clue is found in the expression "glory and splendor" (v. 10). The phrase *hôd wĕhādār* is used in the Hebrew Bible primarily, but not exclusively, with reference to God. Four of the six occurrences are of praise offered to God (Pss 96:6 [par. 1 Chr 16:27]; 104:1; 111:3) but two are used with reference to human beings. In Ps 21:6 (cf. Ps 45:3 [MT 4]) the phrase describes the blessings that God peculiarly bestows upon the king. In Job 40:10 God summons Job, like a king, to put on the regalia of "glory and splendor."[30] The recognition that the endowment with "glory and splendor" is shared in Hebrew Scripture, albeit unequally, by a triad of persons – God, king, and Job – invites us to consider that God is not simply rebuking Job for arrogating to himself that which he can never attain. Instead, God may be understood as summoning Job to a royal responsibility that represents the apex of his vocational calling to image God.[31]

God's speech invites Job to consider his royal responsibilities for governance by subtly calling once more for further exploration of the vision of humankind that is affirmed in Psalm 8. In Job 7:17–21 Job reflected on the psalmist's question "What are human beings?" and proceeded to move outside the affirmations of the psalm to construct an answer from his own experience that envisioned the human creature as little more than a target for divine destruction. Eliphaz returned to the psalmist's question (Job 15:7–16), but in response to Job he too

---

29   On the dual connotations of *mišpāṭ* as both a forensic act, i.e. "judging," and an administrative procedure, i.e. "governance," see S. Scholnick, "The Meaning of *Mišpāṭ* in the Book of Job," *JBL* 101 (1982), 522–23.

30   On the royal imagery that is used with reference to Job in 40:10–13, see Janzon, *Job*, 243–44.

31   Note, e.g., that the collocation in Job 40:10, "*clothe* yourself [*tilbāš*] with glory and splendor," occurs also in Ps 104:1, but with reference to God: "You [God] are *clothed* [*lābāštâ*] with glory and splendor."

moved outside the psalm's assertions to construct an answer. What are human beings? They are sinful, flawed creatures who may claim special status for themselves only if they are willing to violate established boundaries between the divine and the human. God's speech in 40:7–14 puts the psalmist's question once more to Job, this time more specifically framed in terms of Job's capacity to govern: "Have you an arm *like God* [*kāēl*]? Can you thunder with a voice like his [*kāmōhû*]?" Whereas both Job and Eliphaz moved outside the psalm to construct their answers to the question about human identity, God's speech stays inside the claims of the psalm to issue Job a directive: "Deck yourself with majesty and dignity; clothe yourself with glory and splendor [*hôd wĕhādār*]." The latter part of this directive is only a slight variation of the affirmation that is celebrated in Ps 8:25 (MT 6): "You have made them a little lower than God, and crowned them with glory and honor [*kābôd wĕhādār*]."

This subtle echo of Psalm 8 suggests that God summons Job to dispense with all manufactured answers to the question about human identity and vocation. He is to return to the vision of humankind, a vision that is anchored in the primordial design of creation. He is challenged to take up the role that God has specially created for the human being. He is to participate in the governance of the world with a "glory and splendor" that is only a little lower than God's. Such a mandate, however, serves only to invite a further question. What does it mean to participate in the governance of the world with power and glory that is only slightly less than God's?

4. Behemoth and Leviathan are models for Job. Behemoth and Leviathan represent the sixth and final pair of animals that God asks Job to consider. The "poetic logic" of the divine speeches indicates that these two creatures signify the climax of God's revelation to Job.[32] In terms of Johannes Hempel's discernment of what is at stake in the book of Job, the presentation of Behemoth and Leviathan brings the search for the "last truth about God" to the point of ultimate disclosure.[33]

There is substantial support for the general understanding that Behemoth and Leviathan signify the primordial forces of chaos that God defeats to ensure the stability of creation. In this interpretation of Job 40:15–41:34 (MT 26), Job is destined to learn that he, like these mythical opponents, cannot challenge

---

32   Alter has noted that with the presentation of Behemoth and Leviathan, the "poetic logic" of the divine speeches arrives at the climax of the "movement from literal to figurative, from verisimilar to hyperbolic, from general assertion to focused concrete usage" (*The Art of Biblical Poetry*, 107).

33   J. Hempel, "The Contents of the Literature," in *Record and Revelation* (ed. H. W. Robinson; Oxford: Clarendon, 1938), 73.

220   CHAPTER 12

God and survive.[34] It would clearly be unwarranted to argue that there are no grounds for this interpretation. I suggest, however, that here, as throughout the book of Job, the text contains subtle clues that permit a more nuanced understanding.

Unlike the previous animals, Behemoth is introduced with affirmations, not questions (40:15–24). Job is not asked to do anything or to make any response. He is instructed simply to look, listen, and learn.[35] When he looks at this creature Job sees one whom God has made "just as I made you" (v. 15: *ʾăšer ʿāśtî ʿimmāk*; literally "whom I made along with you"). This is the only direct reference to the creation of humans in the divine speeches, thus suggesting that Behemoth represents the one true analogue for humankind that God has placed in the created order.[36] I suggest that Job is invited to understand this particular creature as modeling for him three characteristics that may clarify his own identity and vocation in relation to God.[37]

First, Behemoth is a creature with extraordinary strength and power (40:16–18). With bones like "tubes of bronze" and limbs like "bars of iron," Behemoth is fortified to withstand almost any force that may be brought against it. Its strength, however, resides not merely in its ability to protect itself against life-threatening forces. It also has the sexual potency to generate new life out of its

---

34   On the ancient Near Eastern mythical traditions concerning Behemoth and Leviathan as applied to Job, see O. Keel, *Jahwes Entgegnung an Ijob* (FRLANT 121; Göttingen: Vandenhoeck & Ruprecht, 1978), 127–58; Kubina, *Gottesreden*, 68–75.

35   N. C. Habel, *The Book of Job* (OTL; Philadelphia: Westminster, 1985), 538.

36   The mythical imagery that informs the presentation of Behemoth and Leviathan may contribute an additional perspective on this point. Newsom observes that traditional interpretations have mistakenly focused on whether these two creatures should be viewed as literal animals (e.g., the hippopotamus and the crocodile) or as mythical monsters. She suggests that they are better understood as liminal creatures whose characteristics place them somewhere between mere animals and extraordinary, supernatural creatures ("Book of Job," 615). They are in this respect, I suggest, particularly well suited as models that invite exploration of what it means for human beings to be created "in the image of God," i.e., as mortal creatures who are nevertheless "a little lower than God" (Ps 8:5 [MT 6]).

37   J. G. Gammie has also interpreted Behemoth and Leviathan as models for Job, and I am indebted to him for some of the insights here, although I make the case along somewhat different lines. Gammie suggests that Behemoth and Leviathan are caricatures of Job and as such serve both to rebuke him and to instruct and console him. I am not persuaded that the element of rebuke, which has traditionally been so emphasized, is as prominent as Gammie assumes. See "Behemoth and Leviathan: On the Didactic and Theological Significance of Job 40:15–41:26," in *Israelite Wisdom: Theological Essays in Honor of Samuel Terrien* (ed. J. G. Gammie, et al.; Missoula, Mont.: Scholars Press, 1978), 217–31.

own resources.[38] In short, Behemoth is a creature that is peculiarly endowed for sustaining and generating life.

Second, Behemoth is described as the "first [*rēʾšît*] of the great acts of God" (v. 19). The word *rēʾšît* recalls not only the creation narrative in Genesis 1 (v. 1: *bĕrēʾšît*), which presents God's purposive design for the cosmos, but also the description of Wisdom in Prov 8:22, who celebrates its role as a cocreator that God called forth at the beginning (*rēʾšît*) of the master plan for creation. It should be noted that Eliphaz had rebuked Job for daring to imagine that he could compare himself with the "firstborn [*rîʾyšôn*] of the human race (Job 15:7), thereby claiming for himself a special royal status as a near equal to God. God's description of Behemoth as the "first" of creation's works, however, presents a model of royalty that invites from Job the very self-understanding that Eliphaz would deny. Behemoth is a king in its own domain: the mountains bring forth tribute; the wild animals play as contented subjects of the realm; nature itself serves its sovereign ruler (Job 40:20–22).[39] If Job were to respond to Eliphaz with what God has shown him in this comparison with Behemoth, he might be expected to counter by saying, "Yes, indeed, I *am* like the primal creature who is a near equal God; I am summoned forth and endowed with royal prerogatives and responsibilities."

Third, Behemoth is distinguished among the creatures by the way it responds to aggression and violence. If the river rages against it, it does not flee in fear. If the Jordan should burst forth against it, it trusts (*yibṭaḥ*) in its own resources (Job 40:23). The picture is of one who may be subject to attack, perhaps even by God (cf. vv. 19b, 24), but who nevertheless responds with confident resistance.[40]

It is striking that in this review of Behemoth's distinctive characteristics, this great animal is held up as worthy of praise. If elsewhere Behemoth is portrayed as an opponent of God that must be eliminated or defeated, in the divine speeches something else is indicated. Here God commends Behemoth to Job as an object lesson in what it means to stand before one's maker with exceptional strength, proud prerogatives, and fierce trust. The lesson for Job would seem to be that those who dare to imitate Behemoth may come nearer to realizing God's primordial design for creaturely existence than by following any other model in all of creation.

---

38   It is likely that the description of Behemoth's "tail" (*zānāb*) as "stiff like a cedar" (40:17) is a euphemistic expression for an erection of the penis; see, e.g., Habel, *Job*, 565–66. On the importance of the rhetoric of sexual potency in the Behemoth speech, see Alter, *The Art of Biblical Poetry*, 108.

39   Cf. Perdue, *Wisdom in Revolt*, 222–23; idem, *Wisdom and Creation*, 177.

40   Cf. Gammie, "Behemoth and Leviathan," 220.

The presentation of Leviathan (41:1–34 [MT 40:25–41:26]) may also be understood to offer Job a positive role model. A figure clearly associated with the mythical sea monster, Leviathan is depicted here also as a mortal creature who may teach Job something about his own existence.[41] Unlike the Behemoth periscope, the Leviathan poem includes a number of rhetorical questions that clearly serve to challenge Job in a manner similar to the interrogations of the first divine speech.[42] The latter half of the poem (41:18–34 [MT 41: 10–26]), however, uses declarative sentences to describe positively the distinctive features of Leviathan. Here, as elsewhere in the divine speeches, the rhetoric seems designed primarily not to rebuke and belittle Job but to elicit from him some new and positive articulation of faith that is uniquely informed by his consideration of Leviathan. I suggest that Leviathan models for Job three characteristics that may instruct him in the formulation of a new response to God.

First, Leviathan, like Behemoth, possesses extraordinary strength and power (41:12–32 [MT 41:4–24]). On earth Leviathan is a "creature without fear," a king (*melek*) without peer in its own realm (41:33–34 [MT 41:25–26]).[43] As a royal figure, Leviathan's relation to God is described somewhat ambiguously. Textual uncertainties in 41:10–12 (MT 41:2–4) permit different interpretations. Even so, the main interpretive options yield, in different ways, a common construal of Leviathan's special status in the hierarchy of creation. *Only God* can confront and control Leviathan; or vice versa, *only Leviathan* dares to "stand before" the

---

41   Ibid., 222–25.

42   A series of questions introduced by the interrogative *he* in 41:1–9 (MT 40:25–41:1), ask generally; "Can you, Job, capture Leviathan?" The expected answer is "No, of course not." The questions with the interrogative pronoun *mî* ("who?") in 41:10–14 (MT 41:2–6) ask generally, "If Job, cannot confront and control this beast, who can?" The logic of the question is that Job should answer, "Only you, God, can control Leviathan."

43   The phrase normally translated "on earth" in 41:33 (MT 41:2) is *'al-'āpār*, literally "on dust." Gammie has noted that elsewhere In the book Job is prominently positioned "on the dust" (2:8; 30:19; 42:6). He cites this common rhetoric in support of the argument that Leviathan is presented as a mortal creature, like Job, and thus can serve as a "didactic image" for him ("Behemoth and Leviathan," 224).

The word translated "creature" in Job 41:33 (MT 41:25), *he'āśû*, is difficult. As It stands the word may be taken as an archaic form of the *Qal* passive participle, hence "the one made," i.e. "creature"; cf. R. Gordis, *The Book of Job: Commentary, New Translation, Special Studies* (New York: Jewish Theological Seminary of America, 1978) 490. A similar translation may be derived from an alternative spelling, *he'āśûy*, which is found in some Hebrew manuscripts. Perdue has noted, however, that if the Masoretic pointing is changed slightly to *hā'ōśo*, the reading would parallel 40:19, "the one who made him." The sense of the verse would then be that God, who made Leviathan, has no fear of this creature. Perdue rejects this option as unlikely (*Wisdom in Revolt*, 231).

"WHAT ARE HUMAN BEINGS, THAT YOU MAKE SO MUCH OF THEM?"   223

One who has such demonstrably superior power.[44] Such a description portrays Leviathan as a near equal to God, hence as a figure that invites reflection once more on the theology of Psalm 8. Indeed, in the psalm as in this poem, the creature who enjoys such close proximity to the divine is the object of God's admiration and praise (cf. 41:18–24 [MT 41:10–15]).[45]

Second, the poem affirms that Leviathan's extraordinary power is especially evident in what comes forth from its mouth. Two images in the poem are instructive: one that emphasizes what does not come forth from Leviathan's mouth; the other, that which does. In 41:3–4 (MT 40:27–28) Leviathan is described as a creature that will not be subdued into docile service. In the unlikely event that this creature should ever be captured and forced into domestication, it would not even then make a "covenant" (*bĕrît*) with its master that required it to plead for mercy or to speak "soft words." That which more typically comes from the mouth of Leviathan is vividly described in 41:18–21 (MT 10–13). The rhetoric emphasizes fire and light, smoke and flames, phenomena that are identified with the strong and compelling appearance of divinity.[46] Leviathan, like mythic divine beings, and like YHWH (cf. Pss 18:8–14 [MT 9–15]; 29:7), announces its presence with an awesome fierceness that commands attention and defies coercion. If what does and does not come forth from the mouth of Leviathan is intended to instruct Job, then the lesson commends strong words, not soft or gentle ones, speech that commands recognition, not disregard.[47]

Finally, the description of Leviathan's power and presence culminates with an affirmation of its royal dominion. Leviathan, like Behemoth, is king (*melek*) in its own domain (41:34 [MT 26]). Behemoth's royalty derives from its status as the "first" of God's works, the one to whom all creation offers respectful tribute (40:19–22). Leviathan's royalty is conveyed with images of governance: Leviathan "looks on everyone who is haughty [*kol-gābōaḥ*] (41:34 [MT 26])." In

---

44   The Leningrad text of 41:2b–3 [ET 41: Job–11] is first person speech, "Who can stand before *me* (*lĕpānay*)? Who will confront me (*hiqdîmanî*)?" The emphasis of the speech would be on the incomparability of God, i.e. "Who can contend with God?" In some Hebrew manuscripts the speech is third person, thus "Who can stand before *him* (*lĕpānāyw*)?" In this reading the emphasis would be on the incomparability of Leviathan, i.e. "Who can contend with Leviathan?"

45   On the hymnic style of these verses, see Perdue, *Wisdom and Revolt*, 230–32.

46   Alter suggests that this imagery may be linked to the cosmic imagery of light in the first divine speech (Job 38), which serves rhetorically to counter Job's opening curse of creation (*Art of Biblical Poetry*, 109–10).

47   Cf. Gammie ("Behemoth and Leviathan," 223, 225), who also notes that what comes forth from Leviathan's mouth is a major emphasis in the poem. He suggests that the poet uses this emphasis both to caricature Job's verbal defenses and at the same time to affirm his protests.

224   CHAPTER 12

this respect also Leviathan presents to Job a model for the very challenge that God has extended to him. In 40:7–14 God's speech returned to the rhetoric of Psalm 8 and summoned Job to put on the regalia of "glory and splendor" (v. 10). The success of Job's kingship would be evident if he could "look on all who are proud" (40:11: *rĕʾeh kol-gēʾeh*) and deal with them justly. Now, in this final acclamation of Leviathan as king, God offers Job a worthy example of how to enact the very assignment he has been given.[48]

To summarize, I have suggested that the divine speeches are intended to challenge Job, not to condemn or silence him. What is desired is a fresh articulation of faith, in Brueggemann's terms, a "fresh hunch" about God. After the review of creation's design in the first speech, Job appears to have concluded that there is no significant place or role for suffering humanity in the world that God has crafted. Job responds with silence. But a second divine speech then follows, indicating that Job's initial response has somehow to be extended or enlarged before the divine-human encounter can be complete. God invites consideration of special representatives of the animal world, Behemoth and Leviathan, two figures of power, pride, and dominion, that are celebrated as near equals of God. They may be subject to confrontation and assault, but they will not relinquish their identity nor abandon their creaturely responsibilities. God has power sufficient to combat and to control them, but God does not eliminate them or deny them a meaningful role among the vital life forces in creation's design. The logic of the second speech from the whirlwind is that Behemoth and Leviathan reveal something important about God's design for creaturely existence that belongs in Job's understanding.

3   Job's Final Response: "Now My Eye Sees You"

Job's final response in 42:6 has generally been interpreted as a confession of sin for having wrongly attacked the justice of God. This understanding has been preserved and nurtured by a host of prominent Bible translations, of which the NRSV is but one contemporary example: "therefore I despise myself, and repent in dust and ashes." This rendering of Job's words affirms that God always holds supreme power over frail and flawed humans. Before such a God as this, human discourse is necessarily limited and submissive. Following the counsel of Eliphaz, the proper role for humankind is simply to "agree with God, and be

---

48   Newsom ("Book of Job," 625) has noted that the conclusion of the Leviathan poem, 41:34 (MT 26), forms an *inclusio* with 40:11b.

at peace" (Job 22:21).[49] However ingrained in our consciousness this traditional view of Job's response has become, it can scarcely be regarded as a new or fresh articulation of faith.

Modern commentators now regularly acknowledge and grapple with the intractable ambiguities encoded in Job's last words. No less than five different translations of Job 42:6 should be considered as legitimate possibilities.[50] Whatever Job's final response may be, it must be recognized as anything but a simple admission of sin. I do not intend to debate the strengths and weaknesses of the various alternatives for rendering this verse. I do want to suggest, however, that one of the recognized translations is particularly consonant with the purpose of the divine speeches as I have discerned it in this essay.

Job's final words words in 42:6 may reasonably be translated as follows: "Therefore I retract [my words] and change my mind concerning dust and ashes." Two critical issues must be addressed in order to unlock the meaning of these words. First, the verb *māʾas*, here translated "retract," is active, not reflexive, and ordinarily takes an object. In 42:6 there is no clearly identified object, although one may reasonably assume that an object is implied.[51] Of the alternatives that have been proposed, I am inclined toward supplying "my words" as the object.[52] The specific content of what may be included among Job's "words" is ambiguous, but his previous concession that he has attempted to speak about "things too wonderful" (42:3: *niplāʾôt*) makes it plausible to suggest that the reference is to the wondrous design of God's creation (cf. Job 38:2).[53] Job had cursed this design as being inimical and meaningless for innocent sufferers like him (Job 3). God had countered with a vision of a creation teeming with a variety of intricately balanced life forces. In response to this revelation,

---

49   Cf. Crenshaw (*Old Testament Wisdom*, 111): "In the face of such a blustering deity, who would not be speechless?"

50   The major interpretive options are conveniently identified by Newsom ("Book of Job," 628–29) and Habel (*Job*, 577–78). See further T. Tilley ("God and the Silencing of Job," *Modern Theology* 5 [1989], 257–70), who observes that the multiple translation possibilities for Job 42:6 mean that "Interpreters make, rather than find, the text which they interpret" (260). He concludes that the text interpreters have typically "made" has had the effect of reducing Job to silence.

51   W. Morrow has discussed the philological data, noting that of nearly 70 occurrences of *māʾas* in the *Qal* stem, an object is given in all but four of the cases (Job 7:16; 34:33; 36:5; 42:6) ("Consolation, Rejection, and Repentance in Job 42:6," *JBL* 105 [1986], 214).

52   Cf. S. R. Driver and G. B. Gray, *The Book of Job* (ICC; Edinburgh: T. & T. Clark, 1921), 373; M. Tsevat, "The Meaning of the Book of Job," *HUCA* 37 (1966), 91; G. Fohrer, *Das Buch Hiob* (KAT; Gütersloh: Mohn, 1963), 531; M. H. Pope, *Job* (3d ed.; AB 15; Garden City, N.Y.: Doubleday, 1973) 349; Newsom, "Book of Job," 629. See also the following Bible translations: NAB, JPS, JB, TEV.

53   So also Newsom, "Book of Job," 629.

226   CHAPTER 12

Job may be understood to relinquish his limited discernment of creation's design and to acknowledge that the grander vision he has been granted now requires of him a new assessment.

The key to Job's new assessment is found in 42:6b, where a second critical issue must be addressed. The syntax of the Hebrew words is relatively clear: Job "repents" or "changes his mind" concerning (*niḥamtî 'al*) dust and ashes.[54] What is signified is a reversal or a retraction of a previous decision or position. It is the meaning of the phrase "dust and ashes" that determines finally what Job has decided to *relinquish* and what he now intends to embrace.

The phrase "dust and ashes" (*'āpār wā'ēper*) occurs but three times in biblical Hebrew: Gen 18:27, Job 30:19, and Job 42:6. In each case it signifies something about the human condition vis-à-vis God. In Job 30:19 Job laments that God has thrown him into the "mire" (*ḥōmer*) of human mortality,[55] where human existence is defined as "dust and ashes." In the context of his suffering Job understands this to mean that he is but one small example of the way in which afflicted humans may be banished from society (30:1–8), scorned and terrorized by their peers (30:9–15), and by God (30:16–23). Job's experience leads him to conclude that as "dust and ashes" he is consigned to live in a world where he cries out to God, and God does not answer (30:20). In Gen 18:27 the phrase "dust and ashes" applies to Abraham. In the context of arguing with God about matters of justice, Abraham acknowledges that as a mere creature of "dust and ashes" he has entered into dangerous territory. Abraham's recognition of his status before God is not dissimilar to Job's in 30:19, except that in Abraham's case he persists in questioning God, and God answers.[56] Indeed, the Hebrew text of Gen 18:22, without the *tiqqûn*, invites a dramatic understanding of God's regard for this creaturely interrogator. It says, "Yhwh remained

---

54   On the idiom *nḥm 'al*, as "repent about/concerning," as opposed to the more traditional rendering "repent in," see Morrow, "Consolation," 215–16; D. Patrick, "The Translation of Job XLII 6," *VT* 26 (1976), 370.

55   Cf. Job 4:19; 10:9; 33:6, where the term *ḥōmer* is used with reference to human mortality.

56   For my argument here it is not necessary to resolve the question of whether Job is dependent on Genesis or vice versa. It is sufficient to note that significant parallels between Abraham and Job suggest the likelihood that both texts reflect acute concerns with questions about divine justice that emerged in the postexilic period. See J. Blenkinsopp, who notes that these connections were already noticed by medieval Jewish commentators ("Abraham and the Righteous of Sodom," *JJS* 33 [1982], 126–27; "The Judge of All the Earth: Theodicy in the Midrash on Genesis 18:22 33," *JJS* 41 [1990], 1–12). On the postexilic provenance of Gen 18:22–33 and its connections with Job, see further L. Schmidt, *"De Deo": Studien zur Literarkritik und Theologie des Buches Jona, des Gesprächs zwischen Abraham und Jahwe in Gen 18 22ff. und von Job 1* (BZAW 143; Berlin: de Gruyter, 1976) 131–64.

"WHAT ARE HUMAN BEINGS, THAT YOU MAKE SO MUCH OF THEM?" 227

standing before Abraham."[57] The picture suggests that God, the "judge of all the earth," stands waiting to hear what "dust and ashes" will say on the subject of divine justice. I concur with J. G. Janzen, who observes that in this picture of Creator and creature locked in dialogue over matters of mutual concern, we are given a glimpse of how the divine image may be enacted on earth.[58]

These two images of "dust and ashes" must inform the interpretation of Job's final response to God. Given what God has shown him, Job now changes his mind about "dust and ashes." He previously had concluded that innocent suffering rendered him mute and submissive before a God who permitted neither challenge nor confrontation. In terms of the theology of Psalm 8, he could discern only that to be created in the image of God was more a curse than a blessing. As a human creature a "little lower God," he was destined for death, not life; for the mire, not for the throne; for the misery of silent servitude, not for the "glory and splendor" of royalty.

God's disclosure of creation's design, however, requires of Job a transformed understanding of "dust and ashes." In God's design creaturely existence may entail undeserved suffering, but it does not mandate silence and submission.[59] Like Behemoth and Leviathan, God endows human beings with power and responsibility for their domains. They are and must be fierce, unbridled contenders for justice, sometimes with God and sometimes against God. As near equals of God their destiny is to live at the dangerous intersection between the

---

57   The scribal correction of Gen 18:22 is "Abraham remained standing before YHWH."

58   Janzen, *Job*, 257. See further the similar assessment of this text by E. Ben Zvi: "The text underscores the notion that when the ideal teacher defends the universal order and confronts God with the standards by which God ought to judge the world, he is in fact fulfilling the role God has chosen for him to fulfill" ("The Dialogue Between Abraham and Yhwh in Gen. 18.23–32: A Historical-critical Analysis," *JSOT* 53 [1992], 39).

59   Janzen's discerning interpretation of Job's transformed understanding of "dust and ashes" is perhaps closest to the view I am offering here, although I depart from him in important ways (*Job*, 254–59). He suggests that Job's new understanding of "dust and ashes" teaches him that innocent suffering does not belittle humankind. Rather it is the very condition under which the "royal vocation" to image God can be accepted and embraced. In this respect he suggests that Job comes to a new self-understanding of his suffering that bears a resemblance to the suffering servant in Second Isaiah. In response to Janzen one may argue that he invokes the theology of innocent suffering in a way that does not address adequately the primary issue that is at stake in the book of Job. Job does not suffer on behalf of others. His family does not die on behalf of others. His suffering and their death are "for no reason." It is "without cause," and it can hardly be construed in any normal sense as redemptive. I am more inclined to say that what Job has learned is that humankind may image God not by acquiescing to innocent suffering but rather by protesting it, contending with the powers that occasion it, and, when necessary, taking the fight directly to God. It is just such power, courage, and fierce trust that God seems to commend to Job in the figures of Behemoth and Leviathan.

merely human and the supremely divine. When humans dare to enact this destiny, their appearance before God as "dust and ashes" confirms their heritage as faithful descendants of Abraham. They may be sure that they do not approach an indifferent God; they approach instead One who awaits and desires their arrival. They may speak words of praise; they may speak words of curse. They may also move beyond these two levels of discourse to speak words of resistance and protest. But they may not be silent, for silence is unworthy of those who have stood in the divine presence and have learned that creation has been entrusted to them, because they are a "little lower than God." I submit that this is the foundation for the new articulation of faith that Job announces with the words "now my eye sees you" (42:5).

If this view of God's disclosure from the whirlwind has merit, then I suggest that Brueggemann's summons to attend to the "fresh hunches" about God conveyed by Israel's lament tradition, especially as modeled by Job, does indeed invite a new way of thinking about Old Testament theology. More importantly, it invites a Joban way of imaging God in the world, the neglect of which seriously jeopardizes God's purposive design for creation.

CHAPTER 13

"Will You Condemn Me That You May Be Justified?" – The Character of God in Job

The Book of Job affirms Job's exemplary character at the outset of the story.* Both the narrator (1:1) and God (1:8; 2:3) stipulate that Job is "blameless and upright." The objective of this essay is to ask if the same virtues apply to Job's God. At the end of the story, can one substantiate an affirmation that God's behavior is blamelessly consonant with moral and religious norms, that God's uprightness accords with ethical propriety in the broadest sense? Apart from scattered observations in commentaries and a surprisingly meager number of essays,[1] the question of God's character in the Book of Job has received little attention. I suspect there may be several reasons for this, not the least of which is the Book's own apparent resistance to the question. Who are we, as mere human beings, to pass judgment on God's behavior? By what criteria could we evaluate God's ethics? Such questions appear to anchor God's response to Job at the end of the Book. When God says, "Who is this that darkens counsel without knowledge?" (38:2), must we not admit that limited knowledge constrains us as well as Job? When God says, "Will you even put me in the wrong? Will you condemn me that you may be justified?" (40:8), is there any legitimate response other than Job's: "I have uttered what I did not understand, things too wonderful for me, which I did not know" (42:3)? Confronted with such seemingly impossible questions, I am reminded of Alexander Pope's caution, "Fools rush in where Angels fear to tread."[2]

---

* Originally presented at the national meeting of the Society of Biblical Literature, Atlanta, November 2010.

1 E.g., T. N. D. Mettinger, "The God of Job: Avenger, Tyrant, or Victor?" in L. Perdue, W. G. Gilpin, eds., *The Voice from the Whirlwind: Interpreting the Book of Job* (Nashville: Abingdon, 1992), 39–49; T. Fretheim, "God in the Book of Job," *Currents in Theology and Mission* 26 (1999), 85–93; E. van Wolde, "Different Perspectives on Faith and Justice: The God of Jacob and the God Job," in S. Freyne. E. Van Wolde, eds., *The Many Voices of the Bible* (Concilium 2002/1; London: SCL, 2002), 17–23; K. J. Dell, "Does God Behave Unethically in the Book of Job?" in K. Dell, ed., *Ethical and Unethical in the Old Testament: God and Humans in Dialogue* (LHBOTS 528; New York, London: T & T Clark, 2010), 170–186; cf. D. J. A. Clines, "Job's Fifth Friend: An Ethical Critique of the Book of Job," *Biblical Interpretation* 12 (2004), 233–250, which focuses on the larger question of the ethical integrity of the Book of Job.

2 A. Pope, "An Essay on Criticism," in *Alexander Pope; Selected Poetry*, Selected by D. Grant; Introduction by A. Ross (London, New York: Penguin Books, 1985), 32.

© SAMUEL E. BALENTINE, 2021 | DOI:10.1163/9789004459212_014

The primary question I wish to pose here is this: are there recognizable principles of acceptable and non-acceptable moral behavior that we can deduce from God's words and actions in Job? To frame the question, I invite you to imagine a different introduction to the Book of Job, one constructed from the information about God contained in Job 1–2.

> There once was a G[g]od in the land of Job. One day this God invited the satan, one of the heavenly beings, to consider the virtues of His servant Job who, by God's assessment was blameless and upright, feared God, and turned away from evil. When the satan asked if Job served God for no reason, God agreed that the satan could test Job's fidelity by destroying all his possessions and killing his children, seven sons and three daughters. When Job continued to bless God in spite of these grievous losses, God reaffirmed Job's integrity, even while conceding that the satan had incited Him against Job for no reason. The satan next asked for permission to afflict Job physically. Once again God agreed saying, "Very well, he is in your power, only spare his life." The satan then inflicted loathsome sores that covered Job's body from the sole of his foot to the crown of his head. In his misery, Job sat among the ashes, his only words a question: "Shall we receive the good at the hand of God and not receive the bad?" In the land of Job, whenever God's assessment of one of His blameless and upright servants was questioned, this is what God always did.

If the Book of Job were introduced as the Book of God; if it reported that God spoke and acted towards the blameless and upright in the manner noted above (which in fact is fundamentally consistent with the Prologue we have), would we affirm that this God is "the greatest of all the (gods) of the east" – or the world (cf. 1:3)? More to the point for our purposes today, would we agree that emulating this God's behavior contributes constructively to the virtues requisite for the "very good" world God has created and entrusted to human stewardship?

What follows can be no more than a preliminary probe into these questions. I limit myself to the characterizations of God in the two sections of Job where God speaks and acts – the Prologue/Epilogue (1–2 + 42:7–17) and the divine speeches in Job 38–42. The contributions to this discussion of the dialogues between Job and his friends (3–37), where various aspects of God's character are *spoken about*, must be deferred for subsequent investigation.

"WILL YOU CONDEMN ME THAT YOU MAY BE JUSTIFIED?" 231

1   The Character of God in the Prose Tale of Job

Carol Newsom has argued that the prose tale is "self-consciously concerned with the moral formation of its readers and hearers."[3] Reading the prose tale through the lens of contemporary narrative ethicists, Newsom accents important differences between the genres and rhetorical strategies of the prose tale (Job 1–2 + 42:7–17) and the wisdom dialogue that is the template for the poetry in Job 3–27.[4] The prose tale, which is generically kin to other didactic tales (e.g., Joseph, Tobit, Esther, Daniel, Ahiqar), typically privileges moral perceptions defined by simple assertions, conceptual clarity, and monologic truth, as conveyed by the authoritative narrator who tells the story. The world works this way, the narrator asserts; readers who desire to know how to navigate the complex moral choices between right and wrong behavior are expected to agree and conform to unambiguous truths. By contrast, the dialogue between Job and his friends, with its antecedents in Mesopotamian and Egyptian wisdom parallels, prizes argumentation, debate and discussion, and a skeptical, or at least critically inquisitive, response to authoritative assertions of truth buttressed by hierarchical claims of privilege. The world in which we live defies certainty, these dialogues insist, truth resides in the contradictions between expectations and experiences, and readers are thereby instructed to adapt to a life defined more by moral conundrums than finalized consensus.

Didactic tales like Job, Newsom argues, are typically "character-based" stories in which the established virtues of the primary moral exemplar, in this case, according to the conventional assessment, Job, are threatened by something that "appears to be out of joint with the cultural affirmation of the moral values the hero represents."[5] The testing of Job's virtues, sandwiched between

---

3   C. Newsom, "Narrative Ethics, Character, and the Prose Tale of Job," in Wm. P. Brown, ed., *Character and Scripture; Moral Formation, Community, and Biblical Interpretation* (Grand Rapids, MI, Cambridge, U.K.: Eerdmans, 2002), 121; developed further in idem, *The Book of Job: A Contest of Moral Imaginations* (Oxford: Oxford University Press, 2003), 32–71.

4   Newsom, following R. Gordis (*The Book of Job: Commentary , New Translation, and Special Studies* [New York: Jewish Theological Seminary, 1978], 573–575), regards the report about the friends in Job 2:11–13 and 42:7–10 as an editorial hinge that has been added to the original prose tale to integrate the poetic dialogues; *The Book of Job*, 36.

5   Newsom, *The Book of Job*, 40. Newsom follows, H.-P. Müller, "Die weisheit Lehrerzählung im Alten Testament und seiner Umwelt," *Die Welt des Orients* 9 (1977), 77–98; idem., "Die Hiobrahmenerzählung und ihre altorientalischen Parallelen als Paradigmen einer weisheistlichen Wirklichkeitswahnahme," in W. A. M. Beuken, ed., *The Book of Job* (Louvain: Leuven University Press, 1994), 21–39.

the narrator's affirmation of his character (1:1–5) and God's climaxing decision to reward him for his fidelity (42:11–17), are introduced in two central scenes (1:6–8; 2:1–3), in which God grants the satan permission to destroy Job's possessions and children, then his physical well-being. The primary objective of this test, when assessed according to the expectations of the genre, is to persuade readers that they should be like Job, that if they confront adversity with patience endurance like he does, then they, like he, will not only be good but will also experience the rewards of being good. To encapsulate the objectives of the didactic tale, we may retroject the assessment of Shakespeare's Helena to the grieving widow of Florence: "All's well that ends well."

That said, Newsom draws upon the works of Emmanuel Levinas and more particularly Adam Zachary Newton in order to caution that when reading didactic tales like Job, we should discriminate between the "Said" and the "Saying," between the propositional truths and moral prescriptiveness of the authoritative narrative and the "imaginative play of reading" that invites readers to "face the text as one might face a person."[6] If one not only reads the didactic tale but also faces the Job of the didactic tale as a person, then, as Newsom acknowledges, there is nothing esoteric about its ethical problems.

> That Job should be subjected to such suffering for no cause, that Job's children should be killed as part of the test of his character, that a new family should be represented as restoration when the first children remained dead – all of this strikes some readers as utterly repugnant. That the narrative asks its readers to approve of it is simply immoral.[7]

If the reader's question is "Whom do I want to be like?" in this story, presumably few would say they want to be like God. Both God and the satan treat Job as little more than an object of speculation, more as a laboratory example to be tested scientifically than as a person with real-life feelings who can respond to situations with the full breadth of human decision making. Job is not privy to the heavenly decision to test his virtues. In his innocence, he acts in accordance with a fundamental trust in the reliability of the God he serves, yet it is precisely Job's trust that God's actions subvert. "Deception" on God's part towards a loyal servant becomes in fact the "essential precondition of truth."[8]

---

6   Ibid., 65–66; cf. Adam Zachary Newton, *Narrative Ethics* (Cambridge: Harvard University Press, 1995); E. Levinas, *Otherwise Than Being, or Beyond Essence*, Translated by A. Lingis (Pittsburgh: Duquesne University Press, 1981).

7   Ibid., 66.

8   Ibid., 69.

"WILL YOU CONDEMN ME THAT YOU MAY BE JUSTIFIED?" 233

Most disturbing of all is God's admission that the satan has provoked God to destroy Job (literally, to "swallow" him) "for no reason" (2:3; *ḥinnām*). The exegetical function of these words may be parried, but their insertion into God's speech as a rationale for killing seven sons and three daughters strains to make a virtue out of gratuitous violence.[9]

Newsom is of course not the first reader to note that unjustified violence toward the innocent is a morally repugnant act when committed by anyone. However, when the exemplar of such violence is God, the moral compass for human ethical behavior cannot but spin wildly out of control. Such a God, as Habel says, "contravenes the moral laws of divine behavior" by acting like a "jealous king who is apparently willing to violate human life to gratify personal ends."[10] Lowell Handy describes God as no less guilty of breaking "the norms of cosmic morality" than the Canaanite deities El and Anat.[11] Norman Whybray notes that Job's "deeply flawed" and "immoral" God does not measure up to the readers' "own standards of what is right."[12] Locating himself as "Job's fifth friend," David Clines blames the book "for so naturalizing this outrageous divine behavior that commentators [...] see no sign of an ethical problem." Clines stakes out his position by quoting favorably the words of John Stuart Mill: "I will call no being good who is not what I mean when I apply that epithet to my fellow-creatures; and if such a being can sentence me to hell for not calling him so, to hell I will go."[13]

Such observations notwithstanding, almost all commentators subsume any disconcerting characterizations of God's behavior to the larger, overriding purposes of either the prose tale or the book itself.[14] Perhaps the most

---

9   For further discussion of *ḥinnām* and its hermeneutical import within the Prologue, see S. E. Balentine, "For No Reason," *Interpretation* 57 (2003), 349–369; idem, "Traumatizing Job," *Review and Expositor* 105 (2008), 213–228.

10   N. Habel, "In Defense of God the Sage," in *The Voice from the Whirlwind*, 26.

11   L. K. Handy, "The Authorization of Divine Power and the Guilt of God in the Book of Job: Useful Ugaritic Parallels," JSOT 60 (1993), 117.

12   R. N. Whybray, "The Immorality of God: Reflections on Some Passages in Genesis, Job, Exodus, and Numbers," JSOT 72 (1996), 108.

13   Clines, "Job's Fifth Friend," 234, 240.

14   E.g., Wm. P. Brown (*Character in Crisis: A Fresh Approach to the Wisdom Literature of the Old Testament* [Grand Rapids, MI/Cambridge, U.K.: William B. Eerdmans, 1996]) cautions interpreters to remember that "Job is *primarily* about Job and not someone else, even God" (51; emphasis original). He nuances God's "for no reason" admission in Job 2:3 as the "passionate protest" of a "remorseful God" (citing Gen. 6:6; 56), and of a "struggling Tester" (57). As Fretheim has rightly noted, Brown's argument here "is not grounded in any specific textual reference (unlike the cited Gen. 6:6)" ("God in the Book of Job," 87). K. Dell ("Does God Behave Unethically?") does not dismiss the ethical problems concerning God's behavior in Job 1–2, but in view of God's question to Job at the end

234   CHAPTER 13

sophisticated assessment along these lines comes from Newsom herself.
Accentuating the rhetorical strategies of the didactic tale, she concludes that
"for this narrative the compelling desire to establish the truth about a person
[Job] trumps all other values. It permits everything."[15] Although she recognizes
the "friction" this creates for readers who may wish that the Job of the prose
tale would protest or at least question what has happened to him by uttering
something like the lament in Psalm 13 – "How long, O Lord [...] must I bear
pain in soul and sorrow in my heart?" (vv. 1–2) – she concludes that such words,
"while not exactly wrong," are not the "right words" from the perspective of the
narrative.[16] Even so, as Newsom goes on to say, "The reader, who has been the
recipient of this narration at the expense of Job, may well feel implicated in
and contaminated by the abuses it enacts."[17]

I am in basic agreement with Newsom's reading of the didactic tale.
Nevertheless, I want to press her observations by asking about the cultural
impact on both ancient and contemporary readers of possessing a canon of literature, in this case bequeathed to religious communities as sacred scripture,
which appears to give a divine imprimatur to inflicting suffering, even death,
on the innocent as a means of determining their integrity. The reception history of Job gives us reason to pause in consideration of the question.

The Septuagint translation of Job 1–2, apart from its addition to the speech
of Job's wife (2:9b–e), essentially transmits a Greek version of the story that is
consonant with the MT. However, the *Testament of Job* (first century BCE–first
century CE), arguably the first commentary on the Job, appears to be sensitive to God's problematic behavior in the received story. It omits the dialogue
between God and the satan, and begins instead by reporting that Job himself
decided to engage Satan, fully informed by an angel of God that if he did so, he
would suffer the consequences. Job decides to wage the battle and is assured

---

of the book – "Who is this that darkens counsel by words, without knowledge?" (38:2),
she concludes her essay with a cautionary question addressed to readers: "Are we guilty
of the same accusation if we seek to judge God according to ethical categories?" (185).
For an overview of other "commentarial moves to deflect the force of any critique" of
God's behavior in Job, see Clines, "Job's Fifth Friend," 236–239. Clines's assessment of such
"explanations" for God's behavior is pointed: "The default position of the typical writer
on the book of Job [...] is not to explain or justify the heavenly action against Job, but to
rest content merely with recapitulating the data of the text. The narrative of events in the
heavenly council is for such writers a given, an unexaminable fact that raises no ethical
problems, and needs only to be rehearsed. See no evil, hear no evil, speak no evil is the
watchword of wise monkeys and commentators alike" (239).

15   Newsom, *The Book of Job*, 68.
16   Ibid., 63.
17   Ibid., 70.

"WILL YOU CONDEMN ME THAT YOU MAY BE JUSTIFIED?" 235

in advance by God's angel that he will best Satan, if he will only persevere. From beginning to end, the *Testament* minimizes God's agency in the evil that befalls the biblical Job (cf. Job 2:11 [MT]: "Now when Job's three friends heard of all the troubles [*hara' ah*; literally, "the evil"] that had come upon him [...]"). The *Testament's* demurral may well have been effective for early readers of Job, but it clearly did not silence later "common"[18] readers from critiquing God's behavior in the received form of the text. In recognition of the limits of this venue, I fast forward to modern interpreters who press the question whether the God of Job is a worthy moral exemplar of the ethical behavior requisite for any civilized society.

In his *Answer to Job*, Carl Jung describes the Joban Prologue as the moment when God recognizes that He lacks sufficient self-reflection to make moral judgments.[19] Had God "taken counsel with his own omniscience" when Satan first introduced a "doubting thought" into God's consciousness, then God would not have exposed a faithful servant like Job to such a gratuitous moral test.[20] Yet, as Jung notes, "the really astonishing thing" is that God gives in to Satan's insinuations without thinking.[21] God never rebukes Satan for maliciously slandering Job's integrity. God never expresses disapproval of Satan's murderous actions. Jung explains God's behavior by suggesting that Job's moral superiority forces a jealous God to acknowledge that "man possesses an infinitely small yet more concentrated light than he, Yahweh, possesses."[22] Jung argues that the ramifications of the Prologue drama are consequential for both Job and God. To his horror, Job discovers that God "is not human but, in certain respects less

---

18   I borrow the term "common" reader from Cynthia Ozick ("The Impious Impatience of Job," in C. Ozick, *Quarrel and Quandary* [New York: Alfred A. Knopf, 2000], 59–73). As she notes, "[T]he striking discoveries of scholars – whether through philological evidences or through the detection of infusions from surrounding cultures – will not deeply unsettle the common reader. We are driven – we common readers – to approach Job's story with tremulous palms held upward and unladen. Not for us the burden of historical linguistics, or the torrent of commentary that sweeps through the centuries, or the dusty overlay of partisan interpretation. Such a refusal of context, historical and theological, is least of all the work of willed ignorance; if we choose to turn from received instruction, it is rather because of an intrinsic knowledge – the terror, in fact, of self-knowledge. Who among us has not been tempted to ask Job's questions? Which of us has not doubted God's justice? What human creature ever lived in the absence of suffering? If we, ordinary clay that we are, are not equal to Job in the wild intelligence of his cries, or in the unintelligible wilderness of his anguish, we are, all the same, privy to his conundrums" (59–60).

19   C. G. Jung, *Answer to Job* (Translated by R. F. C. Hull; London: Routledge & Kegan Paul, 1954).

20   Ibid., 20, 19.

21   Ibid., 44.

22   Ibid., 21.

than human."[23] Confronted by Job with the moral superiority of "man's god-likeness," God becomes "unsure of his own faithfulness"[24] and thus is forced to recognize antinomies in the divine nature that require real reflection on God's part.[25] From Jung's perspective the resolution of God's inner struggle is not finally resolved until God decides to "catch up" to "morally higher"[26] creatures by becoming fully human – in Christ's life and suffering. God "must become man precisely because he has done man a wrong."[27]

Jung's prefacing comments to these discernments are worth noting. He says at the outset that he is not concerned with how ancient readers may have read the book but instead with how the modern reader comes to terms with the divine darkness which is unveiled in the Book of Job, and what effect it has on him. Jung's explicit objective is "to give expression to the shattering emotion that the unvarnished spectacle of divine savagery and ruthlessness produces in us."[28] Near the end of his book, Jung is more explicit concerning the moral and ethical challenge the Book of Job presents contemporary readers:

> Everything now depends on man: immense power of destruction is given into his hand, and the question is whether he can resist the will to use it, and can temper his will with the spirit of love and wisdom [...]. This involves man in a new responsibility. He can no longer wriggle out of it on the plea of his littleness and nothingness, for the dark God has slipped the atom bomb and chemical weapons into his hands and given him the power to empty out apocalyptic vials of wrath on his fellow creatures. Since he has been granted an almost godlike power, he can no longer remain blind and unconscious.[29]

Jung's subjective turn in the interpretation of the Joban story is anticipated by H. G. Wells's *Undying Fire* (1919) and Robert Frost's "A Masque of Reason" (1945), and echoed in Archibald MacLeish's *J.B.* (1958), and E. Wiesel's *Trial of God* (1979).[30] In the *Undying Fire*, Wells recasts the Joban story against the

---

23 Ibid., 32.

24 Ibid., 45.

25 Ibid., 10.

26 Ibid., 68.

27 Ibid., 69.

28 Ibid., 4.

29 Ibid., 161, 164.

30 See S. Schreiner's comparison of biblical commentaries with "modern readings of Job" (*Where Shall Wisdom Be Found? Calvin's Exegesis of Job from Medieval and Modern Perspectives* [Chicago, London: University of Chicago Press, 1994], 156–190).

backdrop of the regnant despair wrought by the destruction of World War I. Job Huss, the central figure in the story, looks "squarely at this world" and sees nothing but inexplicable cruelty.

> I have been forced to revise my faith, and to look more closely than I have ever done before into the meaning of my beliefs [...] I have been wrenched away from the habitual confidence in the order of things which seemed the more natural state for a mind to be in [...] I am thrown now into the darkest doubt and dismay; the universe seems harsh and black to me, whereas formerly I believed that at the core of it and universally pervading it was the Will of a God of Light [...]. But this war has torn away the veil of illusion from millions of men.[31]

From Well's perspective Job's perspective signals that "mankind is coming of age" in an amoral universe. "This hell revealed," Job Huss concludes, "is God's creation!"[32]

> Suddenly it seemed to me that the scales had fallen from my eyes and that I saw the world plain. It was as if the universe had put aside a mask it had hitherto worn, and shown me its face, and it was the face of boundless evil.[33]

If there is to be any justice in such a world, it will not come from God. "Everything now depends on man,"[34] but this guarantees no victory against cosmic and human cruelty. Playing off the title of his book, Wells leaves his readers with the haunting suspicion of ultimate defeat: "There is no reason anywhere, there is no creation anywhere, except the undying fire, the spirit of God in the hearts of men [...] which may fail [...] which seems to me to fail."[35]

Robert Frost's *A Masque of Reason* creates a dialogue for an imaginary forty-third chapter of the Book of Job. After a thousand years, God returns to thank Job for "releasing me / From moral bondage to the human race."

---

31 H. G. Wells, *The Undying Fire: A Contemporary Novel* (Norwood, MS: Berwick & South, 1919), 103.

32 Ibid., 84.

33 Ibid., 85.

34 Ibid., 153–154.

35 Ibid.

238   CHAPTER 13

> The only free will there at first was man's
> Who could do good or evil as he chose.
> I had no choice but to follow him
> With forfeits and rewards he understood –
> Unless I like to suffer the loss of worship.
> I had to prosper good and punish evil.
> You changed all that. You set me free to reign.
> You are the Emancipator of your God,
> And as such I promote you to a saint.[36]

Although Job appreciates this retroactive promotion to sainthood, he still wants answers to a lingering question: "Why did you [God] hurt me so? I am reduced / To asking flatly for the reason – outright."[37] God's response is less than satisfactory, as this following exchange makes clear:

> God: I was just showing off to the Devil, Job,
>   As is set forth in Chapters One and Two
>
> Job: 'Twas human of You. I expected more
>   Than I could understand and what I get
> Is almost less than I can understand.[38]

As with Wells's fictional recreation of the Joban story, so too Frost, writing from a post World War II perspective, essentially treats Job's God as more human than divine, more needy of human instruction than sovereign in exemplifying moral behavior. Frost's God can neither command nor inspire virtuous behavior. Like mere mortals, this God, who "in the beginning *was* the Word" must now "wait for words like anyone" else.

Archibald MacLeish's reading of the Joban prologue in *J.B.* imagines God (the Zuss character) as a used-up, washed-out character who has little or nothing to contribute to modern-day Jobs. The words of Zuss and Nickels, his Satan-counterpart, are well-known and have been often critiqued. It is sufficient here to focus on MacLeish's own commentary on the play, in a 1955

---

36   R. Frost, "A Masque of Reason," in *The Poetry of Robert Frost. The Collected Poems, Complete and Unabridged*, ed., Edward C. Lathem (New York. Henry Holt and Company, 1975), ll. 69–79, pp. 475–476.
37   Ibid., ll. 268–269, p. 483.
38   Ibid, ll. 327–328, pp. 484–485; ll. 331–333, p. 485.

"WILL YOU CONDEMN ME THAT YOU MAY BE JUSTIFIED?" 239

sermon delivered in Farmington, CT. "Why did God deliver Job into Satan's hands? Why?" In answering his own question, MacLeish responds as follows:

> Because God had need of the suffering of Job – had need of it for Himself *as God* [...]
> Man depends on God for all things; God depends on man for one. Without man's love, God does not exist as God, only as creator, and love is the one thing, not even God himself, can command.[39]

Here, MacLeish echoes the words of Job's wife, Sarah, at the end of the play:

> You [J.B.] wanted justice, didn't you?
> There isn't any. There's the world [...]
> Cry for justice and the stars
> Will stare until your eyes sting. Weep,
> Enormous winds will trash the water.
> Cry in sleep for your lost children,
> Snow will fall [...].
>
> You [J.B.] wanted justice and there was none –
> Only love [...].
>
> Blow on the coals of the heart.
> The candles in churches are out.
> The lights have gone out of the sky.
> Blow on the coals of the heart
> And we'll see by and by [...].
> [...] and we'll know.[40]

Each of these "ordinary" readers finds the God who hands over Job willy-nilly to the satan to be a flawed character. Such a God, they conclude, is less than the God human beings expect and deserve. As the "face of boundless evil," as Wells puts it, this God endorses and inspires inexplicable cruelty among those who tune their moral compass to divine behavior. Such a God is not only not acting like God; this God is actually less than human, for any reasonable human being would necessarily recoil at the thought of killing innocent children just

---

39   A. B. MacLeish, "God Has Need of Man," in N. Glatzer, ed., *The Dimensions of Job: A Study and Selected Readings* (New York: Schocken, 1969), 284, 285.

40   A. B. MacLeish, *J.B.* (Boston: Houghton Mifflin, 1986), 151, 153.

240 CHAPTER 13

to show off divine powers. As Frost's Job says, "'Twas human of you," but "I expected more." Moreover, such readings of God's character effectively turn upside down a central tenet of the Old Testament's moral vision. It is no longer God as Creator of the world who models the justice and righteousness upon which the covenantal relationship depends, it is now human beings who must teach God how to be God. Instead of setting their moral compass to the words of the One who says "I am your God [...] and you shall be my people," God's people, these readers insist, must now reverse the logic. "We are your people, and you must be a God in whom the best of our virtues are writ large." We may of course assess such readings of the Joban narrative as exegetically deficient, but we cannot silence their voice in the market place of public discourse; they are an important reminder that scholars may inform the public reading and understanding of texts, but we cannot define it.

2   The Character of God in the Divine Speeches

After relinquishing Job into the satan's hands with the words, "Very well, he is in your power; only spare his life" (2:6), God does not speak again until the divine speeches at the end of the book. In the interim between the silence that hangs over the prologue for seven days and seven nights, when "no one spoke a word to him [Job], for they saw that his suffering was very great" (2:13), and the "answer" that comes out of the whirlwind, we may wonder if God could be considered a "judicious spectator." I borrow the term from Martha Nussbaum, who argues that judicious spectatorship should be a prerequisite for judges in the legal system.[41] On the one hand, judges must have the detachment and the neutrality of a spectator. They must assess every case before them without any bias that favors their own goals, projects, or interests. As Nussbaum puts it, judges need "criteria that can be framed and tested as an exercise of reason and not merely as an act of willfulness or will." Every good judgment rests on "reasons that [...] meet a standard of public articulability and principled consistency." In short, the court should never operate as a "naked organ of power."[42] On the other hand, judges must have the capacity to join legal impartiality to the exercise of judicious emotions, such as fear, grief, anger, hope, and love.[43] Among a judge's most important moral faculties "is the power of imagining vividly what it is like to be each of the persons" who appeals to the court for

---

41   M. Nussbaum, *Poetic Justice: The Literary Imagination and Public Life* (Boston: Beacon Press, 1995), 72–78.

42   Ibid., 87.

43   Ibid., 74.

"WILL YOU CONDEMN ME THAT YOU MAY BE JUSTIFIED?" 241

justice.[44] Judges who do not combine external assessment with empathetic identification cannot provide a moral paradigm for public behavior. If judges cannot both assess judiciously and imagine vividly another's person's pain, then they will likely fail to provide an adequate remedy for the situation, let alone a compelling motivation for altering it.[45]

If we apply these criteria to the divine speeches, would God qualify as a judicious spectator in the Joban story? Can we find in these speeches not only a word that breaks the divine silence that hangs over the middle of the book but also an "answer" that clearly articulates an empathetic understanding of Job's losses? To put an edge on these questions, is there anything in this answer that satisfactorily contextualizes God's decision to destroy Job's possessions, his health, and his family "for no reason" (2:3)? To be certain, the objective of God's speeches is elusive and much debated. I do not expect to resolve the issue here, but I am persuaded that what is at stake from an interpretive standpoint is not only Job's integrity in questioning God's moral worldview but also God's integrity in defending it.[46]

The general outline of the divine speeches does not need to be rehearsed here. Suffice it to say that God has two speeches (38:1–40:2; 40:6–41:34), totaling 123 verses; Job has two responses (40:3–5; 42:1–6), nine verses total. Clearly, God dominates the stage in this "dialogue," the last the book records.[47] Both divine speeches begin with questions that challenge Job to "gird up his loins" and answer God like a "hero" (*geber*; 38:3; 40:7). The first speech centers on God's cosmic "design" (*'ēsâ*; 38:2), with specific attention to the stability of the world's foundations (38:4–18), the intricate rhythms of meteorological phenomena (38:19–38), and the instinctive habits of five pairs of animals (38:39–39:40). Commentators often note that God's review of creation accents God's care and nurture of what humans normally regard as either chaotic or threatening. For example, God births the unruly waters of the sea and wraps them in the swaddling bands of darkness and cloud (38:8–11); God hunts prey for the lion, a feared human predator, and provides human corpses for the vulture to feed upon (38:9–11). The second speech focuses on God's governance of the cosmos, the only specific mention of God's justice in the entire speech (*mišpaṭ*;

---

44 Ibid., 73.

45 Ibid., 91.

46 Although I disagree with some of the particulars of Brown's assessment of the divine speeches, I agree with his observation that once God enters into the debate between Job and his friends, both God's character and integrity and Job's are open to scrutiny (*Character in Crisis*, 90–91).

47 Cf. Newsom (*The Book of Job*, 234): "When God speaks, it tends to bring the conversation to an end."

242   CHAPTER 13

40:8), now with a singular focus on two animals, Behemoth and Leviathan. Both these creatures are conventionally identified as chaos monsters, but here again, as commentators have noted, God appears to be on the side of destructive forces that in their own realm humans can never hope to tame or control. To God's first speech, Job responds by acknowledging that he is "small," then placing his hand over his mouth to indicate that he will speak no further (40:3–5). In response to God's second speech, Job acknowledges that he now knows and understands something about God – and himself – that is new. Whether this evokes Job's repentance, as his enigmatic words in 42:6 have been conventionally interpreted, is the crux of the book, but for now, I leave the interpretive options to the side.

For the sake of argument – and perhaps also to stimulate conversation – let us simply stipulate that both divine speeches depict a world in which chaos not only has its place but is also celebrated for its role in God's moral calculus. What does such an affirmation reveal about the horizons of God's ethics, God's moral worldview? To return to Nussbaum's comments about the "judicious spectator," do God's speeches suggest that God has both the necessary detachment to judge Job's situation equitably and the requisite empathetic identification with Job to feel what he feels? The disconnect between God's words and Job's situation has often been noted; thus God's "detachment," to use Nussbaum's language, seems clear enough.[48] If the objective is to demonstrate that God is superior to Job, that God is God and not Job, then the speeches are successful. But what of God's ability to understand what it would mean for God as God to be reduced to the same unhappy situation as Job, "for no reason"?

To address this question, let me return to Frost's "A Masque of Reason," an ordinary reader's imaginative creation of a forty-third chapter to the Book of Job. If God and Job were to have a reunion a thousand years after their original encounter, what would Job say? Frost sets the table with the following words of Job to God:

> You say we groped this out.
> But if you will forgive me the irreverence,
> It sounds to me as if You thought it out,
> And took Your time to do it. It seems to me
> An afterthought, a long-long-after-thought.

---

48   In characterizing God's response to Job, the political commentator William Safire quips: "It as if God appears in a tie-dyed T-shirt emblazoned with the words 'Because I am God, That's why'" (*The First Dissident: The Book of Job in Today's Politics* [New York: Random House, 1992], 22).

"WILL YOU CONDEMN ME THAT YOU MAY BE JUSTIFIED?" 243

I'd give more for one least beforehand reason
Than all the justifying ex-post-facto
Excuses trumped up by You for theologians [...].

The artist in me cries out for design.
Such devilish ingenuity of torture
Did seem unlike You, and I tried to think
The reason might have been some other person's.
But there is nothing You are not behind.
I did not ask then, but it seems as if
Now after all these years You might indulge me.
Why did You hurt me so? I am reduced
To asking flatly for the reason – outright.[49]

In the biblical book, it is God who comes asking questions of Job. Yet, if we stipulate that the divine speeches place God's character and integrity in question as much as Job's, then we might with Frost imagine a reversal of roles in chapters 38–42. What if Job were to ask God the following questions, for example:

Who determined that suffering was the reward for the righteous?
Have You entered into the depths of human grief?
Have You comprehended a parent's loss of ten children?
Do You know what it feels like when despair yields to rebellion?
Have you ever been mocked by those who will not hear Your cries for help?
What do You do when neither wisdom nor faith provide sufficient meaning for life?

Confronted by such questions from Job (which in fact are consonant with those Job asks in the dialogues with the friends), would God respond by saying, "What shall I answer you? I lay my hand on my mouth" (cf. 40:4)? Can we imagine, based on the divine speeches we have, that God would embrace Job's questions and respond by saying, "I have said and done things concerning you that I did not understand. By the hearing of the ear, I had heard about your pain, but now my eye has seen you" (cf. 42:3, 5)?

We are of course reading against the grain of the book, which seems to demand a response from God, perhaps even such an elusive one as we have

---

49   Frost, "A Masque of Reason," 482–483.

received. As Gary Wills observes in his commentary on G. K. Chesterton's Joban parable, *The Man Who Was Thursday* (1907), "There is one thing worse than giving an answer [to Job]. And that is to give an answer. That would turn God into a theologian, reducing Jehovah to the level of Job's friends."[50] Even so, we should pause long enough to let the words of Cynthia Ozick itch at our ears as we ponder the meaning of what God says and does not say to Job at the end of the book:

> So the poet, through the whirlwind's answer, stills Job.
> But can the poet still the Job who lives in us? God's majesty is eternal, manifest in cell and star. Yet Job's questions toil on, manifest in death camp and hatred, in tyranny and anthrax, in bomb and bloodshed. Why do the wicked thrive? Why do the innocent suffer? In brutal times, the whirlwind's answer tempts, if not atheism, then the sorrowing conviction of God's indifference.[51]

3   Which God Should We Emulate?

The Book of Job offers (at least) two asymmetric characterizations of God. The God of the didactic tale willingly enters into dialogue with heavenly beings, like the satan, but does not speak a word directly to Job. Although Job is the focal point of a heavenly "debate," Job himself is objectified as a case study to be examined. God's ultimate responsibility for the test of fidelity imposed on Job is not in question, but even if Job passes the test, and is rewarded for having done so, the suffering he endures "for no reason" raises unavoidable questions about the moral worthiness of God's behavior. Gratuitous suffering will always confound human understanding, but when the Creator of the world admits to being the hand pulling the trigger on the assault weapon, then humility in the presence of divine action crumbles under the weight it is asked to bear. "I am God and no mortal," God says in Hos 11:9. In that context, the affirmation undergirds God's inscrutable decision to extend compassion towards those who do not deserve it. In the context of the Joban story, the same affirmation seems to be a license to kill. Job may pass God's test for virtue, but it is not at all clear that God passes Job's test – or ours – for acting morally and ethically towards others.

---

50   G. Wills, *Chesterton* (Second edition; New York: Doubleday, 2001), 289.
51   Ozick, "The Impious Impatience of Job," 72.

The God of the whirlwind speeches speaks directly, and at great length, to Job. In itself, such an encounter with the Almighty is an experience granted to but a few others in the Old Testament. In this instance, however, God's primary objective seems to be to explain or defend cosmic principles that supersede and relativize the particulars of Job's circumstances. God defends and celebrates the place of chaos in a world adorned with unfathomable complexities, many that can only be sustained at the expense of human creatures, but not once does God identify where an individual who suffers like Job fits into the grand scheme of God's moral governance. Overarching principles trump particular details that may call them into question. "Who is this that darkens (my) design with words lacking knowledge?" God asks Job (38:2). "Would you condemn me so that you may be in the right?" (40:8). Exegetes may argue that the divine speeches effect a positive transformation in Job's character,[52] that they summon Job to an aesthetic appreciation of the sublime beauty of God's world,[53] but the "naked text"[54] we have received invites responses modern exegetes may (justifiably) resist. Jack Miles's Pulitzer-prize winning *God: A Biography* is but one case in point.

> The climax [of the Book of Job] is a climax for God himself and not just for Job or for the reader. After Job, God knows his own ambiguity as he has never known it before. He now knows that, though he is not Bertrand Russell's fiend, he has a fiend-susceptible side and that mankind's conscience can be finer than his. With Job's assistance, his just, kind self has won out over his cruel, capricious self just as it did after the flood. But the victory has come at an enormous price. Job will father a new family, but the family he lost during the wager will not be brought back from the dead; neither will the servants whom the devil slew. And neither will God's innocence. The world still seems more just than unjust, and God still seems more good than bad; yet the pervasive mood, as this extraordinary work ends, is one not of redemption but of reprieve.[55]

So, which God should we aspire to emulate? The God characterized in the didactic tale or the God of the whirlwind speeches? The God who does not speak to Job but makes him the object of underserved suffering for no reason,

---

52 E.g., Brown, *Character in Crisis*, 104–107; idem, *The Seven Pillars of Creation: The Bible, Science, and the Ecology of Wonder* (Oxford: Oxford University Press, 2010), 129–131.

53 Newsom, *The Book of Job*, 234–258.

54 Ozick, "The Impious Impatience of Job," 72.

55 J. Miles, *God: A Biography* (New York: Alfred A. Knopf, 1995), 328.

or the God who privileges Job with divine disclosure that celebrates chaos but reduces him, first to silence, then to an enigmatic utterance that does not clearly explain what he has learned from the encounter? Either or both options confront us with the imperative of dealing with the "dark side" of a God who says and does things that are difficult for most all readers to accept as compatible with divinity.[56] For my part, I resonate with the words of John Barton, who has recently addressed the ethical dilemma the dark side of God presents the modern reader. Does the characterization of God in the Book of Job provide a moral compass that enables us to decide, then act upon, what is right, righteous, and worthy of our highest ethical aspirations? Barton's response – and mine for the time being – is this:

> I hope the answer is yes, but the Old Testament [and the Book of Job] does not make it an easy question to answer; and it gives plenty of ammunition if we want to fight on the other side.[57]

---

56 On the "dark side" side of God, see W. Dietrich, C. Link, *Die dunklen Seiten Gottes: Wilkur und Gewalt* (Second edition; Neukirchen-Vluyn: Neukirchener Verlag, 1997); idem, *Die dunklen Seiten Gottes: Allmacht und Ohnmacht* (Neukirchen-Vluyn: Neukirchener Verlag, 2000).

57 J. Barton, "The Dark Side of God in the Old Testament," in K. Dell, ed., *Ethical and Unethical in the Old Testament: God and Humans in Dialogue* (New York, London: T & T Clark, 2010), 134.

CHAPTER 14

The Joban Theophany and the Education of God

Theophanies are intense experiences of divine disclosure in which God gives and humans receive information unavailable through ordinary encounters. This fact makes it all the more curious that the theophany in Job 38:1–42:6 is introduced not as a divine disclosure but instead as a divine request for knowledge: "Gird up your loins like a man, I [God]¹ will question you, and you will declare to me (*hôdîʿēnî*)" (38:3; 40:7 [repeated by Job in 42:4]). These two references, one introducing the first half of God's speech (38:1–40:2), the other, the second half (40:6–41:34), are the only places in the Old Testament where God says to a human being "make me know," or "teach me" what you know. Ordinarily, God is the one who makes something known to others, e.g., "It was the Lord who made it known to me [*hôdîʿanî*] and I knew [*ʿēdāʿa*]" (Jer 11:18). In the dialogues with the friends, Job himself affirms this typical understanding of God as teacher *par excellence*: "How many are my iniquities and my sins? Make me know (*hōdîʿēnî*) my transgression and my sin" (13:23; cf. 10:2).²

The epistemological question lurking behind the regnant view of God as teacher is this: Can anyone – any mortal – *teach* God anything? Isaiah articulates the implausibility of the idea: "Whom did he [God] consult for enlightenment and who taught him (*wayĕlammĕdēhû*) the path of justice? Who taught him knowledge (*yĕlammĕdēhû daʿat*) and showed him (*yôdîʿennû*) the way of understanding" (Isa 40:14). Job has his own version of the same question: "Who can teach knowledge to God (*halʾēl yĕlammed dāʿat*)?" (Job 21:22).

What then are we to make of God's invitation to Job – actually, according to the imperative verb form, God's *directive* to Job – to teach him something? The predominant approach to this question is to take the supposed tonality of God's leading question in 38:2 as the hermeneutical clue for understanding

---

1   As in the prose Prologue and Epilogue, the narrator uses the divine name Yhwh to introduce both parts of God's speech: "Then the Lord (Yhwh) answered Job out of the whirlwind" (38:1 and 40:3, the latter omitting the words "out of the whirlwind;" cf. 40:1).

2   *yādaʿ* in the Hiphil occurs 71× in the Old Testament; with reference to God as the one making known, 25×: Gen 41:39; Exod 33:12, 13; Num 16:5; Deut 8:3; 1 Sam 16:3; Isa 64:1; Jer 11:18; 16:21; Ezek 20:11; 39:7; Hos 5:9; Hab 3:2; Pss 16:11; 25:4; 39:5; 51:8; 77:15; 90:12; 98:2; 103:7; 143:8; Job 10:2; 13:23; Neh 9:14. Of the 71 total Hiphil occurrences, eight are in the book of Job: two spoken by Job to God (10:2; 13:23); one spoken by Bildad to Job (26:3); two spoken by Elihu to Job (32:7; 37:19); two spoken by God to Job (38:3; 40:3); and one, a repetition of God's words in 40:3, presumably spoken by Job to God (42:4).

© SAMUEL E. BALENTINE, 2021 | DOI:10.1163/9789004459212_015

the entirety of the divine speeches. "Who is this who darkens counsel without knowledge (*bĕlî da'at*)?" God says to Job. It is reasonable to think that God is not asking about the identity of the one standing before him: "Oh, by the way, before we begin, let me ask, 'What is your name?'" The issue does not seem to be Job's missing name tag but instead his missing knowledge; God's words seem to convey irritation, not curiosity.[3] How dare the first year student question the senior professor? The supposed tonality of this question then typically transposes into the barrage of questions that follow in the rest of God's speech. Questions like, "Have you?" "Can you?" "Do you"? would then presuppose answers that only confirm Job's inadequacies. On this reading, God's objective in inviting Job to teach him something would be to make it crystal clear that God has absolutely nothing to learn from him.

But is this necessarily so? We know that it is difficult, if not impossible, to determine the tonality of an ancient text, especially one that dares to imagine the words that God speaks. Grammatical markers may indicate that we are *reading* an interrogative rather than a declarative sentence, but how could we *hear* the sounds that convey the speaker's attitude or mood, whether he is angry or calm, genuinely interested in an exchange of ideas or only pretending to be? What if God's questions from the tempest (*sĕ'ārâ*; 38:1; 40:6) are *not* meant to crush Job's spirit, as Job himself had feared (9:17, with a variant form, *śĕ'ārâ*), but instead to engage him in a mutually beneficial exchange of ideas, a genuine Q and A? By what criteria can we distinguish the tone of Job's words to God in 13:22 – "You call, and I, I will answer; or I will speak and you respond" – from God's virtually identical words to Job in 38:3 and 40:6? Why are they both not saying and expecting, even hoping for, the same thing?

I need not review the arguments for reading God's speeches as a parody of genuine dialogue; they are substantial and perhaps will remain convincing to a majority. But I am curious about this language that suggests it was not unreasonable, inside the ethos of this text, to think about Job teaching God something. What follows are my wonderments about this matter. If there remains some truth in the Socratic axiom that wonder (*thaumazein*) is the beginning of

---

3   It is curious, nonetheless, that elsewhere questions introduced with the words *mi zeh* ("who is this?") do ask for and receive information. They are not merely or only rhetorical (e.g., Isa 63:1; Jer 46:7; 49:14 [= 50:44]; Ps 24:8; Lam 3:37; Esth 7:5; cf. Song 3:6 [= 8:5]; 6:10). Although there are no close parallels to the use of this language in Job, the occurrence in Isa 63:1 is interesting. The one asking the question in this instance is the prophet or sentinel; the one answering it, boldly and with conviction, is God: "Who is this that comes from Edom, from Bozrah in garments stained with crimson? [...] It is I, announcing vindication, mighty to save."

THE JOBAN THEOPHANY AND THE EDUCATION OF GOD

philosophy, the love of learning, then perhaps there is some merit in thinking out loud.

1 "Then the Lord Answered Job Out of the Whirlwind"

We may begin by noting that it is strange to have a theophany at all in a wisdom text, which Job is generally reckoned to be, where the focus is typically on human reason and experience, not divine revelation.[4] God does not speak and makes no appearance in Proverbs or Ecclesiastes (nor in Sirach or Wisdom of Solomon). Neither is there a literary precedent for theophanic divine speech in ancient Near Eastern wisdom texts.[5] The Joban theophany is therefore exceptional in this regard, and we may suspect that the Joban author, familiar with a standard genre, has employed it in an atypical literary context in order to deviate from convention.[6]

Furthermore, the narrator introduces the theophany as God's "answer" to Job. We may surmise that at least from the narrator's perspective the theophany serves 1) to answer Job's many questions throughout the dialogue, thus affirming that God is after all vulnerable to what Job says; and 2) to demonstrate that answering a question with a question, as God does in the Prologue with the satan, is an appropriate and effective way for a deity to engage in substantive discussion with underlings, even if it requires a recalibration of divine agency. "There he is," God says to the satan at the end of dialogue, "he is within you power" (2:6, CEB; cf. 1:12). From the outset then, even before reading the substance of what God says to Job, the narrator serves notice that we must be open to adjusting our expectations about what we are going to hear.

---

4   D. Cox, "Structure and Function of the Final Challenge: Job 29–31," *Proceedings of the Irish Biblical Association* 5 (1981), 65; cf. D. J. A. Clines, *Job 38–42* (WBC 18B; Nashville: Thomas Nelson, 2009), 57: "this may be called a 'stunted' theophany in that it is more of an answer than an appearance."

5   See C. Newsom, *The Book of Job: A Contest of Moral Imaginations* (Oxford: Oxford University Press, 2003), 238: "So far as one can tell, there is no literary precedent for a pair of speeches that set over against one another the voice of a sufferer and the response of his God. What the author of the book of Job has composed is something of a tour de force."

6   On genres in Job and their shaping of expectations, see Newsom, *Book of Job*, 11–15.

250   CHAPTER 14

2   The "Critical Inquisitiveness" of Rhetorical Questions

To convey the "inquisitive attitude"[7] that characterizes the wisdom literature of
the ancient Near East and the Hebrew Bible, the form of the "literary dialogue"
has been shown to be peculiarly apt.[8] The importance of dialogue is clear in
the Joban prose tale (Job 1–2 + 42:7–17) and especially in the poetic "dialogue"
between Job and his friends (4–27), but it is also present in the divine speeches,
where the author has "dialogized" the encounter between Job and God.[9] The
"dialogue" between Job and God has, however, been widely regarded as something of a sham. God speaks for 123 verses, Job for only 9. What kind of dialogue
can this really be? More than word count, it is the extensive use of rhetorical
questions that has convinced most commentators that God is engaging in a
disputation with Job, not a conversation. According to this view, the objective
is not to discuss multiple perspectives on an issue – and certainly not any that
have to do with God's wisdom and justice – but instead to leverage Job toward
one and only one perspective. "Agree with God and be at peace," Eliphaz says
to Job, only in this way will anything good come to you (22:21). As one commentator puts it, "When God speaks, it tends to bring conversation to an end."[10]

Before conceding that the divine speeches are only a parody of dialogue, I
want to lean into these rhetorical questions a bit more. Rhetorical questions
are interrogative sentences that have the force of a declarative statement.[11]
The interrogative opens itself to inquisitiveness; the declarative responds to
inquiry with discovered assertions. The tension between question and answer
is therefore built into the form of this way of speaking. The question may be
resolved, but it remains essential to the thought process. The answer may be
expected, but its force is tethered to the intellectual inquiry it generates.

---

7   I appropriate the terms "inquisitive attitude" (37) and "critical inquisitiveness" (43) from
     G. Bucellatti, "Wisdom and Not: The Case of Mesopotamia," JAOS 101 (1981), 35–47.

8   On the form and function of the "literary dialogue," see, K. van der Toorn, "The Ancient
     Near Eastern Literary Dialogue As a Vehicle of Critical Reflection," in G. J. Reinink,
     H. L. J. Vanstiphout, eds., *Dispute Poems and Dialogues in the Ancient and Medieval Near
     East: Forms and Types of Literary Debates in Semitic and Related Literatures* (Louvain:
     Peeters, 1991), 59–75.

9   On the polyphonic "dialogization" of the book of Job, see Newsom, *Book of Job.*

10   Ibid., 234.

11   L. J. de Regt, "Discourse Implications of Rhetorical Questions in Job, Deuteronomy, and
     the Minor Prophets, in L. J. de Regt, J. de Waard, J. P. Fokkelman, eds., *Literary Structure
     and Rhetorical Strategies in the Hebrew Bible* (Van Gorcum: Eisenbrauns, 1996), 51–78; cf.
     R. Koop, "Rhetorical Questions and Implied Meaning in the Book of Job," *Bible Translator*
     39 (1988), 415–423.

THE JOBAN THEOPHANY AND THE EDUCATION OF GOD
251

We should consider whether the author who constructed the divine speeches and the narrator who construed them as an "answer" to Job were imagining a cognitive process whereby God himself arrives at the declarative by means of engaging the interrogative. Two issues merit further reflection. 1) If we agree the Elihu speeches have been inserted into a book in which Job's words "ended" in Job 29–31, then the divine speeches are structurally located as a response to all that Job has said. They are not a self-addressed soliloquy in which God thinks out loud about no other thoughts than his own;[12] they are not a first-person, finalized declaration of truth – "I know this," "I can do that." They are instead part of the dialogic structure of the book, and in this sense they do not close discussion with Job; in fact, Job has the last word (42:1–6), not God.[13] 2) The amount of detail that accompanies these rhetorical questions hints that God has himself thought deeply about the things he asks Job. Of particular note is God's attention to aspects of life that have troubled Job, e.g., the darkness that shadows or eclipses the light (38:9, 17, 19), the wickedness that permeates the earth like dye in a garment (38:12–15), the hunger and thirst that renders creatures vulnerable to famine and death (38:39–41), the cruelty, rage, and fear that roams wild underneath morning stars that illuminate the deep darkness of the gates of death (38:7, 17, 23; 39:15–16, 22, 24).

Such details are generally lacking in other creation accounts, which are located in monologic or declarative contexts (e.g., Genesis 1–2, Isaiah 40–55; Psalm 8), an observation that invites its own (perhaps rhetorical) question.[14] Were these darker aspects of the world on God's mind *before* Job pressed on him the interrogative mode? Before Job asked, "Do you have eyes of flesh? Do you see as humans see?" (10:4), did God see the world only from one perspective, only from a divine perspective? Could it be that God discovers (or recovers) a thicker knowledge of the world only *after* [as a result of] entering into a dialogue with Job?

---

12   P. L. Arrington, "Soliloquies Divine: God's Self-Addressed Rhetoric in the Old Testament, *Rhetorica* 34 (2016), 223–242.

13   Newsom, *Book of Job*, 28. Newsom argues that the divine speeches respond specifically to Job 29–31, not to the entirety of the wisdom dialogue. She notes in this regard that Job's responses to God in 40:1–5 and 42:1–6 appropriate the words and imagery in chapters 29–31 (238).

14   Psalm 104 could be counted as an exception, as it also acknowledges some of these darker aspects of life, but it does so from a third person perspective, not a first-person divine observation, and within the context of a declarative hymn of praise that makes no room for even rhetorical questions.

252   CHAPTER 14

3   God as Rhetor

We may move from rhetorical questions to the rhetor of the questions. What
are the presuppositions about the nature and character of the God who asks
the questions in Job 38–42? Such a question requires far more attention than
this paper can give it; I limit myself to some preliminary observations about
what Job claims to know about God and what he deduces from this knowledge.[15]
We can stipulate at the outset that Job and all his friends (including Elihu)
fundamentally agree on two metatheistic presuppositions about divinity:
God is immortal, and God's knowledge and wisdom is superior to all others.[16]
God's infinitude always and necessarily surpasses Job's finitude; God's cognitive capacity always and necessarily exceeds Job's comprehension. Job's penultimate words in the book unequivocally affirm both these aspects of God's
divinity. "I know you [God] can do anything" (42:2a), Job says, and I know that
"I have spoken about things I did not understand (*lo' 'ābîn*), about wonders I
did not know (*lo' 'ēdā'*)" (42:3; cf. 38:2). Job therefore affirms the indisputable:
"[God] is not a mortal, like I am" (9:32).[17]

This affirmation, however, serves not to close down all further thinking
about God but instead to evoke more questions. Can mortals discern anything
about the moral code that directs God's behavior? Foreshadowing God's questions to him, Job directs his own (rhetorical) questions to God, for example, in
10:3–7.[18] The expected, yet unspoken, answer from God to each of Job's questions is "No," but the questions themselves hint at Job's thought process, and,
I would argue, a corresponding thinking he invites and expects from God.

---

15   Clines (*Job 38–42*, 52) among others, has rightly discerned that the *dialogue*, or as Clines
      would put it, the *dispute* between God and Job, has fundamentally to do with knowledge,
      the superiority of God's knowledge and the limitation of Job's.

16   On the concept of "generic Godhood" in the ancient Near East and in the Hebrew
      Bible, see J. Gericke, *The Hebrew Bible and Philosophy of Religion* (Atlanta: Society of
      Biblical Literature, 2012), 259–292; M. Smith, *The Origins of Biblical Monotheism: Israel's
      Polytheistic Background and the Ugaritic Texts* (New York: Oxford University Press,
      2001), 6–9.

17   On the use of this language elsewhere in the Old Testament, see S. E. Balentine, "'I am a
      God and Not a Human Being': The Divine Dilemma in Hosea," in K. Spronk, H. Barstad,
      eds., *Torah and Tradition. Papers Read at the Sixteenth Joint Meeting of the Society of Old
      Testament Study and the Oudtestamentish Werkgezelchap, Edinburgh 2015* (Leiden, Boston:
      Brill, 2017), 54–69.

18   For a word-by-word tabulation and assessment of the questions in Job applying the
      method *Sprachwissenschaft*, see P. Ritter-Mueller, *Kennst du die Welt? – Gottesantwort an
      Ijob* (Münster, Hamburg, London: LIT Verlag, 2000).

THE JOBAN THEOPHANY AND THE EDUCATION OF GOD 253

(1). "Does it seem good to you to act unjustly (*hăṭôb lĕkâ kî taʿăšok*)?" (10:3a).
What constitutes goodness in the judgment of God? By what criteria does God
decide that certain divine behaviors are just and others are not? Do human
values like goodness and justice have any meaning at all in the ethos of divinity? Job has presumably thought about these matters. Presumably, he expects
God to say something like this: "No, it is not good to act unjustly; to be good is
instead to do justice, which means ___." How might God fill in the blank?

To answer this question, we must look to the divine speeches, especially to
40:8–14, where we find the book's only first-person account of what God would
acknowledge as good or just justice. With a series of rhetorical questions and
evocative imperatives, God invites Job to understand that the justice on which
the world relies requires godlike *power* (v. 9a: "an arm like God"), *words* (v. 9b:
"thunder with a voice like his [God's]"), and *majesty, dignity*, and *glory* (v. 10). It
also requires righteous anger (vv. 11–13), like that which God displays in bringing down the proud and the wicked, who arrogantly presume they can abuse
others without penalty (cf. Job's complaint in 21:28–30; 24:1–12). The last words
of God's challenge (v. 14) invite close inspection, for they suggest that *if* Job can
image God's power, words, majesty, and anger, *then* God will acknowledge that
his quest for justice is not only principled but also effective: "Then even I will
praise you, for your own right hand has brought you victory."

Must we take all of these words as rhetoric designed only to rebuke Job for
his hubris and to mock his simplistic understanding of divine governance?
Perhaps so, but we should note that like Job, and in response to Job, God has
also thought deeply about what it means to act justly.

(2). "Do you have eyes of flesh or do you see like a human sees (*hă'ênê bāśār
lak 'im-kir'ôt 'ĕnôš tir'eh*)?" (10:4). How does God perceive reality? Even if God
does not see physically *though* human eyes, is it possible for God to see *as if*
he were human? Does God see only from a divine perspective, only from a
point of view that transcends all human limitations? Or is God's insight into
human life fully informed by the very limitations God transcends? It is unlikely
that Job expects God either to confirm or deny the ocular capacity of divinity. Job's primary concern is whether God can understand what it feels like
to experience the deaths of seven sons and three daughters "for no reason"
(2:3; cf. 9:17). We may think of Lear's admonition to his would-be comforters:
"If thou wilt weep my fortunes, take my eyes" (*King Lear*, IV. 6). If Job were to
step into Lear's role, his lines would be still more pointed: "Look at me and be
horrified" (21:5).

The truth Job has learned about the caprice of suffering is inscribed in the
natural order for all to see. "Ask the animals (*bĕhēmot*), Job says, "and they will
teach you" (12:7). "Who among all these does not know that the hand of God
has done this?" (12:9). Job is addressing the friends, not God, and perhaps his

254   CHAPTER 14

anguish has pushed him to satire – does he really expect the friends to question birds and plants and fish? – but he has imagined that creation itself is a source for revelation both *from* and *to* God about the way the world works. We might argue that when God looks at the natural order and disorder manifest in the world, God sees essentially the same truth Job sees, even if, now that Job has called his attention to it, God sees a mysterious majesty in Job's world that Job has yet to comprehend. When God then appropriates Job's words for divine speech, "Look at Behemoth (*běhēmôt*), whom I made just like you" (40:15), we can ask, who is teaching whom?

(3). "Are your days like the days of a human or your years like the days of a mortal (*hăkîmê 'ĕnôš yāmêkâ 'im šĕnôtêkā kîmê gabber*)?" (10:5). Job does not expect God to say, "Yes, gods like me typically live X years and then we die and are no more. Yes, we too move from the womb to the grave; we know therefore that life is both precarious and precious." Nothing in Job's intellectual world would have tempted him to think that God was mortal. Nevertheless, even though Job's questions ultimately lead him to an expected affirmation of God's immortality, we can imagine that he reaches his destination by way of wonderment about what kind of life God lives. If God lives in a world of eternity, unbounded by the constraints of ordinary time – birth and death and the ordinary vicissitudes of the days, months, and years in between – then what can God know in any intimate way about what it means to live in between beginnings and endings? Can God understand the vulnerabilities of finitude, the "days that are swifter than a weaver's shuttle and come to their end without hope," the "months of emptiness" and "nights of misery" (7:3, 6; cf. 9:25) that exhaust themselves in faint questions about the meaning of life: "Why did I not die at birth," Job says, "come out of the womb and expire?" (3:11; cf. 3:12, 16, 20, 23; 10:18–19). In eternity, does God ever yearn for a death that will not come (3:21)?

It is instructive to place Job's questions to God *in dialogue with* God's questions to Job. God's address to Job begins with questions about the beginnings of the cosmos that provides Job's habitat. Was Job present when God laid the foundations? God knows and Job knows that he was not present, but God is not checking the primordial roll to see if Job was enrolled in the class. Instead, questions about the design of creation manifest a thought process that moves from the macro structure of cosmic order to the intricate details of a single creature's life cycle, from the cornerstone and pillars and outermost limits of heaven and earth, to the number of months in the gestation cycle of a mountain goat (39:1–4). Does God comprehend the finitude of life, Job has asked. God has thought deeply about the question. From the questions God asks in response to Job's questions, it is clear that God watches over every step in a creature's life.

THE JOBAN THEOPHANY AND THE EDUCATION OF GOD   255

4   Dueling Banjos

At the end of the Joban theophany, Job announces what he *knows* (*yādaʿtî*, 42:2a) about God's design for the world, what he has *heard* God say (42:5a), and what he has *seen* or perceived about God (42:5b). The substance of Job's new knowledge is buried in the words of 42:6, which can be translated in such different ways that its meaning defies comprehension, but there can be little doubt that Job has experienced a cognitive shift of some sort. But what has God learned from Job? If Job has in some way been God's teacher, imparting knowledge that God would not have had in the same way without Job's help, then does God also experience a cognitive shift as result of this exchange with Job? What does God *know, hear,* and *perceive* about divinity – and about human beings – as a result of this theophanic experience with Job?

I imagine the dialogue of questions between Job and God as a biblical version of "Dueling Banjos," the instrumental bluegrass composition by Authur Smith (1955) famously featured in the movie "Deliverance" (1972). Two banjo players face each other. One is a young "local boy" who lives in the backwoods of Georgia; he is poor, uneducated, and appears to those who see him to have a pitiful "genetic deficiency." The other is a middle-aged businessman who has driven out to the country for a weekend of fun with his mates. His education and resources give him access to a social class the local boy cannot hope to attain. The businessman begins tuning his banjo, random, half strokes, a preliminary test before he begins to play seriously. The young boy listens to these inchoate sounds, mimics them on his own banjo, and adds a few notes of his own, which the man then repeats.

This process continues through several more rounds; each time the boy plays a few more notes of his own; each time the man follows his lead, repeating what he has heard. Gradually, the man takes the lead and begins a riff that becomes increasingly complicated. The boy repeats everything he hears, not note for note, but with variations that invite the man to reciprocate. Back and forth the two go; the tempo accelerates; with widening smiles they struggle to keep up with each other. At one point the man cries out, "I'm lost;" the boy grins and keeps playing. The man laughs and refocuses, intent on demonstrating his superior skill.

They finish simultaneously. Neither thinks of claiming victory over the other. They share a mutual joy at having created music that could only have come from the happy fusion of their distinctive perspectives.[19] The man, the

---

19   Davis Hankins makes a similar point by using the topological model of the Möbius strip to argue that God and Job stand on two sides of the same surface. Neither one needs to cross over an edge to arrive at the other side. In Hankins' words: "At the end, YHWH and Job

one who had started everything with a few simple strokes on his banjo, speaks the last words of the scene. I imagine them as God's words to Job, (perhaps without the opening expletive): "Goddamn, I could play all day with this guy. You wanna play another one?"

It seems appropriate to end an essay such as this with a question, although in this particular situation, I am pretty sure the man's question is real, not rhetorical.

---

remain two different figures, and one does not require the other's destruction. Instead, the truth of each of their positions is ultimately found on the side of the other." Put more simply, "Both Yhwh and Job finally assume the truth of the other's speech as the truth of their own;" *The Book of Job and the Immanent Genesis of Transcendence* (Chicago: Northwestern University Press, 2015), 224.

PART 6

Preaching Job and Job's God: "Listen Carefully to My Words"

∴

CHAPTER 15

Moral Rebellion or Reverent Submission?
(Job 23:1–9, 16–17)

Job's speech in chapters 23–24 holds in tension two seemingly dissonant affirmations: God is absent, and there must be justice.* The first statement is the basis for one of the most rending complaints about God's abandonment of the world and of human beings found anywhere in scripture (23:3, 8–9). On the heels of this complaint, Job's second affirmation sustains a scathing indictment of God's failure as the moral judge of the universe (24:1–17). The cotter pin of defiant faith that strains to hold these two affirmations together is 23:17: "But I am not destroyed by the darkness." Readers may find it instructive to reflect on what it means to be stewards of Job's faith and to be held accountable for acting or not acting on it. In pondering the consequences of either choice, it is important to keep one ear cocked toward God's response (23:4–5), the other toward the cries for help of the wounded and the dying (24:12).

Job's *compelling hope* is that he might find a God who is more present than the One he now knows (23:1–7). Previously, Job has conceded that he has neither the strength (9:4, 19) nor the piety (16:15–17) to stay the course with a God who is determined to destroy him "for no reason" (cf. 2:4) and with "no mercy" (16:13). In his despair he had wanted nothing so much as the consent of his conscience simply to give up and die (3:11–13, 20–22; 6:8–9; 7:15–16; 10:18–22; 16:22–17:1). Now, however, that same despair fuels a new resolve. He determines to find the place where God is hiding and to press his presence on God's until the veil that separates them is lifted. Surely God will honor the arguments of a truly "upright person" like Job (v. 7; cf. 1:1, 8; 2:3), for a God of justice must be guided by reason and fair play, not power and petulance.

Job's *lingering fear* is that the absent God who unjustly terrorizes him is all there is (23:8–16). In search of God, Job sets forth on an imaginative journey to the four points of the compass. He turns to the east ("forward") and the west ("backward"), then to the north ("left") and the south ("right"), but the God

---

* This essay originally appeared in the "Between Text and Sermon" section of *Interpretation* 53 (1999), 290–293. The Joban text was assigned by the editors of the journal. The author's assignment for the essays in this section of the journal is to stand "between" the exegesis of the text and a "sermon" that might emerge from it. The essay "sets the table" for the sermon; it is not itself the sermon.

© SAMUEL E. BALENTINE, 2021 | DOI:10.1163/9789004459212_016

260   CHAPTER 15

he seeks is nowhere to be found. The sad result of his quest is reported in a sequence of deadening truths: "he is not there"; "I cannot perceive him"; "I cannot behold him"; "I cannot see him" (vv. 8–9). The friends have tried to explain away God's absence with two recurring arguments: 1) Job's sin has driven God away, and his repentance will bring God back again (8:3–6; 11:13–19; 22:23–28); and 2) God's wisdom is necessarily too deep and too high for mere mortals to grasp (8:8–9; 11:7–9; 15:7–8: cf. 33:12–14; 37:21–24). Job should not misread transcendence as absence, they insist. If he will only submit obediently to what God gives and withholds, then he can be "at peace" with God and with himself (22:21). Job is not persuaded. After listening to his friends' arguments for 205 verses, his take on God is similar to the ruminations of Doris Betts: "I have never found life, faith, or art really so neat. I continue to outlive many days surveying this world with the suspicion that Deus has really absconded. With the funds."[1]

In the second half of his speech, Job turns from the complaint about God's hiddenness to God's indictable failure as a fair and reasonable judge of the world. He begins with a critical question that authentic faith permits no innocent sufferer to leave unasked: "Why?" (24:1). Why do those who know God is just never see the judgment that confirms God is God? Why do the wicked run free, leaving their victims to cry for help to a God who sees nothing wrong with the way the world is working (24:2–12)? Why do those who "rebel against the light" have license to subvert the moral order of the cosmos by using darkness as a cover for their criminality (24:13–17)? By any normal definition of justice, such evidence requires God's intervention. Yet the violations go on, and God remains silent.

The last section of Job's speech (24:18–24) is problematic. Many commentators assume that these verses belong to one of the friends, not to Job, because they express a certainty about the punishment of the wicked that is inconsistent with Job's argument in this chapter. It is preferable, however, to follow the ancient versions (LXX, Vulgate, Peshitta) and understand these words as Job's attempt to *evoke*, that is, to *actualize* the judgment he believes God must implement if God is to act like God. The NJPS, which renders these verses as Job's curse upon the wicked ("May they be flotsam on the face of the water; May their portion in the land be cursed"), gives the reader the best chance of hearing Job's defiant insistence that justice can remain neither hidden in heaven nor absent on earth. On the chance that he has erred in his discernment, Job takes his stand inside the gap between what he hopes and believes

---

1   Doris Betts, "The Fingerprints of Style," *Black Warrior Review* 10 (1983), 179. See the discussion in W. Dale Brown, *Of Fiction and Faith* (Grand Rapids: Eerdmans, 1997), 17–18.

MORAL REBELLION OR REVERENT SUBMISSION? 261

is the truth about God and his deepening fear that he hopes and believes too much (24:25).

Job's move from complaint to defiant faith rests on the thin edge of a daring decision. In 23:17, he declares that he will not be "destroyed by the darkness" that threatens to collapse the boundaries between life and death (see the marginal note in NRSV). Even if "thick darkness" should cover his face so that he can neither see nor be seen, he will be a *presence* that God cannot ignore. If God does not see that something is wrong when the wicked steal from the poor, then Job will be God's eyes. If God cannot hear the cries for help, then Job will speak words that scratch at God's ears until they are heard and understood. Even if his words can no longer "fork" the lightning, as Dylan Thomas puts it, he will "rage against the dying of the light." He will "not go gentle into that good night."[2]

Job's abiding sense of God's absence is hardly confined to the land of Uz. Indeed, "east of Eden" it may seem even more imperative than ever before that the journey of faith be plotted in what Richard Friedman has described as a "postrevelation world."[3] Like Moses we are permitted only partial glimpses of God at best (cf. Exod 33:12–23). Often we must admit that we see less, hear less, and are less certain about God's active involvement in the affairs of the world and of humankind. The New Testament asserts that God is incarnate in Jesus. And yet it also reports that even Jesus' faith was shaped by a profound understanding of God's absence. Even though his last words from the cross – "My God, my God why have you forsaken me?" (Matt 27:46; Mk 15:34) – are surely enlarged by the testimony to resurrection, they are not erased from the story. Indeed, without their lingering echo, the Sunday celebration of Easter is like a song in search of a tune. As George Steiner has discerned, Christian faith cannot be fully Christian without "the long day's journey of the Saturday" that waits before the "assured" and still "precarious" words of Jesus' question.[4]

Now, nearly two thousand years after the canons of scripture were closed, the twentieth century limps to its end affirming nothing perhaps so strongly as that God has simply disappeared. On the one hand, the ever-expanding domains of science and technology unlock more and more of the mysteries of the universe, leaving religious claims about God sounding more and more naïve and redundant. On the other hand, two world wars, the incomparable

---

2 D. Thomas, "Do Not Go Gentle Into That Good Night," in *The Collected Poems of Dylan Thomas* (New York: New Directions Books, 1971), 128.

3 R. Friedman, *The Disappearance of God: A Divine Mystery* (Boston: Little, Brown, and Company, 1995), 28.

4 G. Steiner, *Real Presences* (Chicago: University of Chicago Press, 1982), 232.

evil of the Holocaust, and the seemingly endless eruptions of violence and barbarity in the world have heaped such suffering on the scales of human experience that the imbalance between death and life seems more precarious today than ever before. As we stare into the face of a new millennium, we are hard put not to look with the eyes of Clarence Wilmot, John Updike's failed minister turned encyclopedia salesman. The world does indeed seem to be dreadfully full of "bombast and deviltry" and "as empty of divine content as a corroded kettle."[5]

Those who search for God with Job's eyes will refuse to accept that this is the world God intends. They will not agree that God has determined that human beings are simply "born to trouble" (4:7). They will not believe that faith must be forever construed as silent submission to injustice that terrorizes the innocent and subverts the moral foundations of creation. Like Job, they will take their lives in their hands (13:14), fill their mouths with arguments (23:4), and stubbornly insist that the absent God remains committed to a world that has the capacity to be "very good" (Gen 1:31).

What haunts Job and his readers is God's response to faith that is enacted as moral rebellion rather than reverent submission. Does such faith pervert God's understanding of what it means for human beings to exercise "dominion" over the creational design (Gen 1: 26, 28)? Or might such faith be the very requirement of what God means by the commission "to till" the garden and to "keep it" (Gen 2:15)? The Jobs of the world will never lack for "friends" who believe that the answer to the first question is a nonnegotiable "Yes," the answer to the second an equally certain "No." But those who number themselves among Job's children will not be so sure. Like their biblical counterpart, they will not be able to hear or see or understand fully "what is right" until God speaks to them directly (42:7–8).

Until God speaks and settles these matters one way or the other, every steward of Job's faith listens for God with ears attuned to the cries for help of the wounded and the dying. Like Father Gower, Gail Godwin's melancholy Rector of St. Cuthbert's, they will "hollow out" a place for a just God who heals and restores and keep it "raw and deep with unanswered questions."[6] I know of no more striking image of what such faith might look like than the eighteen-foot bronze statue designed by Ossip Zadkine (1890–1967) for the city of Rotterdam. Samuel Terrien, who includes this work in his collection of Joban iconography, notes that when Zadkine saw this city that had been bombed out by the German Air Force in 1940, then rebuilt, he determined to sculpt a

---

5 J. Updike, *In the Beauty of the Lilies* (New York: Alfred A. Knopf, 1996), 23, 7.

6 G. Godwin, *Father Melancholy's Daughter* (New York: Avon Books, 1991), 320.

MORAL REBELLION OR REVERENT SUBMISSION? 263

FIGURE 15.1   Ossip Zadkine (1888–1967). "The City Destroyed." (1954). Bronze statue, Rotterdam
CREDIT: NATIONAL PORTRAIT GALLERY, LONDON, UK/WIKIMEDIA COMMONS

figure that testified not only to the terror of the city's vulnerability but also to its courage to "embrace the inhuman pain" and to go on living by the grace of God.[7] Zadkine depicts a person hollowed out in the center, suggestive of the open wounds that remind the city of an unforgettable defeat. With legs spread apart and braced for support, this figure turns a dislocated body and a broken face toward the sky. Outstretched arms reach upward with flattened palms, as if straining to deny the violence a place in a city that will not accept its defeat. This figure provides a striking commentary on the Joban-like faith of those whose hands are heavy with groaning (23:2) yet who refuse to be silenced by a God who "is not there" (23:8) but should be, must be, will be.

---

7 S. Terrien, *The Iconography of Job Through the Centuries. Artists as Biblical Interpreters* (University Park: The Pennsylvania State University Press, 1996), 269.

CHAPTER 16

Preaching Job's God

In 1955, three years before the premier of his Pulitzer Prize-winning play *J.B.*, Archibald MacLeish preached a sermon at the First Church of Christ, Farmington, Connecticut. The title of the sermon was "The Book of Job." MacLeish begins with these words: "To preach is to speak with something more than one's own voice – something that only ordination can give, that only the relation of minister to congregation can make possible."[1] MacLeish immediately goes on to say that he is not a preacher, not even a religious person in any ordinary sense; he is a poet whose art requires him to think about the meaning of life, in other words, about the things that concern religion. And yet, I find it instructive that MacLeish chose the format of a sermon, not a play, to talk about Job's God. He frames the *whence* and *whether* of his thoughts as follows:

> How can we believe in our lives unless we can believe in God, and how can we believe in God unless we can believe in the justice of God, and how can we believe in the justice of God in a world in which the innocent perish in vast meaningless massacres, and brutal and dishonest men foul all the lovely things?

And then these words, now more directly focused on the Book of Job:

> Job's sufferings are unjustified. They are unjustified in any human meaning of the word justice. And yet they are God's work – a work that could not be done without the will of God [...]. If the universe is unjust, if God permits our destruction without cause, how are we to believe in life? And if we cannot believe in life, how are we to live?[2]

Surely there are many sermon topics to be mined in the Book of Job, but I suspect most of us would agree to some extent with MacLeish: sooner or later we have to figure out how to preach about Job's God. How can we believe in life

---

1 A. MacLeish, "The Book of Job," (Farmington, Conn: First Church of Christ, 1955), reprinted as "God Has Need of Man," in N. Glatzer, *The Dimensions of Job: A Study and Selected Readings* (New York: Schocken Books, 1969), 278. Subsequent references are to the edition of the sermon in Glatzer.

2 Ibid., 283.

© SAMUEL E. BALENTINE, 2021 | DOI:10.1163/9789004459212_017

if we cannot believe in God? And if we cannot believe in life – or God – then how are we to live?

The Prologue and Epilogue of Job (Job 1–2 + 42:7–17) reads like a set piece.[3] Its flat prose, strategically guided by an omniscient narrator, seems focused on a single, but virtually unswallowable, message: suffering pays. "Blameless" and "upright" persons, persons who "fear God" and "turn away from evil" with complete integrity, may lose everything; their children's lives may be snuffed out "for no reason;" but if they persist in humility, then they will be doubly rewarded in the end. The ending might well have been scripted by Walt Disney. In the Disney version of life, the world is just fine as it is; all injustice is temporary; all suffering makes sense; and when questions arise, consolation is always preferable to truth. The connections between what is and what ought to be remain essentially untroubled; they may tremble momentarily, but in the end they kiss and make up. From a contemporary perspective, the Czech novelist Milan Kundera describes this Walt Disney reading of life as kitsch, crudely, but perhaps effectively defined, as the "absolute denial of shit."[4]

Presumably, ancient sensibilities were somewhat similar. The history of transmission of the Book of Job suggests that the Prologue-Epilogue version of the story was not adequate for its readers. Thus, in the final form of the book, the prose framework is spliced with a lengthy poetic debate, between Job and his friends (Job 4–27, 32–37), and between Job and God (Job 38–42). It seems that the "all's-well-that-ends-well" conclusion, which affirms a world in which divine providence always works, is hardly ever sufficient. In William Kennedy's recent novel, *Chango's Beads and Two-Tone Shoes*, Daniel Quinn is a newspaperman caught between the objectivity required by his profession and the cynicism his real life imposes. Perhaps he speaks for all readers, ancient and modern, when he concludes that "the simple declarative sentence is an illusion."[5]

The only "dialogue" between Job and God occurs in Job 38:1–42:6. God dominates the dialogue (123 verses are allotted to God; nine verses to Job). If preachers want to take the pulse of the conversation between the God who afflicts Job "for no reason" and the Job who insists on asking God, "Why?" the fraught dialogue that emerges from this interchange is the first place to begin.

---

3   For exegetical details here and throughout this essay, see Samuel E. Balentine, *Job* (Macon, Georgia: Smyth and Helwys Bible Commentary, 2006).

4   M. Kundera, *The Unbearable Lightness of Being*. I am indebted to Susan Neiman, *Moral Clarity: A Guide for Grown-Up Idealists* (Princeton: Princeton University Press, 2009), 422–437) for this way of framing the issue.

5   W. Kennedy, *Chango's Beads and Two-Tone Shoes* (New York; Viking Press, 2011).

PREACHING JOB'S GOD

The structure of the dialogue is easy to discern. There are two divine speeches and two responses from Job. God's first response (Job 38:1–40:2) begins with a series of seemingly impossible questions addressed to Job: "Where were you?" "Can you?" "Have you?" "Do you know?" Multiple interpretations are possible, but for this occasion I cite the assessment of John Holbert, who speaks directly to the issues we are addressing here:

> God preaches a poor sermon, not because of poor content but because of poor style. God simply does not take with any seriousness the receptive position of the divine audience. Like too many modern preachers, God does not pay careful enough attention to the context and audience of the address, and consequently it falls on unwillingly ears.[6]

Mark Twain's essay, "Thoughts of God," adds stinging contemporary commentary:

> It is plain that there is one moral law for heaven and another for the earth. The pulpit assures us that wherever we see suffering and sorrow which we can relieve and do not do it, we sin, heavily. *There was never yet a case of suffering or sorrow, which God could not relieve.* Does He sin, then? If He is the source of Morals he does – certainly nothing can be plainer than that, you will admit. Surely the Source of Law cannot violate law and stand unsmirched; surely the judge upon the bench cannot forbid crime and then revel in it himself unreproached. Nevertheless we have this curious spectacle: daily the trained parrot in the pulpit gravely delivers himself of these ironies, which he has acquired at second-hand and adopted without examination, to a trained congregation which accepts them without examination, and neither the speaker nor the hearer laughs at himself [...].[7]

Job had asked whether there was justice in this world; can seven sons and three daughters be killed "for no reason" and there be no outrage in heaven, no outcry on earth (cf. 16:18–19)? God's first response evades the question with a sheer assertion of reality. An unfathomable cosmic design provides the foundation for a seemingly amoral symbiosis of order and chaos. There are stars and thunder, mud and ice, lionesses feeding cubs with maternal care and

---

6 J. Holbert, *Preaching Job* (St. Louis, MO: Chalice Press, 1999), 131.

7 M. Twain, "Thoughts on God," *The Oxford Book of Essays*. Chosen and edited by J. Gross (Oxford: OUP, 1991), 268–269.

careless ostriches leaving their eggs in the dirt. The warhorse lusts for battle, while vultures wait to feed on human corpses. This speech about cosmic design reveals the Creator's pride; whereas Genesis merely reports that God's creation is "very good," the Voice from the Whirlwind speaks of creation's beauty and wonder. But of justice, God says not a word. To Job's questions about the moral order that *ought* to be in the world, God responds by declaring simply the way the world *is*. To be charitable, such a response may not be kitsch exactly, but one cannot help but wonder if God has not missed the point. Like Voltaire's Dr. Pangloss, God seems to be saying that what is what ought to be, that this is indeed the best of all possible worlds. An earthquake in Lisbon may leave innocent bodies strewn everywhere, but, as Pangloss would say, "[A]ll is for the best. For if there's a volcano at Lisbon, it couldn't be anywhere else. For it's impossible for things not to be where they are. For all is well."[8]

All is for the best? All is well? As Holbert notes, even God seems to be "disappointed in God's own performance in the first speech [...]. Job cannot, will not, hear such things [God's parade of wonders] in such a way. And so, God speaks again, because God *must* speak again."[9]

God's second response to Job (40:6–41:34) addresses, at long last, Job's questions about justice. At the start of the speech the rhetoric is much the same as in the first. God summons Job to a dialogue – "I will question you, you declare to me" (40:7; cf. 38:3) – a dialogue that once again appears to begin with impossible questions. Here, however, God follows these questions with a series of imperatives to Job that seem genuinely to invite a response, an engagement that goes beyond the silence to which Job had retreated after God's first speech (40:4–5). The summons is for Job to understand and to enact, if he can, the very justice he demands from God. If Job can pursue justice with godlike *power* (v. 9a, "an arm like God"), *words* (v. 9b, "thunder with a voice like [God's]"), if he has the courage to live into the *majesty*, *dignity*, and *glory* of having been created as God's near-equal (v. 10; cf. Job 7:17 and Ps 8:4–5), and if Job can respond with *righteous anger* when the wicked presume they can abuse others without penalty (vv. 11–13), then God will acknowledge that Job's quest for justice is both principled and effective.

As if to provide a concrete illustration of what such creaturely nobility looks like, God directs Job's attention to Behemoth and Leviathan, two liminal creatures whose attributes place them somewhere between mere earthly creatures

---

8   Voltaire, *Candide*, trans. L. Blair (New York: Bantam Books, 1981), 30; cf. Neiman, *Moral Clarity*, 425.

9   Holbert, *Preaching Job*, 132 (emphasis original).

PREACHING JOB'S GOD 269

and supernatural figures that belong to the world of myth and legend.[10] Behemoth, "the first of the great acts of God," is a creature of extraordinary strength and power (40:16–18); when confronted by aggression and violence, it stands its ground and trusts in its own God-given resources. To be sure, God can best Behemoth, if necessary, but no earthly creature can dictate its movements or frighten it into submission. "Look at Behemoth," God says to Job, "which I made just as I made you" (40:13). When Job looks at Behemoth, he should learn something about himself.

Leviathan functions as a similar model for Job. No one can domesticate this creature by forcing it into a covenant of "soft words" (41:3–4). Instead, when it opens its mouth, it sends forth fire and light, smoke and flames, phenomena elsewhere associated not only with the strong and compelling presence of ancient Near Eastern deities but also with YHWH. It is speech that demands respect, not disregard. If Job is looking for an exemplar of what it means "to look on all who are proud and bring them low" (40:12), he need look no farther than Leviathan, a creature that "surveys everything that is lofty" and rules like a "king over all who are proud" (41:34).

Job responds to God's second speech by saying that he now "sees" more about God, and presumably more about the requisite of "justice" in God's design for the world, than he did before (42:5). Preachers may find it useful to hit the "pause" button at this point, suspending consideration of Job's enigmatic last words in 42:6, in order to create space for reflection on what God's second "sermon" adds to this story.

To seed this reflection, let me begin by returning to Archibald MacLeish's 1955 sermon. "How can we believe in our lives unless we can believe in God, and how can we believe in God unless we can believe in the justice of God?" MacLeish answers his own ruminations by arguing that God needs Job's loyalty, Job's inextinguishable love, in order to be God. Without Job's love, precisely in the face of innocent suffering, "God does not exist as God, only as creator, and love is the one thing, not even God Himself, can command." MacLeish explicates as follows:

> It is for this reason that God, at the end of the poem, answers Job not in the language of justice but in the language of beauty and power and glory, signifying that it is not because He is just but because He is God that he deserves His creature's adoration [...].

---

10   C. Newsom, "The Book of Job," NIB, Vol. 4 (1996), 615; idem, *The Book of Job: A Contest of Moral Imaginations* (Oxford: Oxford University Press, 2003), 248.

270　　　　　　　　　　　　　　　　　　　　　　　　　　　　　　　CHAPTER 16

The principal concern, then, according to MacLeish is love, not justice.

> To speak of "justice" is to demand something for ourselves and to ask
> something of life, to require that we be treated according to our dues.
> But love, as Saint Paul told the Corinthians, does not "seek her own"
> (1 Cor. 13:5). Love creates even God, for how else have we come to Him,
> any of us, but through love?[11]

MacLeish's humanistic reading of Job has been widely criticized, perhaps
rightly so. It is the case that MacLeish seems to account only for God's first
speech, God's reiteration of realism, but not for God's second speech, which is
certainly a summons to consider whether and to what extent realism must be
leavened with justice. Even so, MacLeish is not the only interpreter to propose
that God's creation cannot be all that God expects and desires without the
contributions of human beings.

Throughout this presentation, I have been working along the edges of Susan
Neiman's search for "moral clarity" in the Book of Job, what she refers to as the
conjunction between God's "is" and Job's "ought."[12] "Am I wrong," God asks Job,
"because you are right?" Neiman suggests that we should not interpret this as
necessarily an either-or question. By reminding Job of the reality of the world,
God affirms that the world is full of forces we cannot tame, which means that
life itself is a gift. And if life itself is a gift, then the more Job participates in it,
through grace and struggle, then the more he shows his thanks to God. Telling
it like it is is a good and necessary thing; God is "right," not wrong, to reiterate
realism. But Job is also "right" to insist that "the moral order that comes from
human reason needs to be in the world as well."[13] In other words, both God and
Job are right; both speak truth: "One tells it like it is, one tells it like it should
be."[14] Neiman unfolds the consequences of such a discernment in this way:

> If Job speaks truth, as God admits, the truth may be this one: There is
> no moral order in the world as it is, and there ought to be some. If God
> speaks truth, as Job admits, it may be to say that creating moral order in
> the world is just what we're meant to give back to it. If there's going to be
> reason in the world, it is we who have to put it there.

11　　MacLeish, "The Book of Job," 285.
12　　Neiman, *Moral Clarity*.
13　　Ibid., 427.
14　　Ibid.

PREACHING JOB'S GOD 271

> The book of Job's most important message is that morality is neither a divine category nor one reflected in nature; morality is – ought to be – human.[15]

Moral simplicity, like kitsch, is easy to come by. It requires nothing more than simplistic assertions about the world and God, like those the friends espouse, which are painfully uninformed by experience, like the "trained parrot[s] in the pulpit" of whom Mark Twain writes, who "gravely deliver [themselves] of ironies, which they have acquired second-hand and adopted without examination." Neither the friends nor "trained parrots" can speak "what is right" about God (42:7, 8), because they trust in the inertia of dogma; what they offer in response to the gift of the complexity of life is a "form of ingratitude."[16]

Moral clarity, on the other hand, is always difficult to obtain. It requires making complex distinctions between knotty ethical problems. It means working to make sense of things that are nonsensical; it means seeing things we do not want to see; knowing things we do not want to acknowledge. And it almost always means deciding on a course of action without ever knowing fully if it is right. In sum, "human attempts to construct moral order are always precarious," precisely because they are human attempts. As Neiman puts it, "Moments of moral clarity are rare in life, and they are exceedingly precious. They usually follow upon hours – years – of moral confusion; they seldom arrive all at once or definitively; and they are never accompanied by a lifetime guarantee."[17]

Job did not need God to persuade him that as a mere mortal he is but a small cog in the vast machinery of the cosmos. He is but one person, his sufferings, however horrendous, however unjust, are the experiences of one person. Even so, negotiating the world with the frail and always flawed moral reasoning of a mere human is all that Job can do. It is precisely what God has created him to do.

"What are human beings, that you make so much of them?" (Job 7:17), Job asks. Before God spoke, the question conveyed lament, the deadening conviction that human beings are no more than targets for the exercise of raw, divine power. After God spoke, and especially after God directed Job's attention to Behemoth and Leviathan, Job undergoes a cognitive shift, "not a change of heart, but a change of mind. He 'sees' God freshly and understands something about the divine nature" that he had not known before.[18] The text is mute on

---

15   Ibid., 429, 430.
16   Ibid., 431.
17   Ibid., 433.
18   W. S. Green, "Stretching the Covenant: Job and Judaism," *RevExp* 99 (2002), 575.

exactly what Job saw in the whirlwind, but like Job, preachers are summoned to gird up their loins and "declare" what they have learned from immersion in this text.

Two primary lessons may be suggested: 1) relationship with God is not "an automated interaction with a unidimensional deity obsessed with conformity and obedience. God is more complex, complicated, and inscrutable than humans can imagine;" 2) Job's fidelity to God is not blind and uninformed; it is driven by a longing for moral clarity, by an irrepressible yearning to know and understand "things too wonderful" (*nipla'ot*; Job 42:3), things beyond complete human comprehension but not beyond the human aspiration to perform (cf. Deut 30:11–20). As William Scott Green puts it, "Job's insistence on God's justice yields unremitting demand for explanation that forces the deity to speak, to reveal himself in unexpected ways. Job draws God into a conversation about the divine self and makes cognition into a religious act."[19]

Preaching Job's God is a summons to preach as adults, not as children, as those who understand that the way the world is is always and necessarily leavened with real-life experience that causes us to yearn and strive for what ought to be, with God and when necessary against God. Real grown-ups, like Job, will insist that we stand ready to call any of our teachers, including God, into question.[20] As Nieman puts it, "if the alternative is inertia, outrage against injustice may keep [us] alive."[21]

---

19   Ibid., 576. This entire paragraph, even when not quoting directly, is informed by Green's cogent assessment of the whirlwind speeches.

20   Neiman, *Moral Clarity*, 437.

21   Ibid., 431.

CHAPTER 17

The Church of Saint Job

"Can you tell me how to find the Church of San Giobbe?" This was the question I asked the museum staff at the Galleria dell' Accademia in Venice. I was on a sabbatical leave, doing research on the Book of Job, and I had come specifically to see a painting of Job by Giovanni Bellini that I had studied in my books at home. I found the painting and discovered from a plaque on the wall that it had hung originally in the Church of San Giobbe (Saint Job) in Venice. A very kind assistant told me that the church still existed and gave me directions.

I took a vaporetto to the train station. Walking north, I followed the canal outside the city center for about six blocks. Just before the sidewalk ran out I turned left and walked down a narrow and deserted ally of closed-up shops and shuttered homes until I came to a small piazza. There stood San Giobbe, a large, well-kept fifteenth-century church. The front door was wide open.

On the right wall were four altarpieces depicting Saint Francis and other Franciscan saints in various scenes. Included among the four was a painting by Lattanzio Querena (1768–1853) of the "Theophany of Job," which I had never seen before. I was in the process of photographing the work when a priest suddenly emerged from the back of the church. Uncertain how he might react to what I was doing, I hurriedly tried to put away my camera before he saw me. Too late. He headed straight for me. I explained that I was working on a commentary on Job and that I was particularly interested in Joban art and iconography. To my surprise (and relief) the mention of the word Job brought a wide-eyed smile to his face. He immediately gestured for me to follow him out the front door. When we were outside he turned and pointed to the tympanum on the front portal.

There, above the main entrance to the church, were two figures, which I later learned were sculpted in the late fifteenth century by Pietro Lombardo. I immediately recognized the person on the left as Saint Francis. Dressed in the traditional robe of the Franciscan monks, he is kneeling before a rock. His head tilts to the left as his eyes look toward the sun that radiates downward from the center of the scene. On his hands are the stigmata. His left hand holds the conventional cross-shaped staff. The figure on the right is Job. He is naked, except for the garment around his waist that drapes down his right side. His body is firm, even muscular, suggesting the physique of a well-trained athlete. His beard is trim, his jaw is set, his hands are clasped together in prayer. Like

© SAMUEL E. BALENTINE, 2021 | DOI:10.1163/9789004459212_018

FIGURE 17.1   Main portal to the church of San Giobbe
CREDIT: SAMUEL E. BALENTINE, PERSONAL PHOTOGRAPH

Francis, Job kneels before the rock and looks toward the light from heaven with a serenity that conveys both resolve and expectation.

I must confess that I did not recognize the person on the right as Job, until the priest explained the scene to me. Sadly, nothing in my study or in my experience had prepared me to see Job as one of the saints whose prayers marked the entrance to Church.

1   Ruminations on What Goes on Inside the Church of Saint Job

I will always regret that my stay in Venice did not afford me the opportunity to attend a service at the Church of Saint Job. I wonder: What kinds of people would be in the congregation on a typical Sunday? What hopes and expectations would they bring with them when they entered the sanctuary? What would the liturgy be like? What scripture would be read? What kind of prayers would be heard? What affirmations would be offered? What kind of sermons would be preached? What ministry opportunities would be promoted in the "announcement time"?

Although I do not have any information on what goes on inside the present-day Church of Saint Job, I have learned a little of its history from a booklet I picked up in the church's vestry. The church has existed since 1493. It was originally associated with a San Giobbe hospital, which may have been established on the same site as early as 1378. The name Giobbe identified both the church and the hospital not only with the biblical Job but also with the section of the city that was home for the poor and afflicted persons who made up the underclass of Venice. These persons, known as "giopen," apparently comprised the majority of the population in this part of the city, though whether this was by choice or by decree the booklet does not say. Presumably there was a time when if someone asked where Giobbe was, they would be directed to the same remote corner of the city that I visited and find the Jobs of Venice and those committed to care for them, body and soul.

It seems reasonable to suppose that the heritage continues to inform what goes on inside the Church of Saint Job. For the purpose of this essay, at least, let us imagine what it might be like to sit in the pew of a church that has its historical and theological roots in the biblical story of the legendary character from the land of Uz.

(1) *Any church that bears the name of Job must surely be open to having Jobs attend in large numbers.* These Jobs know what it means to be consigned to life's ash heap of brokenness and loss. Some have fallen from high positions; others have been defeated before they had a fair chance to succeed. All can say in good faith that they have come to this point in their life "for no reason" (cf. Job 2:3).[1] They know the truth in the saying "the Lord gives and the Lord takes away" (cf. 1:21), and they therefore know the need to be patient when they cannot balance this equation in any way that makes sense. They also know that patience "is a virtue very apt to be fatigued by exercise."[2]

These Jobs know the conventional language of praise and blessing, but we may imagine that they find such language does not resonate with the grief and misery that shapes their deepest thoughts. They know, for example, that poets of faith look at the world and marvel that God has crowned human beings with such "glory and honor" (Ps 8:5). They know that in the poet's world the possibility and the promise that God holds in trust for human beings is cause for astonished praise: "What are human beings that you [God] are mindful of them, mortals that you care for them?" (Ps 8:4). In the world of these Jobs, however, the same thought will likely be heavy with vexed ambiguity. It may be cause for astonishment, but not praise. When Jobs look at the world from the ash heap, they may feel they have been assigned the role of "slave" (Job 7:2), not king. They may have good reason to think they are destined for "emptiness" and "misery" (7:3) rather than glory and honor. When they consider the question

---

1   All scripture quotations are the author's own translation, unless otherwise noted.
2   The words of the character Jenny in Henry Fielding's *The History of Tom Jones. A Foundling*, Vol. 1 (New York: P. F. Collier & Son, 1917), 19.

"What are human beings that you [God] make so much of them?" (7:17), they may be tempted to answer that God has targeted them for destruction, not compassion (7:20). Instead of petitioning God to be more present in their lives, they may be able to say nothing more to God than "Let me alone" (7:16, 19).[3] We may imagine that in the Church of Saint Job conventional doxologies of praise echo with undertones of disbelief, perhaps even sarcasm.

These Jobs are also familiar with the language of lament, but we should not be surprised if they find that even lament must be pushed beyond conventional forms if it is to reach the deepest level of what they need to say. They surely know how to question God, even to accuse God of horrific brutality, and they look to their biblical counterpart to find words that convey their rumblings of discontent:

> Why did I not die at birth, come forth from the womb and expire? (3:11; cf. 3:18)
> Why is light given to one in misery, and life to the bitter in soul? (3:20)
> I shall be condemned; why then do I labor in vain? (9:29)
> Let me know why you [God] contend against me. (10:2b)
> Why do you [God] hide your face, and count me as your enemy? (13:24)

> God gives me up to the ungodly, and casts me into the hands of the wicked,
> I was at ease, and he broke me in two; he seized me by the neck
> and dashed me to pieces; he set me up as his target; his archers surround me.
> He slashes open my kidneys, and shows no mercy;
> he pours out my gall on the ground.
> He bursts upon me again and again; he rushes at me like a warrior (16:11–14; cf. 19:7–12).

> Though I am blameless, he [God] would prove me perverse (9:20b).

> Know then that God has put me in the wrong [...]
> He has stripped my glory from me,
> and taken the crown from my head (19:6a, 9).

---

3   For further reading on the rhetorical links between Job 7 and Psalm 8, see M. Fishbane, *Biblical Interpretation in Ancient Israel* (Oxford: Clarendon Press, 1985), 285–286; idem, "The Book of Job and Inner-biblical Discourse," *The Voice From the Whirlwind. Interpreting the Book of Job*, ed. L. Perdue, W. Gilpen (Nashville: Abingdon Press, 1992), 87–90; P. E. Dion, "Formulaic Language in the Book of Job: International Background and Ironical Distortions," *SR* 16 (1987), 187–193.

THE CHURCH OF SAINT JOB 277

But having dared to challenge God in such radical ways, these Jobs may nonetheless be tempted to still greater despair. It may appear that God is impervious to their every effort. They could search to the farthest points on the compass, but they would not find God (23:8–9). They could stitch the mourner's sackcloth into their skin and cry until their eyes were red-raw, and God would take no notice of their prayer (16:15–17). They could scream out "Violence!" and hope there was someone to hear and come to their rescue, but there would be no answer, and they would get "no justice" (19:7).

When the conventions of lament do not connect them to God's compassion or God's justice, these Jobs may insist that they have not only a moral but a legal suit against the "Judge of all the earth" (cf.Gen. 18:25). They know, of course, that the odds are stacked against them, for in God's court "might (not truth) makes right" (9:14–24). They know that there is no "umpire" to arbitrate the inequalities between themselves and God (9:23). And still they prepare their case against God as if they were going to receive a fair and impartial hearing (13:18–23). They know that even if they were to file a thousand charges, God would not respond to a single one (9:3; REB). And still they fill their mouths with arguments (23:3) in the desperate belief that any judge worthy of the responsibility will pay attention to the claims of the upright. They have to believe that a God of justice will be guided by reason and fair play, not power and petulance (23:6–7). They know that they cannot count on witnesses to give testimony in support of their claim, for the general consensus among their friends is that they are guilty of wrongdoing, not God (22:4–5). But if they cannot expect their friends to validate their innocence, they will appeal to creation itself – heaven and earth – to cry out for justice on their behalf (16:18–19). They know that they can take an oath of innocence. They can swear by everything that is holy that they have committed no crimes against God or their human companions (31:1–34, 38–40) and that God would merely stand in silence as they presented their case (30:20). And still they take the oath and file the charges and demand a formal acquittal from the Judge. They dare to imagine that continued indifference to their claim will prove the Judge's guilt and their innocence (31:35–37).

For all the obvious reasons these Jobs know that bringing suit against God borders on being both blasphemous (8:3: "Does God pervert justice?") and insane (9:32: "God is not as I am, not someone I can challenge, and say, 'Let us confront one another in court';" REB). We may imagine, therefore, that when they step into the breach to contend with God, they do so with a divided mind. They have good reason to believe that "there is no justice" (19:7), and yet they cannot let go of the hope that "there is a judgment" (19:29). Inside the dark chasm, between reality and hope, they carry still one more anxious conviction.

They know that there is a "redeemer" (*gōʾēl*) and that in the end ("at the last") this redeemer will successfully obtain their vindication (19:25–26).

Should they look to God as the redeemer who will come to their aid? They know that their religious heritage celebrates this possibility (e.g. Exod 6:6; 15:13; Ps 119:154; Isa 43:1, 14: Jer 50:34; Lam 3:58), and yet their experience provides no reason to believe that God will play this role for them. Should they expect family and friends to be their redeemer? They know that their legal traditions stipulate that this should be so (e.g. Lev 25:25–28, 47–49; Num 35:22–27; Deut 19:6–12; Ruth 3:12–13; 4:3–6), and yet experience teaches them that their family and friends may be the first ones to abandon them (19:13–20; 30:9–15). Should they expect some interested third-party, perhaps even some heavenly intercessor (cf. 33:23–24), to come to their defense against God and the friends? They have weighed the pros and cons of the possibility (9:33: "there is no umpire;" 16:19: "my witness is in heaven"), but no such person has yet volunteered to be their redeemer. And so they file their charges alone, convinced in spite of the evidence that crying out "Violence!" (19:7) and "Have pity!" and "Why?" (19:21–22) makes a down payment on the final purchase of justice that someone, somewhere, some time, will feel duty-bound to honor.

We may imagine then that in the Church of Saint Job both praise and lament are conflicted, discordant, unmanageable, and for all these reasons, desperately candid and urgent. When summoned to speak the conventional words of praise, we may hear these Jobs say that "Evil's evil, and sorrow's sorrow, and you can't alter its nature by wrapping it up in other words."[4] When cautioned against pushing their lament too far, against pressing their case for justice too hard, we may hear them respond by saying "The weight of this sad time we must obey/ Speak what we feel, not what we ought to say."[5]

(2) *Any church that welcomes the Jobs of the world will surely have a large number of persons wanting to be numbered among the "friends of Job."* We may assume that the "friends of Job" all have their Jobs' best interests at heart, but we should not be surprised if they do not agree on what to say or do to help them.

Some come to "console (*nûd*) and comfort (*niham*; piel)" the Jobs of their community (the same expressions occur 1:14 and 42:11). They do not speak, for they discern that some suffering is too deep to be touched by anything they might say. Instead, they weep and wail and enter sympathetically into their friends' sorrow and affliction (cf. 1:12–13). They may offer the fellowship of a meal, some tangible expression to convey their active communion, some

---

4   The words the narrator gives to Adam Bede in G. Eliot, *Adam Bede*. Edited with an Introduction by Stephen Gill (New York: Penguin Books, 1985), 529.

5   The words of the Duke of Albany upon witnessing Lear's demise in *King Lear*, v, iii, 322–323.

THE CHURCH OF SAINT JOB 279

material gifts to help rebuild a shattered life (cf. 42:11). They ask nothing in return: no confessions, no explanations, no promises. They know that what the despairing most yearn for is the loyalty of their friends, whether they have lost faith in God or not (6:14; cf. NIV, NEB, TEV). Toward that end, these comforters are more concerned to honor suffering than to resolve or remove it.

Others console and comfort in different ways. They sense that the affliction in their midst raises serious moral and theological issues their community cannot ignore. Because their faith is so deep and their convictions so fervent, they instinctively draw upon the resources of their religious tradition. They take comfort in the truth that God's moral governance of the world can be trusted. Even when the innocent suffer inexplicable tragedies, they may remain secure in the knowledge that God will not abandon them forever (cf. 4:7; 5:17–27; 8:20–22; 11:15–19). Even when the wicked prosper, the righteous may know that God will not forever delay the punishment that is required to balance the scales of justice (15:20–35; 18:5–21; 20:2–29).

In good faith these friends may abstract from general truths some specific suggestions for acts of piety that may sustain the afflicted in the interim between suffering and restoration. They may recommend praise of God and confidently model how it should be offered (5:8–16; 36:24–28). They may urge patience (4:5; 5:2), humility (4:17–19; 8:9; 11:7–12; 15:7–16; 22:2; 25:4–6; 36:22–23), and due caution against letting suffering slip into rebellion against God (8:2–3; 11:3; 15:12–13; 18:4; 33:13; 36:17–23). They do not begin by doubting the integrity of those who suffer (4:6; 8:6), but the more they sense resistance to their counsel, the more suspicious they may become that guilt – not innocence – must be the root of the problem (11:6; 15:5–6; 22:5–10; 34:34–37).

One by one these friends may shift their objectives. They may feel compelled to do less comforting and more interrogating (11:8; 15:9, 12, 14; 22:13, 17; 25:4). Whatever questions and doubts about God and the world these sufferers may present, the friends may resolve them by retreating to a time-honored theology that is never threatened by uncertainty. If there is suffering, then sin must be cause. If there is to be a restoration, then there must be a confession:

> *If* your children sinned against him [God],
>   then he delivered them into the power of their transgression.
> *If* you will seek God
>   and make supplication to the Almighty,
> *If* you are pure and upright,
>   *surely then* he will rouse himself for you
>   and restore to you your rightful place.
>   8:4–6

280   CHAPTER 17

If iniquity is in your hand, put it far away,
    and do not let wickedness reside in your tent.
  Surely then you will lift up your face without blemish;
    you will be secure, and will not fear.
You will forget your misery;
    you will remember it as waters that have passed away.
And your life will be brighter than the noonday;
    its darkness will be like the morning.
And you will have confidence, because there is hope;
    you will be protected, and take your rest in safety.
You will lie down in safety, and no one will make you afraid;
    many will entreat your favor.

    11:14–19

If you return to the Almighty, you will be restored,
    if you remove unrighteousness from your tents [...]
then you will delight in the Almighty,
    and lift up your face to God,
You will pray to him, and he will hear you,
    and you will pay your vows.

    22:23, 26–27

When sufferers refuse to accept their place in this "if-then" theology, their friends may deem it necessary to move from cautious sympathy to thinly disguised contempt (cf. 12:5), from suspicions of guilt to allegations of moral failure (22:6–11; cf. 29:11–17; 31:13–23) and theological error (22:12–14) that adjust the facts to fit their theology.

We may imagine then that in the Church of Saint Job all those who come to comfort and console the Jobs of their community are earnestly conflicted about what they should say or do. Perhaps some take their cue from their patron Saint Francis of Assisi. His sculpted presence above the entrance of the sanctuary of the Church of Saint Job may keep them mindful that obedience to God's call means living according to the Gospel of Matthew 10:7–8:

The kingdom of heaven has come near. Cure the sick, raise the dead, cleanse the lepers, cast out demons. You received without payment; give without payment.

Like Francis, they will know that the call to discipleship is a call to care for the outcasts of the world. Their theology of mission follows Francis' simple

THE CHURCH OF SAINT JOB   281

instruction: "Always and everywhere present the gospel, if necessary, with words." Others may remember that caring for the outcasts cost Francis his inheritance, his place in the community, and ultimately his life. They too want to live out the gospel by caring for the outcasts, but they may choose to do so by living in strict obedience to a different theological certainty: always and everywhere wisdom requires "fear of the Lord"; always and everywhere understanding comes by "departing from evil" (Job 28:28). When they look to the sculpted presence of the other "saint" above the entrance to their sanctuary, they may be encouraged to believe that if the Jobs of their community learn to kneel in humble prayer before their maker (cf. 1:20–22), then, and only then, can they find the wisdom and understanding they need for life on the ash heap. Informed by this truth, Jobs' friends may claim a theological imperative to speak and to speak forcefully. Like the friends of the biblical Job, they may be so "full of words" that they will burst open if they do not release them (33:18–20; cf. 4:2: "Who can keep from speaking?").

(3). *Any church that provides sanctuary for Job and Job's friends will surely need and expect to hear a word from God.* Because the suffering in their midst is so great, and because the need for clarity and direction is so urgent, we may imagine that every Job and every friend will be engaged in a "personal struggle for the last truth about God."[6] We may wonder whether God will reveal that truth. Will God establish clear rules of conduct for sufferers like Job? Will God make clear, or at least partially clear, what the church should say or do for the Jobs of the world?

It would of course be presumptuous for anyone to imagine themselves into God's perspective on such matters. Even if people were to restrict their musings to the God they see or think they see in the Book of Job, they may discover that "last truths" are painfully elusive. Still, if those who gather in the Church of Saint Job dare to believe and act upon the first truth God discloses about humankind – that we are created "in the image of God" – then perhaps they believe that striving for last truths is precisely what God expects them to do. If we walk in the footsteps of their quest, for the purpose of this essay at least, what may we expect to learn about the God of Saint Job?

Will we learn that God targets the Jobs of the world – those whom God knows to be "blameless and upright" – for suffering? Are we to understand that God can be manipulated into the silent oversight of a person's destruction "for no reason" (2:3)? When "the satan" (*haśśāṭan*; – God's adversary in the heavenly council) questions God about whether the Jobs of the world "fear God

---

6   J. Hempel, "The Contents of the Literature," *Record and Revelation*, ed. H. W. Robinson (Oxford: Clarendon Press, 1938), 73.

for nothing" (1:9), can we be confident that God already knows the answer? Or should we worry that God may doubt the integrity of those who "fear God" and "turn away from evil" (1:1, 8; 2:3)? Is it always necessary for God to inflict pain in order to know whether piety is real and genuine? Each question is disturbing, and we may imagine that those who ponder them inside the Church of Saint Job would gladly welcome some preemptory divine revelation that would put them out of mind. When we tune ourselves to the story that gives this church its name, we may find instead that, once God gives up the Jobs of the world to affliction, God seems to retreat behind a veil of silence. We may wonder if it is not this great silence in heaven that compels the Church of Saint Job to gather itself on earth.

Will we learn that God has a carefully prescribed plan for dealing with the Jobs of the world? Will we discover that God has plotted a grid of acceptable and unacceptable conduct, with fixed, straight-line projections of matching rewards and punishments? Must all Jobs be silent, submissive, and contrite if they want to be blessed and restored? Must they refuse to question, complain, and contend with God if they want to live into the fullness of what it means to be created in the image of their Maker? If this is God's plan, then the friends who offer comfort without confrontation may worry that they have failed both the Jobs of the world and God. They have been sympathetic, but have they been faithful to the truth? Perhaps the true friends are those willing to challenge, correct, and, when necessary, condemn those Jobs who refuse to accept their place in God's master plan. Even if their words offer no comfort, these friends may believe they have imparted the wisdom of God.

Will the God of Saint Job remain silent, aloof, and inaccessible? Or can the Jobs of the world and their friends expect to hear some word, however distant and difficult to apprehend, that will clarify what the church should do or say? Will God respond by asking questions that invite a close inspection of the world's order and disorder, its coherence and its ambiguity (cf. Job 38–39)? If the Jobs and their friends concede that they are too small to understand what they have seen, too overwhelmed by the challenge to offer any answers (cf. 40:4), will God be satisfied to end the questioning there? Or will God press the case with further questions about what it means to live in this complex world with "majesty and dignity," with "glory and splendor" (40:10; cf. Ps. 8:5)? If God singles out for special praise creatures like Behemoth and Leviathan who are endowed with exemplary strength, confidence, pride, and dominion (cf. 40:15–24; 41:1–34), what response is God hoping for? Surely some in the Church of Saint Job will be confident that God hopes for nothing so much as the contrition and repentance of the Jobs in their midst (thus the traditional interpretation of Job 42:6). Those same friends, however, may be perplexed when God then says to them, "You have not spoken of me what is right, as my servant Job has done" (42:7, 8). If Job has repented, which is what the friends have urged from the very beginning, then how can they be wrong? And if they are wrong, what has Job said that can possibly be right?

I do not know what goes on inside the present-day Church of Saint Job. If the Book of Job is regularly read there, then I imagine that there is a good deal of lament that reverberates with the hope for a reason to praise. I imagine, however, that on any given Sunday there is such hurt and brokenness that no lament will be adequate for what some people feel. I imagine that God is often put on trial in the Church of Saint Job. I suspect that there are friends who will volunteer to testify on God's behalf for the defense. I suspect that others will not testify for the Jobs who bring charges against God unless they receive a subpoena. I would expect God to be present in the Church of Saint Job, although I suspect that God's presence in the midst of a congregation that takes innocent suffering so seriously raises as many questions as it answers. I imagine that the words "now my eye sees you" (42:5) will mean different things to different people. On the lips of the Jobs in the community the words may be the preface to testimony about how suffering has changed them and their view of God. Some friends may use the words to explain why they have learned to open their hearts and their arms to the Jobs in their community. I suspect other friends will use the same words to explain why they have been compelled to open their mouths and teach these Jobs about the mysteries of God.

I do not know what goes on inside the Church of Saint Job. I do know that the church has had a ministry on the same site in Venice for more than 500 years. And I know that its doors are still wide open, inviting all who will to enter into the peculiar cacophony that makes it a sanctuary.

2   Ruminations on What Goes on Inside the Church of the "Lectionary Job"

My visit to Venice caused me to wonder if there are other churches, perhaps closer to home, whose historical or theological roots may be traced back to the biblical Job. Are there sanctuaries where the memory of Job is important enough to be placed at or near the top of the church's understanding of its role in the world? My curiosity focuses not so much on whether Job is represented in the church's art and iconography, although if this were the case it would be an important discovery. Instead, I wonder whether and to what extent Job's story informs and shapes the Church's message and mission. I have not done

284   CHAPTER 17

a systematic study of this matter, and thus I am prepared to offer little more than general impressions and discernments. To avoid being purely subjective and anecdotal, I base these thoughts on the readings from Job that appear in the Revised Common Lectionary (RCL). Although lectionary readings do not provide a complete picture of Job's place in the Church, they are one important indicator of how Christian liturgy preserves and presents Job's witness.[7]

The RCL lists a total of five readings from Job for Year B. Four of the five are given as the primary readings from the Old Testament: 1:1 + 2:1–10 (Proper 22 [27]); 23:1–9, 16–17 (Proper 23 [28]); 38:1–7, (34–41) (Proper 24 [29]); 42:1–6, 10–17 (Proper 25 [30]). One is given as an alternate reading: 38:1–11 (Proper 7 [12]). In addition to these five, Job 19:23–27a is listed as an alternate reading for Year C (Proper 27 [32]). In each case Old Testament readings from Job (and Psalms) are juxtaposed to New Testament lessons from the Gospels and the Epistles. The combination of readings invites worshipers to bring Job's story into the orbit of Christian scripture and to enlarge the Christian story by connecting it to the shared heritage of faith in the God of Israel. The liturgical presentation of Job is therefore different than the story that is preserved in Job 1–42. The differences provide an important clue for understanding how the Church has looked to this old story for instruction on how to become a sanctuary for the Jobs of today's world.

The first reading in Year B (1:1 + 2:1–10) presents Job as a model of heroic faith and trust. By God's own estimation, no one on earth exemplifies such complete devotion and integrity as Job (2:3; cf. 1:1). Job is worthy of such praise, because when suffering strikes him unawares and "for no reason" (2:3), he refuses to yield to the temptation to curse God (2:9). Whatever comes his way, whether good or bad, Job accepts it as what God intends for him (2:10). The New Testament lessons invite worshipers to connect Job's model of piety with what they learn from Jesus and his teaching. The Epistle lesson, Hebrews 1:1–4, 2:5–12, contrasts how God spoke "long ago to our ancestors" with the way God speaks "in these last days [...] by a Son" (1:1–2). By the grace of God Jesus was crowned with "glory and honor," because he was willing to suffer the

---

7   The readings are different, for example, in the Episcopal and Roman Catholic lectionaries, although the variations are modest and do not substantially alter the picture one gets from the RCL. Moreover, many churches do not follow lectionary readings consistently, if at all, and so it is possible that in the course of a year there may be more attention devoted to Job than the readings from the RCL suggest. Of course, the opposite may also be true. For further reading on the presentation of Job in the liturgy, see P. Rouillard, "The Figure of Job in the Liturgy: Indignation, Resignation òr Silence," in *Job and the Silence of God* [*Concilium* 169,9/1983], ed. C. Duquoc, C. Floristan (New York: Seabury, 1983), 8–12; S. E. Balentine, "Who Will Be Job's Redeemer?" *Perspectives in Religious Studies* 26 (1999), 269–289.

THE CHURCH OF SAINT JOB   285

humiliation of death (2:9; cf. 2:6–8 with Ps 8:4–6 and Job 7:17–18). Through his suffering Jesus creates the path on which his followers are to walk. Like Job, Jesus becomes a "pioneer" for humankind; he is made "perfect through sufferings" (2:10). The Gospel reading from Mark 10:2–16 shifts the focus to a vignette from Jesus' teaching ministry that offers insight into how his followers should gather around him. Some, like the Pharisees, come with questions (e.g., about divorce) that are meant to test Jesus' knowledge of the law. Jesus rebukes them, because they are more interested in preserving their own understanding of what is and is not right in God's eyes than with doing God's will (10:2–12). Others, like children, come not with questions but with unassuming trust. Jesus blesses such child-like faith and admonishes all who would enter the kingdom to live their lives in accordance with this model (10:13–16). In bringing together these texts about Job, Jesus, and children, the lectionary offers three examples of faithful submission to God's inscrutable will that all should strive to imitate.

The second reading (23:1–9, 16–17) profiles Job's relentless search for God. Driven by bitterness, Job fills his mouth with arguments that he desires to present to God (23:2–4). He is convinced that God will not be indifferent to the complaints of an "upright person" (23:6–7), yet he despairs that the God he seeks cannot be found anywhere (23:8–9). The New Testament readings effectively respond to Job's complaint with two affirmations. First, the Epistle lesson from Hebrews 4:12–16 counters the complaint about God's absence by emphasizing that God's word is "living and active." Moreover, it is not we who judge God but God who "judge[s] the thoughts and intentions of [our] heart" (v. 12). As the Hebrews writer puts it, "All are naked and laid bare to the eyes of the one to whom we must render an account" (v. 13). It is through Jesus, "who in every respect has been tested as we are, *yet without sin*" (v. 15; emphasis added), that we may approach the throne of God to "receive mercy and find grace in time of need" (v. 16). Second, the Gospel lesson from Mark 10:17–31 affirms that not everyone who claims to be without blemish under the law will be able to enter the kingdom. Some will not be able to relinquish their status as persons worthy of recognition in order to be a true disciple (vv. 17–22). Others will be prepared to renounce everything for the sake of the kingdom of God, and they will be richly rewarded in this life and in the eternal life to come (w. 28–30). The Gospel text ends with a reversal saying: "many who are first will be last, and the last will be first" (v. 31). Given the lectionary's emphasis on Job's futile search for God, the last word from the Gospel lesson invites readers to consider whether his bitterness and complaint number him among the first of those who will enter the kingdom or among the last.

The third reading introduces God's revelation from the whirlwind (38:1–7, 34–41; cf. the alternate reading for Proper 7 [12] from Job 38:1–11). Both the tone

286   CHAPTER 17

and theme of the verses from Chapter 38 suggest that God responds to Job with questions that challenge him for speaking "words without knowledge" (38:2). The questions call attention to God's intricate design of creation ("foundation," "measurements," "cornerstone"). Does Job have the requisite "wisdom" (38:36) to understand the mystery of the world God has created? Can he provide, for example, for the lion and the fledgling raven (38:39–41), each of which depends on God for food and sustenance? The questions are rhetorical, and yet they invite Job (and those who follow his story in the liturgy) to imagine how anyone could or should respond to such a challenge. As readers ponder the challenge, the Epistle lesson from Hebrews 5:1–10 invites them to consider the example of Jesus. In his earthly life Jesus cried out for attention from God, and he was heard because "of his reverent submission" (v. 7). Jesus "learned obedience through what he suffered" and thus "became the source of eternal salvation for all who obey him" (v. 8). The Gospel reading from Mark 10:35–45 effectively extends the consideration of Jesus' model for discipleship. When James and John ask for positions of honor at the throne of God, Jesus says to them, "You do not know what you are asking" (vv. 37–38). The glory they seek is not what Jesus has in mind. All who truly want to be his disciples must surrender their aspiration for greatness and embrace instead the model of the servant (vv. 43–44). That model of the servant is best exemplified in Jesus himself, who did not say to God "I want you to do for me whatever I ask" (cf. the disciples' question in v. 35), but instead took up the cross of suffering and gave "his life a ransom for many" (v. 45). At the conclusion of these three readings then, Job and James and John are linked together as those who ask questions without full knowledge of what they are doing. God and Jesus are joined in the readers' mind as offering revelation that enlarges and corrects their understanding of what is required for authentic discipleship.

The fourth reading (Job 42:1–6, 10–17) provides Job's response to God's revelation from the whirlwind, followed by the account of Job's restoration. Job begins by confessing that God has the power to execute any plan God chooses, including those "too wonderful" for Job to comprehend (vv. 2–3). He follows this with a second confession in which he acknowledges that he has now seen something new about God (v. 5). This new "seeing" in turn leads him to amplify his confession by stating what it means for him: "therefore I despise myself, and repent in dust and ashes" (v. 6).[8] The lectionary reading immediately follows

---

8 From a critical perspective Job's confession in 42:6 is extremely ambiguous and may be legitimately translated and interpreted in a variety of ways (for a convenient summary of the possibilities, see C. Newsom, "The Book of Job," *The New Interpreter's* Bible, Vol. IV (Nashville: Abingdon Press, 1996), 628–629. Lectionary readings are not designed to present the

THE CHURCH OF SAINT JOB

Job's confession with a description of God's restoration of Job's fortunes ("twice as much as he had before") and his family ("seven sons and three daughters;" vv. 10–17). The two New Testament readings offer what may be understood as a parallel account to Job's confession and restoration. The Epistle reading from Hebrews 7:23–28 contrasts the efficacy of the levitical priests, who "were prevented by death from continuing in office" (v. 23), and that of Jesus, who "is able *for all time* to save those who approach God through him" (v. 25; emphasis added). The Gospel lesson from Mark 10:46–52 provides an example of Jesus saving those who draw near to him. The blind beggar named Bartimaeus cried out to Jesus for mercy (v. 47). When Jesus asked him "What do you want me to do for you?" he responded that he wanted to be able to see again (v. 51). Jesus sent him on his way with the assurance that his faith has been the agent of his healing. His faith and his restored sight, both reminiscent of Job's new "seeing" (Job 42:5), culminate in a resolve to follow Jesus (v. 52).

To these four readings from Job we may consider also Job 19:23–27a, which is given as an alternate Old Testament text for Proper 27 [32] in Year C. In this text Job declares emphatically that he knows his future vindication is assured, because his "Redeemer lives" (v. 25). The capitalization of the word "redeemer" ($gō'ēl$)) in some modern translations (e.g. NRSV, NIV; cf. NAB: "Vindicator") will almost inevitably invite Christians to associate the one to whom Job refers with Christ. The two lectionary readings from the New Testament can be expected to reinforce this association. The Epistle lesson from 2 Thessalonians 2:1–5, 13–17 begins with the words "As to the coming of our Lord Jesus Christ" and proceeds to assure the believers at Thessalonica that the day of the Lord's coming is still in the future. In the meantime they are encouraged to "stand firm and hold fast to the traditions" they have been taught (v. 15). They may know that God, through Christ, has given them "eternal comfort and good hope" (v. 16). The Gospel lesson from Luke 20:27–38 focuses the worshiper still more specifically on the issue of resurrection. In a confrontation with the Sadducees, Jesus gives instruction on what it means to be "worthy of a place [...] in the resurrection from the dead" (v. 35). Those who are "children of the resurrection," even though they are part of "this age," may know that they will be raised with Christ in "that age" to new life (vv. 34–36).

If we take the lectionary readings as representative of the Church's understanding of Job's importance for its mission to the world, what conclusions might we draw? We may begin by affirming that readings from the Book of Job

---

subtleties of biblical exegesis. We may reasonably anticipate, therefore, that most worshippers, guided by the NRSV (and most other modern translations) will be naturally inclined toward the conventional understanding that Job is humbly repenting of sin.

have a place in the Church's liturgy. In churches following the RCL for Year B, for example, worshipers will hear parts of Job's story read on four consecutive Sundays. This affirmation, however, invites a further question. In the church of the "lectionary Job," what parts of Job's story will the congregation hear proclaimed as scripture? What parts of the story will not be included in the scripture that informs their understanding of Job's place in the church's mission?

Worshipers *would be encouraged to remember* Job's patient acceptance of suffering (Job 2:1–10), and they would be reminded that Jesus, who was himself made "perfect through sufferings" (Hebrews 2:10), blesses those who follow in his footsteps with a child-like faith (Mark 10:15). They *would not be invited to remember* Job's vexed wonderments about God's sinister intentions (Job 7:17), or his pained laments about God's inexplicable brutality and injustice (e.g. Job 19:7–12).

Worshipers *would be invited to reflect on Job's quest for God* (Job 23), and they *would be encouraged to take comfort* in the affirmation that it is not we who must search for God, but God who searches for us (Hebrews 4:12–16). They *would not be encouraged to remember Job's complaint that God hides* from those who are blameless and upright, because God inexplicably regards them as enemies (e.g. Job 13:24). They would be invited to learn that those who are not prepared to relinquish everything – status, honor, integrity – for the sake of God will not enter the kingdom (Mark 10:17–31). They *would not be encouraged to remember Job's complaint* that *God inexplicably strips persons of their glory and honor* (e.g. Job 19:9) and makes them slaves to lives of misery and mistreatment (Job 7:2).

Those who gather in the church of the lectionary Job, *would hear a word from God* (Job 38:1–7, 34–41), which would give assurance that God will not remain forever silent and distant from the Jobs of the world. They *would be invited to ponder God's questions* about the design of the world, and they would be encouraged to probe the limits of their own wisdom in order to declare what they can and cannot comprehend. *They would not hear God's summons* to the Jobs of their community to put on "majesty and dignity" and "glory and honor" (40:10). *They would not hear God's commendation* of those creatures that have been specially endowed with the strength, confidence, and pride to live in this complex world "without fear" (cf. 40:15–24; 41:1–34). Instead, *they would hear of Jesus' "reverent submission"* (Hebrews 5:7) to suffering, and of his *rebuke of disciples who aspire for their own honor and glory* rather than the servanthood Jesus models for them (Mark 10:35–45).

They *would be invited to consider Job's confession of God's inscrutable power and his repentance* in the face of the new insight he received (Job 42:1–6). They

THE CHURCH OF SAINT JOB   289

would be invited to consider the promise that Jesus can "save for all time those who approach God through him" (Hebrews 7:25). In the description of Job's restoration (Job 42:10–17) and Bartimaeus' healing (Mark 10:46–52), *they would be reassured* that no one who cries out to God for mercy will be turned away empty-handed. They *would not be invited to ponder God's affirmation of Job's journey in faith*: "you [Job's friends] have not spoken of me what is right, as my servant Job has done" (42:7, 8). They *would not be invited to reflect on how Job had been "right"* in what he had spoken about God or on how the friends had been "wrong." They *would not be invited to consider what God meant by saying that Job's prayers were the ones God would accept* (42:8–9).

Finally, we may note that on at least one Sunday in the year worshipers *would be invited to remember Job's emphatic declaration that his "Redeemer" lives* (Job 19:23–27a). *They would be invited* to associate Job's declaration with the "eternal comfort and good hope" that is tied to the "coming of our Lord Jesus Christ" (2 Thess 2:1–5). They *would be instructed to learn* from Jesus' admonition that those who would be "worthy of a place [...] in the resurrection of the dead" should live in "this age" as if they are promised an inviolable place in "that age" (Luke 20:34–36). *They would not be invited to listen to Job despair* that no one, neither God nor his friends, seems willing to be the redeemer he expects and needs. *They will not hear Job say that "there is no justice"* (19:7) for him from any source he seeks. They *will not hear Job say that he believes God has uprooted his every hope* like a tree (19:10). They *will not hear Job complain that his heart grows weary* with the search for a redeemer who seems always just beyond his reach (19:27b).

Let us imagine that a church of this "lectionary Job" opened its doors to those who have been consigned to the ash heaps of life "for no reason." Would such a church provide sanctuary for those whose brokenness had exhausted their capacity for patience? Would those who had searched for God in every place they could imagine be reassured to hear that God's absence is in fact a providential testing designed to determine the purity of their quest? Would those who never hear Job's anguished questions about God's presence, God's justice, and God's compassion have reason to believe that their questions are worthy of being included among the authentic expressions of faith that can be brought into the sanctuary? Will those who have lost hope for justice be comforted by the promise that reverent submission to suffering in this life makes them "worthy" of comfort in the next life? Will those who long for a redeemer they can see and touch to stand by their side be comforted by the instruction to "stand firm and hold fast to the traditions" until Jesus comes? In short, will those who sit in the pews where these lectionary readings are scripture be

290   CHAPTER 17

encouraged to think of the biblical Job as their patron saint whose faith and doubt they can own? Or will they learn to think of Job as their patron sinner whose belated submission to God's mysterious providence teaches them how to avoid repeating his mistakes?

3   Can You Tell Me How to Find the Church of Saint Job?

In J. B., Archibald MacLeish's contemporary recreation of the Joban story, Mr. Zuss and Nickles debate whether there is enough interest in today's world to restage this ancient drama. Mr. Zuss, the God-character, decides the question by observing, "Oh, there's always someone playing Job." Nickles does not need persuading on this point; still he wonders what role he is to play if they go through with their plans to reenact the story:

> There must be
> Thousands! What's that got to do with it?
> Thousands –
> Millions and millions of mankind
> Burned, crushed, broken, mutilated,
> Slaughtered, and for what? For thinking! [...]
> There never could have been so many
> Suffered more for less. But where do
> I come in?

Mr. Zuss begins to shuffle uncomfortably as Nickles confirms the truth he has just stipulated. Then Nickles seems to grasp what his role is to be. He states the matter more as a question than an affirmation: "Play the dung heap?"

Mr. Zuss responds to this query with an oblique affirmation that is worthy of his counterpart in the biblical story:

> All we have to do is start.
> Job will join us. Job will be there.

Once again Nickles immediately sees the truth in this assessment, and yet he is still perplexed about what Mr. Zuss seems to be asking of him:

> I know. I know. I know. I've seen him.
> Job is everywhere we go.

THE CHURCH OF SAINT JOB   291

> His children dead, his work for nothing,
> Counting his losses, scraping his boils,
> Discussing himself with his friends and physicians,
> Questioning everything – the times, the stars,
> His own soul, God's providence.
> What do I do?[9]

This fictional interchange between Mr. Zuss and Nickles provides a provocative perspective for the church to consider. If God and the Church were to engage in conversation about the merits of restaging Job's story, would the Church agree that everywhere it turns there is always someone playing Job? Would the Church be able and willing to say, "I have seen him"? Could the Church give eye-witness testimony to Job's horrendous losses? Could it name his dead children? Could it feel the pain that covers his body from head to toe? Could it say that it has listened to his questions, not only to those that sunder his soul, but also those that fray his faith in God? Most importantly, would the Church be willing to ask, "What do I do?"

What if the Church were to conclude that God wants it to play the role of the one who sits on the dung heap? What would such a Church look like? What would its message to the Jobs of the world sound like?

I have ruminated on two models for the Church of Job. One church I have seen in Venice places the figure of Job above its front entrance. I do not know what goes on inside this church, but given its long history of ministry in the midst of a community of Jobs, I imagine that it is filled with the strange cacophony of faith that joins Jobs and friends and God in a restless search for truth about life on the dung heap. The other is a Church that does not advertise its alliance with Job by anything that is external or visible. I do not know for certain what goes in this Church, but if lectionary readings are any clue, then I can imagine that Job has at least a liturgical presence here as well. If I had only these lectionary readings to go on, I would conclude that this Church's truth about life on the dung heap resides somewhere in the harmonious blends of patient suffering, obedient servanthood, humble confession, and the promise of a place with Christ in the resurrection of the dead.

The question the Church might do well to consider is which of these models will be true to what God intends and expects? I must confess that my own inclinations lead me to suspect that those who sit on the ash heap with Job will be more at home with cacophony than harmony. But then I also confess that I

---

9 A. MacLeish, *J.B.* (Boston: Houghton Mifflin Company, 1956), 12–13.

have never actually experienced worship in a church that did not seem more intent on giving assurance than on encouraging restlessness. Perhaps the true test of whether any church deserves to be known as the "Church of Saint Job" is whether the Jobs of the world can be found sitting on the pews Sunday in and Sunday out.

"Play the dung heap?"
"All we have to do is start. Job will join us. Job will be there."

I wonder [...] Can anyone give me directions to the Church of Saint Job?

PART 7

Epilogue: "All's Well That Ends Well" ... or Is It?

CHAPTER 18

Re(reading) Job's Story in a Post-Holocaust World

There is nothing so whole as a broken heart.
RABBI NAHMAN

• • •

Though a child of survivors, I am parent to the interpretation of their survival.
C. P. SUCHER, "History is the Province of Memory"

• • •

How could they [Job's second children] live in a house filled with tragedy? How could Job and his wife live with their memories?
E. WIESEL, "Some Words for Children of Survivors"

• •
•

How does anyone write an "Epilogue" to Job? When a story, whether sacred scripture or fiction, begins with God's confession that innocent suffering happens "for no reason," what conclusion can be constructed that is adequate, let alone convincing? The narrator of the Joban epilogue opts for a "happy ending" that strives to tie up loose ends.[1] In two didactic assessments, the narrator declares that Job, not the friends, has spoken "what is right" about God (42:7–9), and that, consequently, God rewards Job by restoring his wealth, property, and status (42:10–17). This "all's-well-that-ends-well" ending invites reflection on the interchange between Shakespeare's widow of Florence and Helena:

Widow: Lord how we lose our pains!
Helena: All's well that ends well yet,
　　　Though time seems so adverse and means unfit.
All's Well That Ends Well, 5.1.24–26

1　K. N. Ngwa, *The Hermeneutics of the "Happy" Ending in Job 42:7–17* (BZAW 354; Berlin: Walter de Gruyter, 2005).

© SAMUEL E. BALENTINE, 2021 | DOI:10.1163/9789004459212_019

296   CHAPTER 18

Even if we can settle into this happy ending, Shakespeare's telltale "yet," and the trailer words "adverse" and "unfit," may give us pause. David Clines poses the question the epilogue begs:

> What, in the end, becomes of Job? After all he has endured, after all his vigor to clear his name, after the encounter with God that has proved so disappointing [...] He steps back into the world of the prologue to the book, the world of the naïve fairytale, and closes the door for ever on the world of intensity, intellectual struggle – lucidity – that he has inhabited since the day of his curse on life (chap. 3). Has this been a happy outcome for him? [...] Is this enough to constitute happiness?[2]

A number of subtle clues indicate that the epilogue, whatever closure it may have intended, continues to invite multiple readings that add to the characterizations of God, the friends, Job, and his children.

God. The first clue about God occurs in the narrator's opening statement. The words "After the Lord had spoken these words to Job" (42:7) direct readers back to the to the divine speeches in 38:1–40:34, not to Job's last words in 42:1–6. Does God accept Job's last words as a worthy response to divine revelation? The narrator does not say, an omission that may be read in different ways. Perhaps God chooses to ignore what Job has said. Perhaps God's acceptance is assumed.[3] The only explicit information we are given is that God is angry. Job feared that God would confront him in anger (14:13; 16:9; 19:11), but it is surprising that God never directly expresses anger toward Job. Instead, God is angry with the friends, because they have not spoken "what is right (*nĕkônâ*)." The term refers to what is "correct" or "truthful," not only in an intellectual sense but also with reference to facts that are established and consistent with reality (cf. Deut 17:4; 1 Sam 23:23).[4] God's anger indicates that the friends' error is not trivial; as Clines notes, "in defending the doctrine of retribution, [the friends] were advocates of a theology hostile to the divine designs."[5] But if retributive justice is not the undergirding moral principle of God's governance of the world, then what is? If blessing the righteous and punishing the wicked is not consistent with reality, then what does justice mean for an innocent sufferer

---

2 D. J. A. Clines, *Job 1–42* (Word Biblical Commentary; Nashville: Nelson (1989), Vol. 3:206.

3 Cf. E. van Wolde, "The Reversal of Job," in *The Book of Job*, ed. W. A. M. Beuken (BETL 114; Leuven: Leuven University Press/Peeters, 1994), 223–250.

4 For the use of this term and its derivatives elsewhere in the Hebrew Bible and in Job, see Duck-Woo Nam, *Talking About God: Job 42:7–9 and the Nature of God in the Book of Job* (New York: Peter Lang, 2003), 22–24.

5 Clines, *Job 1–42*, 3:197.

like Job? God's reaction to the friends subtly returns readers to the prologue, where, by God's own admission, the words "for no reason" (2:3; cf. 1:9) must somehow be factored into a theology that is not hostile to God's intentions.

God's anger is further manifest in God's willingness to deal with the friends in distinctly un-Godlike ways. Before Job prays for the friends, God is intent on "doing foolishness" (*ʿăśôt nĕbālâ*; 42:8). The word *nĕbālâ* normally refers to reprehensible or outrageous behavior that subverts acceptable social ethical norms and brings dishonor and judgment on the perpetrator.[6] The occurrence in 42:8 is the only instance in the Old Testament where God is said to be the one doing *nĕbālâ*. The conventional view (reflected in NRSV: "to deal with you according to your folly") is that the *friends'* foolishness, not *God's*, needs changing or forgiving. A straightforward reading suggests, however, that Job's unrecorded prayer may have been something like this: "O Lord, do not do anything foolish when you deal with the friends."[7] When the epilogist reports that God "accepted Job's prayer" (42:10), he suggests that God's intentions have changed. In short, Job's prayer restores both the friends and God to a relationship that is different than that which would have existed if Job had not stepped into the breach between them. Job's participation, which comes at God's invitation, enables God to be more God-like.[8]

Another aspect of God's character is disclosed in the report that God restores Job's fortunes by giving him "twice as much as he had before" (42:10). The doubling may be only a rhetorical flourish designed to connect the epilogue with the prologue (1:3), where Job's possessions are a tangible witness to his piety. Perhaps it is no more than a characteristic feature of conventional stories about the reward that comes eventually to those who remain faithful to

---

6 The collocation *ʿāśâ nĕbālâ* occurs frequently in the Old Testament, always with a strong negative connotation (e.g., Gen 34:7; Deut 22:21; Josh 7:15; Judg 20:6; Jer 29:23). See further, W. M. W. Roth, "NBL," VT 10 (1960), 394–409; A. Phillips, "*Nebalah* – A Term for Serious Disorderly and Unruly Conduct," VT 25 (1975), 237–242; M. Saebo, "*nābāl*, fool," in E. Jenni, C. Westermann, TLOT, Vol. 2 (Trans. M. E. Biddle; Peabody, MS: Hendrikson Publishers, 1997), 712. The comments of Driver (*A Critical and Exegetical Commentary on the Book of Job* [Edinburgh: T and T Clark, 1921], 26) are instructive: "[T]he fault of the *nābhāl* was not weakness of reason, but moral and religious sensibility, an invincible lack of sense or perception, for the claims of either God or man."

7 Cf. M. Pope, *Job* (Anchor Bible 15; Garden City, NY: Doubleday, 1979), 347; J. G. Janzen, *Job* (Interpretation; Atlanta: John Knox, 1985), 266; E. Good, *In Turns of Tempest: A Reading of Job with a Translation* (Stanford, CA: Stanford University Press, 1990), 383. There is a suggestive echo here of Job's rebuke to his wife in 2:10 for talking like a "foolish woman" (*nĕbālôt*) by urging him to curse God. Just as Job dismisses his wife's counsel as foolishness, so now he appears to be unwilling to accept God's "foolish anger" toward the friends.

8 S. E. Balentine, "My Servant Job Shall Pray For You," *ThTo* 58 (2002), 502–518; idem, *Job* (Smyth and Helwys Bible Commentary; Macon, GA: Smyth & Helwys, 2006), 712–713.

298   CHAPTER 18

God in the midst of hardship.[9] It is nonetheless hard to overlook the connection elsewhere in the Old Testament between double compensation for losses and an admission of wrongdoing. "It is a wry touch," F. Anderson says, "that the Lord, like any thief who has been found out (Exod 22:4), repays Job double what he took from him."[10]

The doubling likely also extends to the epilogist's report that "After this Job lived one hundred and forty years" (42:16). If 70 years is a normal life span (Ps 90:10), then it appears that following this encounter with suffering and with God, Job now begins life again. His former life is over. God grants him a fresh start, as if he can now begin anew unencumbered by what he has experienced and learned about life in relation to God. When he dies, "old and full of days" (42:17), Job, like Israel's revered ancestors – Abraham (Gen 25:8), Isaac (Gen 25:29), and David (1 Chr 29:28) – will be full and satisfied. A number of underlying and unaddressed questions linger. Can a restored Job simply forget his losses? Will replacement children compensate for the deaths of seven sons and three daughters? Can Job, should he, simply resume a life of blessing the God who gives and takes away? What assurance does Job have that his new life will be invulnerable to the same seemingly capricious disruptions of a God who can be incited to act against him "for no reason"? Clines sharpens the question that the epilogue invites but does not answer.

> [I]f fire could fall from heaven on his [Job's] flocks and herds one day, who is to know that it will never again in 140 years? It is a little naïve, is it not, to believe that lightning never falls in the same place twice.[11]

Job and His Friends. The epilogue condemns the three friends, represented here by their lead spokesperson Eliphaz, for not having spoken the truth about God. Job alone has done so. The question remains, however: what has Job said about God that is "right"? Was Job right to bless God in the face of undeserved suffering (1:21)? If so, then how could he also be right when he cursed the day of his birth and by implication the Creator who summons forth all life (3:1–10; cf. 3:11 and 10:18)? Was Job right to accuse God of savage indifference to the justice of the wronged (10:1–17; 16:6–17; 19:6–22; 27:2–12)? If so, then why does God criticize Job for questioning divine justice (40:8)? If Job was right to defer

---

9   See, for example, the apocryphal Book of Tobit (second century BCE), a story of a righteous Jew living in exile, who, like Job, suffers the loss of his property, his standing in the community, and his health. His restoration includes a doubling of his life span (14:1–2).

10   F. I. Anderson, *Job: An Introduction and Commentary* (TOTC; Leicester, England: InterVarsity Press, 1976), 293; cf. Clines, *Job 1–42*, 3:202.

11   Clines, *Job 1–42*, 3: 205.

RE(READING) JOB'S STORY IN A POST-HOLOCAUST WORLD 299

in silence to God's first words from the whirlwind (40:5), then why does God
continue to seek Job's response with a second speech (40:6)? If Job's second
response in 42:6 is right, then it is at best enigmatic, and readers are left to
wonder why God does not say more, either to affirm or explain what Job understands now that he did not before. The transmission history of the prose and
poetry of the book may mitigate the contradictory answers these questions
pose, but at a fundamental level the different options remain largely irrecon-
cilable. Perhaps we should settle for a minimalist reading: Job is right that God
does not govern according to the principles of retributive justice; to claim otherwise, as the friends do, is clearly wrong. But then, the price Job pays for being
right casts an even more unsettling pall over the story: seven sons and three
daughters, dead "for no reason," except to teach Job a lesson? How could a righteous God fault Job for refusing to learn such a lesson, even if he is wrong?
Dostoevsky's Ivan responds to his brother Alyosha in a scenario that imagines
a Joban-like refusal to pay the cost obedience to God seems to require.

> I don't want harmony [with God's world], for love of mankind I don't want
> it. I'd rather remain with my unrequited suffering and my unquenched
> indignation, *even if I am wrong*. Besides, they have put too high a price
> on harmony; we can't afford to pay so much for admission. And therefore
> I hasten to return my ticket. And it is my duty, if only as an honest man,
> to return it as far ahead of time as possible. Which is what I am doing.
> It's not that I don't accept God, Alyosha, I just respectfully return him
> the ticket.[12]

The Joban epilogue does not contemplate such a response, although here again
readers may wonder why not.

Instead, God instructs Job to pray for his friends, which by all accounts, he
does willingly. Two issues emerge. First, why should Job pray for the wrong-
doings of Eliphaz, Bildad, and Zophar? The composite story assumes that Job
has no knowledge of either why he was afflicted or why he has been restored.
He knows nothing of God's repudiation of his friends' counsel. He has no evident reason to pray for their forgiveness, apart from what we may assume is
his unwavering commitment to be God's faithful "servant" (42:7, 8 [3×]; cf. 1:8;
2:3). What does he owe those who have abused him? Why should he pray for
the forgiveness of those who condemn him in the name of God? Perhaps the
lesson to be learned is that authentic fidelity to God should be disconnected

---

12   F. Dostoevsky, *The Brothers Karamazov* (Trans. and annotated R. Pevear, L. Volokhonsky;
      New York: Vintage Books, 1990), 245 (emphasis original).

from every expectation of divine blessing and reward. At least on first reading, this is the implicit connection between the satan's presenting question – "Does Job fear God for no reason (*ḥinnām*)?" (1:9) – and God's decision to explore the answer to the question by submitting Job to suffering "for no reason (*ḥinnām*)" (2:3). The fidelity that binds together God and human beings is, according to this reading, a tensive probing of the limits of divine capriciousness. The underlying and unaddressed question is this: if Job should refuse to pray for his friends, whose fidelity suffers the greater loss, Job's to God or God's to Job?

Second, what does it mean to be an authentic friend of Job?[13] Eliphaz, Bildad, and Zophar try to "comfort and console" (2:11) Job with theological maxims about God's inscrutable justice. They fail. As Job says, they "whitewash" the truth with lies (13:4). The epilogue accents instead the community of "brothers, sisters and friends" who offer the "consolation" and "comfort" Job's other erstwhile friends would not or could not provide. It records no exchange of words concerning "all the evil that the Lord has brought upon him [Job]" (42:11). It reports only that these friends share a meal together, an indication that they welcome Job's presence in the routines of everyday fellowship, and that they contribute to his material needs with tangible gifts, a modest amount of money and a gold ring.[14] In sum, they comfort Job with acts not words, with communion not theology. What has become of Job's quest for justice? The narrator leaves open the question, which appears now to be subsumed to the larger imperative of getting on with life – "eating, drinking, begetting, dying"[15] – a blessing that exceeds (and nullifies?) anything Job has experienced thus far.

Job's Children. Job's restoration includes the replacement of his dead children with seven new sons and three new daughters (42:13–16). The narrator names the daughters, but not the sons: Jemimah ("dove;" cf. Song 2:14); Keziah ("cinnamon;" cf. Exod 30:24; Ps 45:8); and Keren-happuch (presumably a reference to the black powder used to beautify the eyes; cf. 2 Kgs 9:30; Jer 4:30). It is unclear what we should make of these names or of the narrator's intention in singling out the daughters.[16] What is clear is that Job bequeaths to his children,

---

13   On the theology of friendship in Job, see my discussion, "'Let Love Clasp Grief Lest Both Be Drowned,'" *Perspectives in Religious Studies* 30 (2003), 381–397; idem, *Job*, 445–451.

14   The amount signified by the term *qĕśîṭâ* ("a piece of money") is uncertain. Jacob, for example, pays the sum of 100 *qĕśîṭâ* to purchase a piece of land (Gen 33:19; Josh 24:32). LXX uses a word that means "lamb," which suggests an amount equivalent to the monetary value of such an animal.

15   Clines, *Job 1–42*, 3:208.

16   In a patriarchal world, which the book of Job assumes, daughters typically inherit only when there are no sons (Num 26:33; cf. Num 27:1–11; 36:1–12; cf. Z. Ben-Barak, "Inheritance

RE(READING) JOB'S STORY IN A POST-HOLOCAUST WORLD   301

specifically the named daughters, an "inheritance" (*naḥălâ*; 42:15) that requires
the stewardship of sustaining the memory of his experiences with God – what
God has given and what God has taken away – through four generations (42:16).

1   "You ... Did Not Comprehend the Extent of Your Sleeping Power"

What is the stewardship required of Job's children? The *Testament of Job*, arguably the first "commentary" on the book, recasts the biblical story as Job's last
words of counsel and advice to his children. Before he dies, he settles all his
affairs with a full account of "the things which the Lord did with me and all
the things which have happened to me" (*T. Job* 1:4). The *Testament's* epilogue
reports that on his death, Job's new seven sons and three daughters, "accompanied by the poor and the orphans and all the helpless," delivered a eulogy –
"Who then will not weep over the man of God?" – then laid him in his tomb,
his legacy henceforth to be "renowned in all generations forever" (*T. Job* 53:4,
8). Thus begins the stewardship of Job's story by his children.

I have commented on various aspects of this stewardship, second, third,
fourth, and more readings and re-readings of Job's story.[17] Here, I conclude
with specific attention to post-biblical Jewish contributions to lessons learned,
imperatives considered, and responses that may be authentically faithful
for those who believe Job's legacy is alive, not buried. Margaret Susman has
argued that the history of the Jewish interpretation of Job is a "seismograph

---

by Daughters in the Ancient Near East," JSS 25 [1980], 22–33). It is not clear why the
epilogue indicates Job does not follow this convention. Some commentators argue
that the epilogue appropriates an old epic motif (N. M. Sarna, "Epic Substratum in the
Prose of Job," JBL 76 [1957], 24; M. D. Coogan, "Job's Children," in *Lingering Over Words;
Studies in Ancient Near Eastern Literature in Honor of William L. Moran*, eds. T. Abusch,
J. Huehnergaard, P. Steinkeller [Atlanta: Scholars Press, 1990], 146–147). Others debate
whether the inheritance of the daughters subverts patriarchal convention or repre-
sents it (cf. J. Chittister, *Job's Daughters: Women and Power* [New York: Paulist Press,
1990], I. Pardes, *Countertraditions in the Bible: A Feminist Approach* [Cambridge: Harvard
University Press, 1994], 145–156; and W. S. Morrow, "Toxic Religion and the Daughters of
Job," JR 27 [1998], 263–276). On the embellishment of the daughters' role in the *Testament
of Job*, see P. Machinist, "Job's Daughters and Their Inheritance in the Testament of
Job and Its Biblical Congeners," in *The Echoes of Many Texts: Reflections on Jewish and
Christian Traditions. Essays in Honor of Lou H. Silberman*, eds. W. G. Dever, J. E. Wright
(Atlanta: Scholars Press, 1997), 67–80.

17   See, for example, "Prologue," in S. E. Balentine, *Have You Considered My Servant Job?
Understanding the Biblical Archetype of Patience* (Columbia, SC: University of South
Carolina Press, 2015), 1–12.

302   CHAPTER 18

of nations."[18] Emil Fackenheim extends this insight by arguing that everyone in the post-Holocaust generation, Gentile or Jewish, is one of Job's children.[19]

Czar Alexander II was assassinated in 1881. His death, followed by the succession of his son Alexander III, marked a watershed for Russian Jews. Russian officials accused Jews of conspiring in the assassination and immediately launched a wave of pogroms throughout Russia and beyond. Violence, sustained by anti-Jewish regulations, severely limited their options. Of those who survived, many emigrated. Many turned inward, seeking identity, if not comfort, in biblical history – suffering is validation that God's Chosen People had been chosen to suffer.[20] Others creatively explored the imperatives of Jewish themes and traditions in Yiddish literature, which not coincidentally begins to flower in the late nineteenth century.[21] Y. L. Perets (1852–1915) straddled the latter two of these options. Unwilling to abandon the pietistic heritage of the Jewish Enlightenment (*Haskala*), Perets exploited Yiddish as means of religious and social critique.

Perets published the Yiddish text of "Bontsye Shvayg" ("Bontsye the Silent") in 1893. A second edition, published in 1901, contains significant variants. Multiple English translations, including a television rendition and a 1953 Broadway play by Arnold Perl, confirm that a story Perets intended to be timely has proved to be "timeless."[22] Perets makes only one explicit reference to Job in "Bontsye the Silent," but Joban themes are implicit throughout the story.[23]

---

18   M. Susman, *Das Buch Hiob und das Schicksal des jüdischen Volkes* (Basel, Wien: Herder Bücherie, 1969), 68.

19   E. Fackenheim, *God's Presence in History: Jewish Affirmations and Philosophical Reflections* (New York: New York University Press, 1970); idem, *To Mend the World: Foundations of Future Jewish Thought* (New York: Schocken Books, 1982). See also, A. L. Berger, *Children of Job: American Second-Generation Witnesses to the Holocaust* (Albany: State University of New York Press, 1997).

20   B. Zuckerman, *Job the Silent: A Study in Historical Counterpoint* (Oxford: Oxford University Press, 1991), 63.

21   S. Liptzin, *The Flowering of Yiddish Literature* (New York: Yoseloff, 1963).

22   E. Wiesel, "Victims of God," review of *Selected Stories by I. L. Peretz*, eds. I. Howe, E. Greenberg, *The New Republic* (September 21, 1974), as cited in I. Abrahamson, *Against Silence. The Voice and Vision of Elie Wiesel*, Vol. 2 (New York: Holocaust Library, 1985), 321.

23   Zuckerman, *Job the Silent*, 34, 187. On commentators who have pursued Zuckerman's insights, see Balentine, *Job*, 709; J. L. Crenshaw, *Reading Job: A Literary and Theological Commentary* (Macon, GA: Smyth and Helwys, 2011), 34–35; G. Oberhänsli, "Job in Modern and Contemporary Literature on the Background of Tradition: Sidelights of a Jewish Reading," in K. Dell, W. Kynes, ed., *Reading Job Intertextually* (Library of Hebrew Bible/ Old Testament Studies 574; New York: Bloomsbury, 2013), 278–279.

Bruce Zuckerman reads Bontsye as a "Super-Job."[24] From the day he was born, Bontsye suffers without complaint. Throughout his life, he endured one calamity after another, unlike Job, never once raising his voice: he "lived silently and silently he died; like a shadow passing through our world."[25] His life of suffering silence reflects the human condition; it was nothing special, simply a given of life in the world God has created. He was but one "grey particle of sand on the seashore [...] Mutely born, mutely lived, mutely died and more mutely buried" (183, 185). If his life and death creates no cause for notice on earth, it nevertheless makes a "great impression" (185) in heaven, where a heavenly council convenes to consider Bontsye's post-mortem fate: "even God himself knew that Bontsye the Silent was coming!" (185). Father Abraham welcomes Bontsye with a warmhearted greeting, "Peace be with you" (187). A Defending Angel makes the case for Bontsye's entry into God's presence. The Presiding Judge, God, prepares to render the final verdict.

> My child! [...] you have always suffered and kept silent! There is not a single member, not a single bone in your body without a wound, without a bloody welt, there is absolutely no secret place in your soul where it shouldn't be bleeding [...] and you always kept silent [...].
>
> There, no one understood all this. Indeed, you, yourself, perhaps did not realize that you can cry out; and due to your cry, Jericho's wall can quake and tumble down! You, yourself did not comprehend the extent of your sleeping power [...].
>
> In the other world your silence was not compensated, but this is the *Realm of Lies*, here in the *Realm of Truth* you will receive your compensation!
>
> On you the Supreme Assembly shall pass no judgment; on you it will make no ruling; for you it will neither divide nor apportion a share. Take whatever you want! *Everything* is yours! (193)

Bontsye's silence constitutes a moral lien against heaven that Bontsye himself does not understand. One cry for justice from him would require compensation greater than the Realm of Truth could pay. No doubt Heaven breathes a sigh of relief when Bontsye speaks for the first time.

---

24   Zuckerman, *Job the Silent*, 34–45.

25   Y. L. Peretz, "Bontsye the Silent, 183." In Zukerman, *Job the Silent*, 181–195. All subsequent parenthetical references are to Zukerman's translation.

Bontsye, for the first time, raises his eyes! He is just about blinded by the light on all sides; everything sparkles, everything flashes, beams shoot out from everything: from the walls, from the vessels, from the angles, from the judges! A kaleidoscope of suns!

He drops his eyes wearily!

"Are you sure?" He asks, doubtful and shamefaced.

"Absolutely!" the Presiding Judge affirms! "Absolutely, I tell you; for everything is yours; everything in Heaven belongs to you! Choose and take what you wish. You only take what belongs to you, *alone!*"

"Are you sure?" asks Bontsye once more with growing confidence in his voice.

"Definitely! Absolutely! Positively! They affirm to him on every side.

"Gee, if you mean it," smiles Bonstye, "what I'd really like is, each and every morning, a hot roll with fresh butter!"

Judges and angels lowered their heads in shame; the Prosecutor burst out laughing. (193, 195)

The ending of the story, like the ending of Job, is oblique. Is Bontsye's request the measure of a simpleton? Is he the ultimate schlemiel, a fool who can imagine nothing better than a hot buttered roll? If so, perhaps the Prosecutor laughs because he realizes, with palpable relief, that Bontsye is not a saint with virtuous demands on heavenly justice; he is simply stupid. Is Bontsye's request a poignant testimony to what Jews suffered during the Russian pogroms, to the ravages of hunger that reduce human life to the cravings of the stomach? If so, then Bontsye represents the ultimate victim, and what he has been denied, his basic rights as a human being, shames everyone – on earth and in heaven – who stood by in complicit silence.

Zuckerman makes a strong case for reading Perets' story as a parody of nineteenth century Jewish piety.[26] It unmasks two absurdities.[27] First, it is absurd to believe that anyone could or should endure suffering like Bontsye's without crying out in pain and protest. Many Russian Jews did not acquiesce in silence to their persecutors, and it is they, not Bontsye, who model the virtue of resistance. Silence in the face of unjust suffering is silly, Perets may be saying, and the laugh is on everyone who thinks that patience is an adequate substitute for action. Second, it is absurd that when offered the world, Bontsye asks only for something for himself. What of the suffering of the "thousand million" (183)

---

26   Zukerman, *Job the Silent*, 44.

27   Ibid. 64.

others who wait for someone to cry out on their behalf? If but one cry can bring down Jericho's walls, what might concerted protest do to collapse the powers of injustice? Perhaps the Prosecutor, the Judge of the world, laughs to keep from crying,[28] because Bontsye's request makes the quest for justice – on earth and in heaven – no more important than a breakfast side dish.

However Perets may have intended his story to be read in the nineteenth century, its meaning cannot but be transformed in a post-Holocaust world. In the wake of 1945, "events have robbed Perets' story of its absurdities by turning them into realities, and in doing so, has changed what was originally meant as a parody into history before its time."[29] To read it as a parody would be a sacrilege.[30] "The force of history" demands a re-reading and a re-evaluation; Bontsye the "silent" must have a voice.[31] Zuckerman discusses multiple re-readings of "Bontsye the Silent." I single out two.

First, Elie Wiesel, widely regarded as the most articulate spokesperson for the post-Holocaust generation, interprets Bontsye's silence as a "screaming silence, a shouting silence" that speaks more than words.[32] The most profound truth imposed by the Holocaust is that some suffering cannot be transmitted; it can only be experienced.

> In 1945 I felt we cannot really communicate the experience, that all we can do is show the impossibility of communicating the experience – if you take these two facts together, you have a certain need for silence. But the silence is not against language; it is a remedy to language. It tries to purify it, tries to redeem it, to give it back its innocence, its weight.[33]

---

28   Ibid., 39.

29   Ibid., 67.

30   "What has happened to the [Yiddish] parodic tradition after the Holocaust is that no one is able to get the joke anymore. That is because everything Yiddish has automatically been shrouded in an aura of holiness. After the Great Destruction we can no longer view the Yiddish world as a paradise lost. All the archetypes are now protected by the Holocaust, so that parody of any kind becomes sacrilege" (D. G. Roskies, "The People of the Lost Book; A Cultural Manifesto," *Orim* 2 (1986), 23; as cited in Zuckerman, *Job the Silent*, 68).

31   Zuckerman, *Job the Silent*, 68.

32   L. Edeleman, "The Use of Words and the Weight of Silence," interview of Elie Wiesel in *National Jewish Monthly* (November 1973) in I. Abrahamson, "Introductory Essay," *Against Silence: The Voice and Vision of Elie Wiesel* (3 vols; ed. I. Abrahamson; New York: Holocaust Library, 1985), vol. 2, 82 (as cited in Zuckerman, *Job the Silent*, 66).

33   Elie Wiesel, interview with H. Broun in 1974 in I. Abrahamson, "Introductory Essay," *Against Silence; The Voice and Vision of Elie Wiesel*, vol. 1, 56 (as cited in Zuckerman, *Job the Silent*, 65–66).

Even a "screaming silence," however, as Wiesel goes on to say, as long as it remains merely metaphorical, is ultimately inadequate: "the generation that is mine could have shouted so loud that it would have shaken the world. Instead it whispered, content with its 'buttered roll'."[34]

A second example is the Yiddish poet Eliezer Greenberg. His 1946 poem, "Y. L. Perets and Bontsye Shvayg in the Warsaw Ghetto," imagines how Perets would have characterized Bonstye, had he lived to see him sitting, Job-like, on a pile of ashes in what became of his adopted hometown, Warsaw. Greenberg suggests that Bontsye would have cried out not only to his literary creator, Perets, but also to God. Greenberg's Bontsye would not settle for the role of "the eternally silent one;" he would instead demand a new trial in which he, not the Defending Angel of the original story, argues the case for justice before the heavenly tribunal.

> I want, now, to cry out all the years of silence,
> I want you to give me a tongue, to give me a voice! [...]
>
> To be a witness to how the world kept silent, to how silent the Creator
>   kept
> When our race was mowed down – with kith and kin – the poor just as
>   the rich!
> O my creator, call once more the whole world to a Tribunal,
> But let me – the eternally silent one – be their Defender! [...]
>
> Let me open these eternally sealed lips,
> Which for a lifetime have been locked with silence!
> Let me throw open my heart, which has sobbed for a lifetime
> In silence – locked with a thousand locks [...].[35]

The case that Greenberg's Bontsye would argue is no longer defined by his own personal need for food; it is has now been enlarged by the imperative cries for justice of a generation murdered, a generation whose voices have been unsuccessfully silenced by unspeakable violence.

---

34 E. Wiesel, "Victims of God," review of *Selected Stories by I.L. Peretz*, ed. by I. Howe, E. Greenberg, *The New Republic* (September 21, 1974) in Abrahamson, *Against Silence; The Voice and Vision of Elie Wiesel*, vol. 2, 321 (as cited in Zuckerman, *Job the Silent*, 66).

35 E. Greenberg, "Y. L. Perets," stanzas 18, 19–20 (as cited in Zuckerman, *Job the Silent*, 69).

RE(READING) JOB'S STORY IN A POST-HOLOCAUST WORLD

His [Bontsye's] lamentation rises and turns into a wild howling,
His voice now pounds like a wolf-and-dove roaring.
Until the morning starts to burn with feverish madness –
And Perets wails and Bontsye wails – and all is frozen still.[36]

2 "We Won't Allow Your Blood to Be Covered"

H. Leivick (1882–1962), perhaps the most revered of Yiddish poets, was born in Belarus and received a traditional Jewish education in czarist Russia. In 1905, at the age of 23, he joined the Jewish underground and was subsequently arrested and sentenced to four years of forced labor and exile in Siberia. During exile, he adopted Yiddish as the language of the people and began composing his first dramatic poems and plays. He escaped to the United States in 1913, where he spent the rest of his life.

As a "poet of conscience," Leivick merged the suffering he experienced during his prison years with traditional Jewish themes and symbols, sin and sacrifice, exile and redemption. In 1957, at the age of 69, he gave an address to a conference of writers and intellectuals in Jerusalem entitled "The Jew – The Individual." His speech connects the major themes he addressed in the body of his published work, twenty-one plays and ten volumes of poetry, with a traumatic childhood experience. When he was seven years old and walking to the *ḥeder* on the synagogue street, he forgot to take off his hat when he passed a Polish church. A Polish man immediately began to beat him with his fists. Leivick escaped and arrived, crying, at the school. The lesson for the day was the story about Abraham and the sacrifice of Isaac.

> The teacher began the lesson for the day, the verses about the sacrifice of Isaac. Isaac accompanies his father Abraham to Mount Moriah, and now Isaac lies bound upon the altar waiting to be slaughtered. Within me my heart weeps even harder. It weeps out of great pity for Isaac. And now Abraham raises the knife. My heart is nearly frozen with fear. Suddenly – the angel's voice: Abraham, do not raise your hand against your son; do not slay him. You have only been tested by God. And now I burst into tears. "Why are you crying now?" the teacher asked. "As you see, Isaac was not slaughtered." In my tears I replied, "But what would have happened had the angel *come one moment too late*?" The teacher tried to console me

---

36   Ibid (as cited in Zuckerman, *Job the Silent*, 69).

308 CHAPTER 18

with the reassurance that an angel cannot be late. But the fear of coming too late stayed with me.[37]

He concludes by reflecting on his existence, his "fate" as a post-Holocaust Jew.

> I have seen – we all have seen – six million Isaacs lying under knives, under axes, in fires, and in gas-chambers; and they were slaughtered. The angel of God did come too late. Six million slaughtered Isaacs are beyond my comprehension. But I can comprehend one Isaac waiting to be slaughtered and thereby living through the horrors of six million slaughtered, as though he were himself slaughtered six million times [...].
> Have we not had enough of sacrificial altars? I ask, have we not had enough? [...][38]

Leivick's play, *In the Days of Job*, explores the connections between Isaac and Job. Through most of the play, Leivick basically follows the biblical script, but he splices the conventional dialogues between Job and his friends with an intense, surreal, conversation between Job, Isaac, and the sheep offered for slaughter. This dramatic shift begins when Leivick's Job responds to Bildad by citing the words of Job 16:18.

> Let me ask you again:
> Do you really think you know
> Something I do not?
>
> What if I complain?
> My complaint is to God,
> To the almighty; to Him, and not to you.
> I have cried out, nor will I stop complaining.
> O earth. You shall not cover my blood.[39]

The first response comes from "outside" voices, voices Job's friends characterize as the "strange, wild cries" of an ugly mob of the "blind, the leprous, and the diseased" (130).

---

37 H. Leivick, "The Jew The Individual," as cited in J. C. Landis, *Three Great Jewish Plays* (New York: Applause Theatre Book Publishers, 1986), 116.

38 Ibid., 118.

39 H. Leivick, *In the Days of Job* in *A Treasury of Yiddish Poetry*, ed., I. Howe and E. Greenberg (New York: Schocken Books, 1969), 130. Subsequent references are given parenthetically in the text.

Voices: We won't allow your blood to be covered.
We won't allow. We won't [...].

It carries everywhere
It reaches us everywhere.
Cry louder. Louder still.
Nor stop your lamentation for an instant. (130)

When Isaac appears on stage, he seems at first little different from Job's other friends. The conversation is casual and cordial, but as it unfolds Job becomes increasingly agitated. "Did you curse when you cried out?" Job asks. Before Isaac can respond, Job answers his own question: "You lay there like a sheep, with no outcry. Like a sheep. Go away [...] away. Out of my sight" (138, 139). Isaac explains that he went to the altar of sacrifice because he was obedient to the temptation God presented his father Abraham, a temptation, Isaac suggests, not unlike the test God has presented to Job. Job is not consoled; Isaac was tied by his father's hands, Job has been bound by the "hand of God Himself" (140), and he wants to know why. Why did Isaac not cry out with a lamentation that might have stopped the testing of a righteous man? A single cry of protest, Leivick suggests, might have changed the course of history. If Isaac had truly wanted to do something that would now comfort Job, then he would have cried out to God "with my [Job's] voice" (140).

Leivick gives the last words of the play to the sheep, Isaac's replacement sacrifice. It is the voice of the one placed on the altar, the one vulnerable to sacrifice. It is the voice of the one who provides the "first inkling" of the fate of six million Jews who would face the knife, but unlike the sheep, be killed, because the sparing angel came too late.

Take a good look. See how deeply
My throat has been carved. Was not
Your father's knife your knife as well?
Or is the blood of a sheep not really blood?
Perhaps I am an incarnation of yourself,
A living prophecy regarding you;
The first inkling of the razor's edge
That must inevitably cut your throat [...]
If not now, then later [...] later.
What if the knife of Mount Moriah missed you?
Has not its sharpness revealed the slaughter
Being readied for you generations hence
By knives as long as the night? (144)

310   CHAPTER 18

When the sheep exits, Leivick adds a final directorial note: "Abel appears
in his place" (145). The ending evokes not only the memory of Job's words in
Job 16:18 – "O earth do not cover my blood; let my cry find resting place" – but
also the generative testimony of Gen 4:8–10. Murdered by Cain, Abel's blood
cries out to God for justice. According to the Genesis account, God responds
by punishing Cain for subverting God's design for the moral order of creation.
In the Genesis account, as in Job's evocation of its abiding legacy, God determines that Cain's violence, and Abel's cry for restitution, subjects the world to
the harshest judgment recorded in scripture (Gen 6:11–13), reinforced by God's
unconditional promise that the shedding of innocent blood will "never again"
(Gen 8:21–22) go without a reckoning from God (Gen 9:5–6).[40] Leivick's conclusion insists that Abel's blood, and Job's cries, still seek a response – from
heaven or earth – that changes the destiny of those who are Job's children.

3   "We Know His [Job's] Story for Having Lived It [...]. Whenever We
       Attempt to Tell Our Own Story, We Transmit His"

Because I have decided to focus on post-Holocaust readings and re-readings of
Job, I have been from the outset of this chapter inching into sacred territory.
I turn now to the writings of Elie Wiesel, which brings me, perhaps, as close
to the inner sanctum of Jewish history as a Gentile may be permitted. Wiesel
himself presses the caution that itches at my conscience as I try to enter into
the world of Joban interpretation post-Auschwitz.

> Accept the idea that you will never see what they have seen – and go on
> seeing now, that you will never know the faces that haunt their nights,
> that you will never hear the cries that rent their sleep. Accept the idea
> that you will never penetrate the cursed and spellbound universe they
> carry within themselves with unfailing loyalty.
>   And so I tell you: You who have not experienced their anguish, you
> who do not speak their language, you who do not mourn their dead,
> think before you offend them, before you betray them. Think before you
> substitute your memory for theirs.[41]

The caution may be reduced to a simple fact about those who dare to enter
into the now fashionable discussion of holocaust "literature": those who know

---

40   For commentary on Job's evocation of Genesis 4, see Balentine, *Job*, 257–260.
41   E. Wiesel, *A Jew Today* (New York: Random House, 1978), 207–208.

RE(READING) JOB'S STORY IN A POST-HOLOCAUST WORLD 311

do not speak; those who speak do not know.[42] Speaking "without knowledge" is what God accuses Job of doing (Job 38:2). Inasmuch as Job was, it seems, a Gentile himself, and given Wiesel's argument that Job is in some sense our "contemporary"[43] (211), I venture the following comments on Wiesel's reading of Job. At best, I hope not to betray the memories that shape Job's children.

Wiesel says that after World War II he was "preoccupied with Job." "He [Job] could be seen on every road in Europe. Wounded, robbed, mutilated. Certainly not happy. Nor resigned" (233–234). The last phrase – "nor resigned" – is critical. Wiesel admires the story of Job's "passionate rebellion," but he is offended by the book's ending and its description of Job's resignation. "The fighter," he says, "has turned into a lamb. A sad metamorphosis [...]" (233). Wiesel imagines and desires a different ending.

> Job's resignation as man was an insult to man. He should not have given in so easily. He should have continued to protest, to refuse the handouts. He should have said to God: Very well, I forgive You, I forgive You to the extent of my sorrow, my anguish. But what about my dead children, do they forgive You? What right have I to speak on their behalf? Do I have the moral, the human right to accept an ending, a solution to this story, in which they have played roles that You imposed on them, not because of them, but because of me? By accepting Your inequities, do I not become your accomplice? Now it is my turn to choose between You and my children, and I refuse to repudiate them. I demand that justice be done to them, if not to me, and that the trial continue [...] Yes, that is what he should have said. Only he did not. He agreed to go back to living as before. Therein lay God's true victory: He forced Job to welcome happiness. After the catastrophe Job lived happily in spite of himself. (234)

Wiesel is neither a theologian nor a historian. He considers himself a story-teller. If we want to understand how and why he imagines such an ending to Job, how and why such an ending embodies Wiesel's own story, then we must look to the tales he tells, particularly in the series of six novels he published between 1958 and 1968.[44] Each book, as Wiesel says, is a "kind of testimony of

---

42   R. M. Brown, *Elie Wiesel: Messenger to All Humanity* (Notre Dame, London: University of Notre Dame Press, 1983), 3.

43   Wiesel, "Job: Our Contemporary," in *Messengers of God: Biblical Portraits and Legends.* Translated by M. Wiesel (New York: Touchstone, 1976), 211. Subsequent citations are given parenthetically in the text.

44   I cite here the English titles, although all six books were first published in French: *Night* (New York: Avon, 1969); *Dawn* (New York: Avon, 1970); *The Accident* (New York: Avon,

312   CHAPTER 18

one witness speaking of his own life, his own death."[45] Each book explores the
options for speaking after Wiesel decided to break his ten-year vow of silence
following his liberation from Buchenwald. The first, probably the most widely
read book in all of Holocaust "literature," appeared in Yiddish in 1956 with the
title *And the World Remained Silent*; a significantly abridged version appeared
in French in 1958 under a new title, *La Nuit*, and in English in 1960 as *Night*.
A well-known passage marks the beginning of Wiesel's journey.

> Never shall I forget that night, the first night in camp, which turned my
> life into one long night, seven times cursed and seven times sealed. Never
> shall I forget that smoke. Never shall I forget the little faces of the chil-
> dren, whose bodies I saw turned into wreathes of smoke beneath a silent
> blue sky.
> Never shall I forget those flames which consumed my faith forever.
> Never shall I forget that nocturnal silence which deprived me for all
> eternity, of the desire to live. Never shall I forget those moments which
> murdered my God and my soul and turned my dreams to dust. Never
> shall I forget these things, even I am condemned to live as long as God
> himself. Never.
> *Night*, 44

The words are searing – "flames which consumed my faith forever;" "silence
which deprived me [...] of the desire to live;" "moments which murdered my
God and my soul." They can be read, but they do not yield to commentary,
except perhaps to Wiesel's own. In reflecting on his work some twenty years
later, Wiesel says *Night* is the "center" for everything else he would write.[46]
Each of his subsequent stories circles round the same question, "Where is God
now?" (*Night*, 76). In *Night*, Wiesel takes the perspective of the victim whose
faith in God has been consumed by the inexplicable deaths of the innocent.
How should one respond when human barbarity murders the soul, dreams for
the future, the will to live, and God is silent? Wiesel's first probe for an answer
is to pray, in spite of himself, "to that God in whom I no longer believed"
(*Night*, 104), yet as the conclusion of the book indicates, Wiesel wonders if this
response is adequate.

1970); *The Town Beyond the Wall* (New York: Avon, 1969); *The Gates of the Forest* (New York:
Avon, 1969); *A Beggar in Jerusalem* (New York: Avon 1971). Subsequent parenthetical references are to the English publications cited here.

45   *Harry James Cargas in Conversation with Elie Wiesel* (New York: Paulist Press, 1976), 86, as
cited in Brown, *Elie Wiesel: Messenger to All Humanity*, 51.

46   Ibid., as cited in Brown, *Elie Wiesel: Messenger to All Humanity*, 51.

RE(READING) JOB'S STORY IN A POST-HOLOCAUST WORLD   313

> I looked at myself in the mirror. A skeleton stared back at me.
> Nothing but skin and bone.
> It was the image of myself after death. It was at that instant that the will
> to live awakened within me.
> Without knowing why, I raised my fist and shattered the glass, along
> with the image it held [...].
> But [...]
> [T]en years after Buchenwald, I ask myself the question, Was I right to
> break that mirror?[47]

The subsequent novels explore other options. "In *Dawn* I explore the political action; in *The Accident*, suicide; in *The Town Beyond the Wall*, madness; in *The Gates of the Forest*, faith and friendship; in *A Beggar in Jerusalem*, the return."[48] Others have analyzed these mileposts in Wiesel's journey; I need not replicate their assessments.[49] For my purposes here, I single out *A Beggar in Jerusalem*, a story of a "return" to Jerusalem.

The narrator of the story is David, a Holocaust survivor, who has made his way to Jerusalem during the Six-Day War. His alter-ego, Katriel, tells him a parable about a man who leaves home in search of a city that promises adventure and fulfillment. By the time he arrives in Jerusalem and joins the Jewish forces that are trying to regain the city, the parable has begun to gnaw at David. It reminds him of a beggar who once told him that the "day someone tells you your life" (*Beggar in Jerusalem*, 159) marks the day when you have not much longer to live. As he stands before the ancient wall of the temple, David imagines all those who stood there before him, "kings, prophets, warriors and priests, poets and philosophers, rich and poor" (239). He realizes for the first time in his life that the dead have a living presence in Jerusalem, that despite history's evils, remembering, fighting for life can be an ally, not an enemy, in the hope to survive. As Wiesel says in his memoirs, survivors are like the parchments of the Holy Book, "So long as they exist, so long as some of them are

---

47   See also Wiesel's comments on this passage in the first volume of his memoirs, E. Wiesel, *All Rivers Run to the Sea: Memoirs* (New York: Alfred A. Knopf, 1995), 321.

48   *Harry James Cargas in Conversation with Elie Wiesel*, 86, as cited in Brown, *Elie Wiesel: Messenger to all Humanity*, 51.

49   See especially the analysis in Brown, *Elie Wiesel: Messenger to All Humanity*, who follows Wiesel's own characterization of these novels with a systematic discussion of the options he pursues. See also Wiesel's reflections in his memoirs, *All Rivers Run to Sea* and *And the Sea is Never Full: Memoirs 1969–* (Trans. M. Wiesel; New York: Alfred A. Knopf, 1999).

314 CHAPTER 18

alive, the others know – even if they do not always admit it – that they cannot trespass certain boundaries."[50]

At the end of *a Beggar in Jerusalem*, David says that "a page has been turned. The beasts in the heart of man have stopped howling, they have stopped bleeding. The curse has been revoked in this place, and its reign terminated" (252). Jerusalem has been saved, not only because its army won the Six Day War but also and more importantly because "Israel [...] could deploy six million more names in battle" (244). David realizes that Jerusalem's victory "does not prevent suffering from having existed, nor death from having taken its toll" (254). Nothing can change the facts of history, but a new vision may keep the future open. "What is important," David says, "is to continue," even when there remain more questions than answers.

> [T]he mystery of good is no less disturbing than the mystery of evil. But one does not cancel out the other. Man alone is capable of uniting them by remembering. (254)

Wiesel, like David, may have turned a page when he wrote *A Beggar in Jerusalem*. His personal journey had taken him from his hometown in Sighet to Buchenwald to Jerusalem. From a death camp, where flames consumed his faith in God's justice (*Night*, 56), Wiesel comes to the city of peace, where David places a note, addressed to the living dead, in the Wall in the Old City. He asks them "to take pity on a world which has betrayed and rejected them." They are powerful enough to do whatever they want. They may "Punish. Or even forgive" (*A Beggar in Jerusalem*, 252).[51] And yet. And yet. The words Wiesel gives to David at the close of the book are thick with nuance. The mysteries of good and evil may not cancel out each other, but can they ever be united in an affirmation of God's justice? David suggests that "man alone" is capable of attending to these mysteries, through the act of faithful remembering. If the

---

50   Wiesel, *All Rivers Run to the Sea*, 327.

51   Wiesel records the following in his diary about his first visit to Jerusalem in 1967 and the experiences that triggered the writing of *A Beggar in Jerusalem*.

"And here I am in Jerusalem. It took me a long time to get here, but here I am. I dream that I'm dreaming. I dream that my words become jumbled on my lips and that they burn my tongue.

And yes, it is both a privilege and a duty to speak of Jerusalem.

Of the heart that is full, so full that if it doesn't open it will burst. Of the alleyways of the Old City, which have made me want to sing like a madman, to sob like a child. To paraphrase Rabbi Nahman of Bratslav, I will have to make words of my tears." (*All Rivers Run to the Sea*, 390).

RE(READING) JOB'S STORY IN A POST-HOLOCAUST WORLD   315

capacity belongs to man *alone*, then how does Wiesel answer the presenting and still lingering question in *Night*: "Where is God now?"

The question, as Wiesel concedes, stands at the center of everything he has written. He may have turned a page with the publication of *A Beggar in Jerusalem*, but Wiesel has spent a lifetime pondering what can be said about God after Auschwitz. Wiesel chooses, ultimately, not to speak *about* God; this is the task of theologians. Instead, he takes his cue from the Talmudic account of God's gift of the Ten Commandments.

> On the morning of the day when all Israel was to have gathered at the foot of the mountain, some men were still asleep in their tents. And so God first manifested Himself with thunder and lightning in order to shake, to awaken those who were foolish enough to sleep while time and the heart of mankind opened to receive the call of *Him who lends mystery to all things*. Then, abruptly, there was a silence. And in this silence a Voice was heard. God spoke. What did he speak of? His secret work, His eternally imperceptible intentions? No, He spoke of man's relationship to man, of one's individual duties toward others. At this unique moment God wished to deal with human relations rather than theology.[52]

For Wiesel, how we treat human beings is more important than how we theologize about God. As he puts it, "Whoever betrays humanity, whoever torments one's fellow man, denies the existence of God."[53]

Wiesel insists on addressing God, not speaking about God. In this commitment, he is compelled to articulate what he calls "the agony of the believer."[54] A selection of Wiesel's comments explicates his journey.

> The Jew in my view may rise against God provided he remains within God. One can be a very good Jew, observe all *mitzvot*, study Talmud, and yet be against God [...] as if to say: You, God, do not want me to be Jewish? Well, Jewish we shall be nevertheless, despite Your will.[55]

> From inside his community [the Jew] may say anything. Let him step outside it, and he will be denied this right. The revolt of the believer is

---

52   Wiesel, *Messengers of God*, 194–195 (emphasis added).

53   E. Wiesel, "A Personal Response," in *Face to Face: An Interreligious Bulletin* 6 (1979), 37.

54   E. Wiesel, *One Generation After* (New York: Random House, 1970), 166.

55   E. Wiesel, "Jewish Values in the Post-Holocaust Future: A Symposium," *Judaism* 16 (1967), 299.

not that of the renegade; the two do not speak in the name of the same anguish.[56]

I prefer to blaspheme in God than far from him.

The Town Beyond the Wall, 176

I don't believe in art for art's sake. For me literature must have an ethical dimension. The aim of literature I call testimony is to disturb. I disturb the believer because I dare to put questions to God, the source of all faith. I disturb the miscreant because, despite my doubts and questions, I refuse to break with the religious and mystical universe that has shaped my own. Most of all, I disturb those who are comfortably settled within a system – be it political, psychological, or theological. If I have learned anything in my life, it is to distrust intellectual comfort.[57]

How then does the Jew who revolts against God address God? One of Wiesel's own prayers provides a touchstone for reflection.

I no longer ask You for either happiness or paradise; all I ask of You is to listen and let me be aware of Your listening.

I no longer ask You to resolve my questions, only to receive them and make them part of You.

I no longer ask You for either rest or wisdom, I only ask You not to close me to gratitude, be it of the most trivial kind, or to surprise and friendship. Love? Love is not Yours to give.

As for my enemies, I do not ask you to punish them or even to enlighten them; I only ask You not to lend them Your mask and Your powers. If You must relinquish one or the other, give them Your Powers. But not Your countenance.[58]

I conclude this summary of Wiesel's works by returning to his reflections on "Job: Our Contemporary." As noted above, Wiesel admires Job's resistance but is offended by his supposed submission as recorded in the Epilogue. His first inclination is to wonder if the Book's original ending has been lost in transmission. If we had this ending, surely it would confirm that Job did not humiliate himself by repenting, that he died in grief uncompromised by his fidelity to his protest about God's injustice. Since this original ending seems to have been

---

56 E. Wiesel, *Souls on Fire* (New York: Random House, 1972), 111.

57 Wiesel, *All Rivers Run to the Sea*, 326–327.

58 Wiesel, *One Generation After*, 189.

RE(READING) JOB'S STORY IN A POST-HOLOCAUST WORLD   317

lost, Wiesel imagines its reconstruction. If the reconstruction is unconvincing, then the only recourse is to salvage the biblical ending by reinterpreting it:

> [I]n spite or because of appearances, Job continued to interrogate God. By repenting sins he did not commit, by justifying a sorrow he did not deserve, he communicates to us that he did not believe in his own confessions; they were nothing but decoys. Job personified man's eternal quest for justice and truth – he did not choose resignation. Thus he did not suffer in vain; thanks to him we know that it is given to man to transform divine injustice into human justice and compassion.
>
>   "Job: Our Contemporary," 235

In what sense then, according to Wiesel, is Job our contemporary? The concluding words of Wiesel's essay on Job are these.

> Once upon a time, in a faraway land there lived a legendary man, a just and generous man who, in his solitude and despair found the courage to stand up to God. And to force Him to look at his creation. And to speak to those men who sometimes succeed, in spite of Him and of themselves, in achieving triumphs over Him, triumphs that are grave and disquieting.
>
>   What remains of Job? A fable? A shadow? Not even the shadow of a shadow. An example, perhaps.
>
>   "Job: Our Contemporary," 235

What exactly is the difference between a fable, a shadow, a shadow of a shadow, and an example? We may speculate, but Wiesel suggests that the only ones who can provide definition are Job's children. If, as Wiesel says, Jews are summoned to "celebrate the memory of silence, but to reject the silence of memory,"[59] then breaking silence, even if in protest against God, is the equivalent of obedience to a divine commandment.

4   "Have You Considered My Servant Job?"

The question that launches Job's story is posed at the outset by God to the satan: "Have you considered my servant Job?" (1:8; 2:3). From a literary standpoint, we may assume that God knows Job's story already. The narrator has sketched its basic outline (1:1–5), and God twice affirms that the basics are correct (1:7–9; 2:3). The satan suggests the basics merit reconsideration; God

---

59   Wiesel, *All Rivers Run to the Sea*, 339.

318   CHAPTER 18

agrees. Thus begins, at God's invitation, the stewardship of reading and re-reading, evaluating and re-evaluating the story of "the greatest of all the people of the east" (1:3).

Questions, and the answers they solicit, provide the foundation for conversation that enlarges understanding, even when, perhaps especially when, there is disagreement and debate. The mere existence of the book of Job confirms that the conversation continues. The narrator's prose account is in dialogue with the poetic center of the book. Elihu engages the readings of Eliphaz, Bildad, and Zophar. Job conforms to the words the narrator gives him, then speaks his own very different words to the three friends and to God. God retreats in silence, then reappears with words so forceful that they presumably silence everyone who has spoken thus far. However we may judge the book's compositional history and the canonical process that resulted in the 42 chapters we now read, we may sure that the "culture of exegesis" it has generated continues long past the "finalization" of the story.

Septuagint translators add to the prose and nuance the meanings of the poetic dialogues. The *Testament of Job* recasts the story by accenting certain aspects and omitting others. The Church Fathers, following Gregory's lead, adopt a Christological approach, and medieval Jewish commentators such as Saadiah Gaon and Maimonides, who debate "conservative" and "liberal" interpretations of God's providence, do much the same, for different reasons. Artists, beginning at least in the Greco-Roman period, painted and sculpted their own interpretations of Job. Novelists, playwrights, poets, and musicians – Jews, Christians, Muslims, and secular, from virtually all points on the globe – have added their own distinctive readings. "Have you considered my servant Job?" The first answer to this question, as this book has tried to demonstrate is, "Yes, we have."

Will there ever be an end to the reading of Job? Is it possible to conceive a time in the future when there will be no Jobs in this world, when the imperative to think deeply about innocent suffering will be nullified, either by answers that are so persuasive they silence all complaint or by the universal acknowledgment that justice has eradicated the problem once and for all? All readers of Job's story may hope for such a time. In the fraught interim between now and then, we continue to read and think, to assess and reassess the imperative that comes with responding to the initiating question, "Have you considered my servant Job?" and if you have, what can you contribute to the ending of his story that enlarges and enriches it?

The Joban epilogue returns readers to the prologue. In doing so, it extends God's presenting question with another. Once we have immersed ourselves in the story of one who, by God's admission, has suffered his reported losses "for no reason," can we ever go back to the beginning and start over again? Job's story begins in Uz, a literary metaphor for Eden, where the "very good" world of God's creation is pristine, seemingly free of any evil that may corrupt or destroy it. His story ends somewhere "east of Eden," to appropriate John Steinbeck's language, with the report that he returns to his origins and begins life anew. Perhaps, in the aftermath of Joban-type losses, we can and should build a new life, with the hope and promise that it will ultimately end "old and full of days" (Job 42:17).

The objective in this last chapter, which addresses how we read Job in a post-Holocaust world, is to raise the question whether east of Eden, we can ever go home again. Our entrance into the "very good" world of God's hopes and expectations is forever barred by the flaming cherubim that God inscrutably places between us and the tree of life (Gen 3:24). In the meantime, we read Job's story and it reads us.

Scripture Index

Old Testament/Hebrew Bible

Genesis

1–3	188n, 210n
1–2	251
1:1–2:4a	133n, 137
1	7, 11, 21, 136, 210n, 212, 215
1:1	221
1:2, 3, 7, 14, 15, 21	139
1:2	10n, 211n
1:3	138
1:6–9	14
1:22, 28	12, 148
1:24–27	185
1:26–30	8
1:26, 28	262
1:26	188n
1:28	210n
1:31	7, 137, 138, 262
2–3	7, 8, 9, 12, 20, 21
2:3	137
2:5	8, 9
2:8	136, 210n
2:9	8
2:15	8, 137, 262
2:17	8
2:19–20	171, 184
3–11	213n
3:4	9
3:12-13	9
3:17	65
3:24	319
4:8–10	155, 310
4:10	65
6–8	9
6:6	233n
6:11–13	310
6:18	177n
8:20	112, 140
8:21–22	310
9:5–6	310
9:9–17	177n
17:2, 4, 9–13, 21	177n
18:22–33	156
18:22–23	226n
18:22	187n, 226
18:23–32	187n, 227n
18:23	179n
18:25	157, 187n, 277
18:27	156, 186, 186n, 226
22:2, 13	112, 140
24:12, 14	63, 89
24:49	63
25:8	149, 298
25:29	149, 298
29:15	15
31:54	112, 140
32:11	63
33:19	300n
34:7	297n
41:39	247n
46:1	112, 140
50:10	142

Exodus

2:24	177n
3:18	187n
5:1, 3	187n
5:5	278
5:22	176n
6:6	35, 95
7:16	187n
8:8, 25–26	176n
8:23, 24	187n
9:29, 33	176n
10:18	176n
14:11, 12	187n
15–18	187n
15:13	35, 95, 278
15:22	187n
16:2, 32	187n
19:2	187n
19:6	108, 175
20:6	63, 89
22:4	159, 160, 298
25–31	133n, 136, 175
28:36–38	117
29	117, 141n
30:24	300

SCRIPTURE INDEX

Exodus (cont.)

32:11–13	176n
33:7–11	176n
33:12–23	261
33:12, 13	247n
33:19	18
34:6	63, 90
34:28	141n
34:29–35	65
35–40	133n, 136, 175
39:28	117

Leviticus

1–15	182n, 191
1–16	113n, 175, 176n
1:1–17	140n
4:1–5:13	121n
4:1–35	179n
5:14–6:7	121n
5:5	176n
6:2–6	182n
6:7–16	182n
6:17–23	182n
7:1–7	182n
7:11–21	182n
7:38	187n
8	117, 141n
8:9	117, 141n
8:22–30	122, 130
11–15	120n
11:1–23, 41–42	182n
11:2–23	165
11:16	169
12:1–8	182n
13	121, 181
13–14	110, 119, 119n, 120, 124, 125, 142, 181
13:1–59	182n
13:1–44	119, 120
13:6, 13, 23, 28, 34, 35, 37, 38, 40	123
13:17	123
13:18–23	116, 119, 142
13:45–46	119, 123
14	121, 130
14:1–57	182n
14:1–32	119, 120, 130
14:2–8	122
14:9	122

14:10–32	122
14:12–18	122
15:1–32	182n
16	117, 141n
16:1–10	114
16:11–28	114
16:21	176n
16:22	187n
17–27	175, 191
17–22	176n
18:5	123
19:2	191
20:20, 21, 25	142
21:17–23	123n
21:17, 18, 21, 23	142
22:19	140n
22:19, 21	112n
25:25–28, 47–49	278
25:25–28	34
22:25	123n
25:28	95
25:47–49	34, 95

Numbers

1–10	133n
1:1, 19	187n
3:4, 14	187n
5:1–4	123
5:21–22	176n
6:22–26	65, 176n
9:1, 5	187n
10:12, 31	187n
11–25	187n
11:15	15
12:1–5	120, 142
12:12	121
12:13	121
12:15–16	121
12:16	187n
14:2, 16, 29, 32, 33, 35	187n
15:2	187n
16:5	247n
16:13	187n
19:2	112n, 140n
21:5, 11, 13	187n
26–36	133
26:33	160, 300n
26:64, 65	187n

SCRIPTURE INDEX

27:1–11	160, 300n
27:3, 14	187n
32:13, 15	187n
33:8, 11, 13, 15, 36	187n
35:19–27	35
35:22–27	278
36:1–12	160, 300n

Deuteronomy

1:39	8
5:10	63, 89
6:4–5	52
7:9, 12	63, 89
8:3	247n
14:3–20	165
14:15	169
17:4	296
19:6–12	35, 278
21:1–9	176n
22:21	297n
24:17	65
26:2–10	176n
30:11–20	272
32:33	169n

Joshua

2:14	63
7:15	297n
24:32	300n

Judges

20:6	297n

Ruth

3:12–13	34, 95, 278
4:3–6	34, 95, 278
4:5	34, 95

1 Samuel

1:3, 10–15	176n
16:3	247n
23:23	296
26:19	15, 198n
31:3	142

2 Samuel

2:6	63, 89
14:17, 20	8
19:36	8
24:1	15, 198n

1 Kings

3:6	63, 89
8:5, 12–64	176n
8:23	63, 89

2 Kings

5:25–27	120, 142
9:30	300
25:18–21	116
25:21	195

1 Chronicles

6:14–15	116
6:16–34	176n
15:16–24	176n
16:4–43	176n
16:27	218
29:28	149, 298

2 Chronicles

6:14	63, 89
24:15	149
26:16–21	142
26:16	120

Ezra

9	192

Nehemiah

1:5	63, 89
9	192
9:14	247n
9:32	63, 89

Esther

7:5	248n

Job

1–42	284
1–20	114n, 115n, 140n, 180n, 213n
1–2	xi, 17, 116n, 127, 136, 137, 139, 140, 141n, 147, 178, 197, 210n, 230, 231, 233n, 234, 250, 266
1:1–5	11, 11n, 137, 210n, 232, 317
1:1, 3	136
1:1	12, 112, 113, 148, 229, 284

324   SCRIPTURE INDEX

Job (*cont.*)

1:1, 8	12, 140, 259, 282
1:2–3	148, 210n
1:2, 8	182
1:3	112, 148, 210n, 230, 297, 318
1:4–5	148, 179n
1:5	112, 121, 140, 180
1:5, 10, 11, 21	81, 138
1:5, 11	138, 211n
1:6–12	11n, 13, 115, 137, 141, 210n
1:6–8	232
1:6	114
1:7–9	318
1:7	12
1:8	12, 14, 69, 115, 148, 229, 299, 317
1:9	14, 69, 113, 115, 147, 199n, 200, 211, 282, 297, 300
1:10	14, 115, 217n
1:10, 21	138, 211n
1:11	14, 15, 115, 167
1:12–13	278
1:12	12, 14, 249
1:13–22	11n, 137, 210n, 211n
1:13–19	14, 115
1:13–15	211n
1:14	278
1:16	211n
1:17	211n
1:18–19	12, 211n
1:20–22	281
1:20	141
1:21–22	181
1:21	12, 109, 141, 143, 148, 211, 275, 298
1:22	86, 87, 202
2:1–10	284, 288
2:1–7a	11n, 14, 137, 210n
2:1–6	13, 115, 141
2:1–3	232
2:1	114
2:2	12
2:3	xi, 6, 12, 13, 14, 15, 16, 16n, 69, 72, 84, 113, 113n, 115, 140, 147, 148, 179, 182, 197, 197n, 198,

	198n, 199n, 200, 202, 211, 229, 233, 233n, 241, 253, 259, 275, 281, 282, 284, 297, 299, 300, 317, 318
2:3, 9	112n, 141n
2:4	259
2:5	15, 115, 116, 167
2:5, 9	81, 138, 211n
2:6	12, 15, 69, 124, 240, 249
2:7	110, 116, 119, 142, 181
2:7b–10	11n, 137, 210n
2:8	148, 222n
2:9–10	148
2:9	284
2:9b–e	234
2:10	13, 86, 113, 137, 181, 202, 284
2:11–13	11n, 52, 54, 84, 137, 148, 210n, 231
2:11	12, 104, 113, 235, 300
2:12	54, 85, 142
2:13	137, 138, 181
3–37	xi, 165, 230
3–31	136, 152
3–27	148, 198, 231
3	30, 54, 72, 138, 165, 197n, 210n, 211n, 225
3:1–42:6	196
3:1–10	81, 138, 211, 298
3:1	86, 138
3:2	181
3:3–13	138n, 139n, 211n
3:3–5	182
3:3	117
3:3, 4, 5, 6–7, 8, 9, 15	139
3:3a, 4–5	211
3:4	138
3:6–9	182, 211
3:11–13, 20–22	259
3:11–12	87
3:11	72, 254, 276, 298
3:11–26	82, 138, 211
3:11, 12, 20	182, 211
3:12, 16, 20, 23	254
3:16	87
3:16, 23	182
3:18	276

SCRIPTURE INDEX

3:20	87, 276	7:16, 19	276
3:21	254	7:17–21	66, 212, 218
3:23	217n	7:17–18	285
3:26	62, 138, 211	7:17	72, 268, 271, 276, 288
4–31	142	7:18	212
4–27	182, 266	7:20	276
4–14	58, 91, 133	8:2–3	279
4:1–3	90	8:3–6	260
4:2	58, 281	8:3	91, 277
4:3–5	118	8:4–6	279
4:5	279	8:5–7	136
4:6–7	58	8:5–6	122, 182
4:6	279	8:6	279
4:6, 8	38	8:8–19	58, 92
4:7–11	58	8:8–10	166
4:7–9	92	8:8–9	260
4:7	262, 279	8:9	279
4:10–11	166	8:11–19	165
4:17–21	72, 213	8:14	166
4:17–19	212, 279	8:20–22	279
4:19	186n, 226n	8:20	140
5:2	279	8:22	30
5:8–16	279	9–10	30, 183, 197n, 211n
5:17–27	279	9:2	35
6–7	62, 211n	9:3	277
6:8–9	259	9:4, 19	259
6:11–12	66	9:14–24	277
6:11	72	9:15, 20–21	213
6:13	62	9:17	197n, 199n, 253
6:14–30	62	9:20–21, 30–21	182
6:14	62, 66, 89, 147, 279	9:20, 21, 22	140
6:15–21	63	9:20b	276
6:15–17	64	9:23	124, 277
6:15	91	9:25	254
6:18–20	64	9:26	166
6:21	64	9:28	35
6:24	121	9:29	276
6:25–26	182	9:32	154, 218, 252, 277
6:28	94, 124	9:33	35, 154, 278
7	212n	9:34	174n, 185n
7:1–6	66	10:1–17	124, 298
7:2	275, 288	10:1–7	39
7:3	275	10:1–2	182
7:3, 6	254	10:1a	182
7:5, 12	166	10:2	247, 247n
7:11–15	182	10:2b	276
7:15–16	259	10:3–7	252
7:16–21	39	10:4	251, 253
7:16	39, 182, 225n	10:5	254

SCRIPTURE INDEX

Job (cont.)

10:9	186n, 226n
10:13–17	124
10:13	35
10:15	213
10:16	166
10:18–23	39
10:18–22	259
10:18–19	254
10:18	72, 298
10:18, 20	39
11:3	279
11:6	279
11:7–12	279
11:7–9	165, 166, 260
11:8–9	166
11:8	279
11:11	58, 92
11:12	166
11:13–20	136, 142
11:13–19	260
11:13–15	182
11:13, 15	123
11:14–19	280
11:14	142
11:15–19	279
11:15	142
12–14	30
12:2–3	91
12:4	57, 90, 144, 213
12:5	127, 280
12:7–10	58
12:7–12	166
12:7–9	165
12:7	167, 253
12:9	167, 253
12:10	167
12:13–14, 16	133
12:13	174n
12:17–21	133
12:19	144
12:22	144
12:24	133
13	197n
13:1–44	181
13:2	91
13:3	xi
13:3, 13–17	182
13:4	47, 300

13:4a	91
13:4b	91
13:7–12	32
13:13–25	212n
13:14	262
13:15–16	36
13:15	57, 89
13:17	94
13:18–23	277
13:18–21	35
13:21	174n, 185n
13:22–28	39
13:22	248
13:23	247, 247n
13:24	276, 288
13:28	166
13:45–46	181
14:1–32	181
14:1–6	39
14:1–3	57
14:12	36
14:13–17	36
14:13–16	39
14:13	296
14:18–22	36
15–22	83
15–21	58, 91
15:3	91
15:4–6	59
15:5–6	279
15:7–16	212, 218, 279
15:7–8	260
15:7	213, 221
15:8	213
15:9, 12, 14	279
15:12–13	279
15:14	212
15:16	72
15:17–35	58, 92
15:20–35	279
15:22, 28	122
16	30, 197n
16:1–3	83
16:2	91
16:6–17	124, 298
16:9	166, 296
16:11–14	276
16:13	37
16:13, 18	112, 140

SCRIPTURE INDEX

16:15–17	259, 277
16:15–16	124
16:17	124
16:18–19	51, 267, 277
16:18	34, 36, 155, 182, 310
16:19	35, 278
16:22–17:1	259
17:1–3, 11–15	39
17:2, 6	124
17:15	36
18:4	279
18:5–21	58, 92, 121, 279
18:6, 14, 15	30
18:8–10	166
18:11–13	121
18:17–18	122
19	197n
19:2–5	30
19:2	30
19:2, 12	48
19:4	121
19:6–22	298
19:6–20	31
19:6–12	124
19:6	30, 32, 50, 124
19:6, 29	48
19:6a, 9	276
19:7–12	30, 276, 288
19:7	33, 34, 51, 155, 218, 277, 278, 289
19:9	288
19:10	31, 289
19:11	296
19:12	30, 48
19:13–20	30, 35, 124, 278
19:20–27	39
19:21–29	29, 30, 31, 37, 39, 48
19:21–22	31, 32, 278
19:21–22, 28–29	49, 50
19:21	30, 32, 57, 89
19:21a	32
19:22	30, 31, 32, 50
19:22, 28	31
19:23–27	31, 33, 37, 48
19:23–27a	287, 289
19:23–24	33, 182
19:25–27	31, 36, 39, 40n, 42
19:25–27a	40
19:25–26	38, 40, 278
19:25–26a	36
19:25	29, 31, 34, 49, 95, 155, 287
19:25b	36
19:26b–27	36
19:27b	289
19:27c	37
19:28–29	31, 32, 50
19:28	32
19:29	30, 32, 33, 38, 49, 50, 155, 277
20:2–29	279
20:4–9	58, 92
20:14, 16	166
21–37	199n
21:1–5	182
21:1	59
21:2	94
21:5	94, 103, 124, 253
21:7, 17–19	179n
21:10–11	166
21:17	92
21:22	247
21:28–30	253
22–27	58, 59, 91, 92
22:1–11	212
22:2	279
22:4–5	277
22:5–10	279
22:5	59, 92
22:6–11	280
22:6	199n
22:13, 17	279
22:21–27	136
22:21	59, 74, 93, 124, 182, 225, 250, 260
22:23–28	260
22:23–27	182
22:23, 25–27	123
22:23, 26–27	280
23–24	259
23	37, 288
23:1–9, 16–17	259, 284, 285
23:1–7	182, 259
23:2–4	285
23:2	264
23:3	277
23:3, 8–9	259
23:4–5	259

SCRIPTURE INDEX

Job (cont.)

23:4	262
23:6–7	277, 285
23:7	259
23:8–16	259
23:8–9	260, 277, 285
23:8	264
23:10	57, 89
23:17	259, 261
24:1–17	124, 259
24:1–12	253
24:1	260
24:2–12	260
24:2–8	166
24:12	259
24:13–17	260
24:18–24	260
24:25	261
25:4–6	72, 279
25:4	279
25:6	166
26:3	247n
27:1–6	64, 182
27:2–12	298
27:2–5	19n
27:5	112n, 117, 141n
27:7–12	124
28	196
28:7	151
28:21–22	167
28:28	281
29–31	64, 168n, 197n, 251, 251n
29–30	167
29	62, 64, 168
29:1–10	64
29:2–6	168, 169
29:4	64
29:5	64
29:7–11	169
29:7–10	64
29:11–17	280
29:11–16	64
29:12–17	168, 169
29:14	117, 141n, 169
29:17	64
29:21–25	65
29:24	65
29:25a	65

29:25b	65
30	64
30:1–15	124
30:1–8	168, 169, 226
30:1–8, 29	166
30:1, 9, 16	168
30:2–8	168
30:3b	173
30:5	169
30:9–15	168, 186n, 226, 278
30:16–23	186n, 226
30:16–19	168
30:19	156, 186n, 187n, 222n, 226
30:20–23	30
30:20–21	186n
30:20	156, 226, 277
30:20, 24, 28	168
30:21	168, 169
30:29	168, 169, 173
31	37, 64
31:1–34, 38–40	277
31:6	112n, 117, 141n
31:13–23	280
31:35–37	182, 277
31:38–40	65
31:40	169, 183
32–37	169, 183, 196, 266
32:1, 3, 5, 6, 12, 17, 20	169
32:7	247n
33:6	186n, 226n
33:12–14	260
33:12	183
33:13	279
33:14–30	170
33:15–28	183
33:18–20	281
33:23–28	136
33:23–24	35, 278
33:26	170
33:27	183
34:21–25	171
34:33	225n
34:34–37	279
36–37	169
36:5–15	170, 183
36:5	225n
36:5, 22, 26, 30	170

SCRIPTURE INDEX

329

36:17–23	279
36:22–37:13	183
36:22–23	279
36:24–28	279
36:24–25	170
36:31–32	170
36:33	171
37:2	170
37:3, 11b	170
37:4–5	170
37:6–7, 10	170
37:7–8	183
37:7	171, 183n
37:8	171, 183n
37:11–12	170
37:13	170
37:19	247n
37:21–24	171, 260
37:22	174n
38–39	216n, 282
38	216, 216n, 217n, 223n
38–42	230, 243, 252
38:1–42:6	xi, 171, 266
38–41	22, 37, 64, 70, 83, 124, 172, 214, 215, 216n
38:1–40:34	152, 296
38:1–40:5	214n
38:1–40:2	165, 241, 247, 267
38:1–39:40	167
38:1–11	285
38:1	247n
38:1–7	284
38:1–7, 34–41	285, 288
38:2	125, 225, 229, 234, 245, 247, 252, 286
38:3	152, 215, 241, 247, 247n, 248, 268
38:4–18	152, 172, 215, 241
38:4–7	172
38:7, 17, 23	251
38:8–11	14, 172, 217, 241
38:8a	217m
38:9–11	241
38:9, 17, 19	251
38:12–15	172, 251
38:16–18	172
38:19–38	172, 215, 241
38:25–27	173
38:36	286

38:39–39:40	241
38:39–39:30	70, 152, 171, 172, 184, 215, 216
38:39–41	251, 286
39:1–4	254
39:7	174n
39:7, 18, 22	184n
39:13	173
39:13a	174
39:14–16	174
39:15–16, 22, 24	251
39:16	169
39:17	174
39:18	174
39:19	174n
39:20b	174n, 185n
39:22	174n
39:25	174n
40:1–5	251n
40:1–2	184
40:1	247n
40:2	155, 217
40:3–5	152, 155, 185, 186, 217, 241, 242
40:3–4	22
40:3	247n
40:4–5	179, 268
40:4	125, 243, 282
40:5	23, 299
40:6–41:34	23, 153, 165, 241, 247, 268
40:6	248, 299
40:7–14	218, 219, 224
40:7	125, 152, 185, 215, 217, 241, 247, 268
40:8–14	253
40:8	125, 218, 229, 242, 245, 298
40:9	174n
40:9a	218, 253, 268
40:9b	218, 253, 268
40:10	125, 153, 218, 218n, 253, 268, 282, 288
40:11–13	253, 268
40:11	224
40:11b	224n
40:12	269
40:13	269
40:14	253

330 SCRIPTURE INDEX

Job (*cont.*)

40:15–41:34	173, 219
40:15–41:26	186n, 220n
40:15–24	70, 171, 172, 173, 185, 215, 220, 282, 288
40:15	167, 185, 254
40:16–18	220, 269
40:19–22	223
40:19	221, 222n
40:19b, 24	221
40:20–22	221
40:23	153, 221
40:33	185
41:1–34	171, 172, 185, 215, 222, 282, 288
41:1–9	222n
41:2b–3	223n
41:3–4	153, 185, 269
41:10–14	222n
41:10–12	222
41:12–32	222
41:18–34	222
41:18–24	223
41:18–21	185, 223
41:25–26	184
41:33–34	185, 222
41:33	222n
41:34	223, 224n, 269
42:1–6	152, 241, 251, 251n, 296
42:1–6, 10–17	284, 286
42:2–5	22
42:2–3	286
42:2a	252, 255
42:3	225, 229, 252, 272
42:3, 5	243
42:4	247, 247n
42:5–6	47n, 179
42:5	37, 71, 128, 157, 228, 269, 283, 286, 287
42:5a	255
42:5b	255
42:6	22, 23n, 47n, 156, 186, 186n, 222n, 224, 225, 225n, 226, 242, 255, 269, 282, 286, 286n
42:6b	156, 226
42:7–17	128, 136, 139, 140, 147, 197, 230, 231, 250, 266
42:7–14	xi
42:7–10	146, 231

42:7–9	148, 161n, 295
42:7–8	23, 71, 83, 103, 132, 148, 262, 271, 283, 289, 299
42:7	152, 296
42:8–9	289
42:8	71, 112, 140, 148, 158, 180, 297
42:10–17	160n, 287, 289, 295
42:10	297
42:10, 12	159
42:11–17	232
42:11–12	52
42:11	103, 104, 148, 278, 279, 300
42:11b	104
42:12	81, 138, 138, 148
42:13–16	300
42:13–15	148, 160
42:15	301
42:16	148, 298, 301
42:17	148
42:17	26, 151, 298, 319

Psalms

3:7	65
8	197n, 212n, 214, 217, 223, 227, 251
8:3–5	212
8:4–6	285
8:4–5	268
8:4	71, 275
8:5–6	153
8:5	220n, 275, 282
8:25	219
13	234
13:1–2	234
16:11	247n
18:7–8, 12–15	185
18:8–14	223
21:6	218
23:1	65
24:8	248n
25:4	247n
25:10	63, 89
25:14	64
29:7–9	185
29:7	223
35:7	15
39:5	247n
42	176n

SCRIPTURE INDEX

44–49	176n
44	194
45:3	218
45:8	300
50	176n
51:8	247n
57:3	63, 89
65:2	177
68:5	65
69	194
73–83	176n
74	194
74:2	35, 95
77:15	247n
79	194
80:8–13	14
84–85	176n
87–88	176n
89:14	63, 65, 89
90:10	148, 298
90:12	247n
96:6	218
98:2	247n
102	194
103:7	247n
104	170
104:1	218, 218n
104:27–30	171n
109:3	15
111:3	218
113:2	141
119:154	35, 95, 278
119:161	15
137	194
138:2	63, 89
143:8	247n
144:3	72
148	170, 171n

Proverbs

1	16
1:10–12a	16
1:15–16	16
1:17	15
3:3	63
3:30	16
6:6	167
8:22–31	213
8:22	221
8:25	213
8:27–29	213
8:30–31	213
8:32, 33	213
11:17	169n
12:10	169n
23:10–11	65
23:11	35, 95
24:28	16
25:11	84
26:2	16
27:8	167
30:4	166
30:24–28	167

Ecclesiastes

5:15	12
9:1	167

Song Of Songs

2:14	300
3:6	248n
6:10	248n

Isaiah

1:3	167
1:10–15	116
1:13–15	176n
5:1–7	14
13:22	169
15:2	141
22:12	141
27:1	32
38:20	176n
40–55	7, 9, 10n, 251
40:12–31	216n
40:12–14	166
40:14	247
40:27–31	216n
40:28	10
41:10	167
41:17–20	10
41:20	10
41:20b	167
42:13–17	10
43:1	35
43:1, 14	278
43:16–21	10
43:20	169n
44:1–5	10
44:24–45:25	10

SCRIPTURE INDEX

Isaiah (*cont.*)

45:6b–7	21
45:7	10, 13
45:8	10
45:15	21, 21n
48:6–8	10
49:7–9	35
49:8–12	10
52:3	15
53:1	11
53:2	11
53:8, 10, 12	11
56:7	176n
62:1–4, 10–12	10
62:3	117
63:1	248n
64:1	247n
65:17–25	10
66:20–24	10

Jeremiah

1:17	216
4:23–26	138n, 139n, 211n
4:30	300
6:23	169n
7:29	141
8:7	167
9:10–11	169
9:24	63, 89
10:22	169
11:18	247, 247n
12:1–4	197n
12:1	179n
12:5	217n
16:6	141
16:21	247n
20	197n
20:14–18	138
22:13	15
27:8	32
29:23	297n
30:14	169n
32:6–8	34
42:10	19n
43:3	15, 198n
44:13	32
46:7	248n
49:14	248n
50:34	35, 95, 278

50:42	169n
52:24–27	116

Lamentations

3	197n
3:37	248n
3:58	35, 95, 278
4:3	169
4:11–13	116
4:13	173

Ezekiel

6:10	15, 196, 197, 197n, 198
7:18	141
12:22	21
14:23	15, 196, 197, 197n, 198
18:1–32	179n
20:11	247n
28	213n
39:7	247n
43:22–23	112n, 140n

Daniel

9	192
9:4	63, 89

Hosea

4:4–17	116
5:9	247n
11:9	244

Amos

5:21–23	176n
8:10	141

Micah

1:8	169
1:16	141
3:9–12	116
6:8	191

Habakkuk

3:2	247n

Zechariah

1–8	117n, 141n
3:1–10	116, 141n
3:1	155
3:3	141n

SCRIPTURE INDEX

3:4–5	125		24:18	98
3:5	116n		24:19–24	98
3:6–7	117		24:31	98, 103
7:9	63, 68		24:35	43, 99
			24:36–53	99
Malachi			24:36–43	99
1:10	15		24:39	43, 100
			24:41	100

New Testament

John

11:25	39n
12:31	17n

Matthew

10:7–8	280
27:46	261

Acts

7:60	149

Mark

10:2–16	285
10:2–12	285
10:13–16	285
10:15	288
10:17–31	285, 288
10:17–22	285
10:28–30	285
10:31	285
10:35–45	286, 288
10:37–38	286
10:43–44	286
10:45	286
10:46–52	287, 289
10:47	287
10:51	287
10:52	287
15:34	261

Romans

8:28	96
14:7–8	40n

1 Corinthians

13:5	270
15	40
15:20	40
15:21	29
15:51–52	40
15:52–53	41
15:54b	41
15:55–56	41
15:57	41, 96

2 Thessalonians

2:1–5	289
2:1–5, 13–17	287
2:15	287
2:16	287

Luke

9:10–17	100
10:29–37	52
14:13	99
16:19–31	95
20:27–38	287
20:34–36	287, 289
20:35	287
22:45	97
23:18–21	98
23:34	149
23:49	97
23:53	97
24	43
24:12	97
24:13–35	97

Hebrews

1:1–4	284
1:1–2	284
2:5–12	284
2:6–8	285
2:9	285
2:10	285, 288
2:14–15	17n
4:12–16	285, 288
4:12	285
4:13	285
4:14–15	108

Scripture Index

Hebrews (cont.)

4:15	285
4:16	285
5:1–10	286
5:7	286
5:8	286
7:23–28	287
7:23	287
7:25	287, 289
9–10	110
9:11	110

James

5:11	13, 54, 81, 85

1 Peter

2:9	108

1 John

3:8	17n
4:7, 20	68
4:20	108

Revelation

12:9	17n
20:1–3	17n

Apocrypha and Septuagint

Sirach/Ecclesiasticus

22:12	142
40:1	12
42–43	170n
42:15–43:33	170
43:27–30	171n

Tobit

14:1–2	298

Pseudepigrapha

Testament of Job

40:3	38
52:10	38
53:2–4	66
53:4, 8	301

Apostolic Fathers

1 Clement

25:1	38
26:1	38

Printed in the United States
By Bookmasters